# THE LAW

OF

# SUBROGATION.

BY

HENRY N. SHELDON.

*SECOND EDITION.*

BOSTON:
THE BOSTON BOOK COMPANY.
1893.

University Press:
John Wilson and Son, Cambridge.

# PREFACE TO SECOND EDITION.

In preparing this new edition, I have carefully examined the later decisions, and have also gone over the whole subject anew, and have made such additions and such changes and emendations as seemed to be called for. The number of cases cited has been considerably more than doubled, and the text has been much enlarged. Many sections have been practically rewritten; and many of my former statements have been much condensed. I have tried to state the law as briefly and as correctly as was within my power. The unexpected favor with which this little work has been received has made me the more anxious to spare no pains in its improvement.

H. N. S.

Boston, January 31, 1893.

# PREFACE TO FIRST EDITION.

It has been my endeavor, in the composition of this book, to state the doctrines which have been laid down by the courts in applying the law of subrogation, without going, beyond the most limited extent, outside of the adjudications of this country and of England. Regarding it as the distinguishing feature of our system of law that it is established by judicial decisions *a posteriori*, and not deduced from *a priori* reasonings, I have made no attempt to go further than the courts have gone; but I have desired to state, as correctly as might be, and with sufficient fulness to be intelligible, the general principles which have been declared by the courts, and the important applications which have been made of these principles.

The most logical division which could be made of this subject would be, as it seems to me, to divide it into two heads: first, the subrogation of junior creditors of a common debtor, or of parties holding subordinate interests in the same property, to the rights and remedies of senior creditors, or of persons holding paramount

claims upon the property, after such junior parties have
for the protection of their own interests satisfied the
superior claims; secondly, the subrogation of one of
several debtors who has, either under compulsion or for
the protection of his property, satisfied a common creditor or a creditor holding a charge upon his property as
well as upon that of others, against those debtors by
whom, or the owners of that property from which, he
ought to have been indemnified, in whole or in part,
against the burden which he has thus discharged.  The
first of these classes would include the subject-matter
of my second chapter, on the subrogation of persons
holding successive claims upon the same property, most
of the cases of the subrogation of devisees and legatees, and probably the subrogation of insurers.   Under
the second head would be included the subrogation of
sureties, of co-sureties, of joint debtors, of parties to
bills and notes, and most cases which arise in the administration of trusts.   But it has on the whole seemed
best to me, for practical convenience, after defining
the subject and after a general chapter upon the subrogation of different parties having successive claims
upon the same property by mortgage, lien, or purchase,
to consider separately subrogation in cases of suretyship, among joint debtors, among parties to bills and
notes, in the administration of estates, under contracts
of insurance, and in favor of strangers.   Also for purposes of practical convenience, and because the subjects
have often been discussed together by the courts, I

have treated under these different heads the substitution of a creditor to the remedies and securities which are held by the surety of his debtor, or by his debtor against one who, by agreement with the debtor, has assumed the burden of the debt, although I am aware that this is not strictly part of the law of subrogation, being rather the converse of that doctrine.

My subject being a small one, I have endeavored to make a copious citation of authorities, even at the risk of seeming needlessly to multiply references for the support sometimes of undisputed propositions.

H. N. S.

Boston, April 11, 1882.

# ANALYSIS OF CONTENTS.

## CHAPTER I.

## CHAPTER II.

## CHAPTER III.

# CHAPTER V.

## CHAPTER VI.

## CHAPTER VII.

## CHAPTER VIII

# TABLE OF CASES.

d

# THE LAW OF SUBROGATION.

## CHAPTER I.

### DEFINITION AND GENERAL NATURE.

§ 1. **Definition of Subrogation.** — Subrogation is a doctrine primarily of equity jurisprudence,[1] although its principles are now often applied in courts of common law,[2] especially in those States in which equitable remedies are administered through the forms of law.[3] It is a substitution, ordinarily

---

[1] Brown, *ex parte*, 58 Ala. 536; Meyer *v.* Mintonye, 106 Ills. 414; Talbot *v.* Wilkins, 31 Ark. 411; Eaton *v.* Hasty, 6 Nebraska, 419; Gadsden *v.* Brown, 1 Speers Eq. (So. Car.) 41; Hewitt, *in re*, 25 N. J. Eq. 210.

[2] See Coles *v.* Bulman, 6 C. B. 184; Brown *v.* Hodgson, 4 Taunt. 189; Granite Bank *v.* Fitch, 145 Mass. 567; Hart *v.* Western R. R. Co., 13 Met. 99; Mason *v.* Sainsbury, 3 Doug. 61; Hall *v.* Nashville & Chatt. R. R. Co., 13 Wallace, 367; Burr *v.* Beers, 24 N. Y. 178; Union Ins. Co. *v.* Burrell, Anth. Cas. (N. Y.) 128; Edgerly *v.* Emerson, 23 N. H. 555; Stevens *v.*

King, 84 Maine, 291; Hatch *v.* Kimball, 16 Maine, 146; Darst *v.* Thomas, 87 Ills. 222; Croft *v.* Moore, 9 Watts (Penn.), 451.

[3] A good illustration of this extension is found in the increasing inclination to hold that the payment of a debt by one entitled to subrogation does not extinguish it as against the primary debtor, but that the right may be enforced, not only by bill in equity, or by retaining independent collateral securities, but also by action at law directly upon the original obligation, which has thus been paid. See *postea*, §§ 45, 135 *et seq.*, 180.

the substitution of another person in the place of a creditor,[1] so that the person in whose favor it is exercised succeeds to the rights of the creditor in relation to the debt.[2]  More broadly, it is the substitution of one person in the place of another, whether as a creditor or as the possessor of any other rightful claim.[3]  The substitute is put in all respects in the place of the party to whose rights he is subrogated.[4] It has been adopted from the civil law by courts of equity.[5] In this country, under the initial guidance of Chancellor Kent, its principles have been more widely developed, and its doctrines more generally applied, than in England.[6]  It is treated as the creature of equity,[7] and is so administered as to secure real and essential justice without regard to form,[8] independently of any contractual relations between the parties to be affected by it.[9]  It is broad enough to include every instance in which one party pays a debt for which another is primarily answerable, and which, in equity and good conscience, should have been discharged by the latter;[10] but it is not to be ap-

---

[1] 2 Bouvier's Law Dic., *verb. cit.*

[2] King *v.* Dwight, 3 Rob. (La.) 2.

[3] Devens, J., in Jackson *v.* Boylston Ins. Co., 139 Mass. 508, 510; Gans *v.* Thieme, 93 N. Y. 225; Acer *v.* Hotchkiss, 97 N. Y. 395, 402; Sidener *v.* Hawes, 37 Ohio St. 532; Smith *v.* Foran, 43 Conn. 244; Stiger *v.* Bent, 111 Ills. 328; Braden *v.* Graves, 85 Ind. 92.

[4] Ohio Ins. Co. *v.* Winn, 4 Md. Ch. Dec. 253; Hodges *v.* Hightower, 68 Ga. 281.

[5] Shinn *v.* Budd, 14 N. J. Eq. 234; Springer *v.* Springer, 43 Penn. St. 518; Easterly *v.* Auburn Bank, 3 Thomp. & C. (N. Y.) 366; Furnold *v.* Missouri Bank, 44 Mo. 338.

[6] Enders *v.* Brune, 4 Rand. (Va.) 438, 447; Douglass *v.* Fagg, 8 Leigh (Va.), 588, 598; Furnold *v.* Missouri Bank, 44 Mo. 338.

[7] Clowes *v.* Dickenson, 5 Johns. Ch. (N. Y.) 235; s. c., 9 Cow. (N. Y.) 403; Scott *v.* Patchin, 54 Vt. 253; Mosier's Appeal, 56 Penn. St. 76; *Chapman, J.*, in Amory *v.* Lowell, 1 Allen (Mass.), 504; Meyer *v.* Mintonye, 106 Ills. 414; Terry *v.* Wooding, 2 Patton & H. (Va.) 178; Smith *v.* Harrison, 33 Ala. 706.

[8] Acer *v.* Hotchkiss, 97 N. Y. 395, 402; Hewitt, *in re,* 25 N. J. Eq. 210; Furnold *v.* Missouri Bank, 44 Mo. 338; Swan *v.* U. S. Bank, 2 Marshall, 293.

[9] Matthews *v.* Aikin, 1 N. Y. 595; Hoover *v.* Epler, 52 Penn. St. 522; Kyner *v.* Kyner, 6 Watts (Penn.), 221; Eaton *v.* Hasty, 6 Nebraska, 419.

[10] Harnsberger *v.* Yancey, 33 Gratt. (Va.) 527; Miller *v.* Winchell, 70 N. Y. 437; Stevens *v.* Goodenough, 26 Vt. 676; Lewis *v.* Palmer, 28 N. Y.

plied in favor of one who has, officiously and as a mere volunteer, paid the debt of another, for which neither he nor his property was answerable,[1] and it is not allowed where it would work any injustice to the rights of others.[2]

§ 2. **Definition in the Civil Law.** — In the civil law, the definitions of which have in the main been followed by our courts, subrogation has been defined as that change by which another person is put into the place of a creditor, so that the rights and securities of the creditor pass to the person who, by being subrogated to him, enters into his right.[3] It is a legal fiction, by force of which an obligation extinguished by a payment made by a third person[4] is treated as still subsisting for the benefit of this third person, who is thus substituted to the rights, remedies, and securities of another.[5] The party who is subrogated is regarded as entitled to the same rights, and indeed as constituting one and the same person with the creditor whom he succeeds.[6] It takes place for the benefit of a person who, being himself a creditor, pays another creditor whose debt is preferred to his by reason of privileges or mortgages,[7] being obliged to make the payment, either as standing in the situation of a surety, or that he may remove a prior

271; Smith v. Foran, 43 Conn. 244; Darst v. Thomas, 87 Ills. 222; Greenwell v. Heritage, 71 Mo. 459; Redington v. Cornwell, 90 Calif. 49.

[1] Harrison v. Bisland, 5 Rob. (La.) 204; Fort v. Union Bank, 11 La. Ann. 708; Roth v. Harkson, 18 La. Ann. 705; Stiewell v. Burdell, 18 La. Ann. 17; Brice v. Watkins, 30 La. Ann. 21; Gadsden v. Brown, 1 Speers Eq. (So. Car.) 41; Shinn v. Budd, 14 N. J. Eq. 234; Griffin v. Proctor, 14 Bush (Ky.), 571.

[2] Knouf's Appeal, 91 Penn. St. 78; Bender v. George, 92 Penn. St. 36; Lloyd v. Galbraith, 32 Penn. St. 103; McGinniss's Appeal, 16 Penn. St. 445;

Keely v. Cassidy, 93 Penn. St. 318; Hatch v. Kimball, 16 Maine, 146; Reilly v. Mayer, 12 N. J. Eq. 55; Kelly v. Kelly, 54 Mich. 30; Longfellow, in re, 17 N. B. R. 27.

[3] Domat, Civ. Law, pt. I., l. III., t. l, § 6; King v. Dwight, 3 Rob. (La.) 2.

[4] New Orleans Bank v. Eagle Cotton Co., 43 La. Ann. 814.

[5] Guyot, *Répertoire Universelle*, *Subrogation*, § 2; Merlin, *Inst. de Droit, Subrogatio*.

[6] Massé, *Droit Commerciel*, Payment in subrogation.

[7] Spiller v. Creditors, 16 La. Ann. 292.

incumbrance from the property on which he relies to secure his payment.[1]

**§ 3. Who will be subrogated.** — Subrogation, as a matter of right, independently of agreement, takes place for the benefit of insurers;[2] of one who, being himself a creditor, has satisfied the lien of a prior creditor;[3] of a purchaser who has extinguished an incumbrance upon the estate which he has purchased;[4] of a co-obligor or surety who has paid the debt which ought, in whole or in part, to have been met by another;[5] of an heir who has paid the debts of the succession;[6] of one who has paid his own debt, the burden of which has, for a valuable consideration, been assumed by another;[7] or of a creditor, who is thereby enabled to subject to the payment of his demand securities or remedies held for its payment by those who are under merely a subsidiary liability to himself.[8]  And there will be no subrogation unless the payment was made either under compulsion, or for the protection of some interest of the party making the payment, and in discharge of an existing liability.[9]  The demand of a creditor which is paid with the money of a third person, without any agreement that the security shall be assigned or kept on foot

---

[1] Griffin v. Orman, 9 Fla. 22; Shinn v. Budd, 14 N. J. Eq. 234; Silver Lake Bank v. North, 4 Johns. Ch. (N. Y.) 370.

[2] *Postea,* § 221, *et seq.*

[3] Ellsworth v. Lockwood, 42 N. Y. 89; Mosier's Appeal, 56 Penn. St. 76; Miller v. Whittier, 36 Maine, 577.

[4] Kirkland, *in re,* 14 N. B. R. 139; Corbally v. Hughes, 59 Ga. 493; Armentrout v. Gibbons, 30 Gratt. (Va.) 632; Hays v. Dalton, 5 Lea (Tenn.), 555.

[5] Cottrell's Appeal, 23 Penn. St. 294; Young v. Vough, 23 N. J. Eq. 325; Silk v. Eyre, Irish Rep. 9 Eq. 393.

[6] Clowes v. Dickenson, 5 Johns.

Ch. (N. Y.) 235; Brigden v. Cheever, 10 Mass. 450; Mitchell v. Mitchell, 8 Humph. (Tenn.) 359; *Tilghman, C. J.,* in Guier v. Kelly, 2 Binney (Penn.), 294, 299; Jenness v. Robinson, 10 N. H. 215.

[7] Kinnear v. Lowell, 34 Maine, 299; Henson v. Reed, 71 Tex. 726.

[8] *Postea,* §§ 85, 154 *et seq.*

[9] Webster's Appeal, 86 Penn. St. 409; Mosier's Appeal, 56 Penn. St. 76; Sanford v. M'Lean, 3 Paige (N. Y.), 117; Gadsden v. Brown, Speers Eq. (So. Car.) 37; Faurot v. Neff, 32 Ohio St. 44; Spray v. Rodman, 43 Ind. 225; Bunn v. Lindsay, 95 Mo. 250; Roth v. Harkson, 18 La. Ann. 705.

for the benefit of such third person, is absolutely extinguished;[1] but the doctrine of subrogation will be applied to reimburse one who has been compelled to pay the debt of a third person in order to protect his own rights or to save his own property.[2] It will not be used to reimburse a father for the expense of supporting and educating his own children.[3] And it will be applied only in favor of one who has actually performed the obligations of another,[4] and thereby entitled himself to the rights and advantages incident to the discharge of such obligations. The mere extinguishment of another's right by legal means is not enough.[5] Consequently, a prior mortgagee acquires no right, by the foreclosure of his mortgage, to redeem from a lien subsequent to his own,[6] or to hold the surplus proceeds on the foreclosure of a junior mortgage.[7]

§ 4. **It is a Mode of Equitable Relief.** — Subrogation is an exercise of the equitable powers of the court, to relieve a meritorious creditor, who might otherwise be subjected to loss by his funds being applied to pay another's debt,[8] or by the operation of proceedings at law against the estate or funds of one who is indebted both to him and to others.[9] This remedy is allowed only when it does not conflict with the legal or equitable rights of other creditors of the common debtor; and the principle is one of equity merely, and will be carried out in the exercise of a proper equitable discretion,[10]

[1] Shinn v. Budd, 14 N. J. Eq. 234; Webster's Appeal, 86 Penn. St. 409; McClure v. Andrews, 68 Ind. 97; Guy v. Du Uprey, 16 Calif. 195.

[2] Cole v. Malcolm, 66 N. Y. 363; Ellsworth v. Lockwood, 42 N. Y. 89; Bishop v. O'Conner, 69 Ills. 431; Suppiger v. Garrels, 20 Ill. Ap. 625; Whithed v. Pillsbury, 13 N. B. R. 241.

[3] Nunn v. Berger, 76 Ga. 705.

[4] Soulié v. Brown, 13 La. Ann. 521; Judah v. Judd, 1 Conn. 309; Hoover v. Epler, 52 Penn. St. 522; Carter v. Neal, 24 Ga. 346; Lee v. Swepson, 76 Va. 173.

[5] As in Parke v. Hush, 29 Minne. 434; Swan v. Emerson, 129 Mass. 289; and Lewis v. Caperton, 8 Gratt. (Va.) 148.

[6] Goodman v. White, 26 Conn. 317; Townsend v. Ward, 27 Conn. 610; Morris v. Oakford, 9 Penn. St. 498.

[7] Firestone v. State, 100 Ind 226.

[8] Evans v. Robertson, 54 Miss. 683; Campau v. Miller, 46 Mich. 148; Fulton v. Nicholson, 7 Md. 104.

[9] Postea, §§ 12, 61.

[10] Crawford v. Richeson, 101 Ills. 351; Greer v. Bush, 57 Miss. 575;

with a due regard to the legal and equitable rights of others.[1] One who claims this equity must be governed by the common maxim, *Sic utere tuo ut alienum non lædas*.[2] Being a doctrine of mere equity and benevolence, it will never be enforced at the expense of a legal right.[3] Thus, where the claim of a surety for money paid by him on a judgment against his principal has been defeated at law, the surety cannot in equity be substituted to the rights of the creditor in the original judgment,[4] as would otherwise be the case.[5] Nor can one by subrogation acquire the right to alter the disposition of a fund which has already been fixed by law.[6] And since no one can rest a claim to equitable redress upon his own wrong,[7] a collector of internal revenue who has, contrary to law, deposited taxes collected by him in a savings bank which has since failed, and who has thereupon paid the amount due to the United States from his own funds, will not be subrogated to the rights of the United States as a preferred creditor of the bank.[8] But upon making good to the government, in pursuance of his obligation so to do, the amount of a check lawfully received from a government debtor and subsequently dishonored, he may be subrogated to the rights of the government against that debtor.[9]

§ 5. **Doctrine adopted in Louisiana.** — In Louisiana, subrogation to the rights of a creditor in favor of a third person who pays him is either conventional or by operation of law.[10]

Ritter *v.* Cost, 99 Ind. 80; Forest Oil Co.'s Appeal, 118 Penn. St. 138; Blake *v.* Traders' Bank, 149 Mass. 250; Drake *v.* Paige, 127 N. Y. 562.

[1] Wagner *v.* Elliott, 95 Penn. St. 487; Rankin *v.* Coare, 46 N. J. Eq. 566; Dillow *v.* Warfel, 71 Iowa, 106; Jones *v.* Covington, 84 Va. 778.

[2] *Chambers, J.*, in McGinniss's Appeal, 16 Penn. St. 445, 447.

[3] Blake *v.* Koons, 71 Iowa, 357. *Postea*, §§ 63, 65, 79.

[4] Fink *v.* Mahaffy, 8 Watts (Penn.), 384.

[5] *Postea*, §§ 135–137.

[6] Williams *v.* Aylesbury Railw. Co., L. R. 9 Ch. 684. See Cooke, *in re*, 19 Fed. Rep. 88.

[7] *Postea*, § 44. Martin *v.* Parsons, 50 Calif. 498.

[8] Wilkinson *v.* Babbitt, 4 Dillon, C. C. 207.

[9] McBride, *in re*, 19 N. B. R. 452.

[10] See Nugent *v.* Potter, 21 La. Ann. 746.

Conventional subrogation, which is equivalent to an absolute transfer or assignment of the debt with its accessories,[1] takes place when the creditor, upon receiving payment from a third person, subrogates him to his own rights and remedies against the debtor;[2] this subrogation will not be implied, but must be formally expressed at the same time as the payment.[3] Legal subrogation, or subrogation by operation of law, takes place only for the benefit of one who, being himself a creditor, pays another creditor whose claim is preferable to his own by reason of privileges or mortgages; of a purchaser of immovable property who employs the purchase-money in paying mortgages upon the property; of one, who being bound with others or for others for the payment of a debt, had an interest in discharging it;[4] and of the beneficiary heir who has paid with his own funds the debts of the succession.[5] Thus, an agent who has paid over to his principal from his own funds the amount due upon a mortgage-note intrusted to him, no express subrogation having been made because the principal supposed that the money came from the debtor, acquires no interest in the note, but both that and the mortgage are extinguished;[6] if the agent's payment had been made in consequence of a legal obligation, subrogation might have been allowed.[7] And full payment of the amount agreed upon is a condition precedent of conventional, as well as of legal subrogation.[8]

§ 6. **Follows the Discharge of an Obligation. Adds Nothing to the Right.** — Subrogation to the rights of a creditor differs from an assignment of the debt, in that the latter assumes

---

[1] Lynch v. Kitchen, 2 La. Ann. 843; Jack v. Harrison, 34 La. Ann. 736; Oakey v. Sheriff, 13 La. Ann. 273.

[2] Virgin's Succession, 18 La. Ann. 42.

[3] Harrison v. Bisland, 5 Rob. (La.) 204; Sewall v. Howard, 15 La. Ann. 400; Virgin's Succession, 18 La. Ann. 42; Hoyle v. Cazabat, 25 La. Ann.

438; Brice v. Watkins, 30 La. Ann. 21.

[4] Miss. & Mex. G. S. Canal Co. v. Noyes, 25 La. Ann. 62.

[5] Stiewell v. Burdell, 18 La. Ann. 17.

[6] Brice v. Watkins, 30 La. Ann. 21.

[7] Postea, § 10 a.

[8] Soulié v. Brown, 13 La. Ann. 521.

the continued existence of the debt, while the former follows only upon its payment.[1] Before the right of subrogation accrues, the legal obligation resting upon the ultimate debtor must be discharged.[2] But the subrogation of an insurer to the remedies of the insured for the destruction of the insured property proceeds rather upon an implied assignment than upon a satisfaction of the cause of action.[3] And the party for whose benefit the doctrine of subrogation is exercised can acquire no greater rights than those of the party for whom he is substituted;[4] if the latter had not a right of recovery, the former can acquire none.[5]

§ 7. Instances. Subrogation of a Sheriff. — Where a sheriff upon a void execution collected the amount due upon a valid judgment and paid it over to the judgment-creditor, the sheriff, upon the judgment-debtor's recovering a judgment against him for the amount so collected, was subrogated for his protection to the rights of the original judgment-creditor,[6] and also to the rights of the original defendant against the original plaintiff.[7] If a sheriff, at the request of the defendant in an execution which has been committed to him for collection, neglects to make a levy and collect the money and return the execution according to its command, thus making himself personally liable for the amount of the judgment, and then,

---

[1] *Sutherland*, J., in Ellsworth v. Lockwood, 42 N. Y. 89, 97; *Colt*, J., in Lamb v. Montague, 112 Mass. 353.

[2] *Simrall*, J., in Staples v. Fox, 45 Miss. 667, 680. *Postea*, § 45.

[3] Mason v. Sainsbury, 3 Doug. 61; London Ass. Co. v. Sainsbury, 3 Doug. 245; Yates v. Whyte, 4 Bing. N. C. 272; Hall v. Nashv. & Chatt. R. R. Co., 13 Wallace, 367; Hart v. Western R. R. Co., 13 Met. 99; Peoria Ins. Co. v. Frost, 37 Ills. 333.

[4] Knapp v. Sturges, 36 Vt. 721; Cooke v. Moore, 2 So. Car. 52; City

Bank v. Smesson, 73 Ga. 422; Teague v. Corbitt, 57 Ala. 529; Campbell v. Elliott, 52 Tex. 151.

[5] Brown v. Houck, 41 Hun (N. Y.) 16; Miller v. Stout, 5 Del. Ch. 259; Harrington v. Fulton, *Id.* 492; Franklin Savings Bank v. Taylor, 131 Ills. 376; Alliance Ins. Co. v. Louisiana Ins. Co., 8 La. 11; Bank of Kentucky v. Milton, 12 B. Mon. (Ky.) 340; Simpson v. Thomson, 3 App. Cas. 279.

[6] Gillette v. Hill, 102 Ind. 531.

[7] Shaw v. Holmes, 4 Heisk. (Tenn.) 692.

on compulsion of the creditor, pays the judgment, he may be subrogated to all the rights of the judgment-creditor against the defendant,[1] especially if he took an assignment of the judgment.[2] He will be subrogated to all the rights of his deputy, for whose default he has been made liable,[3] though the deputy's right to subrogation rests on a different footing.[4] And if, after he has, by his neglect to collect the execution, become himself liable to pay it, he takes out an *alias* for his own use, he has been subrogated to the rights of the creditor.[5] So, if he has been compelled to pay a judgment in consequence of having neglected to assign a bail-bond to the creditor, he may be subrogated to the rights of the creditor in this bail-bond.[6] He may be subrogated to the benefit of a judgment which he has paid under a mistaken belief of his legal liability therefor, if he cannot recover back his payment at law.[7] But this right of subrogation, where no assignment of the judgment has been taken, cannot as a matter of course be enforced at law.[8] And the bare payment by a sheriff with his own funds of an execution put into his hands will not subrogate him to the lien of the judgment as against subsequent creditors of the same defendant.[9] His bare payment of the amount of an execution to the judgment-creditor without any

---

[1] Staples v. Fox, 45 Miss. 667; Bellows v. Allen, 23 Vt. 169; Allen v. Holden, 9 Mass. 183; People v. Onondaga, 19 Wend. (N. Y.) 79; Rees v. Eames, 20 Ills. 282; Bray v. Howard, 7 B. Mon. (Ky.) 467; Taylor v. Hardin, 4 B. Mon. (Ky.) 363.

[2] Heilig v. Lemley, 74 Nor. Car. 250. See also Grant v. Ludlow, 8 Ohio St. 1; Smith v. Miller, 25 N. Y. 619; Rhea v. Preston, 75 Va. 757; Hall v. Taylor, 18 W. Va. 544; Garrow v. Maxwell, 6 Jones Law ( Nor. Car.) 529; Lintz v. Thompson, 1 Head (Tenn.), 456; Poe v. Dorrah, 20 Ala. 288.

[3] Downer v. South Royalton Bank, 39 Vt. 25.

[4] Lee County v. Fulkerson, 21 Gratt. (Va.) 182.

[5] Evarts v. Hyde, 51 Vt. 183; Beard v. Arbuckle, 19 W. Va. 135.

[6] Higgins v. Glass, 2 Jones Law (Nor. Car.), 353.

[7] Farmers' Bank v. Grantham, 3 Harr. (Del.) 289.

[8] Stout v. Dilts, 1 Southard (N. J.), 218; Walker v. Bradbury, 57 Mo. 66.

[9] Clevinger v. Miller, 27 Gratt. (Va.) 740; Martin v. Gowdy, 1 Hill (So. Car.), 417; Harwell v. Worsham, 2 Humph. (Tenn.) 524.

stipulation that it shall be kept alive for his benefit will give him no right of subrogation; [1] nor will his payment made by arrangement with the debtor upon other security taken for his protection.[2] And this subrogation, though allowed against the judgment-creditor, has been limited so as not to override junior liens of other creditors nowise in fault.[3] If the liability of the sheriff is for not paying over to the creditor the avails of the defendant's property which he has sold on the execution, then he cannot be subrogated.[4] Nor can the sheriff be subrogated before he has made full payment, or had judgment rendered against him.[5] And his right of subrogation has been denied.[6] A judgment-debtor who has, in consequence of the sheriff's misconduct, been compelled to pay the judgment twice, may be subrogated for his remedy to the creditor's rights against the sheriff.[7] A tax-collector may be subrogated like a sheriff.[8]

§ 8. **Subrogation of one who has advanced Money for the payment of an Incumbrance.** —Where money has been loaned upon a defective mortgage for the purpose of discharging a prior valid incumbrance, and has actually been so applied, the mortgagee may be subrogated to the rights of the prior incumbrancer whom he has thus satisfied,[9] there being no

[1] Bigelow v. Provost, 5 Hill (N. Y.), 566; Albany Bank v. Kearney, 9 Hun (N. Y.), 535; Arnett v. Cloud, 2 Ga. 53; Finn v. Stratton, 5 J. J. Marsh. (Ky.) 364; Garth v. McCampbell, 10 Mo. 154; Bailey v. Gibbs, 9 Mo. 45; Rutland v. Pippin, 7 Ala. 469.

[2] Rogers v. Nuttall, 10 Ired. Law (Nor. Car.), 347; Reed v. Pruyn, 7 Johns. (N. Y.) 426.

[3] Feamster v. Withrow, 12 W. Va. 612; Sherman v. Shaver, 75 Va. 1.

[4] Bellows v. Allen, 23 Vt. 169; Wright v. Fitzgerald, 17 Ohio St. 635.

[5] Beal v. Smithpeter, 6 Baxter (Tenn.), 356; Pool v. Hunter, 4 Jones Law (Nor. Car.), 144.

[6] Jones v. Wilson, 3 Johns. (N. Y.), 434; Menderback v. Hopkins, 8 Johns. (N. Y.) 436; Carpenter v. Stilwell, 11 N. Y. 61; Whittier v. Heminway, 22 Maine, 238; Albany Bank v. Kearney, 9 Hun (N. Y.), 535; Carpenter v. Fifield, 14 R. I. 73; Evans v. Billingsley, 32 Ala. 395; Roundtree v. Weaver, 8 Ala. 314.

[7] Harvey v. Warren, 31 Neb. 155. *Postea*, § 91.

[8] Meyer v. Burritt, 60 Conn. 117; Hook v. Richardson, 115 Ills. 431; White v. State, 51 Ga. 252; Thomas v. Hammer, 13 Lea (Tenn.), 620; Turner v. Teague, 73 Ala. 554.

[9] Lockwood v. Marsh, 3 Nevada,

intervening incumbrances.[1] But it is necessary both that the money should have been advanced for the purpose of discharging the prior incumbrance, and that it should actually have been so applied.[2] So, where a husband and wife gave a mortgage for money lent to them for the purpose of discharging a prior incumbrance, which was accordingly done, and the wife turned out to have been an infant at the time of the new mortgage, the mortgagee was subrogated to the rights of the prior incumbrancer as against the wife.[3] And if it is expressly agreed that the old incumbrance shall be kept alive as security for the new advance, but the debtor in fraud of his agreement procures it to be discharged, the person making the advance may be subrogated to the benefit of the prior lien, even against other incumbrancers prior to himself, whose rights have not been acquired on the faith of the apparent discharge.[4] One who had lent his notes to the purchaser of land to pay the price thereof was allowed upon payment of the notes to be subrogated to the benefit of a mortgage given by the purchaser to the vendor to secure their payment.[5] So, one who has, at the request of the owner of goods, advanced the money to discharge a lien thereon may retain possession of the goods until he shall be reimbursed.[6] But these are ex-

138; Clark v. Clark, 58 Miss. 68; Emigrant Savings Bank v. Clute, 33 Hun (N. Y.), 82; s. c., affirmed in 2 Silvernail, N. Y. Ct. Appeals, 340; Bolman v. Lohman, 74 Ala. 507; Everston v. Kansas Bank, 33 Kans. 352; Critten v. Chappel, 35 Kans. 495; Gilbert v. Gilbert, 39 Iowa, 657. In the last case, a mortgage executed by a trustee who had the power to give mortgages for the discharge of a prior incumbrance, was invalid for lack of proper execution, and the plaintiff would have had no redress on his security but for the equitable doctrine of subrogation. The same rule was applied in Chaffee v. Oliver, 39 Ark. 531, and in Levy v. Martin, 48 Wisc. 198, but is not universally adopted. Fry v. Hammer, 50 Ala. 52; Ætna Ins. Co. v. Buck, 108 Ind. 174.

[1] Kitchell v. Mudgett, 37 Mich. 82.

[2] Barber v. Lyon, 15 Iowa, 37; Flannary v. Utley, 5 S. W. Rep. 878.

[3] Snelling v. McIntyre, 6 Abbott, N. Y. Cas. 469.

[4] Downer v. Miller, 15 Wisc. 612. See also White v. Knapp, 8 Paige Ch. (N. Y.) 173; Cole v. Edgerley, 48 Maine, 108.

[5] Chonler v. Smith, 3 Desaus. Eq. (So. Car.) 12.

[6] Edwards v. Frank, 40 Mich. 616.

treme cases.[1] If the title to land conveyed and accepted in discharge of a mortgage upon other property afterwards turns out to be defective, this defect, though it may be the subject of a new demand, cannot operate to revive the original mortgage, even with the mortgagor's consent, to the prejudice of rights acquired by others in the mean time.[2] And where a mortgage has been cancelled and discharged, and a new security upon the same land has been taken for the debt, the mortgage will, unless there are countervailing equities,[3] be regarded as if it had never existed, and intervening incumbrances or attachments will be let in.[4]

§ 9. **Of one who has been compelled to pay the Debt of another.** — A third person who pays off a mortgage-debt for his own protection may be subrogated to the place of the mortgagee, and may retain the mortgage for his reimbursement.[5] One who pays taxes which are a lien upon land to which he must look for the payment of his debt,[6] or in which he has an apparent interest,[7] in order to preserve the property from the lien, will be entitled by subrogation to reimbursement out of the property itself. Where at an auction sale of a debtor's property, the debtor has fraudulently procured a sham bid to be made by an irresponsible person, and has thereby caused the land of another to be afterwards sold for the satisfaction of the debt which ought to have been discharged out of his own property, the party thus injured may, by subrogation to the rights of the original creditor, hold the primary debtor for the amount of his loss.[8] One who in good faith, believing

[1] *Postea,* §§ 240 *et seq.*

[2] Lasselle *v.* Barnett, 1 Blackf. (Ind.) 150.

[3] Charleston Bank *v.* Epstin, 44 Fed. Rep. 403. *Postea,* § 90.

[4] Stearns *v.* Godfrey, 16 Maine, 158; Woollen *v.* Hillen, 9 Gill (Md.), 185.

[5] Coster, *in re,* 2 Johns. Ch. (N. Y.) 503. *Postea,* § 12 *et seq.*

[6] Broquet *v.* Sterling, 56 Iowa, 857; Waterson *v.* Devoe, 18 Kans. 223; Whittaker *v.* Wright, 35 Ark. 511.

[7] Arn *v.* Hoppen, 25 Kans. 707; Weimer *v.* Porter, 42 Mich. 569; Ingersoll *v.* Jeffords, 55 Miss. 37.

[8] Darst *v.* Thomas, 87 Ills. 222.

himself to have an interest in property which is subject to a
lien, pays off the lien to protect that interest, will in equity
be subrogated for his reimbursement to the protection of that
lien, as against the real owner of the property, who has stood
by in silence while the payment was made.[1]  So, a grantee
of land who, through neglect to record his deed, has had the
land taken from him upon a judgment recovered against his
grantor, may by subrogation in equity claim the benefit of a
mortgage held by the judgment-creditor to secure the debt
upon which the judgment was rendered, so far as the same
is not required for the full satisfaction of the debt, and to
the extent of his loss by the levy upon his land.  " The
plaintiff," said Mr. Justice Chapman, " has paid his grantor's
debt, which his grantor ought to have paid himself ; and it
is but just that he should have the benefit of the security
which his grantor had previously given to the creditor for
the debt." [2]

§ 10.  Of a Carrier. — A carrier who has paid the charges of
antecedent carriers for the transportation of goods sent over
successive lines will be subrogated to their rights,[3] even though
he afterwards fails to perform his own contract ;[4] but this
right will extend only to necessary charges for actual transportation.[5]  And if property in a carrier's possession is lost
or destroyed by the fault of another, the carrier will, upon
saisfying the owners for such loss, be subrogated to their
rights.[6]  Thus, where notes issued by a bank had been stolen
while in the course of transportation by an express company,

---

[1] Fowler v. Parsons, 143 Mass.
401 ; Cockrum v. West, 122 Ind.
372.

[2] Wall v. Mason, 102 Mass. 313 ;
Weiss v. Guerineau, 109 Ind. 438.

[3] Lee v. Salter, Lalor's Sup. to
Hill & Denio (N. Y.), 163 ; Hunt v.
Haskell, 24 Maine, 339 ; Briggs v.
Boston & Lowell R. R. Co., 6 Allen
(Mass.), 246 ; White v. Vann, 6

Humph. (Tenn.) 70 ; Wells v. Thomas,
27 Mo. 17.

[4] Western Transportation Co. v.
Hoyt, 69 N. Y. 230.

[5] Steamboat Virginia v. Kraft, 25
Mo. 76.

[6] United States v. Vermilye, 10
Blatchf. C. C. 280 ; Pierce v. Win-
ser, 2 Sprague, 35 ; Brass v. Mait-
land, 6 Ellis & Bl. 470.

and subsequently destroyed, and the company, being liable
for the loss, paid the amount thereof, it was held that, upon
such payment, the property in the notes vested in the express
company; and, upon proof of their destruction, it was
allowed to recover their amount from the bank.[1]  So, where
a carrier has by mistake delivered to one person goods which
had been sold and consigned to another, and the former has
appropriated them for his own use, the carrier, after satisfying the real owner for the loss, may recover the value of the
goods from the person who has thus received them.[2]  The
carrier's agent, who made the mistake which created the
carrier's liability, may, upon the carrier's satisfying the owner
and such agent's reimbursing the carrier, be subrogated in the
same way.[3]  The carrier is subrogated to liens for charges
which he is compelled to pay to obtain or to retain the
goods.[4]  A letter-carrier, who, having delivered to a hotel-
clerk a valuable registered letter, has been held to pay for its
loss arising from the clerk's negligence, will be subrogated to
the remedy against the clerk, the party ultimately liable.[5]

§ 10 a.  Of a Consignee or Agent. — The consignee of property who has sold the same and deposited the proceeds in
bank to the credit of the consignor, if afterwards on the failure
of the bank obliged to pay the amount of such proceeds to the
consignor, will be subrogated to the rights of the consignor
against the insolvent bank and its assignee.[6]  An agent's
payment of the debt of a third party to his principal, made in
discharge of a liability as guarantor or surety, or under compulsion of a judgment, will subrogate the agent to the
principal's remedy against the third party.[7]  So, an attorney,

[1] Hagerstown Bank v. Adams Express Co., 45 Penn. St. 419.
[2] Brown v. Hodgson, 4 Taunt. 189;
Coles v. Bulman, 6 C. B. 184.
[3] O'Neal v. Deese, 23 Ga. 477.
[4] Guesnard v. Louisville & Nashville R. R. Co., 76 Ala. 453.

[5] Joslyn v. King, 27 Neb. 38.
[6] Stoller v. Coates, 4 West. Rep.
600.
[7] Bank of Scotland v. Dominion
Bank, (1891) 1 App. Cas. 592; Nichols v. Wadsworth, 40 Minne. 547.

having become personally liable to his client for the amount of a judgment by reason of having neglected to compel the sheriff to pay over the amount collected thereon, is, by payment to his client, subrogated to his client's rights against the sheriff, and may for his own benefit enforce payment from the latter.[1]

§ 11. **General Doctrine of Subrogation.** — In short, the doctrine of subrogation is that one who has been compelled to pay a debt which ought to have been paid by another is entitled to exercise all the remedies which the creditor possessed against that other,[2] and to indemnity from the fund out of which should have been made the payment which he has made.[3] To the creditor they may have been both equally liable; but if, as between themselves, there is a superior obligation resting upon one to pay the debt, the other, after paying it, may use the creditor's securities to obtain reimbursement. The doctrine does not depend upon privity,[4] nor is it confined to cases of suretyship, though in Massachusetts it has been refused at law on the ground of a lack of privity.[5] It is a mode which equity adopts, to compel the ultimate discharge of a debt by him who in equity and good conscience ought to pay it, and to relieve him whom none but the creditor could ask to pay.[6] Although, as between debtor and creditor, the debt may be extinguished, yet, as between the person who has paid the debt and the other parties, the debt is kept alive, so far as may be necessary to preserve the securities.[7] The payment of the money due upon a debt will operate as a discharge of the indebtedness, or as subrogating

---

[1] Governor v. Raley, 34 Ga. 173.

[2] City Bank v. Crossland, 65 Ga. 734; Thomas v. Bridges, 73 Mo. 530; Weiss v. Guerineau, 109 Ind. 438.

[3] Allen v. Williams, 33 N. J. Eq. 584; Darst v. Thomas, 87 Ills. 222.

[4] Eldridge v. Wright, 55 Calif. 531. *Postea*, § 93.

[5] Beck v. Gallagher, 114 Mass. 28; Holmes v. Day, 108 Mass. 563.

[6] *Strong, J.*, in McCormick v. Irwin, 35 Penn. St. 111, 117; Heart v. Bryan, 2 Dev. Eq. (Nor. Car.) 147.

[7] *Chapman, J.*, in Wall v. Mason, 102 Mass. 316.

him who pays it to the place of the creditor, as may best
serve the purposes of justice and the just intent of the
parties.[1] But the burden is always on one who claims this
equity to show that he is entitled to it.[2]

---

[1] *Parker, J.*, in Robinson *v.* Leavitt, 7 N. H. 99; Bacon *v.* Goodnow, 59 N. H. 415; Danville Poor District *v.* Montour County, 75 Penn. St. 35; Houston Bank *v.* Ackerman, 70 Tex. 315.

[2] Wilkinson *v.* Babbitt, 4 Dillon, C. C. 207; Hunnicutt *v.* Summy, 63 Ga. 586; Binford *v.* Adams, 104 Ind. 41; Griffith *v.* Townley, 69 Mo. 13.

# CHAPTER II.

SUBROGATION IN CASES WHERE DIFFERENT PARTIES HAVE SUC-
CESSIVE CLAIMS UPON THE SAME PROPERTY, BY MORTGAGE,
LIEN, OR PURCHASE.

2

§ 12. **Subrogation of a Junior Incumbrancer upon Payment of a Prior Incumbrance.** — All persons having an interest in property subject to an incumbrance by which their interest may be prejudiced or lost have a right to disengage the property from such incumbrance by the payment of the debt or charge which creates it;[1] and if such debt be one for which another party is ultimately liable, they will, upon their payment, be subrogated to the right of the creditor against the ultimate debtor,[2] and against the property upon which the debt was a charge.[3] A mortgagee can make no effectual resistance to a claim for subrogation by one who tenders to him his debt and costs, and who has a subordinate interest in the property, which would either be lost or seriously injured without the proposed substitution.[4] So, a second mortgagee who

---

[1] Powers v. Golden Lumber Co., 43 Mich. 468; Smith v. Provin, 4 Allen (Mass.), 516; Green v. Tanner, 8 Met. (Mass.) 411; Morse v. Smith, 83 Ills. 396; Willis v. Jelineck, 27 Minn. 18; Wiley v. Ewing, 47 Ala. 418; Scott v. Henry, 13 Ark. 112.

[2] Southworth v. Scofield, 51 N. Y. 513; Graham v. Dunnigan, 4 Abbott Pr. (N. Y.) 426; Lucking v. Wesson, 25 Mich. 443; Evans v. Saunders, 3 Lea (Tenn.), 734; Exall v. Partridge, 8 T. R. 308.

[3] Denman v. Nelson, 31 N. J. Eq. 452; Coster, in re, 2 Johns. Ch. (N. Y.) 503; Dings v. Parshall, 7 Hun (N. Y.),

522; Page v. Foster, 7 N. H. 392; Downer v. Fox, 20 Vt. 388; Young v. Williams, 17 Conn. 393; Mosier's Appeal, 56 Penn. St. 76; Darst v. Bates, 95 Ills. 493; Goode v. Cummings, 35 Iowa, 67; Darling v. Harmon, 47 Minn. 166; White v. Hampton, 13 Iowa, 259; Carter v. Taylor, 3 Head (Tenn.), 30; Staples v. Fox, 45 Miss. 667; Griswold v. Marshman, 2 Ch. Cas. 170.

[4] Davis v. Cook, 65 Ala. 617; McLean v. Tompkins, 18 Abbott Pr. (N. Y.) 24; Emigrant Savings Bank v. Clute, 33 Hun (N. Y.), 82.

is in danger of losing his security by the foreclosure of the
first mortgage may redeem from the first mortgagee, or pay
the debt secured by the first mortgage, and may thereupon
look to the mortgaged property for his reimbursement,[1] even
against intervening incumbrances.[2]  On the same principle,
the lien of a pledgee will cover freight paid by him upon the
goods pledged;[3] and as a carrier's lien for the carriage of
the specific goods is prior to the vendor's right of stoppage
*in transitu*, and the carrier may insist upon retaining possession until these charges are paid,[4] an officer who pays these
charges to the carrier in order to obtain the goods for the
vendor is substituted to the carrier's right of possession until
he is repaid.[5]  The general rule is that a lien-creditor, on
paying the mortgage or other lien which is prior to his own,
is subrogated by law to the rights of the creditor whose debt
he has paid.[6]  A second mortgagee who, to prevent a foreclosure of the first mortgage, redeems from it will be subrogated to its lien against an intervening or subsequent
attachment,[7] and an assignment of the mortgage will not
be necessary for this purpose.[8]  Though a stranger cannot
set up an outstanding satisfied mortgage as a basis of title to

[1] Bigelow *v.* Cassedy, 26 N. J. Eq.
557; Tarbell *v.* Durant, 61 Vt. 516;
Wood *v.* Hubbard, 50 Vt. 82; Weld
*v.* Sabin, 20 N. H. 533; State *v.*
Brown, 73 Md. 484; Baker *v.* Pier-
son, 6 Mich. 522; Flachs *v.* Kelly,
30 Ills. 462; Marshall *v.* Ruddick, 28
Iowa, 487; Abbott *v.* Union Life Ins.
Co., 127 Ind. 70; Arnold *v.* Foot, 7
B. Mon. (Ky.) 66.

[2] Conn. Ins. Co. *v.* Bulte, 45 Mich.
113; Erwin *v.* Acker, 126 Ind. 133;
Walker *v.* Stone, 20 Md. 195; Allen
*v.* Wood, 31 N. J. Eq. 103; Dillon *v.*
Kauffman, 58 Tex. 696.

[3] Clark *v.* Dearborn, 103 Mass.
335.

[4] See Wolfe *v.* Crawford, 54 Miss.

514; Potts *v.* N. Y. & N. E. R. R. Co.,
131 Mass. 455.

[5] Rucker *v.* Donovan, 13 Kans. 251.

[6] Silver Lake Bank *v.* North, 4
Johns. Ch. (N. Y.) 370; Brainard *v.*
Cooper, 10 N. Y. 356; Brown *v.* Si-
mons, 44 N. H. 475; Armstrong *v.*
McAlpin, 18 Ohio St. 184; Russell
*v.* Howard, 2 McLean C. C. 489;
Southard *v.* Dorrington, 10 Nebraska,
119; Grigg *v.* Banks, 59 Ala. 311;
Ventress *v.* Creditors, 20 La. Ann.
359.

[7] Ward *v.* Seymour, 51 Vt. 320;
Downer *v.* Fox, 20 Vt. 388; Flachs
*v.* Kelly, 30 Ills. 462.

[8] Moore *v.* Beasom, 44 N. H. 215;
Reyburn *v.* Mitchell, 106 Mo. 367.

the property, yet the equitable owner of the land, whose debt it was not, but who has paid it in order to protect his property, may do so.[1] But a release from a prior to a subsequent mortgagee, nothing more appearing, will operate merely as an extinguishment of the mortgage.[2]

§ 13. **Subrogation will be made to serve the Purposes of Justice and the Intent of the Parties.** — "There are cases," said Mr. Justice Parker,[3] "in which a party who has paid money due upon a mortgage is entitled, for the purpose of effecting the substantial justice of the case, to be substituted in the place of the incumbrancer, and treated as assignee of the mortgage, and is enabled to hold the land as if assignee, notwithstanding the mortgage itself has been cancelled and the debt discharged.[4] The true principle, I apprehend, is, that where money due upon a mortgage is paid, it shall operate as a discharge of the mortgage or in the nature of an assignment of it, as may best serve the purposes of justice and the just intent of the parties.[5] Many cases state the rule in equity to be that the incumbrance shall be kept on foot or considered extinguished or merged, according to the intent or the interest of the party paying the money; but the decisions themselves, it is believed, will generally be found in accordance with the principle above stated.[6] There is another class of cases in

---

[1] Peltz *v.* Clarke, 5 Peters, 481; Bacon *v.* Van Schoonhoven, 19 Hun (N. Y.), 158.

[2] Hill *v.* West, 8 Ohio, 222.

[3] Robinson *v.* Leavitt, 7 N. H. 99 *et seq.*

[4] Citing Marsh *v.* Rice, 1 N. H. 167; Peltz *v.* Clarke, 5 Peters, 481; Coster, *in re*, 2 Johns. Ch. (N. Y.) 503; Silver Lake Bank *v.* North, 4 Johns. Ch. (N. Y.) 370; Dale *v.* McEvers, 2 Cow. (N. Y.) 118.

[5] Citing Starr *v.* Ellis, 6 Johns. Ch. (N. Y.) 393. See also Hastings *v.* Stevens, 29 N. H. 564, 573; New Haven Savings Bank *v.* McPartlan, 40 Conn. 90; Devine *v.* Harkness, 117 Ills. 145.

[6] Citing Gardner *v.* Astor, 3 Johns. Ch. (N. Y.) 53; James *v.* Johnson, 6 Johns. Ch. (N. Y.) 425; s. c. on error, 2 Cow. (N. Y.) 246; Burnet *v.* Denniston, 5 Johns. Ch. (N. Y.) 35; Mills *v.* Comstock, 5 Johns. Ch. (N. Y.) 214; Freeman *v.* Paul, 3 Greenl. (Me.) 260; Thompson *v.* Chandler, 7 Greenl. (Me.) 377; Harvey *v.* Hurlburt, 3 Vt. 561; Marshall *v.* Wood, 5 Vt. 250; Lockwood *v.* Sturdevant, 6 Conn. 374; Kirkham *v.*

which he who has paid money due upon a mortgage of land
to which he had some title which might be affected or defeated by the mortgage, and who was thus entitled to redeem,
has the right to consider the mortgage as subsisting in himself, and to hold the land as if it subsisted, until others interested in the redemption, or who held also the right to
redeem, have paid a contribution.[1]  And it makes no difference in either of these classes, as I conceive, whether the
party on payment of the money took an assignment of the
mortgage or a release, or whether a discharge was made and
the evidence of the debt cancelled.[2]  The debt itself may be
held still to subsist in him who paid the money, as assignee,
so far as it ought to subsist, in the nature of a lien upon the
land, and the mortgage be considered in force for his benefit,
so far as he ought in justice to hold the land under it, as if
it had been actually assigned to him." [3]

§ 14. **Subrogation upon Redemption from a Prior Incumbrance.** — One who has paid the money due upon a mortgage
of lands to which he had a title that might have been defeated
thereby has the right to hold the lands as if the mortgage
subsisted and had been assigned to him,[4] until he has received
the amount due upon it from some one who has the right to
redeem, whether he took a discharge [5] or an assignment [6] of
the mortgage. The mortgage may, for his benefit, be considered as still subsisting, though formally discharged, so far

Smith, 1 Ves. Sen. 258; Shrewsbury
v. Shrewsbury, 1 Ves. Jun. 227, 233;
Compton v. Oxenden, 2 Ves. Jun. 261,
264; Forbes v. Moffatt, 18 Ves. 384;
Buckinghamshire v. Hobart, 3 Swanst.
186.

[1] Citing Cass v. Martin, 6 N. H.
25; Swain v. Perine, 5 Johns. Ch.
(N. Y.) 482–491; Carll v. Butman,
7 Greenl. (Me.) 102; Taylor v. Bassett, 3 N. H. 294; Russell v. Austin,
1 Paige (N. Y.), 192.

[2] Citing Snow v. Stevens, 15 Mass.

278; Barker v. Parker, 4 Pick. (Mass.)
505; Wade v. Howard, 6 Pick. (Mass.)
492.

[3] Citing Pratt v. Law, 9 Cranch,
456, 498.

[4] Twombly v. Cassidy, 82 N. Y.
155; Mix v. Hotckiss, 14 Conn. 32;
Manwaring v. Powell, 40 Mich. 371;
Taylor v. Heggie, 83 Nor. Car. 244.

[5] Arnold v. Green, 116 N. Y. 566;
Farrell v. Lewis, 56 Conn. 280; Towle
v. Hoit, 14 N. H. 61.

[6] White v. Hampton, 13 Iowa, 259.

as he ought in justice to hold the property.[1] So an incumbrancer may redeem from a paramount tax title, and be subrogated to it for his protection,[2] even against a prior mortgagee until reimbursed for his expenditures.[3] A tenant for life[4] or for years has the right to redeem from a mortgage which is prior to the creation of his tenancy, and upon redemption will be subrogated to the rights of the mortgagee against the mortgagor and the reversioner.[5] And in New Jersey he will have the right, upon redemption, to have the bond and mortgage delivered to him uncancelled, which in equity will be equivalent to an assignment of them to himself.[6] A mortgagee of a leasehold estate will have the right of subrogation upon redemption from a prior incumbrance.[7] But the tenant cannot hold the land against a prior incumbrancer by simply paying the interest as it accrues; nor can he, on paying the debt, require a formal assignment of the incumbrance.[8] He can only redeem, and then claim his subrogation.[9] And he must pay the entire amount of an incumbrance which is senior to his own estate, with whatever costs have accrued.[10]

---

[1] Lewis v. Chittick, 25 Fed. Rep. 176; Cobb v. Dyer, 69 Maine, 494; Johnson v. Elliot, 26 N. H. 67; Heath v. West, 26 N. H. 191; Schissel v. Dickson, 129 Ind. 139; McClain v. Sullivan, 85 Ind. 174; Lamb v. Richards, 43 Ills. 312.

[2] Windett v. Union Ins. Co., 144 U. S. 581; Smith v. Roberts, 91 N. Y. 470; Athens Bank v. Danforth, 80 Ga. 55; Gwinn v. Smith, 55 Ga. 145; Stiger v. Bent, 111 Ills. 328; Pratt v. Pratt, 96 Ills. 184; Johnson v. Payne, 11 Nebraska, 269; Townsend v. Case Threshing Machine Co., 31 Neb. 836; Devin v. Eagleson, 79 Iowa, 269; Stanclift v. Norton, 11 Kans. 218; Sharp v. Barker, 11 Kans. 381.

[3] Fiacre v. Chapman, 32 N. J. Eq. 463.

[4] Crawford v. Carver, 16 Phila. 53.

[5] Averill v. Taylor, 8 N. Y. 44; Loud v. Lane, 8 Met. (Mass.) 517.

[6] Hamilton v. Dobbs, 19 N. J. Eq. 227.

[7] Campbell v. McAlevy, 3 Disney, (Ohio), 574.

[8] Magilton v. Holbert, 52 Hun (N. Y.), 444.

[9] Lamson v. Drake, 105 Mass. 564; Nelson v. Loder, 132 N. Y. 288; Bigelow v. Cassedy, 26 N. J. Eq. 557.

[10] O'Reilly v. Holt, 4 Woods, C. C. 645; Shutes v. Woodard, 57 Mich. 213; Union Ins. Co. v. Kirchoff, 133 Ills. 368; Merritt v. Hosmer, 11 Gray (Mass.), 276; Street v. Beal, 16 Iowa, 68; Massie v. Wilson, 16 Iowa, 390; Knowles v. Rablin, 20 Iowa, 101.

**§ 15. Subrogation of Junior Incumbrancer compelled to pay a Prior Charge.** — A mortgagee who has been compelled, in order to protect his title, to pay the amount due upon a prior mortgage, will be subrogated to the rights of the prior mortgagee, and may hold the land for the sum so paid by himself,[1] even against one whose title to the property has accrued after the discharge of the prior mortgage upon the record, if the whole amount claimed upon both mortgages is not greater than appears to be due by the record.[2] And he may also hold for the payment of the debt secured by the prior mortgage the parties who were personally liable therefor.[3] If his payment was made to the authorized attorney of the first mortgagee, and that attorney embezzled the amount, and then transferred the first mortgage overdue to a stranger, yet the junior mortgagee will be subrogated for his protection to the prior lien of the first mortgage which he has thus paid.[4] The payment by a junior mortgagee will not relieve the real debtor from his obligation.[5] A mortgagee who purchases, at the request of the debtor, a paramount lien on the mortgaged premises, with the express understanding that it shall be tacked to the mortgage and paid out of the fund, is entitled to have it so tacked to his mortgage and paid out of the mortgaged premises.[6] The necessary expenses incurred by a subsequent mortgagee to redeem from a prior mortgage which ought to have been paid by the mortgagor, or to remove a paramount right of dower, are justly chargeable by him upon the mortgaged estate.[7] And if a junior incumbrancer takes up

---

[1] Citizens' Savings Bank v. Foster, 22 Abbott New Cases (N. Y.), 425; Porter v. Vanderlin, 146 Penn. St. 138; Hull v. Godfrey, 31 Neb. 204.

[2] Davis v. Winn, 2 Allen (Mass.), 111.

[3] Georgia Chemical Works v. Cartledge, 77 Ga. 547; Miller v. Aldrich, 31 Mich. 408; Mattison v. Marks, 31 Mich. 421.

[4] Sessions v. Kent, 75 Iowa, 601.

[5] Chandler v. Dyer, 37 Vt. 345, 354.

[6] Cullum v. Mobile Bank, 23 Ala. 797.

[7] Miller v. Whittier, 36 Maine, 577; Pierce v. Faunce, 53 Maine, 351.

a prior incumbrance which was also a lien upon other property than that to which he had himself a claim, he may resort to that other property, and enforce the lien thereon for his reimbursement.[1] If the debt secured by the incumbrance which he has thus paid bore a higher rate of interest than his own, he will be allowed the increased rate of interest on his payment,[2] subject to any legislative change in the rate of interest allowed.[3] This right of a junior mortgagee cannot be defeated by any arrangement between the prior incumbrancer and the mortgagor, or by any adjudication of their respective rights to which the junior mortgagee was not a party.[4]

§ 16. **Duty of Prior to Junior Incumbrancer.** — In England a mortgagee is required to convey and hand over the title-deeds to any person having an interest in the equity of redemption, though only a partial one, by whom he is paid off.[5] But the conveyance should be made subject to the right of redemption of all persons who hold other interests. When the party redeeming has only contracted to purchase an interest in the premises, the mortgagee need not convey until the purchaser has accepted the title.[6] The prior mortgagee ought, without judicial proceedings, to accept an offer of payment made to him by a junior incumbrancer, and thereupon to convey to him the mortgaged estate, with or without the concurrence of the mortgagor.[7] And if he refuses to do so on demand, and subsequently acquires from the mortgagor the equity of redemption, which was of sufficient value to pay the junior incumbrance, he will be himself held for the amount of the latter.[8]

[1] Peter v. Smith, 5 Cranch, C. C. 383.

[2] Dodge v. Fuller, 2 Flippin, C. C. 603; Braden v. Graves, 85 Ind. 92; Harper v. Ely, 70 Ills. 581; Mosier v. Norton, 83 Ills. 519.

[3] Memphis & Little Rock R. R. Co. v. Dow, 120 U. S. 287.

[4] Davis v. Rogers, 28 Iowa, 413; Frost v. Yonkers Bank, 8 Hun (N. Y.), 26; Blakely v. Twining, 69 Wisc. 238.

[5] St. 44 & 45 Vic., § 15. Teevan v. Smith, 20 Ch. D. 724.

[6] Pearce v. Morris, L. R. 5 Ch. 327.

[7] Smith v. Green, 1 Coll. C. C. 555; McCullough v. Staver, 119 Penn. St. 432.

[8] Griswold v. Marshman, 2 Ch. Cas. 170.

§ 17. **Junior Incumbrancer's right of Redemption.** — A junior incumbrancer or claimant has the right to redeem from a prior mortgage by paying the amount which is due according to its terms as recorded ;[1] the facts shown by the record cannot be contradicted to his prejudice.[2] When he offers to redeem, the prior mortgagee cannot tack to his demand another debt due to him from the mortgagor, not a charge upon the premises sought to be redeemed of which the junior incumbrancer was bound to take notice.[3] A latent equity of subrogation cannot be enforced against a subsequent *bona fide* purchaser for value without notice.[4] Even a mortgagee's right of subrogation to the benefit of prior liens discharged by him, if not appearing of record, cannot be enforced against those who have taken interests in reliance upon the record,[5] to an amount greater than the total sum which the record shows to be due.[6] As against the junior incumbrancer, no new terms can be incorporated into the prior mortgage, no new indebtedness can be secured by it.[7] Thus, where the parties to the mortgage stipulated for the payment of a higher rate of interest upon the mortgage-debt than was provided for by the terms of the mortgage as recorded, it was held that the excess of interest could not be made a lien upon the land to the prejudice of subsequent incumbrancers,[8] or of purchasers without notice.[9] Payments made by the mortgagor upon the indebtedness secured by the first mort-

---

[1] Whittacre *v.* Fuller, 5 Minn. 508.

[2] Gibbons *v.* Hoag, 95 Ills. 45; Eagle Beneficial Society's Appeal, 75 Penn. St. 226.

[3] Burnet *v.* Denniston, 5 Johns. Ch. (N. Y.) 35; Lee *v.* Stone, 5 Gill & J. (Md.) 1; McGuire *v.* Wilkinson, 72 Mo. 199.

[4] Richards *v.* Griffith, 92 Calif. 493.

[5] Wilson *v.* Barker, 50 Maine, 447; Ahern *v.* Freeman, 46 Minne. 156; Persons *v.* Shaeffer, 65 Calif. 79.

[6] Davis *v.* Winn, 2 Allen (Mass.), 111.

[7] Trimble *v.* Hunter, 104 Nor. Car. 129; Kistler *v.* Mosser, 140 Penn. St. 367.

[8] Gardner *v.* Emerson, 40 Ills. 296; Perrin *v.* Kellogg, 38 Mich. 720.

[9] Bassett *v.* McDonnel, 13 Wisc. 444; Burchard *v.* Frazer, 23 Mich. 224.

gage cannot afterwards be transferred to another account, to
the prejudice of a second incumbrancer, by the mortgagor
and the first mortgagee.[1] Where property was subject to the
lien of a judgment, and then to four successive mortgages,
and the holder of the judgment agreed with the fourth mortgagee to postpone his lien to that of the fourth mortgagee,
and then sold the property under his judgment to the first
mortgagee, who had no notice of this agreement, it was held
that the first mortgagee was by his purchase subrogated to
the lien of the judgment, and that the fourth mortgagee could
not redeem from him without paying the cost of buying in
the property under the judgment as well as the amount which
was due upon the first mortgage;[2] and though this decision
was reversed on appeal, the general principle was not doubted,
but it was decided on the ground that the purchaser of real
estate sold on execution acquires no other or better title than
would have vested in the judgment-creditor had the latter
purchased the property.[3]

§ 18. When Junior Incumbrancer entitled to Subrogation. —
Although a junior incumbrancer is entitled to redeem from a
prior mortgage, and although, if he is not himself the principal debtor, but is compelled to redeem for the protection of
his own lien upon the premises, he will upon redemption be
subrogated for his reimbursement to the rights of the senior
mortgagee,[4] yet, if the debt secured by his own mortgage is
not yet due or payable, he cannot insist upon his right to pay
off the first mortgage and to be subrogated to the position of
the prior mortgagee, without showing that this is necessary for

[1] York County Savings Bank v.
Roberts, 70 Maine, 384; Hayden v.
Auburn Prison, 1 Sandf. (N. Y.) 195;
Marvin v. Vedder, 5 Cow. (N. Y.)
671; Warner v. Blakeman, 36 Barb.
(N. Y.) 501; Gardner v. James, 7
R. I. 396; Bowman v. Master, 33
N. H. 530; Large v. Van Doren, 14

N. J. Eq. 208. But see Sims v. Lester, 55 Ga. 620.
[2] Frost v. Yonkers Bank, 8 Hun
(N. Y.), 26.
[3] Frost v. Yonkers Bank, 70 N. Y.
553. Postea, § 39.
[4] Antea, §§ 12-15.

his own protection or for the preservation of his own security. Subrogation in equity proceeds upon the ground that it is necessary for the protection of the party who seeks it;[1] and this will be the case when it is necessary for him, in order to get the benefit of his own security, to disengage the property from the previous incumbrance. If his own mortgage is payable, and he cannot get his payment without clearing away the previous incumbrance,[2] or if the prior mortgagee is himself seeking to foreclose, then he may rightfully insist upon redeeming and upon being subrogated to the rights of the prior mortgagee.[3] After a decree for the foreclosure of a prior mortgage has been rendered in proceedings to which the junior incumbrancer was a party, the latter cannot then claim a decree of subrogation, or prevent the sale of the premises, unless he can show that the payment of the prior mortgage or its enforcement by foreclosure and sale would work him an injustice; his application comes too late;[4] as mere junior mortgagee, his rights are sufficiently protected by the opportunity to purchase at the sale, or to pay off the prior incumbrance before the sale.[5]

§ 19. **Subrogation of one advancing Money for the Payment of an Incumbrance.** — Where a person advances money to pay off a mortgage-debt under an agreement with the owner of the equity of redemption or his representative that he shall hold the mortgage as security for his advance, but the mortgage, instead of being assigned to him, is discharged in whole or in part, he is yet entitled as against subsequent parties in interest to be subrogated to the rights of the mortgagee and to enforce the mortgage;[6] though, if he was not intended to

[1] *Antea*, § 4.
[2] Kelly v. Longshore, 78 Ala. 203.
[3] Jenkins v. Continental Ins. Co., 12 How. Pr. (N. Y.) 66.
[4] Searles v. Jacksonville R. R. Co., 2 Woods, C. C. 621. See also Gerrish v. Bragg, 55 Vt. 329; Phelps v. Pope, 53 Iowa, 691.

[5] Bloomingdale v. Barnard, 7 Hun (N. Y.), 459; Ketchum v. Crippen, 37 Calif. 223; Searles v. Jacksonville R. R. Co., 2 Woods, C. C. 621. See Wyckoff v. Noyes, 36 N. J. Eq. 227.
[6] Cottrell v. Finney, L. R. 9 Ch. 541; King v. McVickar, 3 Sandf. Ch. (N. Y.) 192; Detroit Ins. Co. v. As-

have the benefit of the former security for the debt which he pays,[1] or which his grantor has paid,[2] or if the subrogation is not necessary for his protection,[3] or if he relied upon a forged mortgage,[4] or if the agreement had been that he should depend upon a new security which was given to him, he could not be subrogated to the charge which had thus been paid.[5] And where a creditor, having taken on execution his debtor's lands, which were subject to a previous mortgage, subsequently paid off the mortgage with money which he borrowed for that purpose of a stranger, to whom he gave therefor a new mortgage upon the same land, and afterwards his levy proved to be defective, and the new mortgage was accordingly invalid as such, the new mortgagee was held, as against the debtor's grantee, to be subrogated to the rights of the prior incumbrancer, the payment having been necessary to avoid a foreclosure of the first mortgage.[6] The same principle was applied in England in a case in which the plaintiff held a junior charge upon the company's property. A scheme of arrangement was confirmed by the court, by which the company was authorized to issue certain debenture A and debenture B stock. Debenture A stock was to be applied, first, in payment of the mortgage debentures of the company, and of certain costs, the stock applied for these purposes being preferred over the

pinall, 43 Mich. 233; Johnson v. Barrett, 117 Ind. 551; Levy v. Martin, 48 Wisc. 198; Downer v. Miller, 15 Wisc. 612; Morgan v. Hammett, 23 Wisc. 30; Lockwood v. Marsh, 3 Nevada, 138; Fears v. Albea, 69 Tex. 437; Focko v. Weirsheeher, 55 Tex. 33. Contra in Tennessee in the case of a married woman. Owens v. Johnson, 8 Baxter, 265.

[1] Mead's Appeal, 46 Conn. 417; Jeffries v. Allen, 29 So. Car. 501.

[2] Spratt v. Pierson, 4 So. Car. 301.

[3] Edinburg Mortgage Co. v. Latham, 88 Ind. 88.

[4] Byerly v. Humphrey, 65 Nor. Car. 151. *Contra.* Everston v. Central Bank, 33 Kans. 352.

[5] Jones v. Lockard, 89 Ala. 575; Fry v. Hamner, 50 Ala. 52; Loewenthal v. McCormick, 101 Ills. 143; Small v. Stagg, 95 Ills. 39; Wormer v. Waterloo Agricultural Works, 62 Iowa, 699; Watson v. Wilcox, 39 Wisc. 643; Gage v. Ward, 25 Maine, 101; Wooldridge v. Scott, 69 Mo. 669; Cohn v. Hoffman, 50 Ark. 108.

[6] Payne v. Hathaway, 3 Vt. 212. So in Clute v. Emmerich, 26 Hun (N. Y.), 10; Kaiser v. Lembeck, 55 Iowa, 244.

residue of the stock, which residue was to be applied in paying unpaid vendors of land. Debenture B stock was to be applied in paying off debentures of the company which were not secured by mortgage, and in meeting other debts. The net income of the company was to be applied to pay, first, interest on preferred debenture A stock; second, interest on the residue of that stock; third, interest on debenture B stock; and, lastly, such dividends as might be payable to stockholders. The plaintiff contended that he was not bound by the scheme, and that he had a charge on the income prior to the holders of the A and B stocks, on the ground that the original priority of former mortgagees and unpaid vendors of land, who had accepted payment in these new stocks, had been lost by the extinguishment of their original securities. But it was held that though he was not bound by the scheme, yet as it did not lessen his rights, so neither did it increase them; that he was not, therefore, entitled to such priority as he claimed; but that the net income must, in the first place, to an amount equal to the sums due upon liens which had been prior to the plaintiff's, be applied according to the scheme.[1] So the lender of money borrowed by a corporation *ultra vires* may be subrogated to the rights of lawful creditors of the company who have been paid out of such money, and allowed to recover from the company to the extent of the lawful liabilities so paid off.[2] For the prevention of fraud, a person who advances money to pay off a mortgage, believing that it was the only lien upon the land, may be subrogated to the lien of that mortgage,[3] as against a surety who has paid a

[1] Stevens *v.* Mid-Hants Railway Co., L. R. 8 Ch. 1064. So in Campbell *v.* Texas R. R. Co., 2 Woods C. C. 263; Barry *v.* Missouri, K. & T. R. R. Co., 34 Fed. Rep. 829; Hollister *v.* Stewart, 111 N. Y. 644; Humphreys *v.* Allen, 100 Ills. 511.

[2] Brooks *v.* Blackburn Building Society, 9 App. Cas. 857; Blackburn Building Society *v.* Cunliff, 22 Ch. D. 61; Wenlock *v.* River Dee Co., 19 Q. B. D. 155, and 10 App. Cas. 354; Rainsburg Borough *v.* Fyan, 127 Penn. St. 74.

[3] Edwards *v.* Davenport, 20 Fed. Rep. 756; White *v.* Newhall, 68 Mich. 641; Chaffe *v.* Patterson, 61 Miss. 28.

judgment, which was a lien subsequent to the mortgage, and the payment of which appeared by the record to have been otherwise provided for.[1] One who had paid off a mortgage-debt under the mistaken belief that the title to the land was in his wife, while it really belonged to her daughter by a previous marriage, was allowed against the daughter a charge upon the land to reimburse him for this payment,[2] but not for improvements which he had made upon the land.[3] But a husband who, being sued with his wife for her debt contracted before marriage, and secured by a mortgage upon her land, allows himself after her death to be defaulted in the suit and pays the debt on execution, under the mistaken[4] supposition that he can claim the amount of her estate at law, without taking an assignment of the mortgage, cannot be subrogated to the rights of the mortgagee for his reimbursement; for he paid the debt, not to protect an imaginary estate in himself or his wife, but under a mistaken belief of his legal liability therefor.[5] Though a mere volunteer cannot by paying off a mortgage acquire an equitable lien or any right of subrogation, yet if he advances the money to redeem or pay off a mortgage at the request of one who is interested or bound to discharge it, he may be protected against such person by subrogation.[6] A third party, who, at the instance of the mortgagor, pays a part of the mortgage-debt, but takes no assignment of the mortgage, is not thereby subrogated to the rights of the mortgagee as against a subsequent incumbrancer; to effect such a subrogation there must be some-

[1] Green v. Millbank, 3 Abbott New Cas. (N. Y.) 138. And see Burchard v. Phillips, 11 Paige (N. Y.), 66.

[2] Haggerty v. McCanna, 10 C. E. Green (25 N. J. Eq.), 48.

[3] Haggerty v. McCanna, supra; Guckian v. Riley, 135 Mass. 71; O'Brien v. Joyce, 117 Mass. 360.

[4] Warren v. Williams, 10 Cush. (Mass.) 79.

[5] Warren v. Jennison, 6 Gray (Mass.), 559; and see Peters v. Florence, 38 Penn. St. 194.

[6] Gans v. Thieme, 93 N. Y. 225; Robertson v. Mowell, 66 Md. 530; McWilliams v. Bones, 84 Ga. 203; White v. Newhall, 68 Mich. 641; Yaple v. Stephens, 36 Kans. 680; Tolman v Smith, 85 Calif. 280; Fievel v. Zuber, 67 Tex. 275.

thing more than a mere payment of the money, and its silent
receipt by the first mortgagee;[1] nor will he be subrogated to
the benefit of the mortgage as against others who are secured
thereby, by his having furnished the debtor with the means to
make a partial payment of the mortgage-debt,[2] even though
he holds the agreement of the mortgagor that he shall be protected by the mortgage.[3] The mortgagor's agreement cannot
prejudice the mortgagees, though it would bind the mortgagor
himself.[4]

§ 20. **Where New Incumbrance given for old.**— Where a new
mortgage is given for the same debt which was secured by a
prior mortgage, which is thereupon discharged, the execution
of the new and the satisfaction of the old mortgage have
been treated as simultaneous and dependent acts; and if the
new mortgage is invalid, its holder has been subrogated to
the lien of the old mortgage.[5] But if the new mortgage
covers also an additional indebtedness, this subrogation can
protect only what remains due upon the old mortgage-debt.[6]
The same rule is applied where the new and defective mortgage is given to one who at the request of the debtor advances
the money to pay off the prior incumbrance, the transaction
being treated in equity as an assignment of the old mortgage
to the new mortgagee.[7] *A fortiori*, if the old mortgage is re-

---

[1] Commonwealth *v.* Chesapeake &
Ohio Canal Co., 32 Md. 501; Collins
*v.* Adams, 53 Vt. 433; Greer *v.* Chester, 7 Humph. (Tenn.) 77.

[2] Bissell *v.* Lewis, 56 Iowa, 231;
Bockes *v.* Hathorn, 20 Hun (N. Y.),
503.

[3] Child *v.* N. Y. & N. E. R. R. Co.,
129 Mass. 170.

[4] Cameron *v.* Tome, 64 Md. 507;
Haven *v.* Grand Junction R. R. Co.,
109 Mass. 88.

[5] Milholland *v.* Tiffany, 64 Md.
455; Donohue *v.* Daniel, 58 Md. 595;
Lockwood *v.* Bassett, 49 Mich. 547;

Pouder *v.* Ritzinger, 102 Ind. 571;
Gerwig *v.* Shetterly, 64 Barb. (N. Y.)
620; Christie *v.* Hale, 46 Ills. 117;
Kimble *v.* Esworthy, 6 Ills. Ap. 517;
Jones *v.* Parker, 51 Wisc. 218; Crip-
pin *v.* Chappel, 35 Kans. 495; Dillon
*v.* Byrne, 5 Calif. 455; Birrell *v.* Schie,
9 Calif. 104; Hazleton *v.* Lesure, 9
Allen (Mass.), 24; Kalscheuer *v.*
Upton, 43 N. W. Rep. 816.

[6] Carr *v.* Caldwell, 10 Calif. 380;
Birrell *v.* Schie, *supra;* Dillon *v.*
Byrne, 5 Calif. 455.

[7] Swift *v.* Kraemer, 13 Calif. 526;
Carr *v.* Caldwell, 10 Calif. 380; Ho-

tained undischarged and a new mortgage taken to secure both the old debt and the new advances,[1] or if the old mortgage is contemporaneously with the payment assigned by the mortgagee to the one who advances the money to pay him,[2] this will not operate a discharge of the former security.[3] The authority of the California decisions cited above has, however, been somewhat shaken, as to intervening liens of third persons, by a later case in the same State;[4] and elsewhere it has been held that a mortgage once understandingly and intentionally discharged cannot afterwards be reinstated to the prejudice of other claimants or incumbrancers;[5] and that where a mortgage has been discharged and its satisfaction acknowledged, and a new security taken upon the same land for the same debt, the lien of the old mortgage is gone once for all, and the new security must be postponed to such incumbrances as are prior to itself, though junior to the old mortgage.[6] The old security ceases to have any validity upon the taking of a new security as a substitute therefor.[7] If the

mœopathic Ins. Co. v. Marshall, 32 N. J. Eq. 103; Tyrell v. Ward, 102 Ills. 29.

[1] Tenison v. Sweeney, 1 Jones & La Touche, Irish Eq. 710; Hill v. Beebe, 13 N. Y. 556.

[2] White v. Knapp, 8 Paige (N. Y.), 173.

[3] Drury v. Briscoe, 42 Md. 154; Christian v. Newberry, 61 Mo. 446.

[4] Guy v. Du Uprey, 16 Calif. 195; Dingman v. Randall, 13 Calif. 512.

[5] Tracy v Lincoln, 145 Mass. 357; Hobbs v. Harvey, 16 Maine, 80; Fidelity Ins. Co. v. Shenandoah Valley R. R. Co., 86 Va. 1; Gibbes v. Greenville & Columbia R. R. Co., 15 So. Car. 224; Banta v. Garmo, 1 Sandf. Ch. (N. Y.) 383; Frazee v. Inslee, 1 Green (2 N. J. Eq.) 239; Neidig v. Whiteford, 29 Md. 178; Weidner v. Thompson, 69 Iowa, 36.

[6] Gerrish v. Bragg, 55 Vt. 329; St. Albans Trust Co. v. Farrar, 53 Vt. 542; Holt v. Baker, 58 N. H. 276; Westfall v. Hintze, 7 Abbott New Cas. (N. Y.) 236; Woollen v. Hillen, 9 Gill (Md.), 185; Stearns v. Godfrey, 16 Maine, 158; Hinchman v. Emans, 1 N. J. Eq. 100; Barnett v. Griffith, 27 N. J. Eq. 201; Mather v. Jenswold, 72 Iowa, 550; Washington County v. Slaughter, 54 Iowa, 265; Iowa County v. Foster, 49 Iowa, 676; Kitchell v. Mudgett, 37 Mich. 82; Smith v. Bynum, 92 Nor. Car. 108; McKeen v. Haseltine, 46 Minn. 426; Daly v. Proetz, 20 Minn. 411; Hechtman v. Sharp, 3 McArthur (D. C.), 90.

[7] Wynne, in re, Chase's Dec. 227; Ames v. New Orleans R. R. Co., 2 Woods C. C. 206; Morris v. White, 36 N. J. Eq. 324; Gaskill v. Wales,

new security is taken for the express purpose of gaining an advantage which could not have been enjoyed under the first, the first will likewise be extinguished; as where a creditor who held a note secured by a mortgage upon a stock of goods, being told by the debtor that he had a number of notes coming due which he could not pay, delivered up his note and mortgage, and took a new note secured by a new mortgage upon the stock as altered and added to by labor, sales, and purchases, and it was held that he could not, upon the avoidance of his new mortgage, be subrogated to the lien of his former security.[1] But if an intervening incumbrance were created without the knowledge of the beneficiary therein just prior to the execution of the new mortgage, with the fraudulent intention of giving it priority over the latter, it would not be allowed a preference over such new mortgage.[2] And if a first mortgagee has accepted a new mortgage and surrendered his prior security for cancellation in ignorance of the existence of an intervening lien, equity will, upon his prompt application and in the absence of laches or other disqualifying facts,[3] restore him to his original position.[4] If a mortgage has not been formally discharged, but the mortgagor has obtained from the mortgagee possession of it and of the note which it secures, by means of a fraudulent pretence of payment, the mortgagee may yet foreclose the same, both against the mortgagor himself and also against those who have

Id. 527; Wagner's Appeal, 98 Penn. St. 77; Calmes v. McCracken, 8 So. Car. 87; Anglade v. St. Avit, 67 Mo. 434.

[1] Paine v. Waite, 11 Gray (Mass.), 190.

[2] Eggeman v. Eggeman, 37 Mich. 436; Waldo v. Richmond, 40 Mich. 380; Short v. Currier, 153 Mass. 182.

[3] Childs v. Stoddard, 130 Mass. 110; Seymour v. Mackay, 126 Ills. 341; Dutton v. McReynolds, 31 Minn. 66.

[4] Keller v. Hannah, 52 Mich. 535; Sledge v. Obenchain, 58 Miss. 670; Young v. Sharer, 73 Iowa, 555; Clark v. Bullard, 66 Iowa, 747; Bruse v. Nelson, 35 Iowa, 157; Campbell v. Trotter, 100 Ills. 281; Hutchinson v. Swartsweller, 31 N. J. Eq. 205; McKenzie v. McKenzie, 52 Vt. 271; Stafford v. Ballou, 17 Vt. 329; Lambert v. Leland, 2 Sweeny (N. Y.), 218; Wright v. Walter, McArthur & Mackey (D. C.), 343; Wooster v. Cavender, 54 Ark. 153.

acquired rights under him in ignorance of the apparent satisfaction.[1] A formal record discharge of a mortgage improvidently made by the administrator of the mortgagee, without the knowledge of the mortgagor and without consideration, will not necessarily discharge the mortgage, no other rights having intervened.[2] A mortgagee or other lien creditor who has been induced to surrender his security by the mere fraud of his debtor, may in equity have it reinstated and enforced as if no such surrender had been made;[3] but innocent third parties who have, after such surrender and before the revival of the incumbrance, parted with their money upon the faith of the apparent surrender, will not be prejudiced by the revival.[4] The same rule will be applied for the protection of the assignee of a mortgage which, before the recording of the assignment, has by mistake merely been discharged of record by the original mortgagee;[5] and if intervening incumbrancers, having come in without notice of his rights, are entitled to priority over him, he may upon paying them be subrogated to their rights.[6] Where a mortgagor made a subsequent equitable charge upon his equity of redemption, and then requested

[1] Grimes v. Kimball, 8 Allen (Mass.), 153. And see Robinson v. Sampson, 23 Maine, 388; Trenton Banking Co. v. Woodruff, 2 N. J. Eq. 117; Mallett v. Page, 8 Ind. 364.

[2] Hay v. Washington & Alex. R. R. Co., 4 Hughes C. C. 327, and 1 Id. 168; Hammond v. Barker, 61 N. H. 53; Bond v. Dorsey, 65 Md. 310; Moore v. Bond, 75 Nor. Car. 243; Ferguson v. Glassford, 68 Mich. 36; Hanlon v. Doherty, 109 Ind. 37; Liggett v. Himle, 38 Minn. 421.

[3] Short v. Currier, 153 Mass. 182; Clark v. McNeal, 114 N. Y. 287; Stover v. Wood, 26 N. J. Eq. 417; Callahan's Appeal, 124 Penn. St. 138; Crumlish v. Railroad Co., 32 W. Va. 244; French v. De Bow, 38 Mich.

708; Farmers' Ins. Co. v. German Ins. Co., 79 Ky. 598; Sidener v. Pavey, 77 Ind. 241; Fouch v. Wilson, 60 Ind. 64; Rand v. Barrett, 66 Iowa, 731; Hait v. Ensign, 61 Iowa, 724; Ellis v. Lindley, 37 Iowa, 334; Geib v. Reynolds, 35 Minn. 331; Aldrich v. Willis, 55 Calif. 81.

[4] Heyder v. Excelsior Building Association, 42 N. J. Eq. 403; Gaskill v. Wales, 36 N. J. Eq. 527; Harner's Appeal, 94 Penn. St. 489; Charleston v. Ryan, 22 So. Car. 339; Beal v. Stevens, 72 Calif. 451; Edwards v. Thom, 25 Fla. 222; Morris v. Beecher, 1 Nor. Dak. 130; Vannice v. Bergen, 16 Iowa, 555.

[5] Willcox v. Foster, 132 Mass. 320.

[6] Clark v. Mckin, 95 N. Y. 346.

the defendant, who had no notice of the charge, to pay off the
mortgage, which was done, and a receipt was indorsed upon
the mortgage, and the title-deeds were handed over to the
defendant, and the mortgagor then gave to the defendant a
new mortgage to secure both the amount he had thus paid to
the prior mortgagee and also a new advance made by himself
to the mortgagor, it was held that the defendant's subsequent
mortgage had priority over the equitable charge, but only to
the extent of the prior mortgage which he had paid off ; [1] and
even this limitation has since been disapproved.[2]

§ 21.  **Holder under a Judgment Lien subrogated upon paying
Prior Incumbrance.** — Where a judgment-creditor levied his
execution upon land, the whole of which was subject to a
prior mortgage, and the debtor was entitled, as against the
judgment-creditor, to hold part of the land as a homestead,
and had the same set off to himself, and afterwards the creditor was obliged to pay off the whole mortgage, which was
superior to the homestead estate, it was held that the creditor
was subrogated by his payment to all the rights of the mortgagee, and might enforce against the homestead estate the
contribution of its proportional share of the mortgage-debt.[3]
One who levies an execution upon an equity of redemption,
and then pays off the mortgages to which his levy was subject,
becomes by such payment the equitable assignee of the mortgages, and is subrogated to all the rights of the mortgagees
in the mortgaged premises.[4]  So where the purchaser of an

---

[1] Pease v. Jackson, L. R. 3 Ch.
576.  So in·Howell v. Bush, 54 Miss·
437 ; Cansler v. Sallis, *Id.* 446.

[2] Hosking v. Smith, 13 Ap. Cas.
582, overruling on this question Pease
v. Jackson, *supra,* and Robinson v.
Trevor, 12 Q. B. D. 423.  So, also,
Sangster v. Cochran, 28 Ch. D. 298;
Carlisle Banking Co. v. Thompson, 28
Ch. D. 398 ; Fourth City Building
Society v. Williams, 14 Ch. D. 140.

[3] Lamb v. Mason, 50 Vt. 345 ;
Devereux v. Fairbanks, 50 Vt. 700.

[4] Warren v. Warren, 30 Vt. 530 ;
Majury v. Putnam, 4 Dane's Ab.
(Mass.) 183, 676; Tiffany v. Kent, 2
Gratt. (Va.) 231; Hammond v. Leav-
itt, 59 Iowa, 407 ; Lane v. Hallum, 38
Ark. 385 ; Eldridge v. Wright, 55
Calif. 531.

equity of redemption, at a sale thereof on execution against the mortgagor, paid off the mortgage and had it discharged, and then, on payment of the amount for which he had purchased at the execution sale, released to the mortgagor all the right he had acquired under the sale, it was held that he could afterwards recover from the mortgagor the amount which he had thus paid upon the mortgage.[1] One who had purchased, under an execution against the devisee thereof, land which had been devised subject to a charge for a legacy, was allowed in equity, upon the legacy being afterwards charged upon the land, to recover the amount of the legacy from the devisee.[2] But the creditor will not be allowed to use his right of subrogation for any other purpose than to obtain reimbursement for what he has paid upon the prior incumbrance.[3]

§ 22. **Where Incumbered Lands sold under a Junior Lien.**— When the equity of redemption in mortgaged lands is sold under a judgment or a junior mortgage which constitutes merely a subordinate lien upon the premises, and the sale has been consummated so that no right to redeem therefrom remains in the former owner, the purchaser at such sale is presumed to have bid only to the value of the equity of redemption;[4] and the land which he has thus purchased becomes in equity the primary fund for the payment of the prior incumbrance.[5] Such a purchaser cannot, upon paying and taking an assignment of the prior mortgage, collect the debt secured thereby out of the mortgagor's other property;[6]

[1] Gleason v. Dyke, 22 Pick. (Mass.) 390.

[2] Harris v. Fly, 7 Paige (N. Y.), 431.

[3] Lyons' Appeal, 61 Penn. St. 15; Denman v. Jayne, 16 Abbott Pr. N. s. (N. Y.), 317; Bailey v. Warner, 28 Vt. 87; Mallory v. Danber, 83 Ky. 239; White v. Butler, 13 Ills. 109.

[4] Krueger v. Ferry, 41 N. J. Eq. 432; Dauchy v. Bennett, 7 How. Pr. (N. Y.) 375; Dodds v. Snyder, 44 Ills.

53; Vanscoyoc v. Kimler, 77 Ills. 151; Roberts v. Hughes, 81 Ills. 130; Vaughn v. Clark, 5 Nebraska, 238.

[5] Weaver v. Toogood, 1 Barb. (N. Y.) 238; Carpenter v. Koons, 20 Penn. St. 222; Robins v. Swain, 68 Ills. 197; Hanger v. State, 27 Ark. 667; Sturges v. Taylor, 15 La. Ann. 285.

[6] McKinstry v. Curtis, 10 Paige (N. Y.), 503; Dollar Savings Bank v. Burns, 87 Penn. St. 491; Cooley's

the prior incumbrance is discharged by his payment, to the
extent of the value of the property;[1] on the contrary, if payment of the mortgage-debt is then enforced by its holder from
other property of the mortgagor, the latter will be subrogated
to the mortgagee's lien upon the land, that he may indemnify
himself out of the mortgaged premises,[2] as he will be if upon
his payment he takes an express assignment of the mortgage
which he has given.[3] And such a purchaser has no equity to require the mortgagee to apply to the satisfaction of his demand
personal property which is also embraced in his mortgage.[4]
But the rule is different before the consummation of the sale,
while the junior incumbrance remains merely a subordinate
lien upon the premises; then the owner of the equity, if he
wishes to preserve his estate, must redeem it from all the
incumbrances to which it is subject;[5] and the junior incumbrancer may pay off the debt secured by the prior lien, and
enforce it against the property.[6] But there is no personal
charge upon such a purchaser of the equity of redemption: if
he takes an assignment of the prior mortgage, and forecloses
it, and sells the property for less than the amount of the debt
secured thereby, he can then maintain an action for the balance of the debt against the mortgagor; though the land has
become the primary fund for the payment of the debt, yet the
original debtor remains liable for what the land fails to pay.[7]
And the original debtor will have no defence to an action at
law by the first mortgagee against him to collect the indebtedness secured by the mortgage, although another creditor has

Appeal, 1 Grant, Pa. Cas. 401; Se-
mans v. Harvey, 52 Ind. 331.

[1] Booker v. Anderson, 35 Ills. 66;
Waddle v. Cureton, 2 Spears (So.
Car.), 53.

[2] Hart v. Chase, 46 Conn. 207;
Funk v. McReynolds, 33 Ills. 481;
Cox v. Wheeler, 7 Paige (N. Y.), 248;
Tice v. Annin, 2 Johns. Ch. (N. Y.)
125.

[3] Barker v. Parker, 4 Pick. (Mass.)
505.

[4] Lovelace v. Webb, 62 Ala. 271;
Dirks v. Humbird, 54 Md. 399.

[5] Rogers v. Meyers, 68 Ills. 92.

[6] Southworth v. Scofield, 51 N. Y.
513.

[7] Southworth v. Scofield, supra.

levied on his equity of redemption; he cannot compel the purchaser at the execution sale to redeem from the prior mortgage; he must himself, where the law gives him the power to do so, redeem both from the prior mortgage and from the execution sale, or lose the land.[1] So, one who levies upon part of an equity of redemption, and then pays off and takes an assignment of the mortgages to which his levy was subject, becomes thereby entitled to the rights of the mortgagees in the whole of the premises.[2] Where mortgaged land was successively attached by two different creditors of the mortgagor, and the first attaching creditor, having obtained judgment, levied on the equity of redemption, and sold it on his execution subject to the mortgage, and then the mortgagee released and quitclaimed his right in the land to the mortgagor, it was held that the original mortgagor became thereupon invested as to the land with the character of a mortgagee, and that a deed of release and quitclaim given by him to the purchaser of the equity of redemption at the execution sale vested the whole title to the land in the latter to the exclusion of the second attaching creditor.[3]

§ 23. **Subrogation of an Assignee in Bankruptcy.** — Assignees in bankruptcy will, upon redeeming pledges made by the bankrupt, be subrogated to the rights of the pledgees, until the fund for general distribution is made good from the proceeds of the pledges redeemed.[4] If the property of a bankrupt was subject both to attachments and to subsequent levies, it has been said that the dissolution of the attachments by the bankruptcy proceedings will not advance the levies, but the assignee will be subrogated to the priority of the dissolved attachments,[5] though this proposition is neither self-evident

---

[1] Rogers v. Meyers, 68 Ills. 92.

[2] Tichout v. Harmon, 2 Aik. (Vt.) 37; Wheeler v. Willard, 44 Vt. 640; Tuttle v. Brown, 14 Pick. (Mass.) 514.

[3] Bullard v. Hinckley, 5 Greenl. (Me.) 272.

[4] McLean v. Cadwalader, 15 N. B. R. 383; Longfellow, in re, 17 Id. 27.

[5] Matter of Klancke, 4 Benedict,

nor universally admitted.[1] And if a creditor of the bankrupt holding security for the payment of his debt proves it as an unsecured demand, and thereby waives his security, this will not extinguish the security for the benefit of other parties claiming the property subject to the rights of the creditor, but paramount to the title of the assignee; but the assignee will, for the benefit of the general fund, be subrogated to the security thus waived by the creditor.[2] But it is only the assignee who will be thus subrogated; a junior claimant of the security thus waived will acquire no advantage by the waiver.[3] A junior lien, though valid against the assignee, will not be advanced by the assignee's avoidance of the prior lien.[4] If the secured creditor proves his whole claim against the bankrupt's estate, and thus diminishes the dividend of the general creditors, they, or the assignee as their representative, will be subrogated to his rights under his security and allowed to enforce the same against those whose rights were subject to his.[5] A creditor who has proved his demand against the bankrupt estate of one who was under a subsidiary liability for the debt, though entitled to receive his dividend, may yet be compelled by the assignee either to proceed himself at law against the ultimate debtor, or to allow the assignee to do so in his name.[6]

§ 24. **Subrogation of a Mortgagor against a Purchaser of the Equity who has assumed the Mortgage.** — Where the purchaser of an equity of redemption who has agreed with the mortgagor to assume and pay the mortgage-debt, fails to do so, the mort-

---

326; Steele, *in re*, 7 Bissell, 504; s. c. 16 N. B. R. 105; Nelson, *in re*, 16 N. B. R. 312.

[1] See the opinion of the court in Grant *v.* Lyman, 4 Met. (Mass.) 470, 474; Hull, *in re*, 14 Blatchford, C. C. 257; s. c. 18 N. B. R. 1; Beadle, *in re*, 2 Sawyer, C. C. 351.

[2] Hiscock *v.* Jaycox, 12 N. B. R.

507; Wallace *v.* Conrad, 3 N. B. R. 41.

[3] Cook *v.* Farrington, 104 Mass. 212.

[4] Beisenthal, *in re*, 14 Blatchford, C. C. 146.

[5] *Thayer, J.*, in Wallace *v.* Conrad, *supra*.

[6] Babcock, *in re*, 3 Story, C. C. 393.

gagor, if he is himself compelled to pay it, will be subrogated to the rights of the mortgagee against the mortgaged premises, and may enforce the mortgage upon them,[1] or he may look to the personal responsibility of the purchaser,[2] even though the purchaser has since sold the property;[3] for, as between the mortgagor and such a purchaser from him, the debt rests upon the latter; and where one person pays a debt for another, being legally obliged to pay it, or having an interest in paying it, he is subrogated to all the rights of the creditor whom he has paid.[4] So, according to the generally received doctrine, the mortgagee may himself enforce the performance of such an agreement by the purchaser.[5] If the mortgagor in such a case, upon making the payment, obtains from the mortgagee a deed of release of the estate, he will, even at law, be regarded as the assignee of the mortgage.[6] Where a mortgagee agreed with a mortgagor to look solely to the mortgaged premises for the payment of his debt, and to hold the mortgage-bond merely as evidence of the debt, but in violation of his agreement took judgment on a warrant of attorney which accompanied the bond, and collected the whole amount of the debt from the mortgagor personally, the mort-

[1] Kinnaird v. Trollope, 39 Ch. D. 636; Kinnear v. Lowell, 34 Maine, 299; Dean v. Toppin, 130 Mass. 517; Marsh v. Pike, 10 Paige (N. Y.), 595; McLean v. Towle, 3 Sandf. Ch. (N. Y.) 117; Stillman v. Stillman, 21 N. J. Eq. 126; Morris v. Oakford, 9 Penn. St. 498; Baker v. Terrell, 8 Minn. 195; Flagg v. Geltmacher, 98 Ills. 293; Wright v. Briggs, 99 Ind. 563; Risk v. Hoffman, 69 Ind. 137; Baldwin v. Thompson, 6 La. 474.

[2] Locke v. Homer, 131 Mass. 93; Furnas v. Durgin, 119 Mass. 500; Braman v. Dowse, 12 Cush. (Mass.) 227; Pike v. Brown, 7 Cush. (Mass.) 133; Fiske v. McGregory, 34 N. H. 414; Bassett v. Bradley, 48 Conn.

224; Taintor v. Hemmingway, 18 Hun (N. Y.), 458; Dorr v. Peters, 3 Edwards Ch. (N. Y.) 132; Bolles v. Beach, 22 N. J. Law, 680; Taylor v. Preston, 79 Penn. St. 436; Whithed v. Pillsbury, 13 N. B. R. 241.

[3] Reed v. Paul, 131 Mass. 129; Lowry v. Smith, 97 Ind. 466.

[4] Curry v. Hale, 15 W. Va. 867; Comstock v. Drohan, 71 N. Y. 9; Ferris v. Crawford, 2 Denio (N. Y.), 595; Flagg v. Thurber, 14 Barb. 196; Orrick v. Durham, 79 Mo. 174; Begein v. Brehm, 123 Ind. 160; Joselyn v. Edwards, 57 Ind. 212; Baldwin v. Thompson, 6 La. 474.

[5] *Postea*, § 85.

[6] Kinnear v. Lowell, 34 Maine, 299.

gagor was, as against a second mortgagee from a later owner of the premises, subrogated to the rights of the first mortgagee in the mortgaged premises.[1] If a purchaser from the mortgagor has agreed to assume and pay the mortgage-debt, such purchaser and the original mortgagor stand to each other in the relation of principal and surety; the latter is *quasi* surety for the former for the payment of the mortgage-debt.[2] The rule is the same if the payment, instead of being made by the mortgagor personally, is realized from the proceeds of collateral security deposited by him with the mortgagee,[3] or by the levy of execution upon other property of the mortgagor.[4] Each successive purchaser of the premises who assumes the payment of the mortgage becomes in his turn the party ultimately liable to bear the burden of the debt,[5] and his payment will extinguish the debt;[6] but such a purchaser's grantee with warranty, who has not assumed the mortgage and did not know of its existence, is not subject to the same equity as the original purchaser.[7]

§ 25. **Rights of Mortgagor against Mortgagee and such a Purchaser.** — When a purchaser of mortgaged premises has assumed the payment of the mortgage-debt, the mortgagor cannot require the creditor to foreclose, but must himself, if the creditor so requires, pay his debt according to his agreement.

---

[1] Conrad *v.* Mullison, 24 N. J. Eq. 65.

[2] Union Ins. Co. *v.* Hanford, 143 U. S. 187; a. c. 27 Fed. Rep. 588; Francisco *v.* Shelton, 85 Va. 779; Paine *v.* Jones, 76 N. Y. 274; s. c. 14 Hun (N. Y.), 577; Calvo *v.* Davies, 73 N. Y. 211; a. c. 8 Hun (N. Y.), 223; Marshall *v.* Davies, 78 N. Y. 414, reversing s. c., 16 Hun, 606; Bentley *v.* Vanderheyden, 35 N. Y. 677; Ayres *v.* Dixon, 78 N. Y. 318; Cornell *v.* Prescott, 2 Barb. (N. Y.) 16; Flagg *v.* Thurber, 14 Barb. (N. Y.) 196; Blyer *v.* Monholland, 2 Sandf. Ch. (N. Y.) 478; Hoys-radt *v.* Holland, 50 N. H. 433; Corbett *v.* Walerman, 11 Iowa, 87.

[3] Ferris *v.* Crawford, 2 Denio (N. Y.), 595; Brewer *v.* Staples, 3 Sandf. (Ch. N. Y.) 579.

[4] Woodbury *v.* Swan, 58 N. H. 380.

[5] George *v.* Andrews, 60 Md. 26; Young *v.* Hawkins, 74 Ala. 370; Knox *v.* McCain, 13 Lea (Tenn.), 197; McLean *v.* Towle, 3 Sandf. Ch. (N. Y.) 117; Wood *v.* Smith, 51 Iowa, 156.

[6] Shinn *v.* Fredericks, 56 Ills. 439.

[7] Bock *v.* Gallagher, 114 Mass. 28.

He may then proceed against the land and the purchaser thereof for his indemnity. He can also proceed in equity, to compel the purchaser, as to whom he stands in the position of a mere surety, to pay the debt for his protection.[1] But the mortgagee may, if he choose, rely upon the personal liability of his debtor;[2] his rights are not affected by the agreement between the mortgagor and the purchaser;[3] for the principal debtor cannot acquire the rights of a surety against the creditor without the latter's consent.[4] The mortgagee is not bound to look after or to protect the mortgaged premises; and if he finally forecloses the mortgage, the mortgagor is entitled to credit only for the net proceeds realized therefrom, and remains liable for any deficiency.[5] The mortgagee can enforce for his payment both the personal liability of the mortgagor, and the security of the mortgaged property;[6] equity will not, unless for special reasons, compel him to elect between his remedies.[7] The mortgagor would have been protected in payment of the debt by his right of subrogation to the mortgage, which, as between himself and his grantee, would not be extinguished by being transferred to him.[8] But he cannot be subrogated to the mortgage lien against his

[1] Rubens v. Prindle, 44 Barb. (N. Y.) 336. See Resor v. McKenzie, 2 Disney (Ohio), 210.

[2] James v. Day, 37 Iowa, 164; Gillmann v. Henry, 53 Wisc. 465.

[3] Shepherd v. May, 115 U. S. 505; Meyer v. Lathrop, 10 Hun (N. Y.), 66; Waters v. Hubbard, 44 Conn. 340.

[4] Swire v. Redman, 1 Q. B. D. 536; Boardman v. Larrabee, 51 Conn. 39; Gay v. Blanchard, 32 La. Ann. 497. The contrary is held in Ireland (Maingay v. Lewis, Ir. Rep. 5 Com. Law, 229, overruling s. c. 3 Id. 495), and New York (Millerd v. Thorn, 56 N. Y. 402; Colgrove v. Tallman, 67 N. Y. 95), on the authority of Oakely v. Pasheller, 4 Clark & Fin. 207, and 10 Bligh, N. s. 548, which, however, was said in Swire v. Redman, supra, to have been decided on the ground that the creditor was a party to the new arrangement. See Overend v. Oriental Financial Corporation, L. R. 7 Ho. Lds. 348.

[5] Marshall v. Davies, 78 N. Y. 414; s. c. 58 How. Pr. (N. Y.) 231.

[6] Boyce v. Hunt, 19 La. Ann. 449.

[7] Micou v. Ashurst, 55 Ala. 607. See Wadsworth v. Lyons, 93 N. Y. 201; Wilson v. Bryant, 134 Mass. 291.

[8] Ely v. Stannard, 44 Conn. 528; Welton v. Hull, 50 Mo. 296; Smith v. Ostermeyer, 68 Ind. 432; Stillman v. Stillman, 21 N. J. Eq. 126.

grantee, until the mortgagee has been fully paid.[1]  And if the
mortgagor has himself taken a second mortgage from his
grantee, and has then assigned this for value to the first mortgagee, who took it without any knowledge of the assumption
of the first mortgage by that grantee, the original mortgagor
will not upon paying the first mortgage acquire any rights by
subrogation prior to the lien of the second mortgage in the
hands of the first mortgagee.  The original mortgagor's subrogation in such a case will be only against his grantee who
had assumed the first mortgage.[2]

§ 26. **Subrogation of the Mortgagor against his Grantee subject to the Mortgage.** — A conveyance of mortgaged premises
by the mortgagor, subject in terms to the incumbrance, though
the payment of this is not assumed by the grantee, will make
the mortgaged premises, as between the mortgagor and the
grantee, the primary fund for the payment of the mortgage-
debt.[3]  And if the mortgagee with notice of the facts releases
the land after such a conveyance, he thereby releases the
liability of the mortgagor.[4]  A second mortgagee who has
taken a conveyance of the equity of redemption in terms subject to the payment of the mortgages cannot, after paying off
the notes secured by the first mortgage, maintain any action
upon them against the debtors thereon;[5] his purchase of the
mortgage extinguishes it and the debt it secures.[6]  The land
is the primary fund for the payment of the mortgage-debt in
the hands of a mere assignee of the equity of redemption,[7] or
a purchaser thereof who has retained the amount of the debt

---

[1] Massie v. Wilson, 17 Iowa, 131.
[2] Knoblauch v. Foglesong, 38 Minn.
459.
[3] Sweetzer v. Jones, 35 Vt. 317;
Hopkins v. Wolley, 81 N. Y. 77;
Brewer v. Staples, 3 Sandf. Ch. (N. Y.)
579; Stevens v. Church, 41 Conn.
369; Townsend v. Ward, 27 Conn.
610; Scheppelman v. Fuerth, 87 Mo.
351; Hutchinson v. Wells, 67 Iowa,
430; Colby v. Place, 11 Nebraska,
348.
[4] Townsend Savings Bank v. Mun-
son, 47 Conn. 390.
[5] Viles v. Moulton, 11 Vt. 470.
[6] Speer v. Whitefield, 10 N. J. Eq.
107; Crowley v. Harader, 69 Iowa, 83.
[7] Sheffy's Appeal, 97 Penn. St.
317.

out of his purchase-money.[1] If the mortgagor is afterwards obliged to pay the debt, he will be subrogated to the lien of the mortgage for his indemnity ;[2] but there will be no personal liability upon the grantee for its payment ;[3] the risk of the latter is limited to the estate in his hands.[4] Such a purchaser cannot, upon paying off the mortgage-debt, have the mortgage assigned to himself, and avail himself of it against his grantor, the original mortgagor,[5] unless for special reasons.[6] A conveyance of the mortgaged premises, made to the mortgagee by the mortgagor's grantee, who had assumed the mortgage, will operate a merger of the mortgage and a payment of the debt secured thereby,[7] so that no action can be maintained thereon against the mortgagor.[8] But if the grantor has warranted against the mortgage, or if it was agreed between the grantee and the grantor that the mortgage-debt should be paid by the grantor, the original debtor, then the grantee,

[1] Manwaring v. Powell, 40 Mich. 371; Andrews v. Fiske, 101 Mass. 422; Drury v. Tremont Improvement Co., 13 Allen (Mass.), 168; Murray v. Marshall, 94 N. Y. 611; Harris v. Jex, 66 Barb. (N. Y.) 232; Kostenbader v. Spotts, 80 Penn. St. 430; Drury v. Holden, 121 Ills. 130.

[2] Moore's Appeal, 88 Penn. St. 450; Hermann v. Fanning, 151 Mass. 1; Greenwell v. Heritage, 71 Mo. 459; Gerdine v. Menage, 41 Minn. 417; Weeks v. Garvey, 56 N. Y. Super. Ct. 557; Johnson v. Zink, 52 Barb. (N. Y.) 396; s. c. affirmed on appeal, 51 N. Y. 333.

[3] Middaugh v. Bachelder, 33 Fed. Rep. 706; Smith v. Cornell, 111 N. Y. 554; Bennett v. Bates, 94 N. Y. 354; Northern Dispensary v. Merriam, 59 How. Pr. (N. Y.) 226; Tillotson v. Boyd, 4 Sandf. (N. Y.) 516; Girard Ins. Co. v. Stewart, 86 Penn. St. 89; Randall v. Bradley, 65 Maine, 43; Laurence v. Towle, 59 N. H. 28; Rapp

v. Stoner, 104 Ills. 618; Rourke v. Colton, 4 Ills. App. 257; Ritchie v. McDuffie, 62 Iowa, 46; Cleveland v. Southard, 25 Wisc. 479; Hall v. Morgan, 79 Mo. 47; Patton v. Adkins, 42 Ark. 197. *Contra*, Canfield v. Shear, 49 Mich. 313.

[4] Fiske v. Tolman, 124 Mass. 254; Taylor v. Mayer, 93 Penn. St. 42; Hubbard v. Ensign, 46 Conn. 576; Stebbins v. Hall, 29 Barb. (N. Y.) 524; Baumgardner v. Allen, 6 Munf. (Va.) 439; Tichenor v. Dodd, 3 Green (4 N. J. Eq.), 454; Johnson v. Monell, 13 Iowa, 300.

[5] Atherton v. Toney, 43 Ind. 211; Eaton v. George, 2 N. H. 300; Bier v. Smith, 25 W. Va. 830.

[6] As in Carter v. Holahan, 92 N. Y. 498.

[7] Lynch v. Kirby, 36 Mich. 238.

[8] Dickason v. Williams, 129 Mass. 182; Buckley's Appeal, 48 Penn. St. 491.

if obliged to pay the incumbrance, may set it up against his grantor,[1] and the grantor's payment will not entitle him to subrogation against the grantee.[2]

§ 27. **Rights of Co-mortgagees against each other.** — Where a third mortgage was held by three, one of whom also held the first and second mortgages, and the latter began to foreclose the first mortgage, as he had a right to do,[3] the other two were allowed against him to redeem from the first and second mortgages, with the privilege, if he refused to contribute to the redemption, of holding the premises against him until he should contribute his share, being subrogated by their redemption to the same rights against him which before redemption he held against them.[4]  If a mortgagor has a demand against the mortgagee, which he has a right to set off against the notes secured by the mortgage, and these notes are in the hands of different assignees, the set-off should diminish the amount to be paid to each assignee ratably;[5] and if one of them has extinguished the set-off, and the mortgaged estate is not sufficient to pay all, its proceeds should be so distributed that all shall contribute ratably to the extinguishment of the set-off, and receive ratable shares of the surplus.[6]

§ 28. **Subrogation of the Purchaser of an Equity of Redemption on his payment of a Prior Incumbrance.** — The purchasers of an equity of redemption, which was subject to the incumbrance of four different liens, the payment of which they did not assume, having paid off the first two charges and a portion of the third, were held to be subrogated by their payments to the rights of the creditors under their respective liens, to the

[1] Estabrook v. Smith, 6 Gray (Mass.), 572; Wolbert v. Lucas, 10 Penn. St. 73.
[2] Ruggles v. Barton, 16 Gray (Mass.), 151.
[3] Sanford v. Bulkley, 30 Conn. 344; Cronin v. Hazletine, 3 Allen (Mass.), 324.

[4] Saunders v. Frost, 5 Pick. (Mass.) 259.
[5] Kilpatrick v. Dye, 4 Sm. & M. (Miss.) 289.
[6] Campbell v. Johnston, 4 Dana (Ky.), 177.

extent to which they had paid off the same, and were allowed to set them up against the holder of the fourth charge,[1] on the principle that where one who is not personally liable for a debt secured by a mortgage or other lien is compelled to pay it in order to preserve his own property, and does pay it, he may be subrogated to the lien,[2] although it has not been assigned to him;[3] though, if he takes an assignment of it, this of course will only strengthen his position.[4] This right of subrogation will also pass to a grantee of such a purchaser.[5] And where the holder of the first incumbrance waived his claim to actual payment for the sole benefit of one holding an interest in the equity of redemption, and discharged his mortgage of record to such person without consideration, it was held that the incumbrance was not thereby extinguished as to a subsequent incumbrancer,[6] but the holder of the equity in whose favor the waiver was made was subrogated to its benefit, and could set it up as a subsisting title.[7] If a party who has the right to require an assignment of a mortgage pays the mortgage-debt, and takes a discharge of the mortgage, the mortgage may be regarded as a subsisting security for his protection; he will be subrogated to the rights of the mortgagee.[8] The rule that the payment of a mortgage-debt by the owner of the equity of redemption will extinguish the mortgage does not apply to the payment of an incumbrance which existed before the conveyance to the owner of the equity, and which the latter is under no obligation to pay.[9] If such an

---

[1] Walker v. King, 45 Vt. 525. So in Ayers v. Adams, 82 Ind. 109.

[2] Hancock v. Fleming, 103 Ind. 533; Warren v. Hayzlett, 45 Iowa, 235.

[3] McCormick v. Knox, 105 U. S. 122; Watson v. Gardner, 119 Ills. 312; Wilson v. Kimball, 27 N. H. 300; Bell v. Woodward, 34 N. H. 90; Peet v. Beers, 4 Ind. 46; Watts v. Symes, 1 De G., Mac. & G. 240.

[4] Davis v. Pierce, 10 Minn. 376; Dutton v. Ives, 5 Mich. 515.

[5] Bell v. Woodward, 34 N. H. 90.

[6] Paulsen v. Manske, 126 Ills. 72; Wood v. Wood, 61 Iowa, 256.

[7] Spaulding v. Crane, 46 Vt. 292.

[8] Rigney v. Lovejoy, 13 N. H. 247, 252, Parker, C. J.; Drew v. Rust, 36 N. H. 335.

[9] Abbott v. Kasson, 72 Penn. St. 183; Holten v. Lake County, 55 Ind.

owner of the equity of redemption pays the debt, the mortgage is to be treated as assigned to him, if this is manifestly for his interest, and not inconsistent with the justice of the case, and if no contrary intent is clearly expressed or necessarily implied.[1] And he will be entitled to the benefit of a personal judgment already recovered against the mortgagor for the debt.[2]

§ 29. **Rights of such a Purchaser.** — Where the purchaser from a mortgagor pays off the mortgage and has it discharged without more, equity will not subrogate him to the rights of the mortgagee against an incumbrancer whose lien is subject to the mortgage, but prior to the purchase.[3] If, however, the purchaser has paid off the mortgage in ignorance of the subsequent incumbrance, he could in spite of its discharge claim the benefit of subrogation to its lien;[4] much more, if he made his payment and took the discharge relying upon the statements of the subsequent incumbrancer that the latter held no claim upon the property.[5] One who purchases property subject to the lien of three mortgages, the first two of which he pays out of his purchase-money and has discharged, the third mortgage having been given to the indorser of certain promissory notes to secure their payment by the mortgagor so as to save the mortgagee harmless by reason of his indorsement thereof, and then takes a discharge of the third mortgage from such indorser, the mortgagee therein, cannot be subrogated to the lien of the two prior incumbrances which he has paid, against the holders of the notes which were secured by the third mortgage, although the discharge of the third mort-

---

194; Knox v. Easton, 38 Ala. 345; Ryer v. Gass, 130 Mass. 227.

[1] *Ames*, J., in Ryer v. Gass, *supra*, citing Hinds v. Ballou, 44 N. H. 619; Leavitt v. Pratt, 53 Maine, 147.

[2] Greenough v. Littler, 15 Ch. Div. 93.

[3] Guernsey v. Kendall, 55 Vt. 201; Bentley v. Whittemore, 18 N. J. Eq.

366; Garwood v. Eldridge, 2 N. J. Eq. (1 Green) 145; Carter v. Goodin, 3 Ohio St. 75.

[4] Young v. Morgan, 89 Ills. 199; Barnes v. Mott, 64 N. Y. 397; McNeil v. Miller, 29 W. Va. 480; Cameron v. Holenshade, 1 Cincin. (Ohio) 83.

[5] Bunting v. Gilmore, 124 Ind. 114.

gage was in equity inefficacious against such holders;[1] the
only way in which he could have kept the prior liens alive
against the parties interested in the third mortgage was by
having them assigned to him.[2] The bare purchaser of an
equity of redemption, in terms subject to the mortgage-debt,
cannot be subrogated to the benefit of other securities held by
the mortgagee for its payment; having purchased the equity
of redemption and nothing more, he acquires by his purchase
no equitable control over such other securities.[3] As between
the original purchaser and such mortgagor the land is the
primary fund for the payment of the mortgage-debt;[4] and the
mortgagor, if compelled to pay it, will be subrogated to the lien
upon the land and entitled to reimbursement therefrom.[5]

§ 30. **Purchaser, if his Purchase avoided, subrogated to Lien
which he has paid.** — The purchaser of real estate who, in
order to save his property, has paid off a valid lien thereon,
is entitled to be subrogated to this lien as against those who
turn out to have a title to or lien upon the property superior
to his own but subject to the incumbrance which he has discharged,[6] though the enforcement of this equity has been
refused at law in Massachusetts.[7] Where the purchase-money
paid for real estate, under a sale which is afterwards avoided,
has been applied in the extinguishment of a valid mortgage,
such purchaser will be subrogated to the rights of the mortgagee to the extent of the purchase-money which has been so
applied;[8] and the owner will not be allowed to avail himself
of the payment thus made by a purchaser under a voidable
sale and to recover the property free of the incumbrance,
without making compensation to the purchaser to the extent

[1] *Postea*, §§ 154, 155, 187.
[2] Boyd v. Parker, 43 Md. 182.
[3] Stevens v. Church, 41 Conn. 369.
[4] *Antea*, § 26.
[5] Jumel v. Jumel, 7 Paige (N. Y.), 591.
[6] Matzen v. Shaeffer, 65 Calif. 81; Muir v. Berkshire, 52 Ind. 149; Webb
v. Williams, Walker (Mich.), 544; Valle v. Fleming, 29 Mo. 152.
[7] Wade v. Howard, 11 Pick. (Mass.) 289.
[8] French v. Grenet, 57 Tex. 273; Hull v. Hull, 35 W. Va. 155; Goring
v. Shreve, 7 Dana (Ky.), 64, 66.

of the payment which has gone to the benefit of the owner.[1]
If the purchaser of an equity of redemption has paid off the
mortgage-debt, but has neglected to record his deed from the
mortgagor, until after a creditor of the mortgagor has
attached the equity of redemption, he will be subrogated to
the lien of the mortgage upon the premises, for the reimbursement to him of the amount which he has paid upon the
mortgage-debt.[2] But if the attachment had been made prior
to the purchase, though actually unknown to the purchaser,
such purchaser, having really bought subject to the attachment, could not, after the land had been sold upon the
attachment, have the sale vacated, and set up against the
attachment the lien of a paramount incumbrance, which he
had paid out of his purchase-money.[3] So the purchaser by
parol of part of a mortgaged tract of land, who has paid off
the mortgage to prevent a sale of the mortgaged estate, will
be subrogated to the lien of the mortgage upon the whole
tract, and to the benefit of a judgment recovered thereon.[4]
The same rules will be applied to a purchaser whose money
has discharged an incumbrance upon personal property.[5]

§ 31. **Purchaser under a Mortgage or Charge subrogated to its
Lien.** — Purchasers of property under a valid decree in favor
of creditors will be subrogated to the rights of those creditors;[6] and if the creditors had no notice of a lien upon the
property and so are not bound by it, the purchasers will
not be affected by such lien, though notified of its existence

[1] *Fagg*, J., in Wade v. Beldmeir, 40 Mo. 486, 488, explaining Valle v. Fleming, 29 Mo. 152.

[2] Slocum v. Catlin, 22 Vt. 137.

[3] Wade v. Baldmeir, 40 Mo. 486.

[4] Champlin v. Williams, 9 Penn. St. 341.

[5] Crescent City Ice Co. v Stafford, 3 Woods, C. C. 94; St. Louis Min-ing Co. v. Sandeval Mining Co., 116 Ills. 170.

[6] Taylor v. Agricultural Associa-tion, 68 Ala. 229; Cheek v. Waldrum, 25 Ala. 152; Jones v. McKenna, 4 Lea (Tenn.), 630; Bodkin v. Merit, 102 Ind. 293; Watkins v Winings, 102 Ind. 330; Johnson v. Sandhoff, 30 Minn. 197; Frische v. Kramer, 16 Ohio, 125; Grapengether v. Fejervary, 9 Iowa, 163; McCammon v. Worrall, 11 Paige (N. Y.), 99; Raymond v. Holborn, 23 Wisc. 57; Jones v. Smith, 55 Tex. 383.

before their purchase.[1] If mortgaged property has been sold under a decree of foreclosure, and the sale has been confirmed by the court which ordered it, but subsequently on appeal this decree is reversed, and the mortgaged property is ordered to be again sold for the payment of the mortgage-debt, the original purchaser, if he has paid his purchase-money and it has been applied in payment of the mortgage-debt, is entitled to be subrogated to the position of the creditor,[2] and to be treated as the assignee of the mortgage, to the extent of the payment of the debt which he has thus made.[3] And if the mortgagee had himself purchased at such sale, and had accordingly entered satisfaction upon his mortgage, the mortgage would, upon the sale being subsequently set aside, be set up again and enforced in equity.[4] The purchaser at a sale made for the enforcement of a mortgage or other lien is subrogated to the rights of the original lien-holder,[5] even though the proceedings were invalid and his purchase has been avoided.[6] Unless he secures a title under his purchase, the sale is treated as an equitable assignment of the mortgage to him,[7] and his grantee takes the same

---

[1] Smith v. Jordan, 25 Ga. 687; Shepherd v. Burkhalter, 13 Ga. 443; Martin v. Jackson, 27 Penn. St. 504; Sharp v. Shea, 32 N. J. Eq. 65; Case v. Woolley, 6 Dana (Ky.), 17.

[2] Jones v. McKenna, 4 Lea (Tenn.), 630; Davis v. Roosevelt, 53 Tex. 305.

[3] Martin v. Kelly, 59 Miss. 652; Wilson v. Brown, 82 Ind. 471; Miller v. Hall, 1 Bush (Ky.), 229; Crosby v. Farmers' Bank, 107 Mo. 436; Johnson v. Robertson, 34 Md. 165.

[4] Zylstra v. Keith, 2 Desaus. Eq. (So. Car.) 140; Stackpole v. Robbins, 47 Barb. (N. Y.) 212.

[5] Brobst v. Brock, 10 Wallace, 519; Dearnaley v. Chase, 136 Mass. 288; Brown v. Smith, 116 Mass. 108; Dutcher v. Hobby, 86 Ga. 198; Logansport v. Case, 124 Ind. 254;

Shannon v. Hay, 106 Ind. 589; Hines v. Dresher, 93 Ind. 551; Ingle v. Culbertson, 43 Iowa, 265; Loney v. Courtnay, 24 Neb. 580; Merriam v. Rauen, 23 Neb. 217; Bonner v. Lessley, 61 Miss. 392; Clark v. Wilson, 56 Miss. 753; Gregory v. Bartlett, 55 Ark. 30; Turman v. Bell, 54 Ark. 273.

[6] Brobst v. Brock, 10 Wallace, 519; Sloan v. Sewell, 81 Ind. 180; Parker v. Goddard, 81 Ind. 294; Jackson v. Bowen, 7 Cow. (N. Y.) 13; Gilbert v. Cooley, Walker Ch. (Mich.) 494; Russell v. Hudson, 28 Kans. 99; St. Louis v. Priest, 103 Mo. 652; Honaker v. Shough, 55 Mo. 472; King v. Brown, 80 Tex. 276.

[7] Marimuttu v. De Soysa, (1891) 1 Ap. Cas. 69; Smith v. Robertson,

right.[1]  If the proceeds of a sheriff's sale made upon existing
mortgages have been applied in satisfaction of prior incumbrances, a subsequent mortgagee, who got nothing by reason
of the insufficiency of the proceeds, cannot disregard the sale
because the purchaser has failed to record his deed.   Such a
subsequent mortgagee would not, under any circumstances,
be allowed to have the land resold without reimbursing the
price of the former sale which had been applied upon the
prior incumbrances.[2]  But if the purchaser ought himself to
have paid the debt for which the sale was made, he cannot
set up any title through the prior lien, but it will be deemed
to have merged.[3]  And one who has purchased, not under a
paramount incumbrance, but under an adverse claim, will not
be subrogated to the former, merely because it was afterwards,
without his privity, paid off out of his purchase-money.[4]

§ 32.  **Rights of such a Purchaser in California.** — It was held
in California, after a foreclosure sale had been avoided
because the owner of the mortgaged premises had not been
made a party to the foreclosure suit, that the purchaser at
such sale must seek his relief from the consequences of the
invalidity of the decree for the sale by proceedings in the
foreclosure suit; because by his purchase he had submitted
himself to the jurisdiction of the court in that suit as to all
matters connected with the sale.  Upon his application, the
court might set the sale aside and cancel the satisfaction of
the mortgage, and authorize a supplemental bill for a resale
of the premises to be filed, and conducted in the names of the
original complainants for the benefit of the purchaser, causing

89 N. Y. 555; Childs v. Childs, 10
Ohio St. 339; Brewer v. Nash, 16 R.
I. 458; Curtis v. Gooding, 99 Ind.
45; Ulrich v. Drischell, 88 Ind. 354;
Ray v. Detchon, 79 Ind. 565; Wells
v. Lincoln County, 80 Mo. 424;
Rogers v. Benton, 39 Minn. 39;
Walker v. Lawler, 45 Tex. 532;
Wilson v. White, 84 Calif. 239.

[1] Osborne v. Taylor, 60 Conn. 107;
Jellison v. Halloran, 44 Minn. 199;
Cooke v. Cooper, 18 Oreg. 142.
[2] Wolf v. Lowry, 10 La. Ann. 272.
[3] Thompson v. Heywood, 129
Mass. 401. *Postea*, § 46.
[4] Waples v. Hays, 108 U. S. 6;
Huse v. Den, 85 Calif. 390 ; Lowe v.
Rawlins, 83 Ga. 320.

all parties interested in the premises to be brought in as parties, or make such other orders as should protect the rights of all parties and mete out exact justice.[1] In that State it has also been held, with less show of reason, that the purchaser of property at a judicial sale made under a decree for the foreclosure of a mortgage is not entitled, merely as such purchaser, to have the satisfaction of the judgment under which the sale was made set aside, and to be subrogated to the rights of the plaintiff in the judgment, simply because the sale at which he purchased was void, and he acquired no title thereby: his money has gone to pay the plaintiff's debt, but he is without remedy.[2] The general rule is otherwise.[3]

§ 33. **Instances of such Subrogation.** — Mortgaged land, upon the default of the mortgagor, was sold by the mortgagee to a purchaser, who afterwards conveyed the land to a second vendee with warranty. The mortgagor's heirs avoided the foreclosure sale by suit and recovered the land from the second vendee. The second vendee then sued the heirs of the first purchaser upon the covenants in his deed, and recovered judgment against them, which they paid. The heirs of the first purchaser then brought suit against the grantees with notice of the mortgagor's heirs, to have the land sold for the payment of the original mortgage-debt; and it was held that these plaintiffs should be regarded as the equitable assignees of the mortgage by subrogation to the rights of the mortgagee, the court saying, through *Biddle, C. J.*, that though subrogation is not allowed to voluntary purchasers or to strangers, unless there is some peculiar equitable relation in the transaction, and never to mere volunteers,[4] yet a person who has paid a debt under a colorable obligation to do so, and in order to protect his own claim, should be subrogated to the rights of

---

[1] Boggs *v.* Hargrave, 16 Calif. 559. And see Burden *v.* Johnson, 81 Mo. 318.

[2] Branham *v.* San José, 24 Calif. 585.

[3] *Antea,* § 31, and cases there cited.

[4] *Postea,* §§ 240 *et seq.*

the creditor, and that since subrogation is allowed for the benefit of a purchaser of an immovable, who uses the price which he pays in paying the creditors to whom the inheritance was mortgaged,[1] this purchaser's heirs should be subrogated to the rights of the mortgagee whose debt had been paid by his purchase.[2] The same principle was applied in Michigan for the protection of one who had purchased mortgaged premises from the widow of the mortgagor, in consideration of his paying her a small sum of money and redeeming from the mortgage, and he was allowed against the mortgagor's heirs upon their avoidance of his purchase a lien upon the land for the amount which he had paid to redeem it with interest, less the value of the use and occupation which he had enjoyed.[3]

§ 34. **Purchaser ordinarily subrogated to all the Rights of his Vendor.** — A purchaser will ordinarily be subrogated to all the rights of his vendor in the property, even though they are not expressly conveyed to him.[4] Though he had notice of outstanding equities, he will not be bound by them, if his grantor could have defended against them as a *bona fide* purchaser without notice.[5] Thus, one who holds property in pledge has a special property which may be sold or assigned; and his assignee will be subrogated to the rights of the original pledgee.[6] The assignee of one who has agreed to sell land is subrogated to his vendor's right of rescission.[7] So, one

[1] *Antea,* § 5.
[2] Muir v. Berkshire, 52 Ind. 149.
[3] Webb v. Williams, Walker (Mich.), 544.
[4] Chicago v. Tebbetts, 104 U. S. 120; McKeage v. Hanover Ins. Co., 81 N. Y. 39; Sickles v. Flanagan, 79 N. Y. 224; Thompson v. Kenyon, 100 Mass. 108; Ruggles v. Barton, 13 Gray (Mass.), 506; Murdock v. Chapman, 9 Gray (Mass.), 156; Butler v. Barnes, 60 Conn. 170; Loomis v. Knox, 60 Conn. 343; Murphy v. Adams, 71 Maine, 113; Logan v. Taylor, 20 Iowa, 297; Kemp v. Kemp, 85 Nor. Car. 491; Pettit v. Black, 8 Neb. 52; Stanton v. Quinan, 91 Calif. 1; Creanor v. Creanor, 36 Ark. 91; Heinlen v. Martin, 53 Calif. 321; Peters v. Clements, 52 Tex. 140.
[5] Brown v. Cody, 115 Ind. 484; Drey v. Doyle, 99 Mo. 459.
[6] Talty v. Freedmens' Savings Co., 93 U. S. 321; Merchants' Bank v. State Bank, 10 Wall. 604; Lewis v. Mott, 36 N. Y. 395; Donald v. Sackling, L. R. 1 Q. B. 585.
[7] Castle v. Floyd, 38 La. An. 583.

who has in good faith and for a valuable consideration purchased the whole or a portion of a mortgaged estate from the
mortgagee in possession will be regarded as the equitable
assignee of the mortgage to the extent of his purchase-money,
both against the mortgagor seeking to redeem the estate,[1] and
against parties interested in the estate by subsequent conveyances.[2] The vendee of one who holds a bond for title to land
acquires by his purchase all the interest of his vendor, that
is, the right to require a conveyance from the owner of the
land upon payment of the price stipulated in the bond;[3] and
the owner of the land and the holder of the bond, having
notice of his rights, cannot rescind their contract so as to
deprive him of this equity.[4] The assignee of one who held
a contract for the purchase of land will be subrogated to the
equitable lien of his assignor upon the land for the return of
a portion of the purchase-money which he had advanced, upon
the contract failing through the default or the inability of
the vendor.[5] Such an assignee may also, upon making full
payment of the price, be subrogated to the rights of the original vendor against the original purchaser.[6] The assignee of a
debt will take as an incident the equitable right[7] to the collateral obligation of a third person,[8] or to any collateral security held by the original creditor for its payment,[9] even though

[1] McSorley v. Larissa, 100 Mass.
270; Ruggles v. Barton, 13 Gray
(Mass.), 506; Grover v. Thatcher, 4
Gray (Mass.), 526; Wyman v. Hooper, 2 Gray (Mass.), 141; Raymond
v. Raymond, 7 Cush. (Mass.) 605.

[2] Smith v. Hitchcock, 130 Mass.
570.

[3] Graves v. Graves, 6 Gray (Mass.),
391; Fulcher v. Daniel, 80 Ga. 74;
Shaw v. Foster, L. R. 5 Ho. Lds.
321.

[4] Shaver v. Shoemaker, Phillips
Eq. (Nor. Car.) 327; Chickering v.
Fullerton, 90 Ills. 520.

[5] Tompkins v. Seeley, 29 Barb.
(N. Y.) 212.

[6] Dillow v. Warfel, 71 Iowa, 106.

[7] Not always the legal right:
Batchelder v. Jenness, 59 Vt. 104.

[8] Lahmers v. Schmidt, 35 Minn.
434.

[9] Payne v. Wilson, 74 N. Y. 348;
Cooper v. Newland, 17 Abb. Pr. (N.
Y.) 342; Hagemann's Appeal, 88
Penn. St. 21; Cathcart's Appeal, 13
Penn. St. 416; Fitzsimmon's Appeal,
4 Penn. St. 248; Miller v. Hoyle, 6
Ired. Eq. (Nor. Car.) 269; Waller v.
Tate, 4 B. Mon. (Ky.) 529; Strother

a formal assignment has not been made.[1] A maritime lien will
pass to an assignee of the debt secured thereby.[2] The claim of
a vendee of land for a defect in the title, a conveyance not yet
having been made, will pass to his grantee. Thus, where the
purchaser at a judicial sale of land paid a part of the purchase-money, and then, before taking a conveyance, sold
his claim under his purchase to an assignee, who paid the
residue of the price, and then a defect in the title was discovered, whereby the sale was avoided, this assignee was
held to be entitled to have the whole amount that had been
paid refunded to him, including the payment made by his
grantor as well as what he had himself paid.[3] If the purchaser of real property at an execution-sale before taking his
deed accepts from a stranger the amount on payment of
which the judgment-debtor would have been entitled to redeem, and assigns to him the certificate of the sale, the
stranger is thereby subrogated to the rights of such purchaser
and entitled to a deed of the property.[4]

§ 35. **Where the Purchaser pays Debts with which the Property was chargeable.** — The purchaser of land who pays off a
lien upon it may be subrogated to the rights of the holder of
the lien as against another incumbrancer, such purchaser not
having assumed either of the debts.[5] He has even been subrogated to an interest in the prior incumbrance upon making
only a partial payment thereof.[6] The purchaser from a devi-

v. Hamburg, 11 Iowa, 59; State v.
Hoshaw, 98 Mo. 358; Taylor v. Nel-
son, 54 Miss. 524; Hurt v. Wilson,
38 Calif. 263; Skyrme v. Occidental
Mill Co., 8 Nevada, 219; Rogers v.
Omaha Hotel Co., 4 Nebraska, 54.
*Postea*, § 185.

[1] Mohle v. Tschirch, 63 Calif. 381;
Wilson v. Boden, 26 Ark. 151.

[2] The American Eagle, 19 Fed. Rep.
879; The Pride of America, 19 Id. 607;
The Sarah J. Weed, 2 Lowell, 555.

[3] Smith v. Brittain, 3 Ired. Eq.
(Nor. Car.) 347.

[4] Eleventh Avenue, *in re*, 81 N Y.
436.

[5] Pierce, *in re*, 2 Lowell, 343; Ste-
vens v. King, 84 Maine, 291; John-
son v. Parmely, 14 Hun (N. Y.), 398;
Robenson v. Urquhart, 12 N. J. Eq.
515; Dircks v. Logsdon, 59 Md. 173;
Sidener v. Hawes, 37 Ohio St. 532;
Bressler v. Martin, 133 Ills. 278;
Planters' Bank v. Dodson, 9 Sm. & M.
(Miss.) 527.

[6] Simpson v. Del Hoyo, 94 N. Y.
189.

see whose purchase-money has been applied in payment of debts of the testator will be subrogated to the rights of the creditors whose demands he has thus satisfied.[1] And in Pennsylvania a purchaser of real estate has been allowed to take an assignment of incumbrances which he had agreed to pay out of his purchase-money, and hold under them against an incumbrance which he had not agreed to pay, but the existence of which he discovered after his purchase.[2] If the purchasers from the importers of dutiable goods have, upon the bankruptcy of the importers, paid the duties in order to obtain the goods, they will be subrogated to the priority of the United States for their reimbursement, even though they have proved their claim against the estate of the importers in bankruptcy as an unsecured one.[3] But this right of purchasers to be subrogated to the benefit of debts which have been paid by themselves or out of their purchase-money is limited to their reimbursement[4] for debts which constitute a prior charge upon the property which they have purchased. If they have voluntarily paid debts which could not have been enforced against them or against the property in their hands, if, for example, the purchasers at a foreclosure-sale have voluntarily paid off a junior mortgage upon the property, they will have no right of subrogation to its lien.[5]

§ 36. **Purchaser compelled to pay his Vendor's Debt subrogated to Creditor's Rights against his Vendor.** — A purchaser of land who, in order to save the property which he has purchased, is compelled to pay a debt which ought to have been paid by his vendor, will be subrogated to the benefit of the debt, and of any charge therefor upon the property of the vendor.[6] And in at least one State this equitable right of

[1] Gibson v. McCormick, 10 Gill & J. (Md.) 65.

[2] Bryson v. Myers, 1 Watts & S. 420. *Contra,* Birke v. Abbott, 103 Ind. 1.

[3] Kirkland, *in re,* 14 N. B. R. 139.

[4] Comstock v. Michael, 17 Neb. 288.

[5] Carpenter v. Brenham, 40 Calif. 221.

[6] Chute v. Emmerich, 99 N. Y. 342; Alford v. Cobb, 28 Hun (N. Y.), 22; Hoke v. Jones, 33 W. Va. 501;

the purchaser has been preferred to the claim of a surety
of the vendor for the debt which constituted the charge upon
the land to be subrogated, upon his payment of the debt, to
the security which was held by the creditor.[1] A purchaser
whose land has been taken upon an execution against his
vendor is entitled, upon paying the debt, to be subrogated to
the lien of the judgment against the remaining land of his
vendor.[2] If, however, he has paid for the land by giving
bonds for its price, which are still unpaid, he may set off
his payment against these bonds, even though they are in the
hands of one to-whom they have been assigned by the vendor;[3] so, too, he may set off such a payment against notes
which he has given for the price of the land, while these
notes are still retained by the vendor, even though the notes
are by statute exempted from levy in the hands of the vendor,
like a homestead estate.[4] But this set-off of such a payment
by the purchaser against bonds given by him for the price of the
land must be made first upon bonds which are retained by the
vendor, before applying it upon those bonds which have been
assigned by him; and if the purchaser, with knowledge of the
assignment of some of the bonds and with notice of the prior
lien upon his land, pays the unassigned bonds to the amount
of the lien, the assigned bonds will be thereby relieved from
all liability on account of the lien.[5]

§ 86 a. **Purchaser's Subrogation does not depend upon the
Validity of his Title.** — The right of subrogation does not
depend upon the validity of the title of the person claiming
to be reimbursed for his payment in discharge of a valid incumbrance.[6] It is merely necessary that his payment should

Shelby v. Marshall, 1 Blackf. (Ind.)
384; Galliher v. Galliher, 10 Lea
(Tenn.), 23; Hurt v. Reeves, 5 Hayw.
(Tenn.) 50.
[1] Rush v. State, 20 Ind. 432;
Armstrong v. Fearnaw, 67 Ind. 429.
[2] Beall v. Walker, 26 W. Va. 472;
McGill, in re, 6 Penn. St. 504.

[3] Armentrout v. Gibbons, 30 Gratt.
(Va.) 632; McGill, in re, 6 Penn. St.
504.
[4] Corbally v. Hughes, 59 Ga. 493.
[5] Armentrout v. Gibbons, 30 Gratt.
(Va.) 632.
[6] Bright v. Boyd, 1 Story, 478;
Fowler v. Parsons, 143 Mass. 401;

have been made in good faith for the protection of an interest which he believed himself to have in the estate, and in discharge of a burden actually resting upon the property,[1] so that his payment has increased the value of the estate for the benefit of those who turn out subsequently to be entitled to the title.[2] The benefit of subrogation has accordingly been allowed to one who held merely an invalid or a verbal contract for the conveyance of the land which he has freed from an incumbrance;[3] to the assignee of one who held such a contract;[4] to one whose only title was under an invalid mortgage,[5] or under a voidable decree;[6] to one who claimed only under a void or a voidable sale,[7] even after the avoidance of the sale by order of court;[8] to an unsecured creditor who has paid off a mortgage-debt in compliance with an erroneous order of court;[9] to a devisee who has only a contingent remainder in the encumbered estate,[10] and to one who holds merely an equitable lien upon the property.[11] If he *bona fide* claims an interest, he is not a mere volunteer, and may be subrogated;[12] but he must show that he had or supposed he had some interest to be protected.[13]

Sunders *v.* Sanders, 2 Dev. Eq. (Nor. Car.) 262; Scott *v.* Dunn, 1 Dev. & Bat. Eq. (Nor. Car.) 425, 427; Gerdine *v.* Menage, 41 Minn. 417.

[1] Guckian *v.* Riley, 135 Mass. 71; Kelly *v.* Duff, 61 N. H. 435; Benedict *v.* Chase, 58 Conn. 196; *Thompson, C. J.,* in Mosier's Appeal, 56 Penn. St. 76, and cases there cited.

[2] Weimer *v.* Porter, 42 Mich. 569; Ingersoll *v.* Jeffords, 55 Miss. 37; Blodgett *v.* Hitt, 29 Wisc. 169, 182 *et seq.:* Wright *v.* Oroville Mining Co., 40 Calif. 20.

[3] Champlin *v.* Williams, 9 Penn. St. 341; Stewart *v.* Fellows, 128 Ills. 480; Dillow *v.* Warfell, 71 Iowa, 106.

[4] Tompkins *v.* Seely, 29 Barb. (N. Y.) 212; Sheen *v.* Hogan, 86 Ills. 16; Fisher *v.* Johnson, 5 Ind. 492.

[5] Brooke *v.* Bordner, 125 Penn. St. 470; Spaulding *v.* Harvey, 129 Ind.

106; Lamb *v.* West, 75 Iowa, 399; Gilbert *v.* Gilbert, 39 Iowa, 657; Davis *v.* Roosevelt, 53 Tex. 305.

[6] Coudert *v.* Coudert, 43 N. J. Eq. 407.

[7] Hutson *v.* Sadler, 31 W. Va. 358; Muir *v.* Berkshire, 52 Ind. 149; Payne *v.* Hathaway, 3 Vt. 212.

[8] Johnson *v.* Robertson, 34 Md. 165. *Antea,* § 31. *Postea,* § 209.

[9] Magill *v.* De Witt County Bank, 126 Ills. 244.

[10] Pease *v.* Eagan, 131 N. Y. 262.

[11] Hackensack Savings Bank *v.* Terhune Manufacturing Co., 45 N. J. Eq. 610.

[12] Harlan *v.* Jones, 104 Ind. 167; Kelly *v.* Duff, 61 N. H. 435; James *v.* Burbridge, 33 W. Va. 272; Arn *v.* Hoppin, 25 Kans. 707.

[13] Wadsworth *v.* Blake, 43 Minn. 509.

§ 37. **Limitation of Purchaser's Right of Subrogation.** — A grantee's cause of action against his grantor for any misrepresentation is personal, and does not pass to any subsequent purchaser from the grantee.[1] The subrogation of the purchaser will not ordinarily extend to a mere right of action which has already become vested in his grantor,[2] such as an action for a deficiency in the quantity of the land which would have entitled the vendor to an action against the original owner for such deficiency. An express or conventional subrogation is necessary to vest this right of the vendor in his purchaser.[3] Nor will one claiming under a quitclaim deed from a mortgagor be thereby subrogated to the mortgagor's right to defend against the mortgage on the ground that it was procured by the fraud of the mortgagee.[4] Nor will the purchaser be subrogated to any right of his vendor of which the law forbids the conveyance,[5] or which is excluded by necessary implication from the terms of the conveyance under which he claims.[6] Where the vendor of land had a lien thereon for the price, which was superior to a mortgage subsequently given by the vendee, but sold the vendee's interest in the property, instead of the property itself, for the unpaid balance of the price, the purchaser of the vendee's interest at this sale was not allowed to prevent a foreclosure of the mortgage on the ground that he was by his purchase from the vendor subrogated to the vendor's equitable lien.[7] The purchaser of the right to redeem from two mortgages or other liens, since he acquires only the interest of the mortgagor,

[1] Livingston v. Peru Iron Co., 2 Paige (N. Y.), 390; Collins v. Suau, 7 Robt. (N. Y.) 623; Lawrence v. Montgomery, 37 Calif. 183.

[2] Willoughby v. Middlesex Co., 8 Met. (Mass.) 296.

[3] Chambliss v. Miller, 15 La. Ann. 713; Davis v. Clark, 33 N. J. Eq. 579.

[4] Fairfield v. McArthur, 15 Gray (Mass.), 526; Bradshaw v. House, 43 Tex. 143.

[5] Mason v. Mason, 140 Mass. 63.

[6] True v. Congdon, 44 N. H. 48; Warren v. Coggswell, 10 Gray (Mass.), 76; Kendall v. Brown, 7 Gray (Mass), 210; Squier v. Shepard, 38 N. J. Eq. 331; Adams v. Friedlander, 37 La. Ann. 350.

[7] Allen v. Phelps, 4 Calif. 256.

cannot, upon taking an assignment of the first mortgage, set it up as a source of title against those who claim under the second mortgage.[1]

§ 38. **Subrogation of the Purchaser at an Execution-sale against the Debtor.** — The purchaser of land at an execution-sale holds merely a lien upon the land while the statutory period of redemption is running; if in the meantime it becomes necessary for the protection of his interest, he may be subrogated, upon discharging a prior lien created by the judgment-debtor, to the benefit of that lien for his reimbursement;[2] and if the proceeds of property irregularly sold at a sheriff's sale have been applied in payment of the owner's debts, that owner cannot recover the property from the purchaser without repaying to him the amount so applied.[3] The purchaser who has bought in good faith and whose bid has discharged an existing lien upon the land is subrogated to the rights of the judgment-creditor to the extent of the lien which he has thus discharged.[4] But if the judgment itself was void and created no lien, and the debt was not a charge upon the land, there is nothing to which the purchaser can be subrogated, and he has no rights against the judgment-debtor.[5] Where a judgment-debtor owned a lot of land, and the sheriff, on an execution against him, sold by mistake another lot to which the debtor had no title, and the purchase-money was paid and applied upon the judgment, and the debtor surrendered his lot to the purchaser, both supposing it to be the one that had been sold

[1] Afton Bank v. Thompson, 72 Iowa, 417; Parker, C. J., in Wade v. Howard, 6 Pick. (Mass.) 492.

[2] Swain v. Stockton Savings Society, 78 Calif. 600.

[3] Blackburn v. Clarke, 85 Tenn. 506; Henry v. Keyes, 5 Sneed (Tenn.), 488; Shepherd v. McIntyre, 5 Dana (Ky.), 574; Hart v. Smith, 44 Wisc. 213; Blanton v. Ludeling, 30 La. Ann. 1232; Dufour v. Camfranc, 11 Martin (La.), 607; Burns v. Ledbetter, 54 Tex. 374.

[4] Paxton v. Sterne, 127 Ind. 289; Short v. Sears, 93 Ind. 505; Ray v. Detchon, 79 Ind. 56; O'Brien v. Harrison, 59 Iowa, 686; Rinehart v. Long, 95 Mo. 396; Meher v. Cole, 50 Ark. 361; Cline v. Upton, 59 Tex. 27; Tappan v. Hunt, 74 Ga. 545.

[5] Northraft v. Oliver, 74 Tex. 162; Two Rivers Manufacturing Co. v. Beyer, 74 Wisc. 210.

upon the execution, but afterwards the debtor, discovering
the mistake, regained the land, and refused to refund the
purchase-money, the purchaser was allowed to recover the
amount of the purchase-money from him.[1]  The purchaser at
an execution-sale of property which is under attachment for
the same debt is entitled, if it is afterwards subjected by a
decree to the payment of the attachment, to be reimbursed
out of the proceeds of the attached property for his payment
upon the execution.[2]  And if the purchaser of attached property pays the price in discharge of liens which were superior
to the attachment, he should be indemnified, if the property
is afterwards decreed to be sold upon the attachment, by the
reimbursement of his money in preference to the attaching
creditor.[3]  So, also, if an execution-creditor takes from his
debtor an assignment of the latter's interest in a personal
estate, this assignment is valid to the amount of his demand ;
and if this creditor, to save his rights, afterwards purchases
the same property from a sheriff, who sells it upon a subsequent levy made under executions senior to his own, though
this latter sale is void, the creditor so purchasing will be
allowed, as against the debtor, to stand in the place of the
senior creditors whom he has thus satisfied, and to be subrogated to their rights.[4]  And generally where an execution-
sale upon a valid judgment is voidable, and the debtor seeks
to recover the property, if there be no fraud on the part of
the purchaser, the latter will not be compelled to restore the
property to the debtor without being reimbursed the amount
which he paid, and which has gone to discharge the judgment-
lien.[5]  And in the same way the purchaser from a judgment-
debtor of property which has been sold on execution will be

[1] McLean v. Martin, 45 Missouri,
393.

[2] Beall v. Barclay, 10 B. Mon.
(Ky.) 261.

[3] Beall v. Barclay, 10 B. Mon.
(Ky.) 261.

[4] Bentley v. Long, 1 Strobh. Eq.
(So. Car.) 43.

[5] Stone v. Darnell, 25 Tex. Sup.
430; Andrews v. Richardson, 21 Tex.
287; Morton v. Welborn, 21 Tex.
772; Howard v. North, 5 Tex. 290

subrogated to whatever right of redemption the debtor has by agreement acquired in the premises.[1]

§ 39. **Subrogation of such Purchaser where the Property recovered by Third Parties.** — It has been considered that the purchaser of property sold under an execution has the right in equity, if the property has been recovered from him or his vendor by another under a superior title, to be substituted for the judgment-creditor to the original judgment-lien, and to have the amount of his purchase-money refunded to him by the defendant in the execution,[2] even though he knew at the time of his purchase that the property belonged to another, and was not liable to be sold on the execution;[3] and that if the property had been thus recovered from a vendee of the purchaser, the purchaser, in his suit for indemnity, need not show that he has reimbursed his vendee, to whom he only, and not the defendant in the execution is liable.[4] But this has also been strenuously denied, and the position maintained, with greater reason, that the purchaser at an execution-sale is not subrogated to the rights of the judgment-creditor against the debtor, if the property is afterwards taken from him by virtue of a paramount title in a stranger,[5] just as he cannot under the same circumstances recover back the amount of his purchase-money from the creditor to whom it has been paid;[6]

[1] Dupuy v. McMillan, 2 Duvall (Ky.), 555.

[2] Julian v. Beal, 26 Ind. 220; Muir v. Craig, 3 Blackf. (Ind.) 293; Geoghegan v. Ditto, 2 Met. (Ky.) 433; Price v. Boyd, 1 Dana (Ky.), 434; McGhee v. Ellis, 4 Litt. (Ky.) 244.

[3] McLaughlin v. McDaniel, 8 Dana (Ky.), 182; semble, in Howard v. North, 5 Tex. 290, 315.

[4] McLaughlin v. McDaniel, 8 Dana (Ky.), 182.

[5] Hawkins v. Miller, 26 Ind. 173; Vattier v. Lytle, 6 Ohio, 477, 478; Perry v. Williams, Dudley (So. Car.),

44; Halcombe v. Loudermilk, 3 Jones Law (Nor. Car.), 491; Goodbar v. Daniel, 88 Ala. 583.

[6] Georgetown v. Smith, 4 Cranch, C. C. 91; Patterson's Estate, 25 Penn. St. 71; Lall v. Matthews, 19 Vt. 322; Leport v. Todd, 32 N. J. Law, 124; Martin v. Martin, 7 Md. 368; Spott v. Commonwealth, 85 Va. 531; Rollins v. Henry, 78 Nor. Car. 342; Andrews v. Murphy, 12 Ga. 431; Anderson v. West, 80 Ky. 171; Bunch v. Grave, 111 Ind. 351; Conner v. Wells, 91 Ind. 197; Burden v. Johnson, 81 Mo. 318; Nugent v. Priebatsch, 61 Miss. 402; Goodbar v.

and this on the ground that he is merely a voluntary purchaser of the debtor's interest in the property, and that it is
only where the person paying a debt has the rights of a surety,
or is compelled to pay it by legal process, or in order to save
his own property, that equity substitutes him, even against
the debtor, to the place of the creditor; and that a mere
stranger or volunteer paying the debt will not be subrogated
to the rights of the creditor, unless there has been an assignment to him or an express agreement for such subrogation.[1]

§ 40. **Rights of a Purchaser whose Purchase is voidable by
the Creditors of his Vendor.** — One who has purchased property
at a sale which may be avoided by the creditors of the vendor,
whether he is an assignee for the benefit of creditors, a purchaser, or a voluntary grantee, will, after satisfying the claims
of the attaching creditors, be subrogated to their rights, so as
to enable him to hold the property against subsequent attachments.[2] His purchase at a sheriff's sale against his grantor
will give him a good title.[3] And if the sale to him was good
as against the vendor, so that he could require the vendor
himself to discharge the debts for which the property was subsequently attached, he may, in New York, upon paying the
judgment rendered under such attachment, take an assignment of the judgment against his vendor and be subrogated
to the rights of the judgment-creditor against his vendor.[4] If
a grantee of land whose deed is voidable by the creditors of
his grantor takes from a prior mortgagee of the property a
quitclaim deed of all the latter's interest in the premises,
though it expressly states that the mortgage is thereby cancelled and discharged, this will, if his grant is avoided by the
grantor's creditors, be construed against them to operate as

Dun, *Id.* 618; Stevens *v.* King, 21
Ala. 429; Fore *v.* Manlove, 18 Calif.
436.
[1] Richmond *v.* Marston, 15 Ind.
134; Childress *v.* Allen, 8 La.
477.

[2] Selleck *v.* Phelps, 11 Wisc. 380;
Lamb *v.* Smith, 132 Mass. 574.
[3] Arrington *v.* Arrington, 102 Nor.
Car. 491.
[4] Cole *v.* Malcolm, 66 N. Y. 363.

an assignment and not as a discharge of the mortgage;[1] his right of subrogation is not destroyed by the avoidance by his grantor's creditors of the conveyance which he has taken.[2] A wife's right of dower is not barred by her having released it in his deed of his real estate which has been subsequently set aside as in fraud of his creditors.[3] This whole doctrine rests upon the principle that merely constructive fraud without an actual wrongful intent will not prevent subrogation, though it would be otherwise with an active participant in the fraud;[4] and this principle has been generally maintained in the later decisions, though with great diversity of application to the varying circumstances, and with much difference of opinion as to the existence of actual participation in the fraudulent scheme.[5] But the fraudulent grantee will not by subrogation or any other device be reimbursed for payments made by him in furtherance of the fraud.[6]

§ 41. **Waiver of the Right of Subrogation.** — The right of subrogation may be lost by the waiver of the party entitled to it.[7] Thus, where one of two whose estates were subject

[1] Crosby v. Taylor, 15 Gray (Mass.), 64. See Mansfield v. Dyer, 133 Mass. 374.

[2] Phillips v. Chamberlain, 61 Miss. 740; Rhead v. Hounson, 46 Mich. 243; Tompkins v. Sprout, 55 Calif. 31; Merrell v. Johnson, 96 Ills. 224.

[3] Wilkinson v. Paddock, 57 Hun (N. Y.), 191; Malony v. Horan, 12 Abbott Pr. N. s. (N. Y.) 289; Lockett v. James, 8 Bush (Ky.), 28; Rupe v. Hadley, 113 Ind. 416; Horton v. Kelly, 40 Minn. 193; Bohannon v. Coombs, 97 Mo. 446; Hume v. Scruggs, 64 Ala. 40.

[4] McCaskey v. Graff, 23 Penn. St. 321; Jackson v. Summerville, 13 Penn. St. 359; Gilbert v. Hoffman, 2 Watts (Penn.), 66; Cook v. Berlin Woolen Mill Co., 56 Wisc. 643; Grant v. Lloyd, 12 Sm. & M. 191. *Postea,* § 44.

[5] See Loos v. Wilkinson, 113 N. Y. 485, reversing s. c., 51 Hun, 74; Baldwin v. Short, 125 N. Y. 553; s. c., 54 Hun, 73; Hamilton Bank v. Halstead, 56 Hun (N. Y.), 530; Newman v. Kirk, 45 N. J. Eq. 677; Levi v. Welsh, *Id.* 867; Williamson v. Goodwyn, 9 Gratt. (Va.) 503; Burton v. Gibson, 32 W. Va. 406; Cutcheon v. Buchanan, 88 Mich. 594; Wallace v. McBride, 70 Mich. 596; Shawano Bank v. Koeppen, 78 Wisc. 533; Fordyce v. Hicks, 76 Iowa, 41; Tuskaloosa Bank v. Kennedy, 91 Ala. 470; Pritchett v. Jones, 87 Ala. 317; Wiley v. Knight, 27 Ala. 336.

[6] Sullivan v. Tinker, 140 Penn. St. 35.

[7] Richardson v. Traver, 112 U. S. 423; Turnbull v. Thomas, 1 Hughes, C. C. 172, 176; U. S. Bank v. Peters, 13 Peters, 123; Campbell v. Sloan, 21

5

to a common lien paid off the whole debt and took an assignment of the mortgage, it was held that he might either regard the mortgage as discharged, and bring an action against the other for contribution, or treat it as a subsisting charge upon the estate until the other should redeem by paying a reasonable contribution.[1] Certain mortgaged premises being subject to a paramount lien for taxes, the first mortgagee, before foreclosure, paid the same, under an agreement with the second mortgagee that the latter, if he purchased the premises at the foreclosure-sale, should repay the amount. The second mortgagee did so purchase; and the estate was conveyed to him. He then refused to refund the taxes; and it was held that the first mortgagee could not now, after his conveyance, be subrogated to the original tax lien.[2] Though in general a junior incumbrancer who pays off the holder of a prior lien is entitled to be subrogated to the benefit of the latter's security, yet this right will be waived by an agreement of the junior incumbrancer that the property shall be otherwise appropriated.[3] A long delay without action will be fatal to a claim of subrogation.[4]

§ 42. **What is not a Waiver.** — The right of subrogation to a recorded mortgage will not be lost by the mere failure to give notice of the claim to a purchaser for value.[5] The fact that one entitled to subrogation obtains also collateral security for his protection is not of itself a waiver of his right.[6] A mortgagee who is entitled to be subrogated to the benefit of a prior lien, which he has discharged, will not be deprived of this right, even though he has taken a new mortgage upon the

---

So. Car. 301; Belcher v. Wickersham, 9 Baxter (Tenn.), 111. *Postea*, §§ 110, 147.

[1] Taylor v. Bassett, 3 N. H. 294.

[2] Manning v. Tuthill, 30 N. J. Eq. 29.

[3] United States Bank v. Peters, 13 Peters, 133.

[4] West's Appeal, 88 Penn. St. 341; Fleming v. Parry, 24 Penn. St. 47; Buffington v. Bernard, 90 Penn. St. 63.

[5] Hurt v. Riffle, 11 Fed. Rep. 790.

[6] Smith v. Dinsmoor, 119 Ill. 656.

same premises for the amount of his payments,[1] and this new mortgage has been afterwards avoided for usury.[2] But it is to be observed that this agreement for usury was not made until after the right of subrogation had vested;[3] if, however, the claim had grown out of the usurious agreement, instead of being prior to it and independent of it, it could have furnished no basis for subrogation.[4] Where one who was in treaty for the purchase of personal property, which was subject to two mortgages, paid off the first mortgage, under an agreement that until the completion of the sale he should stand in the place of the mortgagee and have the benefit of his security, it was held that he was not deprived of this conventional subrogation by the fact that his agreement with his vendor contained a recital that the amount so paid by him had been paid by him out of the purchase-money and in discharge of the mortgage-debt.[5]

§ 43. **Right lost by Negligence resulting in Prejudice to others.** — The fact that the loss of one who seeks to be protected by the application of the doctrine of subrogation arose from his own negligence, and that the granting of his request would now be prejudicial to other innocent creditors or assignees of his debtor, will be fatal to his claim.[6] Thus, where the owner of land conveyed it to another, and took for the purchase-money a mortgage upon the property, and the parties agreed that the deeds should remain unrecorded until the land should be surveyed, and the mortgagor stated to the

[1] Worcester Bank v. Cheeney, 87 Ills. 602; Burchard v. Phillips, 11 Paige (N. Y.), 66; Eagle Ins. Co. v. Pell, 2 Edw. Ch. (N. Y.) 631.

[2] Patterson v. Birdsall, 64 N. Y. 294; affirming s. c. 6 Hun (N. Y.), 632; McWilliams v. Bones, 84 Ga. 203.

[3] See Giveans v. McMurtry, 16 N. J. Eq. 468.

[4] Perkins v. Hall, 105 N. Y. 539; Baldwin v. Moffett, 94 N. Y. 82, and 26 Hun, 209; Farmers' Loan Co. v. Carroll, 5 Barb. (N. Y.) 613, per Welles, J. ; Trible v. Nichols, 53 Ark. 271; postea, § 44.

[5] Watts v. Symes, 1 De G., M. & G. 240.

[6] The Superior, 5 Sawyer, 346; Printup v. Barrett, 46 Ga. 407; Gordon v. English, 3 Lea (Tenn.), 634; State v. Bèal, 88 Ind. 106; Conner v. Welch, 51 Wisc. 431; Schaller, in re, 10 Daly (N. Y.), 57.

mortgagee that he intended to sell the land to one D., and
promised to transfer D.'s mortgage instead of his own, to
which arrangement the mortgagee assented, and the mortgagor did convey to D., who recorded his deed without notice
of the prior mortgage, which was not recorded until after the
conveyance to D., it was held that the original mortgagee was
not entitled to the benefit of the mortgage given by D., in
preference to the other creditors of his debtor's insolvent
estate.[1] And where a grantor sold land, taking no security
for the payment of the purchase-money, and his grantee sold
the land to another, and took divers bonds for the purchase-
money, it was held that although the original grantor, by
virtue of his equitable lien upon the land, might have subjected these bonds to the payment of his claim while they
were in the hands of his grantee, yet he lost this right by
delaying to enforce it until after the bonds had been assigned
to *bona fide* holders for value without notice of his claim.[2]
But the mere fact that the loss of the party seeking to be subrogated arose from his own negligence will not debar him
from the right, unless its enforcement would be prejudicial
to others who are not at fault.[3]

§ 44. **The Party seeking Subrogation must not be in his own
Wrong.** — Any one who seeks the benefit of the equitable doctrine of subrogation must come into court with clean hands.[4]
It will not be applied to relieve a vendee from the consequences of his own wrongful act, or of a wrongful act in which
he has participated,[5] or of the wrongful act of one under
whom he claims.[6] Accordingly, a vendor who seeks to re-

[1] Bussey v. Page, 13 Maine, 459.
[2] Moore v. Holcombe, 3 Leigh
(Va.), 597. *Antea*, § 40.
[3] Willcox v. Foster, 132 Mass. 320;
Wall v. Mason, 102 Mass. 313; Daniel v. Baxter, 1 Lea (Tenn.), 630.
[4] Wilkinson v. Babbitt, 4 Dillon, C.
C. 207; Railroad Co. v. Soutter, 13
Wallace, 517; Griffith v. Townley, 69

Mo. 13; Farmers' Loan Co. v. Carroll,
5 Barb. (N. Y.) 613; Johnson v.
Moore, 33 Kans. 90.
[5] Rowley v. Towsley, 53 Mich. 329;
Spratt v. Pierson, 4 So. Car. 301; Johnson v. Moore, 33 Kans. 90; Devine v.
Harkness, 117 Ills. 145.
[6] Boyer v. Bolender, 129 Penn. St.
324; Wilson v. Murray, 90 Ind. 477.

scind the contract of sale and to recover the property by reason of the fraud of the vendee will not be obliged to reimburse
the fraudulent vendee for his expenditures made to carry out
the fraud, although upon recovering the property he will reap
the benefit of these expenditures by the discharge of a lien
upon the property which they have paid,[1] though it has been
said that in equity where the party seeking to avoid a sale
has been benefited by the fraudulent purchaser's having paid
off incumbrances, the purchaser should be reimbursed for
such payments.[2] Where the second mortgagees of a railroad
company purchased the road under an execution against the
company, formed themselves into a new corporation, and as
such operated the road for their own benefit, and then the
new corporation, to prevent a foreclosure, paid the debt
secured by the first mortgage, after which their own purchase
of the road, at the suit of creditors of the old company, was
set aside as fraudulent and void, it was held that the new
corporation could neither recover back the amount it had
paid to the first mortgagees, nor yet be subrogated to their
rights under their first mortgage.[3] If a creditor who might
otherwise claim to be subrogated to the lien of a mortgage
upon his debtor's property, which he has paid off, has taken
for his security another mortgage from the debtor upon the
same property, which is found to be fraudulent and void as
against the debtor's other creditors, he will not be allowed
such subrogation to the prejudice of parties who have purchased the property at an execution-sale against the debtor.[4]

§ 45. **When One entitled to be subrogated to a Lien may demand an Assignment thereof.** — The right of subrogation to the
benefit of a prior incumbrance is sometimes enforced by
compelling an assignment of the prior lien to the party en-

---

[1] Guckenheimer v. Angevine, 81
N. Y. 394.
[2] White v. Trotter, 14 Sm. & M.
(Miss.) 30; Everett v. Beebe, 37
Iowa, 452.

[3] Railroad Co. v. Soutter, 13 Wallace, 517.
[4] Wiley v. Boyd, 38 Ala. 625.

titled to be subrogated thereto.[1]  But the mere right of redemption and of subrogation will not of itself entitle a party to require an assignment, although this has been maintained in some cases.[2]  The right to demand an assignment is now generally limited to cases in which the party who is entitled to redeem, and thereupon to be subrogated to the benefit of the lien from which he redeems, is also in effect a surety, or is in equity to be regarded as a surety, for the payment of the debt secured thereby.[3]  "Any one having a subsequent incumbrance upon the mortgaged estate can protect his interest by paying the prior mortgage when it is due; and he thereupon succeeds by subrogation, upon settled principles of equity, to the rights and interest of such prior mortgagee in the lands, as security for the amount so paid, without any assignment or transfer by the prior mortgagee.  He is not entitled to an assignment."[4]  Where one is entitled to an assignment of a prior mortgage, he must actually tender the full amount of principal, interest, and any accrued costs to the mortgagee; merely saying what he will do and paying the money into court will not stop the running of interest on the mortgage-debt.[5]  And the right of any parties junior in in-

[1] Twombly v. Cassidy, 82 N. Y. 155; Clark v. Mackin, 95 N. Y. 346; Platt v. Brick, 35 Hun (N. Y.), 121; Knoblauch v. Fogelsong, 37 Minn. 320; Johnson v. Zink, 52 Barb. (N. Y.) 396; s. c. on appeal, 51 N. Y. 333; Mount v. Suydam, 4 Sandford Ch. (N. Y.) 399; Lyons' Appeal, 61 Penn. St. 15; Raffety v. King, 1 Keene, 601.  And see Cilley v. Hare, 40 N. H. 358.

[2] Forest Oil Co.'s Appeal, 118 Penn. St. 138; *Sutherland, J.*, in Ellsworth v. Lockwood, 42 N. Y. 89, 97, citing and criticising Pardee v. Van Anken, 3 Barb. (N. Y.) 536, 537, and Jenkins v. Continental Ins. Co., 12 How. Pr. (N. Y.) 66.

[3] Bigelow v. Cassedy, 26 N. J. Eq.

557; Nelson v. Loder, 132 N. Y. 288; Speiglemeyer v. Crawford, 6 Paige (N. Y.), 254, 257; Cherry v. Monro, 2 Barb. Ch. (N. Y.) 618; Averill v. Taylor, 8 N. Y. 44; Johnson v. Zink, 52 Barb. (N. Y.) 396; s. c. on appeal, 51 N. Y. 333; Vandercook v. Cohoes Savings Institution, 5 Hun (N. Y.), 641; Ellsworth v. Lockwood, 42 N. Y. 89; Holland v. Citizens' Savings Bank, 16 R. I. 734.

[4] Jones on Mortgages, § 792, citing Ellsworth v. Lockwood, 42 N. Y. 89, 96; Burnet v. Denniston, 5 Johns. Ch. (N. Y.) 35; Hubbard v. Ascutney Mill Dam Co., 20 Vt. 402.

[5] Hornby v. Cramer, 12 How. Pr. (N. Y.) 490.

terest to compel the assignment to them of a prior mortgage
has been utterly denied.[1] "The mortgagee," says Mr. Justice Colt, "is not required to observe or to regard the equitable rights to contribution which may exist between parties
having different interests in the equity, or to protect them
by transferring his title to any one.[2] When such rights
exist, they are protected on those settled principles of equity
by which one who assumes more than his share of the common burden is subrogated to the rights of the mortgagee, to
hold, without any assignment or act of transfer, as *quasi*
assignee, for the purpose of compelling contribution. He
becomes in effect the assignee of the mortgage, for the purpose of enabling him to compel a contribution. But the
right of subrogation arises by operation of law only when
there has been a payment and extinguishment of the mortgage by one entitled to redeem.[3] An assignment implies
the continued existence of the debt, and the equitable right
does not arise."[4]

§ 46. **The Real Debtor cannot be subrogated.** — The debtor
upon whom rests the ultimate obligation of discharging the
debt cannot by his payment acquire any right of subrogation;[5] and if, upon making his payment, he takes an assignment of the security, this will be equivalent to a discharge
thereof.[6] One whose duty it is to pay the taxes upon real
estate cannot obtain any title in himself by neglecting to
pay them, and either buying the property himself at the tax
sale or afterwards purchasing it from a third party who had

[1] Chedel v. Millard, 13 R. I. 461; Butler v. Taylor, 5 Gray (Mass.), 455; Lamson v. Drake, 105 Mass. 564; Lamb v. Montague, 112 Mass. 352.

[2] So in Chase v. Williams, 74 Mo. 429; Davis v. Flagg, 35 N. J. Eq. 491.

[3] See *antea*, § 6.

[4] Lamb v. Montague, 112 Mass. 353.

[5] Underwood v. Metropolitan Bank, 144 U. S. 669; Thompson v. Heywood, 129 Mass. 401; Walsh v. Wilson, 130 Mass. 124; Acer v. Hotchkiss, 97 N. Y. 395; N. Y. Ins. Co. v. Vanderbilt, 12 Abbott Pr. (N. Y.) 458; Frye v. Bank of Illinois, 11 Ills. 367; Atkins v. Emison, 10 Bush (Ky.), 9; Hardin, *ex parte*, 34 So. Car. 377; Hardin v. Clark, 32 So. Car. 480; Davis v. Townsend, Id. 112; People's Bank v. Ballowe, 34 La. Ann. 565.

[6] Loverin v. Humboldt Safe De-

bought at such sale.[1] An assignment of a judgment to one
primarily bound to pay it will not keep it alive.[2] One who
has given two mortgages upon the same land with warranty
cannot, after the titles under the two mortgages have been
united in one person and the second mortgage has been foreclosed, redeem from the first mortgage and claim to be an
equitable assignee thereof, and to be subrogated to the rights
of the first mortgagee, so as to enable him to open the foreclosure of the second mortgage;[3] for no debtor can be subrogated against his own warranty,[4] nor can he be subrogated to
the rights of the second against the first mortgagee.[5] A purchaser cannot be subrogated to the benefit of an incumbrance
which he has agreed to pay.[6] One who has assumed and
agreed to pay two incumbrances cannot be subrogated to the
lien of the second,[7] and his agent who made the bargain, and
so knows its provisions, is under the same disability.[8] If he
himself held the first mortgage, that is extinguished by his
assumption of both burdens.[9] So, if the purchaser of land

posit Co., 113 Penn. St. 6; Keim v.
Robeson, 23 Penn. St. 456; Clay v.
Banks, 71 Ga. 363; Carlton v. Jackson, 121 Mass. 592; Hooper v. Henry,
31 Minn. 264; McCarty v. Christie,
13 Calif. 79.

[1] Barnard v. Wilson, 74 Calif. 512;
Barrett v. Amerein, 36 Calif. 322;
Busch v. Huston, 75 Ills. 343; Cho-
teau v. Jones, 11 Ills. 300; Medley v.
Elliott, 62 Ills. 532; Burchard v. Fra-
zer, 23 Mich. 224; Cooley v. Water-
man, 16 Mich. 366; Gaskins v. Blake,
27 Miss. 675; Smith v. Lewis, 20
Wisc. 350; Bassett v. Welch, 22
Wisc. 175; Fallas v. Pierce, 30 Wisc.
443; Fair v. Brown, 40 Iowa, 209;
Porter v. Lafferty, 33 Iowa, 254; Al-
lison v. Armstrong, 28 Minn. 276;
Williamson v. Russell, 18 W. Va. 612;
Franks v. Morris, 9 W. Va. 664;
Magner v. Hibernia Ins. Co., 30 La.
Ann., part II., 1357.

[2] Montgomery v. Vickery, 110 Ind.
211.

[3] Butler v. Seward, 10 Allen
(Mass.), 466.

[4] Sparhawk v. Bagg, 16 Gray
(Mass.), 583.

[5] McIntier v. Shaw, 6 Allen
(Mass.), 83.

[6] Bolton v. Lambert, 72 Iowa,
483; Goodyear v. Goodyear, Id. 329;
Probstfied v. Czizek, 37 Minn. 420;
Martin v. Aultman, 80 Wisc. 150;
Sharp v. Collins, 74 Mo. 266; Converse v. Cook, 8 Vt. 164; Willson
v. Burton, 52 Vt. 394; Munroe v.
Crouse, 59 Hun (N. Y.), 248; Tompkins v. Halstead, 21 Wisc. 118.

[7] Stiger v. Mahone, 24 N. J. Eq.
426; Willson v. Burton, 52 Vt. 394.

[8] Dargan v. McSween, 33 So. Car.
324, 325.

[9] Kneeland v. Moore, 138 Mass.
198.

which is incumbered first by a mechanic's lien and then by a mortgage has assumed and agreed to pay the mortgage-debt, his purchase of the land when sold under a judgment recovered upon the mechanic's lien will give to him or to his grantee no title that can be set up against the mortgage.[1] The purchaser of an equity of redemption is entitled to the benefit of a payment made by any one whose duty, as to him, it is to pay the mortgage-debt.[2] But the mere fact that the money paid to a mortgagee comes from the debtor will not necessarily operate a discharge of the mortgage, if that is, as a part of the same transaction, assigned to a third party for value.[3] Upon payment of a mortgage debt from the funds of the debtor and also from those of a third party, the mortgage can be kept alive only to the extent of the latter funds.[4]

§ 47. **Assignment to One who is bound to pay the Debt tantamount to a Discharge.** — Just as an assignment is not necessary where the right of subrogation exists,[5] so where one who has the right to redeem property from a mortgage or other charge pays the amount due and takes an assignment of the security, this will be treated as thereby discharged or as still subsisting, as the justice of the case may require.[6] The party who is ultimately liable for a debt cannot, upon taking an assignment thereof, enforce payment from one under a merely secondary liability.[7] Thus, an assignment of a mortgage to a former owner of the equity of redemption, who has conveyed the mortgaged premises with warranty, extinguishes the mortgage; the assignee takes it for the

[1] Heim v. Vogel, 69 Mo. 529.
[2] Williams v. Thurlow, 31 Maine, 392; Noyes v. Ray, 64 Ga. 283.
[3] Sheddy v. Geran, 113 Mass. 378; Howe v. Woodruff, 12 Ind. 214; Hall v. Southwick, 27 Minn. 234; Goulding v. Bunster, 9 Wisc. 513; Faulks v. Dimock, 27 N. J. Eq. 65.
[4] Hammond v. Barker, 61 N. H. 53.
[5] Antea, § 45.

[6] Grave v. Bunch, 83 Ind. 4; Dayton v. Rice, 47 Iowa, 429; Bailey v. Willard, 8 N. H. 429; McGiven v. Wheelock, 7 Barb. (N. Y.) 22; Leppo v. Gilbert, 26 Kans. 138; Christy v. Fisher, 58 Calif. 256; Walker v. Stone, 20 Md. 195.
[7] Byles v. Kellogg, 67 Mich. 318; Morse v. Brockett, 67 Barb. (N. Y.) 234.

benefit of his grantee with warranty, and the assignment is tantamount to a discharge.[1] So, if a purchaser of mortgaged premises who has by his deed assumed payment of the mort-gage-debt, or the grantee of such a purchaser,[2] takes an as-signment of the mortgage, this operates a discharge, and the lien of the mortgage is gone;[3] and the same principle will be applied to a tax-title.[4] If the purchaser of mortgaged property, who has agreed with his grantor to assume and pay the mortgage as a part of his purchase-money, causes the conveyance of the property to be made to a third party in-stead of taking it to himself, and then obtains an assignment of the mortgage to himself instead of having it discharged, this will as to the vendor operate an extinguishment of the mortgage;[5] the rights of such third party are no greater than those of the original purchaser.[6] So also one for whom prop-erty is held in trust, and whose equitable duty it is to pay a mortgage upon the property, though he may not be legally bound therefor, cannot, after paying the mortgage-debt, keep the mortgage alive by procuring it to be assigned to himself, or to a third person for his benefit; his payment discharges the mortgage.[7] By an arrangement between two mortgagors, one of them assumed the payment of the whole debt, and gave to the mortgagee a new mortgage upon the same and other property, to secure both the old debt and a new indebtedness of his own, the former joint mortgage be-

---

[1] Mickles v. Townsend, 18 N.Y. 575; Mickles v. Dillaye, 15 Hun (N.Y.), 296; Wadsworth v. Williams, 100 Mass. 126.

[2] Crowley v. Harader, 69 Iowa, 83.

[3] Russell v. Pistor, 7 N.Y. 171; Ely v. McNight, 30 How. Pr. (N.Y.) 97; Kilborn v. Robbins, 8 Allen (Mass.), 466; Hoysradt v. Holland, 50 N.H. 433; Jerome v. Seymour, Harringt. (Mich.) 357; Fretland v. Mack, 76 Iowa, 434; Byington. v.

Fountain, 61 Iowa, 512; Winans v. Wilkie, 41 Mich. 264; Parry v. Wright, 5 Russ. 142.

[4] Bertram v. Cook, 32 Mich. 518; Stinson v. Richardson, 48 Iowa, 541.

[5] Frey v. Vanderhoof, 15 Wisc. 397.

[6] Wright v. Patterson, 45 Mich. 261; Reid v. Sycks, 27 Ohio St. 285.

[7] Putnam v. Collamore, 120 Mass. 454.

ing also retained by the creditor as collateral security. A purchaser of the property covered by the new mortgage then paid off the latter security, and took an assignment of the old joint mortgage; and this transaction was held to operate a discharge of the old mortgage.[1]

§ 48. **Subrogation of a Dowress who has paid a Paramount Lien on the Property.**—A widow who was entitled to dower, but had not yet had it assigned to her, remained in the mansion-house of her deceased husband with her infant children, whom she supported. She then paid a balance of the purchase-money which remained due upon the property, and which was secured by a vendor's lien thereon; and she also paid out money for the taxes upon the property and for improvements: and it was held that she should be subrogated to the liens upon the property which existed respectively for the purchase-money and for the taxes which she had paid, except so far as it was her duty as dowress to pay the same, though she had no lien for what she had spent in making improvements.[2] She is entitled to be subrogated to a lien which she has paid off, in order to preserve the property in which she thus has an interest.[3]

§ 49. **Widow's Right of Dower against a Purchaser who has paid an Incumbrance to which her Dower was subject.** — As the purchaser of an equity of redemption may be subrogated to the lien of prior incumbrances which he has paid in order to preserve his property, without having been under any personal obligation for their payment,[4] so, *a fortiori*, if such a purchaser takes an assignment of a previous mortgage, this will not operate an extinguishment of the lien of the mortgage.[5] And if the mortgagor's widow was entitled to dower or homestead as against such purchaser, but not as against

---

[1] McGiven v. Wheelock, 7 Barb. (N. Y.) 22

[2] Simmons v. Lyle, 32 Gratt. (Va.) 752.

[3] Gatewood v. Gatewood, 75 Va. 407; Roach v. Hacker, 2 Lea (Tenn.), 633; Stinson v. Anderson, 96 Ills. 373.

[4] *Antea,* §§ 13, 28.

[5] Selb v. Montague, 102 Ills. 446; De Lisle v. Herbs, 25 Hun (N. Y.), 485; Simonton v. Gray, 34 Maine, 50.

the mortgagee, then, after such an assignment from the latter to the former, she cannot have her dower or her homestead without redeeming from the mortgage, which, however, she will have the right to do.[1] A quitclaim deed of the mortgaged premises from the mortgagee to such a purchaser, after a breach of the condition of the mortgage, is a sufficient assignment of the mortgage.[2] The mortgage will be kept alive where this is manifestly for the interest of the party who has paid it, and is consistent with the justice of the case, if no contrary intent is expressed or manifestly implied;[3] in other words, the mortgage will be kept alive for the benefit of one who has paid it,[4] where he is evidently entitled in equity to be subrogated to it, and does not appear to have done anything to waive the right,[5] though it is sometimes said that if the purchaser has simply paid off the mortgage and had it discharged, not having taken an assignment of it, or in any way indicated an intention to avail himself of its lien, he cannot set it up against the claim of the mortgagor's widow for dower.[6] The release of dower in a mortgage-deed works an estoppel, not only in favor of the mortgagee and the direct assignees of the mortgage, but also of those who by subrogation become entitled to its benefits.[7] The dower rights of the mortgagor's widow, having been released in the mortgage, though valid against the purchaser of the equity, must remain subject to the mortgage after this has been assigned

---

[1] Lamb v. Montague, 112 Mass. 352; Gibson v. Crehore, 3 Pick. (Mass.) 475; s. c. 5 Pick. (Mass.) 146; Carll v. Butman, 7 Greenl. (Me.) 102; Simonton v. Gray, 34 Maine, 50; Kenyon v. Segar, 14 R. I. 490; Hinds v. Ballou, 44 N. H. 619; Woodhull v Reid, 1 Harrison (16 N. J. L.), 128.

[2] Savage v. Hall, 12 Gray (Mass.), 363; Hinds v. Ballou, 44 N. H. 619; Carll v. Butman, 7 Greenl. (Me.) 102.

[3] Hinds v. Ballou, 44 N. H. 619;

Price v. Hobbs, 47 Md. 359; Bryar's Appeal, 111 Penn. St. 81.

[4] As in Popkin v. Bumstead, 8 Mass. 491.

[5] Antea, § 12.

[6] Cox v. Garst, 105 Ills. 342; Atkinson v. Angert, 46 Mo. 515, 518.

[7] Dearborn v. Taylor, 18 N. H. 153; McMahon v. Russell, 17 Fla. 698; Walker v. Walker, 5 Ills. App. 289.

or quitclaimed to the purchaser.[1]  And a redemption from
the mortgage through process of law by such a purchaser will
give him the same right,[2] to the extent of the actual cost of
the redemption.[3]  If a new mortgage has been given by such
a purchaser expressly as a substitute for the old mortgage,
the widow's rights will be no greater against the holder of
the new mortgage, or against one who has redeemed from it,
than they were against those claiming under the old mortgage.[4]  But where a husband, by falsely representing that he
was unmarried, obtained a loan on a mortgage in which his
wife did not join, and therewith paid off prior liens upon the
premises, the mortgagee's estate was not allowed to override
her inchoate rights of dower;[5] for the wife is not in privity
with her husband in regard to transactions to which she is
not a party;[6] and his frauds cannot be imputed to her.[7]  The
mortgagor's assignee in insolvency is to be regarded as a
purchaser who is not bound to pay the mortgage-debt;[8] and
an assignment of the mortgage to him will not extinguish it
for the benefit of the mortgagor's widow.[9]  The same rules
apply to a purchase of the equity of redemption by the mortgagee as to an assignment or quitclaim of the mortgage to a
purchaser of the equity, as to its effect upon the rights of the
mortgagor's widow.[10]  The mortgage will not be regarded as

[1] Harrow v. Johnson, 3 Met. (Ky.)
578; Woods v. Wallace, 30 N. H.
384.

[2] Everson v. McMullen, 113 N. Y.
293, reversing s. c. 45 Hun, 578;
Sheldon v. Hoffnagle, 51 Hun (N. Y.),
478; Niles v. Nye, 13 Met. (Mass.)
135.

[3] Walker v. Doane, 131 Ills. 27.

[4] Newton v. Cook, 4 Gray (Mass.),
46; King v. Stetson, 11 Allen (Mass.),
407.

[5] Westfall v. Hintze, 7 Abbott
New Cas. (N. Y.) 236.

[6] Tibbetts v. Langley Manufg.
Co., 12 So. Car. 465.

[7] Moore v. Foote, 34 Mich. 443.

[8] Bell v. Sunderland Building
Society, 24 Ch. D. 618.

[9] Sargeant v. Fuller, 105 Mass.
119; Brown v. Lapham, 3 Cush.
(Mass.) 551.

[10] Campbell v. Knights, 24 Maine,
332; Newton v. Sly, 15 Mich. 391;
Decker v. Hall, 1 Edm. Select Cas.
(N. Y.) 279; Hugunin v. Cochrane,
51 Ills. 302; Durval v. Febiger, 1
Cincin. (Ohio) 268; Snyder v. Snyder,
6 Mich. 470; Thompson v. Boyd, 1
Zab. (21 N. J. L.) 58.

extinguished, so as to let in the widow's claim of dower, which was released in the mortgage, unless the debt has been paid by her husband, the mortgagor, or from his means, or by some one who stands in such relation to him as to be in legal effect the debtor, whose duty it is to pay and discharge the mortgage-debt.[1]

§ 50. **Dower let in if Debt paid by one bound to pay it.** — If, however, the mortgage-debt has been paid by one bound to pay it, then the mortgage will be regarded as extinguished, whether or not it has been assigned to the party making the payment.[2] Whether any particular transaction shall be held to operate as a payment which extinguishes the lien, or as an assignment, which preserves and keeps it on foot, does not depend so much upon the form of words used as upon the relations subsisting between the parties advancing the money and the party executing the transfer or release, and their relative duties. If the money is advanced by one whose duty it is, by contract or otherwise, to pay and cancel the mortgage, and relieve the mortgaged premises from the lien of the mortgage, a duty in the proper performance of which others have an interest, it will be held to be a release and not an assignment, although in form it purports to be an assignment.[3] If the payment is made by an heir-at-law of the mortgagor, pursuant to the terms of a bond given by him to the administrator to pay the debts of the deceased, in order to prevent his real estate from being sold therefor, this payment will extinguish the mortgage in favor of the widow's claim to dower.[4] If the mortgage-debt has in substance been paid from the means or estate of the principal debtor, this

[1] *Shaw, C. J.*, in Brown *v.* Lapham, 3 Cush. (Massachusetts) 551; Cockrill *v.* Armstrong, 31 Arkansas, 580.

[2] *Antea*, § 74; McCabe *v.* Swap, 14 Allen (Mass.), 188; Norris *v.* Morrison, 45 N. H. 490; Collins *v.* Torry, 7 Johns. (N. Y.) 278; Atkinson *v.* Stewart, 46 Mo. 510.

[3] *Shaw, C. J.*, in Brown *v.* Lapham, 3 Cush. (Mass.) 551; Hatch *v.* Palmer, 58 Maine, 271.

[4] King *v.* King, 100 Mass. 224.

will let in the widow's claim to dower, which was barred by the mortgage.[1]

§ 51. **The widow may redeem. Her Rights thereupon.** — A widow who is entitled to dower in an equity of redemption may redeem the estate by paying off the whole of the mortgage-debt;[2] and upon so doing she will, without specific proof of her intent at the time of payment to keep the mortgage alive,[3] be subrogated to the place of the mortgagee for her protection and indemnity, until the heirs shall reimburse her their equitable proportion, and thus redeem from her all that is not comprehended in her claim of dower.[4] When another claiming, like herself, under the mortgagor, redeems the mortgaged estate, she may share in the benefit of the redemption, upon paying her equitable proportion of the mortgage-debt, according to the value of her dower interest;[5] or she may be assigned her dower in the excess of the value of the estate over the amount of the mortgage-debt.[6] An assignment of the mortgage to her will not merge her dower interest.[7] And a wife who has joined with her husband in a mortgage of both his land and his personal property, has, after the death of her husband, an equitable right to have the mortgaged personalty first applied to the payment of the mortgage-debt, both against the mortgagee and also against

[1] Peckham v. Hadwen, 8 R. I. 160; Ketchum v. Shaw, 28 Ohio St. 503; Sweaney v. Malony, 62 Mo. 485; Atkinson v. Stewart, 46 Mo. 510.

[2] Davis v. Wetherell, 13 Allen (Mass.), 60; McCabe v. Bellows, 7 Gray (Mass.), 148, overruling in part Van Vronker v. Eastman, 7 Met. (Mass.) 157.

[3] Jefferson v. Edrington, 53 Ark. 545.

[4] Rossiter v. Cossit, 15 N. H. 38; Woods v. Wallace, 30 N. H. 384; Norris v. Morrison, 45 N. H. 490; Mantz v. Buchanan, 1 Md. Ch. Dec.

202; Atkinson v. Stewart, 46 Mo. 510.

[5] Jones v. Gilbert, 135 Ills. 27; Cox v. Garst, 105 Ills. 342; Gibson v. Crehore, 5 Pick. (Mass.) 146; Norris v. Morrison, 45 N. H. 490; Evertsen v. Tappen, 5 Johns. Ch. (N. Y.) 497.

[6] Snyder v. Snyder, 6 Mich. 470; Norris v. Morrison, 45 N. H. 490; Richardson v. Skolfield, & Pratt v. Skolfield, 45 Maine, 386; George v. Cooper, 15 W. Va. 666; Stoppelbeir v. Shulte, 1 Hill (So. Car.) 200.

[7] Hunter v. Dennis, 112 Ills. 568.

the general creditors of her husband's estate ;[1] if she has
given a mortgage of her own real estate, merely to secure a
debt of her husband's, she is entitled to have his interest in
the estate as tenant by the curtesy first sold and applied to pay
the debt, in exoneration of her own interest in the mortgaged
premises, even against another creditor of her husband, who
holds a general lien upon his interest in the premises, created
subsequently to the execution of the mortgage.[2] But if she
has joined with her husband in a mortgage of his real estate,
she is not entitled to have the debt satisfied exclusively out
of her husband's interest in such real estate, so as to give
her dower out of the whole estate, notwithstanding the mortgage ; she can be endowed only in the equity of redemption,[3]
except as against those entitled to her husband's estate, in
the case of the mortgage-debt being his personal debt, which
she may require his representatives to pay out of his personal
estate.[4]

§ 52. **The Rule in Massachusetts.** — The rules adopted in
Massachusetts applicable to all these cases have been suc-
cinctly but fully stated by an eminent judge,[5] as follows : —

" *First.* When a purchaser pays off a mortgage to which
the right of dower would be subject, merely to clear the
estate of the incumbrance, and not by virtue of any obligation
to pay the mortgage-debt, and takes an assignment or a
conveyance of his interests from the mortgagee, he may stand
on the mortgage title if he please, and then no dower can be
assigned without payment of the whole mortgage-debt by the
demandant.[6]

[1] Harrow v. Johnson, 3 Met. (Ky.)
578.

[2] Neimcewicz v. Gahn, 3 Paige
(N. Y.), 614.

[3] Hawley v. Bradford, 9 Paige (N.
Y.) 200; Leavenworth v. Cooney, 48
Barb. (N. Y.) 570; Denton v. Nanny,
8 Barb. (N. Y.) 618, 619.

[4] Campbell v. Campbell, 30 N. J.

Eq. 415; Mantz v. Buchanan, 1 Md.
Ch. Dec. 202; Creecy v. Pearce, 69
Nor. Car. 67 ; Henagan v. Harllee, 10
Rich. Eq. (So. Car.) 285 ; Hunsucker
v. Smith, 49 Ind. 114; Greenbaum v.
Austrian, 70 Ills. 591.

[5] *Wells, J.,* in McCabe v. Swap,
14 Allen (Mass.), 188, 190.

[6] Strong v. Converse, 8 Allen

" *Second.* If in such case the mortgage be discharged, then he will be held to have redeemed, and the widow will take her dower in the equity, or by contribution, as she may elect.[1]

" *Third.* But if the mortgage-debt be paid by the debtor, or from his property or in his behalf, then the payment will be treated as a satisfaction and discharge of the mortgage, and the widow will be remitted to her full right of dower.[2]

" *Fourth.* The payment will be held to be made in behalf of the debtor, when there is an obligation imposed by the grantor upon the purchaser to assume and pay the debt as his own ; or when the grantor furnishes the means for the payment, as where, by the terms of the conveyance, the entire estate is sold, and the seller leaves a sufficient part of the purchase-money in the hands of the grantee for the purpose.[3] In such cases, if the purchaser take an assignment of the mortgage to himself, he will not be allowed to set it up, but the legal title thus acquired will be held to merge in the equity." [4]

§ 53. **Assignment of a Mortgage to the Owner of the Equity of Redemption will not necessarily Extinguish its Lien.** — The payment of the money due upon a mortgage-debt by the owner of the equity of redemption, who is not the debtor, and his taking an assignment of the mortgage, will operate as a payment or as a purchase of the mortgage, as will best serve the ends of justice and the proper intent of the parties.[5] Where the purchaser of an equity of redemption made a second mortgage thereof, and, while this was outstanding, took an assignment of the first mortgage, which he soon after assigned to a third person, it was held that the existence of the second mortgage at the time of these assignments prevented the

(Mass.), 557; McCabe *v.* Bellows, 7 Gray (Mass.) 148.

[1] Newton *v.* Cook, 4 Gray (Mass.), 46. And see Pynchon *v.* Lester, 6 Gray (Mass.), 314 ; Eaton *v.* Simonds, 14 Pick. (Mass.) 98.

[2] Wedge *v.* Moore, 6 Cush. (Mass.) 8.

[3] Brown *v.* Lapham, 3 Cush. (Mass.) 551.

[4] Bolton *v.* Ballard, 13 Mass. 227 ; Snow *v.* Stevens, 15 Mass. 278. And see Hall *v.* Southwick, 27 Minn. 234.

[5] Bullard *v.* Leach, 27 Vt. 491 ; Loud *v.* Lane, 8 Met. (Mass.) 517 ; Duncan *v.* Smith, 31 N. J. Law, 325.

merger of the first mortgage.[1] The assignment of a mortgage
to one who has purchased the equity of redemption will or
will not operate an extinguishment of the mortgage, according to the interest of the party taking the assignment and
the just intent of the parties.[2] If the owner of mortgaged
premises conveys different parts of them to separate grantees,
and one of these pays and takes an assignment of the mortgage, he can, in the absence of circumstances which would
make this inequitable,[3] hold it against all the mortgaged
premises.[4] And if the purchaser of a bare equity of redemption which is subject to two mortgages takes an assignment
of the first mortgage for the protection of his title, this mortgage will not be thereby merged in the equity, so as to give
to the holder of the junior mortgage a preference in payment
out of the proceeds of the mortgaged property.[5] And generally a mortgage which is assigned to one, not being the
debtor, but having an interest in the mortgaged premises, is
not thereby extinguished if it is for the interest of the
assignee to uphold it ;[6] this equitable doctrine of subrogation
has so far been adopted at common law as to prevent a
merger.[7] If the equity of redemption was subject when purchased to an attachment against the mortgagor which was
junior to the mortgage, this will prevent a merger of the
mortgage upon an assignment of the latter to the purchaser
of the equity.[8]

[1] Evans v. Kimball, 1 Allen
(Mass.), 240; Spurgin v. Adamson,
62 Iowa, 661.

[2] Hunt v. Hunt, 14 Pick. (Mass.)
374; Crosby v. Taylor, 15 Gray
(Mass.), 64; Binsse v. Paige, 1
Abbott (N. Y. App. Dec.), 138;
Franklyn v. Hayward, 61 How. Pr.
(N. Y.) 43.

[3] Postea, §§ 75 et seq.

[4] Casey v. Buttolph, 12 Barb. (N.
Y.) 637; Scott v. Webster, 44 Wisc.
185.

[5] Millspangh v. McBride, 7 Paige

(N. Y.) 509; Green v. Currier, 63 N.
H. 563.  And see McKinstry v. Mer-
vin, 3 Johns. Ch. (N. Y.) 466.

[6] Fellows v. Dow, 58 N. H. 21;
Carpenter v. Gleason, 58 Vt. 244;
Van Wagenen v. Brown, 26 N. J.
Law, 196; Rawiszer v. Hamilton, 51
How. Pr. (N. Y.) 297.

[7] Hatch v. Kimball, 16 Maine,
146; Goodwin v. Keney, 47 Conn.
486; Duffy v. McGuinness, 13 R. I.
595; Knowles v. Lawton, 18 Ga. 476.

[8] Grover v. Thatcher, 4 Gray
(Mass.), 526.

§ 54. **Tests by which Merger is determined.** — Nor is it necessary that the intent to keep the mortgage alive should have been manifested at the time of the payment otherwise than by taking an assignment of the security; unless there appears to have been an intention to extinguish it, it will be taken to be subsisting or extinguished, as the interest of the party may require.[1] The merger of a charge in the inheritance will not be presumed, if this would be contrary to the interest of the owner of both the charge and the inheritance.[2] The merger is prevented, and the charge or mortgage upheld, whenever there is a strong equity in favor of it, but never where it is not for an innocent purpose.[3] If they are held in different rights, there will be no merger.[4] When a charge on an estate becomes absolutely vested in the owner of the inheritance, the tests usually applied for ascertaining whether the charge has merged, are, — *first*, whether there has been an actual expression of intention to that effect;[5] *secondly*, whether the acts done by the owner of the estate are only consistent with the maintaining of the charge,[6] and, *thirdly*, whether it is for the interest of the owner that the charge should not be merged in the inheritance.[7]

§ 55. **Incumbrance so assigned, kept alive only for a Good Purpose and to protect a Beneficial Interest.** — The owner of an equity of redemption who has taken an assignment of the

---

[1] Evans v. Burns, 67 Iowa, 179; Strever v. Earl, 60 Hun (N. Y.), 528; Buzzell v. Still, 63 Vt. 490; Pool v. Hathaway, 22 Maine, 85; Hatch v. Kimball, 16 Maine, 146.

[2] Pride, *in re*, Shackell v. Colnett, 2 Ch. D. (1891) 135; Forbes v. Moffatt, 18 Ves. 384; Davis v. Barrett, 14 Beav. 542; Smith v. Roberts, 91 N. Y. 470; Shimer v. Hammond, 51 Iowa, 401.

[3] McClain v. Sullivan, 85 Ind. 174; Hatch v. Kimball, 16 Maine, 146.

[4] Radcliffe, *in re*, 1 Ch. D. (1892) 227.

[5] Lewis v. Hinman, 56 Conn. 55.

[6] See Gunter v. Gunter, 23 Beav. 571; Hatch v. Skelton, 20 Beav. 453; Hood v. Phillips, 3 Beav. 513.

[7] Tyrwhitt v. Tyrwhitt, 32 Beav. 244; Lynch v. Pfeiffer, 110 N. Y. 33; Ann Arbor Bank v. Webb, 56 Mich. 377; Watson v. Dundee Mortgage Co., 12 Oreg. 474.

mortgage cannot keep it on foot to the prejudice of a *bona fide*
purchaser under himself,[1] nor unless some beneficial interest
is shown to require it.[2] And if the payment appears to have
been intended at the time to extinguish the charge, it will
have that effect.[3] When the owner of the equity paid the
amount which was due upon the mortgage, without then
manifesting any intention of keeping the mortgage in force,
and without any agreement for an assignment of the mortgage,
but many years afterwards took an assignment of the mortgage and the notes secured by it, this transaction was held to
operate a discharge of the mortgage.[4] But it is a general
rule that where a discharge of a mortgage has been taken
inadvertently and under a mistake of fact, equity will keep
the mortgage alive and treat the transaction as an assignment, when necessary to protect the rights of the parties.[5]

§ 56. **Mortgage assigned to the Principal Debtor is extinguished.** — If the mortgage-debt is paid by the principal
debtor, or out of his funds, it cannot be kept alive by being
assigned to him or to a mere agent for him.[6] And the
grantee of a mortgaged estate who has accepted a deed of
the equity of redemption without covenants will be held, in
the absence of a special contract, and without some special
circumstances, to take the land charged with the incumbrance, as between himself and his grantor.[7] Accordingly
he cannot, after paying off the debt, keep it alive against his

---

[1] Starr *v.* Ellis, 6 Johns. Ch. (N. Y.) 393.

[2] Gardner *v.* Astor, 3 Johns. Ch. (N. Y.) 53; Starr *v.* Ellis, 6 Johns. Ch. (N. Y.) 393.

[3] Lewis *v.* Hinman, 56 Conn. 55; Agnew *v.* Renwick, 27 So. Car. 562; Champney *v.* Coope, 34 Barb. (N. Y.) 539.

[4] Given *v.* Marr, 27 Maine, 212.

[5] Short *v.* Currier, 153 Mass. 182; Eversen *v.* McMullen, 113 N. Y. 293;

Barnes *v.* Mott, 64 N. Y. 397; Kins-ley *v.* Davis, 74 Maine, 498; Cobb *v.* Dyer, 69 Maine, 494; Hammond *v.* Barker, 61 N. H. 53; Coudert *v.* Coudert, 43 N. J. Eq. 408; Barta *v.* Vreeland, 15 N. J. Eq. 103.

[6] Morse *v.* Bassett, 132 Mass. 502; Angel *v.* Boner, 38 Barb. (N. Y.) 425; Champney *v.* Coope, 34 Barb. (N. Y.) 539; Shepherd *v.* Mc-Clain, 18 N. J. Eq. 128.

[7] *Antea,* § 26.

grantor by having it assigned to himself,[1] so as to enable him to set it off against any unpaid balance that he may owe to his grantor upon his purchase.[2] But if a mortgage has been assigned to the owner of the equity under such circumstances as to be tantamount to an extinguishment of the security, yet this owner, after assigning it as a valid instrument, will be estopped from claiming that it has become merged or extinguished, and such owner's grantee with notice of the circumstances will also be estopped.[3] And an assignment of a mortgage made to the principal debtor merely as an intermediary or a trustee will not necessarily extinguish the mortgage.[4] So, although the purchaser of an equity of redemption has expressly assumed and agreed to pay the mortgage-debt, so that an assignment of the mortgage to him would operate an extinguishment of its lien,[5] yet if, when he pays the debt, he takes an assignment of the mortgage in blank instead of a discharge, and subsequently reissues the mortgage to a creditor of his own, filling up the blank in the assignment with the name of such creditor, the mortgage will be kept on foot even against a subsequent purchaser from him with warranty.[6]

§ 57. **Conveyance of the Equity to the Holder of a Prior Incumbrance will not extinguish it in Favor of a Junior.** — If a prior incumbrancer acquires the absolute title to the incumbered property, his prior charge will not be merged in the absolute title where his interest and the intention of the parties unite to prevent the merger.[7] He may still claim

---

[1] Donk v. Alexander, 117 Ills. 330; Morrison v. Morrison, 38 Iowa, 73.

[2] Atherton v. Toney, 43 Ind. 211.

[3] Powell v. Smith, 30 Mich. 451; Coles v. Appleby, 22 Hun (N. Y.), 72.

[4] Kelly v. Jenness, 50 Maine, 455; Denzler v. O'Keefe, 34 N. J. Eq. 361; Baker v. N. W. Loan Co.,

36 Minn. 185; Angell v. Boner, 38 Barb. (N. Y.) 425.

[5] Mickles v. Dillaye, 15 Hun (N. Y.) 296. *Antea*, § 46.

[6] Kellogg v. Ames, 41 N. Y. 259.

[7] Boardman v. Larrabee, 51 Conn. 39; Holden v. Pike, 24 Maine, 427; Thompson v. Chandler, 7 Greenl. (Me.) 377; Freeman v. Paul, 3 Greenl. (Me.) 260; Marshall v.

under his prior title; and the holder of the junior lien may still redeem from him as before;[1] or the equity of redemption from the junior lien may still be foreclosed.[2] The estates of the mortgagor and of the mortgagee, though united in the same person, will still be treated as distinct, when this is necessary for just purposes and to effectuate the proper intention of the parties.[3] Though the purchase of the equity of redemption by the mortgagee generally operates to extinguish the mortgage-debt and to merge the mortgage-title,[4] this will not be so where it is the intention and the interest of the mortgagee to keep the mortgage alive by reason of intervening incumbrances or otherwise,[5] and this can be done without injury to the mortgagor or to third parties.[6] Even if the mortgagee, in consideration of the conveyance to him of the equity of redemption, gives up the evidence of the mortgage-debt, or acknowledges its satisfaction, this will not

Wood, 5 Vt. 250; Myers v. Brownell, 1 D. Chip. (Vt.) 448; Day v. Mooney, 4 Hun (N. Y.), 134; Wallace v. Blair, 1 Grant (Pa. Cas.), 75; Edgerton v. Young, 43 Ills. 464; Lydecker v. Bogert, 38 N. J. Eq. 136; Thebaud v. Hollister, 37 N. J. Eq. 402; Smith v. Swan, 69 Iowa, 412; Lyon v. McIlvaine, 24 Iowa, 9; Wickersham v. Reeves, 1 Iowa, 413; Besser v. Hawthorne, 3 Oregon, 129.

[1] Thompson v. Chandler, 7 Greenl. (Me.) 377; Kinney v. Ensign, 18 Pick. (Mass.) 232; Fouche v. Swain, 80 Ala. 151; Fuller v. Lamar, 53 Iowa, 477; Strong v. Burdick, 52 Iowa, 630; Rogers v. Herron, 92 Ills. 583.

[2] Cochran v. Goodell, 131 Mass. 464; Cronin v. Hazletine, 3 Allen (Mass.), 324; Doten v. Hair, 16 Gray (Mass.), 149; Palmer v. Fowley, 5 Gray (Mass.), 545; Walters v. Defenbaugh, 90 Ills. 241.

[3] Hutchins v. Carleton, 19 N. H. 487; Bean v. Boothby, 57 Maine,

295; Clos v. Boppe, 23 N. J. Eq. 270; Flanigan v. Sable, 44 Minn. 417; Ætna Ins. Co. v. Corn, 89 Ills. 170; Meacham v. Steele, 93 Ills. 135.

[4] Bleckeley v. Branyan, 28 So. Car. 445; s. c., 26 Id. 424.

[5] Bell v. Tenney, 29 Ohio St. 240; Haggerty v. Byrne, 75 Iud. 499; International Bank v. Wilshire, 103 Ills. 143; Cohn v. Hoffman, 45 Ark. 376; Patterson v. Mills, 69 Iowa, 755; McCrossen v. Harris, 35 Kans. 178; McClaskey v. O'Brien, 16 W. Va. 792.

[6] Adams v. Angell, 5 Ch. Div. 634; Simpson v. Hall, 47 Conn. 417; Delaware & Hudson Canal Co. v. Bonnell, 46 Conn. 9; Campbell v. Vedder, 1 Abbott (N. Y. App. Dec.), 295; James v. Morey, 2 Cow. (N. Y.) 246; Mulford v. Peterson, 35 N. J. Law, 127; Pike v. Gleason, 60 Iowa, 150; Vannice v. Bergen, 16 Iowa, 555; Webb v. Meloy, 32 Wisc. 319; Grellet v. Heilshorn, 4 Nevada, 526.

necessarily extinguish his mortgage for the benefit of the holder of a subsequent lien.[1] In equity a merger will not take place unless the purposes of justice or the intentions of the parties so demand.[2] The manifest intention of the parties at the time of the transaction will determine whether the lien is preserved or extinguished.[3] An express written agreement that there shall be no merger will prevent it.[4] The holder of a mortgage may keep it alive as a part of his title after acquiring the equity of redemption,[5] if this is necessary for the preservation of his rights.[6]

§ 58. **Conveyance of Equity in Payment of Prior, will not advance Junior, Incumbrance.** — A mortgagee having received from the mortgagor a deed of the mortgaged premises which contained a recital that the deed was to cancel the mortgage, and the land having been taken upon an attachment made before the execution of the deed and consummated by a levy afterwards, and the mortgage and the mortgage-notes having been retained by the mortgagee under a parol agreement with the mortgagor to await the result of the attachment, it was held that the taking of this deed did not extinguish the mortgage in favor of the attaching creditor: for one party is not to be estopped by the recitals in a deed which he has taken

[1] Baldwin v. Norton, 2 Conn. 161, 709; New England Jewelry Co. v. Merriam, 2 Allen (Mass.), 390; Hemenway v. Bassett, 13 Gray (Mass.), 378; Richardson v. Hockenhull, 85 Ills. 124; Simpson v. Pease, 53 Iowa, 572; Stanton v. Thompson, 49 N. H. 272; Adams v. Angell, 5 Ch. Div. 634.

[2] Sheldon v. Edwards, 35 N. Y. 279; Bascom v. Smith, 34 N. Y. 320; Waterloo Bank v. Elmore, 52 Iowa, 541; Carpenter v. Brenham, 40 Calif. 221; Woodward v. Davis, 53 Iowa, 694.

[3] Oregon Trust Co. v. Shaw, 6 Sawyer, C. C. 52 and 5 Id. 336; Aldrich v. Blake, 134 Mass. 582; Mexall v. Dearborn, 12 Gray (Mass.), 336; Tower v. Divine, 37 Mich. 443.

[4] Spencer v. Ayrault, 10 N. Y. 202; Fowler v. Fay, 62 Ills. 375; Agnew v. Charlotte R. R. Co., 24 So. Car. 18; Gresham v. Ware, 79 Ala. 192.

[5] New Jersey Ins. Co. v. Meeker, 40 N. J. Law, 18; Lockwood v. Sturdevant, 6 Conn. 374; Polk v. Reynolds, 31 Md. 106; Hoppock v. Ramsay, 28 N. J. Eq. 413; Mobile Bank v. Hunt, 8 Ala. 876.

[6] Jackson v. Evans, 44 Mich. 510.

from giving the truth in evidence to sustain it, against another party who is seeking to go behind the deed to prevent its operation.[1] The retention by a mortgagee of his mortgage and mortgage note or bond, on taking a conveyance of the mortgaged premises, is *prima facie* sufficient evidence of his intention to keep the mortgage alive to prevent a merger.[2] And if he has cancelled his mortgage by reason of the junior incumbrance having been fraudulently concealed from him, he may by seasonable proceedings have the discharge cancelled, and be reinstated in his prior lien over the holder of the junior charge,[3] though this has been refused where no fraud was practised upon him.[4] So he may have the satisfaction cancelled and his mortgage reinstated, if his purchase of the equity, which was the consideration of the satisfaction, is afterwards set aside.[5] If the rights of the parties require it, if for example the conveyance of the equity was made merely for a further security, and it was to be reconveyed upon a fixed payment,[6] equity will regard a mortgage as remaining in force, though a deed of the equity of redemption has been accepted as a foreclosure thereof.[7]

§ 59. **When a Conveyance of the Equity to the Mortgagee will be regarded as a Payment of the Mortgage-debt.** — Whether the mortgage-debt will be considered to have been paid by a conveyance of the equity of redemption to the mortgagee, will depend upon the intention of the parties.[8] Where a mortgagor of land, by deed, for a valuable consideration ex-

[1] Crosby *v.* Chase, 17 Maine, 369.

[2] Dunphy *v.* Riddle, 86 Ills. 22.

[3] Young *v.* Hill, 31 N. J. Eq. 429.

[4] Bleckeley *v.* Branyan, 26 So. Car. 424.

[5] Hemstreet *v.* Burdick, 90 Ills. 444; Corwin *v.* Collett, 16 Ohio St. 289; Kieser *v.* Baldwin, 62 Ala. 526.

[6] McElhaney *v.* Shoemaker, 76 Iowa, 416.

[7] Decatur *v.* Walker, 137 Mass. 141; Worcester Bank *v.* Cheeney, 87 Ills. 602; Stimpson *v.* Pease, 53 Iowa, 572; Rumpp *v.* Gerkens, 59 Calif. 496; Brooks *v.* Rice, 56 Calif. 428.

[8] Germania Building Association *v.* Neill, 93 Penn. St. 322; Huebsch *v.* Scheel, 81 Ills. 281; Sanborn *v.* Magee, 79 Iowa, 501.

pressed therein, conveyed the mortgaged premises to the mortgagee, it was held that, in the absence of evidence that this conveyance was intended by the parties as a payment of the notes which were secured by the mortgage, these notes might still be collected or negotiated by the mortgagee.[1] The owner of an equity of redemption sold it to a purchaser, who assumed the payment of the mortgage; this purchaser gave a second mortgage of the same premises, which was assigned to the first mortgagee, and then conveyed the premises to this mortgagee, with warranty against all persons claiming under him, and a covenant that there were no incumbrances made by him except the second mortgage; and it was held that the first mortgage was not merged by this conveyance, and the mortgagee could still collect the note secured thereby from the original debtor, whatever the value of the premises.[2] But if a party takes from a mortgagor an assignment without recourse of a second mortgage upon the premises, given by a purchaser of the equity of redemption who has assumed the payment of the first mortgage, and who so states in his second mortgage, and if thus holding the second mortgage he then takes an assignment of the first mortgage, he cannot collect the note secured by the first mortgage from the original mortgagor; for this mortgagor would then be subrogated to the priority of the first mortgage over the second, and thus be enabled to get back exactly the amount he would have paid from the party to whom he would have paid it.[3] The cases just cited hold that a conveyance of the mortgaged premises made by the mortgagor to the mortgagee, will not operate a payment of the mortgage-debt, unless it is shown affirmatively that this was the intention of the parties:[4] if that intention does appear, it will be carried into

[1] Van Deusen v. Frink, 15 Pick. (Mass.) 449.
[2] Tucker v. Crowley, 127 Mass. 400.
[3] Swett v. Sherman, 109 Mass. 231.
[4] So in Cattel v. Warwick, 6 N. J. Law, 190; Jackson v. Relf, 26 Fla. 465.

effect.[1] Elsewhere the presumption has been said to be the other way; that the mortgage-debt is paid by such a conveyance unless it appears that the parties intended otherwise.[2] It has even been held that such a conveyance of part of the mortgaged premises will operate an extinguishment of the mortgaged-debt *pro tanto;*[3] but that it will be only *pro tanto* an extinguishment, although this conveyance of part of the mortgaged property comes from one who had purchased that part from the mortgagor, and had agreed to pay off the whole mortgage.[4]

§ 60. **An Intervening Estate will prevent a Merger.** — If the holder of a mortgage which is the oldest lien upon the property, and which is for an amount exceeding the value of the property, takes from the mortgagor a conveyance of the mortgaged premises to save the expense of a foreclosure, this will not operate a merger of his mortgage-title, so as to enable the holder of a junior lien to take the premises without paying the first mortgage-debt.[5] But if the senior mortgagee should purchase the mortgaged premises from the mortgagor and undertake to pay the junior incumbrance, deducting its amount from the price of his purchase, this would postpone the lien of his senior mortgage to that of the junior incumbrance.[6] It has been said to be a general principle that whenever the owner of an estate has also a charge upon it, and there is another intermediate charge or estate between

---

[1] Dickason *v.* Williams, 129 Mass. 182; Hemenway *v.* Bassett, 13 Gray (Mass.), 378; Holman *v.* Bailey, 3 Met. (Mass.) 55.

[2] Bassett *v.* Mason, 18 Conn. 131; Burnet *v.* Denniston, 5 Johns. Ch. (N. Y.) 35; Clift *v.* White, 12 N. Y. 519; Spencer *v.* Harford, 4 Wend. (N. Y.) 381; Seighman *v.* Marshall, 17 Md. 550; Wilhelmi *v.* Leonard, 13 Iowa, 330; McCormick *v.* Bauer, 122 Ills. 573; Lilly *v.* Palmer, 51 Ills.

331; Astley *v.* Milles, 1 Sim. 298; Tyrwhitt *v.* Tyrwhitt, 32 Beav. 244.

[3] Wilhelmi *v.* Leonard, 13 Iowa, 330; Trimmier *v.* Vise, 17 So. Car. 499.

[4] Klock *v.* Cronkhite, 1 Hill (N. Y.), 107.

[5] Campbell *v.* Carter, 14 Ills. 286, 289; Jarvis *v.* Frink, 14 Ills. 396; Adams *v.* Angell, 5 Ch. Div. 634; Troost *v.* Davis, 31 Ind. 34.

[6] Fowler *v.* Fay, 62 Ills. 375.

his own charge and his ownership in fee, then no presumption without some special act can be made of an intention to merge the charge in the fee, for that might be against the interest of the owner, by letting in the intermediate estate;[1] but if the intervening estate were created by the act of the owner himself, this reasoning would have no application.[2]

§ 61. **The Doctrine of Two Funds.** — Where one creditor holds security upon two funds or estates, with perfect liberty to resort to either for the payment of his demand, and another creditor holds a junior security upon one only of these funds, equity will compel the former creditor to exhaust the fund which he alone can hold as security, before coming upon the latter fund, and thereby depriving the latter creditor of his security;[3] and in a decree foreclosing a junior mortgage, the senior mortgagee may be ordered to exhaust for the satisfaction of his claim all the other property described in the senior mortgage, before resorting to that which is covered by the junior mortgage.[4] If one judgment-creditor has two funds out of which he may collect his debt, and a junior judgment-creditor can reach only one of these funds, the prior creditor must first resort to that fund over which he has the exclusive control.[5] The junior creditor may also

[1] Scrivner v. Dietz, 84 Calif. 295; Asche v. Asche, 113 N. Y. 232; Belknap v. Dennison, 61 Vt. 520; Gray v. Nelson, 77 Iowa, 63; Collins v. Stocking, 98 Mo. 290.

[2] Johnson v. Webster, 4 De G., M. & G. 474.

[3] Gibson v. Seagrim, 20 Beav. 614; Lanoy v. Athol, 2 Atk. 446; Fox, in re, 5 Irish Ch. 541; Merchants' Bank v. McLaughlin, 1 McCrary, C. C. 258; Russell v. Howard, 2 McLean, C. C. 489; Warren v. Warren, 30 Vt. 530; York & Jersey Steamboat Co. v. Jersey Co., Hopkins, Ch. (N. Y.) 460; Baird v. Jackson, 98 Ills. 78; Wise v. Shepherd, 13 Ills. 41; Glass v. Pullen, 6 Bush (Ky.), 346; Rust v. Chisolm, 57 Md. 376, 383; Pettibone v. Stevens, 15 Conn. 19; Ball v. Setzer, 33 W. Va. 444; Hannegan v. Hannah, 7 Blackf. (Ind.) 353; Davis v. Walker, 51 Miss. 659; Gusdorf v. Ikelheimer, 75 Ala. 148; Nelson v. Dunn, 15 Ala. 501.

[4] Swift v. Conboy, 12 Iowa, 444; Hamilton v. Schwehr, 34 Md. 107; Terry v. Rosell, 32 Ark. 478; Geller v. Hoyt, 7 How. Pr. (N. Y.) 265; Turner v. Flinn, 67 Ala. 529; Henshaw v. Wells, 9 Humph. (Tenn.) 568; Davenport Plow Co. v. Mewis, 10 Nebraska, 317; Sternberg v. Valentine, 6 Mo. App. 176.

[5] Reynolds v. Tooker, 18 Wend. (N. Y.) 591.

pay off the prior security, and be subrogated to the prior
creditor's rights over both funds.[1]   If the prior incumbrancer
does exhaust the only fund which is pledged to the holder of
the junior lien, the latter is entitled to be subrogated to the
former's lien upon the other fund, or to any balance thereof
remaining after the full payment of the prior lien, of which
the senior creditor might and should have availed himself.[2]
A creditor holding a mechanic's lien, properly perfected,
will be protected by the application of the same doctrine.[3]
A bank holding a judgment against one of its stockholders,
for which, besides its judgment-lien upon his real estate, it
has also a lien upon his stock, may indeed collect its judgment out of his real estate; but his other judgment-creditors,
who are thereby deprived of the opportunity of collecting their
money, shall be subrogated to the rights of the bank, so as to
enable them to hold the debtor's bank stock.[4]   As the creditor
having the choice of two funds ought so to exercise his right
of election as not to injure those creditors who can resort to
only one of these funds,[5] so if he, in the exercise of his legal
right, exhausts that fund, to which alone the other creditors
can resort, equity will place them in his situation, so far as
he has applied their funds to the satisfaction of his claim.[6]

§ 62.   A Creditor whose Fund has been taken to pay a Prior
Debt subrogated to the Lien of that Debt on Other Funds. —

[1] Washburn v. Hammond, 151
Mass. 132; King v. Nichols, 138
Mass. 18, 21.

[2] Mower's Trusts, in re, L. R. 8
Eq. 110; Dolphin v. Aylward, L. R.
4 Ho. Lds. 486; Hunt v. Townsend,
4 Sandf. Ch. (N. Y.) 510; Cheeseborough v. Millard, 1 Johns. Ch.
(N. Y.) 409; Slade v. Van Vechten,
11 Paige (N. Y.). 21; Ingalls v. Morgan, 10 N. Y. 178; Gist v. Pressley,
2 Hill Eq. (So. Car.) 318.

[3] Rust v. Chisolm, 57 Md. 383;
Kenny v. Gage, 33 Vt. 302.

[4] Ramsey's   Appeal,   2   Watts
(Penn.), 228.

[5] The Edward Oliver, L. R. 1 Adm.
& Ec. 379; Hurd v. Eaton, 28 Ill. 122;
Wartz v. Hart, 13 Iowa, 515 ; Lee v.
Buck, 13 So. Car. 178; Messervey v.
Barelli, 2 Hill Eq. (So. Car.) 567.

[6] Alston v. Mumford, 1 Brock.
C. C. 266; Foot, in re, 8 Benedicts,
228; Delaware & Hudson Canal Co.'s
Appeal, 38 Penn. St. 512; Bank of
Kentucky v. Vance, 4 Litt. (Ky.) 168;
Wolf v. Ferguson, 129 Penn. St. 272.

If a prior creditor of two funds satisfies his demand out of that fund which alone is pledged to a junior creditor, and thereby exhausts that fund, equity will subrogate the latter creditor to the former's lien upon that fund which is not exhausted.[1] A debtor against whom there had been issued executions which were liens upon his personal estate, having assigned his property to a trustee for the payment of his debts, and directed that the avails of certain cloth should be applied to pay notes given by him to the vendors of the wool which had been used in the manufacture of the cloth, and this cloth having been taken on the executions, the assignee bid it in, and afterwards sold it for a much larger sum; and it was held that the other parts of the assigned property, as between the vendors of the wool and the general creditors, were the primary funds for the payment of the executions which were liens upon all the assigned property, and that these vendors should be subrogated to the rights of the execution-creditors against the other parts of the assigned property, so far as their cloth had been applied to pay such execution-creditors, and that the assignee should reimburse himself for the amount of his bid to buy in the cloth from the general fund, so as to give to these vendors the benefit of all the proceeds of the cloth, so far as should be necessary to satisfy their notes.[2]

§ 63. **Doctrine of Two Funds not applied, if it would work Injustice to Senior Creditor.** — But this general rule, that a creditor having a prior lien upon two funds will not be allowed so to apply them as to exclude a creditor having a junior lien upon one only of the same funds from the benefit of his lien, will not be applied in any case where it would

---

[1] Hawkins v. Blake, 108 U. S. 422; Bowler, in re, 2 Hughes, C. C. 319; Findlay v. United States Bank, 2 Mc. Lean, C. C. 44; Farwell v. Importers' Bank, 90 N. Y. 483; Milligan's Appeal, 104 Penn. St. 503; The Olympic Theatre, 2 Browne (Penn.), 275; Hunter v. Beach, 80 Va. 361; Ross a. Duggan, 5 Color. 85.

[2] Slade v. Van Vechten, 11 Paige (N. Y.), 21. So in Wolf v. Ferguson, 129 Penn. St. 272.

work an injustice to the creditor having the prior lien to restrict him to only one fund.[1] It is never applied where its enforcement would prejudice the rights of the prior creditor,[2] or where it would delay him in obtaining his payment.[3] It will not be applied against the prerogative right of the government to hold all the property of its debtor.[4] The prior creditor cannot be compelled to confine himself to only one of the funds, unless that fund is shown to be sufficient to satisfy his demand.[5] He will not be compelled to resort to a fund of which he can realize the benefit only by litigation;[6] if he holds both a prior mortgage and also certain promissory notes as collateral security for the same debt, the holder of a junior lien upon the mortgaged premises cannot require him to prosecute suits upon the notes before foreclosing his mortgage.[7] A mortgagee of both the goods and the accounts of his debtor will not be obliged to collect the accounts and apply their proceeds upon his claim against the debtor, in

[1] Woolcocks v. Hart, 1 Paige (N. Y.), 185; James v. Hubbard, 1 Paige (N. Y.), 128; Herriman v. Skilman, 33 Barb. (N. Y.) 378; Van Mater v. Eley, 12 N. J. Eq. 271; Thayer v. Daniels, 113 Mass. 129; Bruner's Appeal, 7 Watts & Serg. (Penn.) 269; McCormick's Appeal, 57 Penn. St. 54; Newbold v. Newbold, 1 Del. Ch. 310; Post v. Mackall, 3 Bland (Md.), 486; General Ins. Co. v. United States Ins. Co., 10 Md. 517; Jones v. Zollicoffer, 2 Hawks (Nor. Car.), 623; Behn v. Young, 21 Ga. 207; Calloway v. People's Bank, 54 Ga. 572; Wolf v. Smith, 36 Iowa, 454; United States v. Duncan, 12 Ills. 523; Morrison v. Kurtz, 15 Ills. 193; Sweet v. Redhead, 76 Ills. 374; Logan v. Anderson, 18 B. Mon. (Ky.) 114; Cannon v. Kreip, 14 Kans. 324.

[2] Sauthoff, in re, 14 N. B. R. 364; Jervis v. Smith, 7 Abbott Pr. N. s. (N. Y.) 217; Slater v. Breese, 36 Mich. 77; Clark v. Wright, 24 So. Car. 526.

[3] Wallis v. Woodyear, 2 Jur. N. s. 179; Pennock v. Hoover, 5 Rawle (Penn.), 391; Detroit Savings Bank v. Truesdail, 38 Mich. 430; Gillians v. McCormack, 85 Tenn. 597; Rogers v. Blum, 56 Tex. 1.

[4] United States v. Duncan, 4 McLean, C. C. 607.

[5] Barnwell v. Wofford, 67 Ga. 50; Coker v. Shropshire, 59 Ala. 542; Mason's Appeal, 89 Penn. St. 402; Briggs v. Planters' Bank, 1 Freem. Ch. (Miss.) 574; Trapnall v. Richardson, 13 Ark. 543.

[6] Walker v. Covar, 2 So. Car. 16; Moore v. Wright, 14 Rich. Eq. (So. Car.) 132, 134; Austin v. Bowman, 81 Iowa, 277; Bryan-Brown Shoe Co. v. Block, 52 Ark. 458; Rogers v. Holyoke, 14 Minn. 220; Kidder v. Page, 48 N. H. 380.

[7] Wolf v. Smith, 36 Iowa, 454.

order to aid other creditors who are unsecured.[1] Or, if the prior mortgagee, in an action for his debt, obtains the additional security of a sufficient attachment, but the validity of this attachment is contested in another action, a junior mortgagee cannot require him to litigate this question before resorting to the mortgaged property.[2] Nor will the prior creditor be compelled to go into another jurisdiction, there to prosecute the fund to which he has the exclusive right.[3] But if the avails of property constituting the first fund, though orginally beyond the jurisdiction, have been brought within the jurisdiction, the senior creditor must resort to them.[4] And it has been said that the principle that one creditor shall not take a part of a fund which would otherwise have been available for all the creditors, and at the same time be allowed a proportionate share of the remainder of that fund with the other creditors, does not apply to a case in which the first creditor by his diligence obtains something which could not form a part of that fund.[5] But the prior creditor must be able to show what disposition he has made of the fund that was exclusively his.[6] And he may not voluntarily put himself in a position where he will be embarrassed by the enforcement of the rights already vested in the junior creditor.[7] The fact that the prior creditor holds also a third lien on the first fund, inferior in date to the junior creditor's lien, will not be sufficient to exempt the prior creditor from the operation of the ordinary rule.[8] The junior creditor's right of subrogation to the securities of which the senior

[1] Emmons v. Bradley, 56 Maine, 333.

[2] Simmons Hardware Co. v. Brokaw, 7 Nebraska, 405.

[3] Morton v. Grafflin, 68 Md. 545; Denham v. Williams, 39 Ga. 312.

[4] Moss's Estate, 138 Penn. St. 646.

[5] Cockerell v. Dickens, 3 Moo. P. C. 98.

[6] Bryan-Brown Shoe Co. v. Block, 52 Ark. 458.

[7] Washburn v. Hammond, 151 Mass. 132, 139, et seq.

[8] Kendig v. Landis, 135 Penn. St. 612; Moss's Estate, 138 Penn. St. 646.

creditor has declined to avail himself will be preserved after the satisfaction of the latter.[1]

§ 64.• **Where One of the Two Funds is itself subject to Prior Incumbrances.** — A creditor who holds security upon two tracts of land, one of which is the debtor's homestead, cannot except by reason of special equities [2] be compelled by another creditor holding a junior security upon the tract which is not a homestead to resort first for the satisfaction of his demand to the homestead, so as to leave the other tract, so far as may be, for the second creditor,[3] and the prior creditor's subsequent purchase of the homestead will not affect his rights.[4] But the creation of the homestead after that of the incumbrances will not affect the rights of the junior creditor.[5] And if the prior creditor had chosen to resort first to the homestead, or even to release the other land and then come upon the homestead, the debtor could not have complained;[6] there is no implied obligation on the holder of a mortgage which covers both a homestead and other property to exhaust first his remedy against the other property,[7] for the equitable rule that a creditor who has a lien upon two funds, upon one of which another creditor has a subsequent lien only, will be required to satisfy his claim primarily out of that fund on which the latter has no lien, has no application as between debtor and creditor;[8] it avails only as be-

[1] King v. McVickar, 3 Sandf. Ch. (N. Y.) 192; Reigle v. Leiter, 8 Md. 405; Dunn v. Olney, 14 Penn. St. 219.
[2] Hodges v. Hickey, 67 Miss. 715.
[3] Wilson v. Patton, 87 Nor. Car. 318; Shell v. Young, 32 So. Car. 462; Armitage v. Toll, 64 Mich. 412; McArthur v. Martin, 23 Minn. 74; Mitchelson v. Smith, 28 Neb. 583; McCreery v. Shaffer, 26 Neb. 173; White v. Fulghum, 87 Tenn. 281; Dickson v. Chorn, 6 Iowa, 19; Smith v. Wait, 39 Wisc. 512; Marr v. Lewis, 31 Ark. 203. *Contra*, in part, State Bank v. Harlin, 18 So. Car. 425.

[4] Linscott v. Lamart, 46 Iowa, 312; Raber v. Gund, 110 Ills. 581.
[5] Abbott v. Powell, 6 Sawyer, C. C. 91; Bowen v. Barksdale, 33 So. Car. 142.
[6] Albright v. Albright, 88 Nor. Car. 238; Creath v. Creath, 86 Tenn. 659; Vaughn v. Powell, 65 Miss. 401.
[7] Chapman v. Lester, 12 Kans. 592; De Negre v. Haun, 14 Iowa, 240; White v. Polleys, 20 Wisc. 503; Tuttle v. Howe, 14 Minn. 145; Worcester's Estate, 60 Vt. 420.
[8] Binns v. Nichols, L. R. 2 Eq. 256; McDevitt's Appeal, 70 Penn. St.

tween different creditors of the same debtor.[1] The rights of
the parties where a homestead is involved will depend in each
State upon the local statutes;[2] in some States the homestead
is favored, and the owner may require even a secured creditor
to resort first to the other property.[3] When a person takes a
mortgage upon land, of which one portion is, and another
portion is not, already incumbered, he acquires the right to
satisfy his debt in the first instance out of that property
which is not incumbered; and this right will not be impaired by a subsequent mortgage of that part to another creditor.[4] The junior mortgagee cannot require him to run the
risk of being obliged to pay off a prior incumbrance before
he can enforce his own security.[5] But if the debtor has
waived his right of redemption against one creditor but not
against another, the latter has been allowed to require the
former to resort first to the exempted property.[6]

§ 65. **Doctrine of Two Funds not applied where it would
be Injurious to Third Parties.** — A junior creditor cannot compel a prior creditor to resort first to that fund which he alone
can make available, in any case where this would injuriously
affect rights that have vested in others.[7] The prior creditor
cannot be compelled to resort first to property which, though
pledged for his demand, belongs to another than his debtor.[8]
Where a debtor gave to a building association a mortgage of

373; Butler *v.* Stainback, 87 Nor.
Car. 216; Plain *v.* Roth, 107 Ills.
588; Witherington *v.* Mason, 86 Ala.
345.

[1] Rogers *v.* Meyers, 68 Ills. 92;
Lee *v.* Gregory, 12 Neb. 282; Richardson *v.* Wallis, 5 Allen (Mass.), 78.

[2] See Grant *v.* Parsons, 67 Iowa,
31; Ebert *v.* Gerding, 116 Ills. 216.

[3] Leak *v.* Gay, 107 Nor. Car. 468;
Horton *v.* Kelly, 40 Minn. 193; Carra-
way, *ex parte*, 28 So. Car. 233.

[4] See Robeson's Appeal, 117 Penn.
St. 628.

[5] Dodds *v.* Snyder, 44 Ills. 53;
Lewis *v.* Hinman, 56 Conn. 55.

[6] Pittman's Appeal, 48 Penn. St.
315; Jones *v.* Dow, 18 Wisc. 241.

[7] Leib *v.* Stribling, 51 Md. 285;
McGinniss's Appeal, 16 Penn. St.
445; McClaskey *v.* O'Brien, 16 W.
Va. 792; Cogbill, *in re*, 2 Hughes, C.
C. 313.

[8] Shinn *v.* Smith, 79 Nor. Car.
310, citing Worth *v.* Gray, 6 Jones
Eq. 4, and Ashe *v.* Moore, 2 Murph.
383; Warwick *v.* Ely, 29 N. J. Eq.
82.

two lots of land and an assignment of five shares of stock as
security for the same debt, and after giving a second mortgage of one of the lots sold his interest in the stock to other
parties, the second mortgagee, although he could require the
association to enforce its mortgage first upon the lot which
was not subject to his charge, had no right to compel it to
appropriate the stock to the payment of its debt;[1] while the
principal debtor still owned the stock, it was liable to be
applied upon the debt secured by the first mortgage, so as to
relieve the security of the second mortgagee;[2] but the burden of this latent equity would not accompany the stock into
the hands of a *bona fide* purchaser thereof for value.[3] The
junior incumbrancer cannot insist that the funds shall be
marshalled, when the effect of this will be to destroy the
remedies or impair the rights of the purchasers or *bona
fide* grantees of one or both of the funds or estates.[4]

§ 66. **Where One of the Funds is primarily liable for the
Payment of Both Debts.** — There can be no subrogation for
the relief of the owner of the fund which is primarily liable
for both debts, the very object of subrogation being to throw
the burden upon those parties or that fund upon which rests
the primary liability.[5] A testator who held one estate in
fee-simple and another estate in fee-tail left an annuity
charged upon all his property. A judgment-creditor of the
testator, whose judgment was a charge upon both estates,
having obtained satisfaction mainly by exhausting the fee-
simple estate, the annuitant was not allowed to marshal the

[1] Reilly v. Mayer, 12 N. J. Eq. 55.

[2] Herbert v. Mechanics' Building
Association, 17 N. J. Eq. 497;
Phillipsburg Building Association v.
Hawk, 27 N. J. Eq. 355; Red Bank
Building Association v. Patterson, 27
N. J. Eq. 223.

[3] Reilly v. Mayer, 12 N. J. Eq. 55;
Mechanics' Building Association v.
Conover, 14 N. J. Eq. 219.

[4] Barnes v. Racster, 1 Yo. & Co.
Ch. 401; Bugden v. Bignold, 2 Yo. &
Co. Ch. 377; Lloyd v. Galbraith, 32
Penn. St. 103; Green v. Ramage, 18
Ohio, 428; Sager v. Tupper, 35 Mich.
134.

[5] *Antea*, §§ 6, 11, 46. Amherst
College v. Smith, 134 Mass. 543;
Iowa Loan Co. v. Mowery, 67 Iowa,
113.

securities as against the remainder-man of the fee-tail estate, so as to recoup out of the surplus proceeds of that estate the amount which had been paid to the creditor out of the fee-simple estate. "To authorize the marshalling," said the Master of the Rolls, "it is obviously necessary, not only that a claim should exist against a fund subject in common with another fund to a paramount liability, but also that those interested in that other fund should not have a right to throw that liability upon the fund of the claimant. A man's own property, in which alone his legatees can claim, must be applied to the payment of his debts, in preference to the property of another, against which the statute merely gives a remedy."[1] So, a junior firm-creditor cannot compel another firm-creditor holding a senior lien on both firm and individual property to exhaust first the latter security,[2] though the contrary was held in an early and doubtful case in Tennessee.[3]

§ 66 a. **Waiver of Right of marshalling Assets.** — Though a junior incumbrancer has the right in equity to compel a senior judgment-creditor to levy on and exhaust the other property of the common debtor, before coming upon that which is bound by the junior lien,[4] yet if such junior creditor neglects to interfere and assert his right until after the property which he could hold has been sold upon the execution, this sale will not afterwards be set aside for his relief.[5] He will be taken to have waived his right to the application of the rule of two funds, unless he presses it before the prior creditor has enforced his securities,[6] and can then have only such protection as he may obtain from subrogation to the prior creditors' rights.[7] The mere neglect of the prior credi-

---

[1] Douglass v. Cooksey, Irish R. 2 Eq. 311.

[2] Bell v. Hepworth, 51 Hun (N. Y.), 616.

[3] White v. Dougherty, Mart. & Yerg. 309.

[4] Antea, § 61.

[5] Baine v. Williams, 10 Sm. & M. (Miss.) 113. So in Searles v. Jacksonville R. R. Co., 2 Woods, 621.

[6] St Joseph Manufacturing Co. v. Daggett, 84 Ills. 556; Turner v. Flinn, 67 Ala. 529.

[7] Antea, § 62.

tor by which his lien upon one of the funds has been lost will not, in the absence of special circumstances, accrue to the advantage of the junior claimant of the second fund.[1] The prior creditor of two funds has a right to expect a notification of the right of a junior claimant of one of the funds, if the latter desire to restrict the action of the former.[2]

§ 67. **Junior Creditor cannot claim the Benefit of a Lien established subsequently to his Own.** — One lien-creditor cannot claim to be subrogated to any security taken by another which had not become a lien when he secured his own: accordingly a subsequent mortgagee, having also taken a bond for his debt, but without a warrant to confess judgment, cannot insist that a prior mortgagee shall enter up judgment upon a bond and warrant of attorney that accompanied his mortgage, in order to throw him upon other property; nor can the subsequent mortgagee object to the waiver of a judgment, subsequently confessed upon the prior bond, though purposely withdrawn in order to make way for other judgment-creditors of the mortgagor, whose liens upon the other property are posterior in date to his lien upon the mortgaged premises.[3] And a junior creditor has no right to object to an appropriation of payments in favor of an earlier lien, so long as the security which he originally had remains undiminished.[4]

§ 68. **Creditor subrogated only to a Fund which ought to have discharged the Debt his Fund has paid.** — One fund cannot be applied to the relief of another by way of subrogation or substitution, unless it is clearly shown that the former fund was liable for the payment of the debt which the latter fund has discharged.[5] The liability of the shareholders in an insurance company being unlimited as to the general

[1] Sandidge v. Graves, 1 Patt. & H. (Va.) 101.

[2] Clarke v. Bancroft, 13 Iowa, 320. *Postea,* § 81.

[3] Miller v. Jacobs, 3 Watts (Penn.), 477.

[4] Johnson's Appeal, 37 Penn. St. 268.

[5] Greenlee v. McDowell, 3 Jones, Eq. (Nor. Car.) 325.

creditors, but restricted as to the policy-holders, the company borrowed money upon the security of certain calls upon its members. Before this debt was paid, the company was wound up; and the debt was subsequently paid out of the calls. The policy-holders desired to have the amount of this debt repaid from the unlimited assets, so as to throw the burden of its payment upon these and not upon the limited assets; but it was held that they had no right ·in equity to have the debt thus thrown upon the unlimited assets.[1] Under such circumstances no call could be made upon the shareholders for the purpose of recouping to the policy-holders the amount of the capital which had been paid to the general creditors; for the liability of the shareholders is only secondary,[2] and the policy-holders could assert no priority in the capital over the general creditors.[3]

§ 68 *a.* **Where each Creditor has a Lien upon the Same One of the Funds.** — This doctrine is applicable only in cases in which the senior creditor has a lien upon two funds, of which the junior creditor can hold only one.[4] The senior creditor cannot be compelled to resort to property not included in his lien, however this might benefit the junior claimant.[5] Accordingly, where auctioneers held in their hands a part of the proceeds of a brewery which they had sold for a customer, subject to their lien for charges thereon, and also held a second fund for the same customer, being the net proceeds of certain personal property which they had also sold for him, it was held that they might well apply the first fund to the payment of their charges, and pay over the second fund to their customer, although the effect of this was to leave unprovided for another creditor of the customer, who held a junior charge on

[1] International Life Ass. Co., *in re*, 2 Ch. Div. 476.

[2] Professional Life Ins. Co., *in re*, L. R. 3 Eq. 668.

[3] State Ins. Co., *in re*, 1 De Gex, Jones & Smith, 634.

[4] Detroit Bank *v.* Haug, 82 Mich. 607; Southern Michigan Bank *v.* Byles, 67 Mich. 296.

[5] State *v.* Aetna Ins. Co., 117 Ind. 251.

the first fund. This junior creditor could not require them
to pay their charges out of the second fund, and thus leave
the first fund available for his benefit, because they had
themselves no lien upon the second fund.[1]

§ 69. **Doctrine of Two Funds applied only if Debtors are the
Same.** — This doctrine of two funds is applied only to cases
in which two creditors have the same common debtor,[2] and
only as between the different creditors, or others who stand
among themselves in the same relation.[3] Where a creditor
can hold the joint and several funds of two debtors for the
payment of his demand, a court of equity will not qualify
this right by limiting the liability of each debtor to one-half
of the debt.[4] If the first creditor has a judgment against A.
and B., and the second creditor has one against B. only, the
latter cannot compel the former to restrict himself to the
property of A., when it does not appear whether A. or B.
ought, as between themselves, to pay the debt due to the first
creditor, and no equitable rights are shown in B. to have the
debt charged upon A. alone.[5] So, also, if one creditor has a
lien for his demand upon the property of two separate debtors,
and another creditor has a junior lien only upon the fund
belonging to one of the debtors, the latter creditor cannot
require the former to collect his claim wholly out of that
debtor whom the latter creditor cannot reach,[6] unless it be
shown that the relations between the co-debtors are such as
to make it equitable that the debtor having but one creditor
should pay the whole of the senior demand; for equity will

---

[1] Webb v. Smith, 30 Ch. D. 192.

[2] Boone v. Clark, 129 Ills. 466;
Carter v. Neal, 24 Ga. 346; Knouf's
Appeal, 91 Penn. St. 78; House v.
Thompson, 3 Head (Tenn.), 512;
Saunders v. Cook, 22 Ind. 436; Geg-
ner v. Warfield, 72 Iowa, 11.

[3] Miller v. Cook, 135 Ills. 190.

[4] Hoys v. Penn, 2 Harr. & G.
(Md.) 473; Markham v. Calvit, 5
How. (Miss.) 427; Gammell v. Mul-
ford, 53 Ga. 78; Prout v. Lomer, 79
Ills. 331.

[5] Kendall, ex parte, 17 Vesey, 314,
520; Dorr v. Shaw, 4 Johns. Ch. (N.
Y.) 17; Lloyd v. Galbraith, 32 Penn.
St. 103.

[6] Parker v. Dennie, 6 Pick. (Mass.)
227; Loudon v. Coleman, 62 Ga. 146.

not sanction a principle which, though it may be just as to the creditors, is unjust as to the debtors.[1] But if a partnership creditor has obtained payment of his demand out of the separate property of one of the partners, whom he held as a surety therefor, the separate creditors of that partner may be subrogated to the rights of the partnership creditor against the firm assets,[2] unless it should appear that the partner whose separate property had thus been taken was then indebted to the firm.[3] And the general rule that courts of equity will marshal securities only among creditors of the same debtor is subject to the exception that equity will enforce a duty on the part of one debtor to pay in exoneration of another, by subjecting first the property of the principal debtor.[4]

§ 70. **Junior Creditor cannot be subrogated until Prior Creditor satisfied.** — Before one creditor can be subrogated to the rights of another, the demand of the latter must be satisfied, so that he shall be relieved from all further trouble, risk, and expense.[5] The creditor holding two funds may avail himself of either of them until he has secured his whole claim.[6] And if one creditor has got his payment from the fund which was available to another, under such circumstances as to entitle the latter to be subrogated to the former's claim against another fund, yet the latter must claim his subrogation before the rights of any assignee of that fund have accrued.[7]

---

[1] Ayres v. Husted, 15 Conn. 504; Cannon v. Hudson, 6 Del. 21, & 5 Del. Ch. 112; Wise v. Shepherd, 13 Ills. 41.

[2] Averill v. Loucks, 6 Barb. (N. Y.) 470.

[3] Sterling v. Brightbill, 5 Watts (Penn.), 229.

[4] Hodges v. Hickey, 67 Miss. 715; Hall v. Stevenson, 19 Oreg. 153; Dorr v. Shaw, 4 Johns. Ch. (N. Y.)

17 ; Kendall, *ex parte*, 17 . Vesey, 514, 520.

[5] Graff's Estate, 139 Penn. St. 69 ; Swigert v. Bank of Kentucky, 17 B. Mon. (Ky.) 268; Carter v. Neal, 24 Ga. 346.

[6] Quackenbush v. O'Hare, 129 N. Y. 485; Taylor's Appeal, 81 Penn. St. 460.

[7] Williams v. Washington, 1 Dev. Eq. (Nor. Car.) 137. *Antea,* § 65.

§ 71. **Application of these Principles to a Case of Several Creditors of Joint and Several Debtors.** — The Pittsburg Bank, having the first judgment against and lien on the real estate of Peter Peterson, Lewis Peterson, and James Kincaid, satisfied its judgment by selling land which was the individual property of Lewis Peterson. The Monongahela Navigation Company had the second, and William Sheer the third, judgment against and lien on the real estate of the two Petersons, but not against Kincaid or on his estate. After these judgments, William Taylor obtained three judgments against the Petersons and Kincaid, on which Thomas Dale became bail for the stay of execution, and as such paid the three judgments, after other judgments had been obtained against the Petersons and Kincaid. Among these was a judgment in favor of Sylvanus Lathrop, upon which the real estate of the Petersons and Kincaid was taken in execution and sold, as also under a prior levy upon the judgment in favor of the Pittsburg Bank. Under these circumstances it was held that the Monongahela Company was entitled to be subrogated to the rights of the bank, and to have its judgment satisfied out of the money arising from the sale; and then that William Speer was entitled to receive the residue of the money towards the satisfaction of his judgment; but that Thomas Dale could not be subrogated to the rights of the bank or receive any portion of the money, in preference to the judgment-creditors of the Petersons and Kincaid, though such judgments might be subsequent to Taylor's judgments.[1]

§ 72. **Release by Prior Creditor of Fund primarily liable to him.** — A prior creditor of two funds, who has notice of such a junior charge upon one of those funds that the junior creditor may require him to resort in the first instance to the other fund, will, by a release of the fund thus primarily liable to him, postpone his lien upon the remaining fund to that of

[1] Lathrop's Appeal, 1 Penn. St. 512.

the second creditor, to the extent of the value of the primary
fund; so far as the subsequent creditor is concerned, the debt
of the prior creditor is *pro tanto* satisfied by such a release.[1]
And the prior creditor's waste or misapplication of his primary fund will, as to the junior creditor, have the same effect
as the express release thereof.[2] Accordingly, where one creditor had a lien upon two pieces of land belonging to the same
debtor, and another creditor had a junior lien upon one only
of these tracts, and the first creditor by his conduct released
his claim upon that tract upon which his was the only lien,
which was more than sufficient to have paid the whole of his
demand, it was held that the debt due to the junior creditor
should be first satisfied out of that tract on which both had
a lien.[3] Where the agent of a judgment-creditor was present
at the sale by the debtor to a third party of certain lands on
which the judgment was a lien, and drew the conveyance,
and was informed of the terms of the sale, and the debtor
afterwards delivered to such agent as security for the payment
of the judgment-debt the notes taken for the purchase-money
of the lands, it was held that this was sufficient constructive
notice to the creditor of the facts, and that the receipt of the
notes by his agent with knowledge of their consideration,
although it did not destroy the creditor's lien upon the land
as security for the payment of his judgment, in case it should
not be otherwise satisfied, imposed upon him in equity the
duty to apply the proceeds of the notes in reduction of the
judgment; and that the creditor was also bound in equity to
retain all other property which had been delivered to him as
security for the judgment, and to apply its proceeds also
upon the judgment, before resorting to the land and taking

---

[1] Washington Building Association
v. Beaghen, 27 N. J. Eq. 98; Dillon
v. Bennett, 14 Sm. & M. 171; Jordan
v. Hamilton Bank, 11 Neb. 499; Hazard v. Fiske, 83 N. Y. 287; s. c., 18
Hun, 277.

[2] Gordon v. Bell, 50 Ala. 213;
Henderson v. Huey, 45 Ala. 275.
[3] Glass v. Pullen, 6 Bush (Ky.),
346.

it away from the purchaser thereof; and that the surrender
by the creditor of any such security, sufficient to have satisfied the debt, discharged the lien of the judgment upon this
land in the hands of the purchaser.[1]

§ 73. **But Release of Primary Fund will not prejudice Prior
Creditor if made in Good Faith and without Notice.** — If, however, the prior creditor's release of the fund primarily liable
to him was made in good faith, and without knowledge of
the facts which established the claim of the junior creditor,
his release will not prejudice his right of precedence in the
common fund over the subsequent creditor.[2] Nor will his
claims upon the secondary fund be prejudiced unless his
rights to the primary fund which he has chosen to abandon
were clear and not seriously contested, and his remedies for
obtaining its application upon his demand were reasonably
efficient.[3] A settlement of a contested litigation made in
good faith, whereby he receives less than its value from the
primary fund, will not interfere with the prosecution of his
right to the secondary fund.[3] Although a second mortgagee
of part of the same property which is covered by the first
mortgage may require the first mortgagee to act with reasonable diligence in enforcing and preserving his rights, yet he
cannot in equity compel the latter to account for the value
of property covered by his mortgage, which has without his
fault been put out of his reach by the mortgagor.[4] The prior
creditor's rights will not be affected by his having released
one fund, if the remaining fund is amply sufficient for the
payment of all the claims.[5]

§ 74. **Purchase of a Portion of an Incumbered Estate; Rights
of the Purchaser.** — The purchaser of land which, in common
with other land, is subject to an incumbrance, for the pay-

[1] Ingalls v. Morgan, 10 N. Y. 178.
[2] Cheeseborough v. Millard, 1
Johns. Ch. (N. Y.) 409.
[3] Kidder v. Page, 48 N. H. 380;
Brown v. South Boston Savings Bank,
148 Mass. 300; Ross v. Duggan, 5
Color. 85.
[4] Shields v. Kimbrough, 64 Ala.
504.
[5] Kelly v. Whitney, 45 Wisc. 110.

ment of which the other land is, or has become by his purchase, the primary fund, acquires by his purchase the right of paying off the lien or other incumbrance, and of being subrogated for his indemnity to the rights of its holder.[1] If the mortgage-debt is not to be charged primarily upon either estate, he can then require a reasonable contribution from the holders of the other land,[2] the general rule being that when the estates of two or more persons are subject to a common incumbrance, for the payment of a common debt, it is to be borne ratably by all,[3] and one who pays the whole for the benefit of all will have the right to hold all the estates thus redeemed, until the others shall reimburse him an equitable proportion of the sum which he has thus paid for their common benefit;[4] or if he has paid his proportion of the debt, and the mortgagee, having sold the other land for enough to pay the remainder, fails to enforce these sales by agreement with the owners of such other lands, the mortgagee cannot afterwards further hold his land for any balance which the other land fails to pay.[5] If, however, the primary liability for the payment of the debt rested upon the estate of him who has satisfied it, then his payment will give him no claim upon the rest of the incumbered property,[6] even though he took an assignment of the mortgage or other charge.[7]

[1] Sergeant v. Rowsey, 89 Mo. 617; O'Brien v. Krenz, 36 Minn. 136; Fletcher v. Chase, 16 N. H. 38; Kilborn v. Robbins, 8 Allen (Mass.), 466; *Lowe, J.,* in Street v. Beal, 16 Iowa, 68, 70; Cheever v. Fair, 5 Calif. 337.

[2] White v. White, 9 Vesey, 554; Jones v. Jones, 5 Hare, 440; Lyman v. Little, 15 Vt. 576; Henderson v. Stewart, 4 Hawks (Nor. Car.), 256.

[3] New Jersey Sinking Fund v. Woodward, 40 N. J. Eq. 23.

[4] *Shaw, C. J.,* in Chase v. Woodbury, 6 Cush. (Mass.) 143, 146; Brown v. Worcester Bank, 8 Met.

(Mass.) 47; Allen v. Clark, 17 Pick. (Mass.) 47; Salem v. Edgerly, 33 N. H. 46; Chittenden v. Barney, 1 Vt. 28; Young v. Williams, 17 Conn. 393; Skeel v. Spraker, 8 Paige (N. Y.), 182; Cheeseborough v. Millard, 1 Johns. Ch. (N. Y.) 409; Stevens v. Cooper, 1 Johns. Ch. (N. Y.) 425.

[5] Jennings v. Vickers, 31 La. Ann. 679.

[6] Merritt v. Richey, 97 Ind. 236.

[7] McIntire v. Parks, 59 N. H. 258; Chase v. Woodbury, 6 Cush. (Mass.) 143; George v. Wood, 11 Allen (Mass.), 41, 42; Cushing v. Ayer, 25 Maine, 383.

**§ 75. Order of Liability of Separate Parcels of Incumbered Estate sold successively.** — When different parcels of premises, the whole of which are subject to the burden of a mortgage or other charge, are successively sold to different purchasers with warranty, the rule almost universally adopted to determine the comparative liability of the different parcels is that any portion retained by the debtor or mortgagor shall be first applied to the payment of the debt secured by the charge or mortgage,[1] and if that is not sufficient, then the other parcels shall be resorted to in the inverse order of their alienation, the parcel last sold being first applied upon the debt,[2] even though a part of the remaining land is situated in another State.[3] The first purchaser from the mortgagor has the prior equity,[4] although he did not actually pay the consideration

---

[1] Savings Bank v. Cresswell, 100 U. S. 630; Orvis v. Powell, 98 U. S. 176; Dougherty v. Richardson, 20 Ind. 419; Edwards v. Applegate, 70 Ind. 325; Gantz v. Toles, 40 Mich. 725; Hoff's Appeal, 84 Penn. St. 40; Lowry v. McKinney, 68 Penn. St. 294; Raun v. Reynolds, 11 Calif. 14; Keirsted v. Avery, 4 Paige (N. Y.), 1.

[2] Holden v. Pike, 24 Maine, 427; Wallace v. Stevens, 64 Maine, 225; Bradley v. George, 2 Allen (Mass.), 392; Pike v. Goodnow, 12 Allen (Mass.), 472; Allen v. Clark, 17 Pick. (Mass.) 47; Sandford v. Hill, 46 Conn. 42; Brown v. Simons, 44 N. H. 475; Deavitt v. Judevine, 60 Vt. 695; Gates v. Adams, 24 Vt. 71; Lyman v. Lyman, 32 Vt. 79; Skeel v. Spraker, 8 Paige (N. Y.), 182; Kellogg v. Rand, 11 Paige (N. Y.), 59; Welch v. James, 22 How. Pr. (N. Y.) 474; Green v. Millbank, 3 Abbott New Cas. (N. Y.) 138; Chapman v. West, 17 N. Y. 125; Keene v. Munn, 16 N. J. Eq. 398; Dawes v. Cammus, 32 N. J. Eq. 456; Mount v. Potts, 23 N. J. Eq. 188; Sternberger v. Hanna, 42 Ohio St. 305; Commercial Bank v. Western Reserve Bank, 11 Ohio, 444; Paxton v. Harrier, 11 Penn. St. 312; Beddow v. De Witt, 43 Penn. St. 326; Jones v. Myrick, 8 Gratt. (Va.) 179; Schofield v. Cox, 8 Gratt. (Va.) 533; Norton v. Lewis, 3 So. Car. 25; Burton v. Henry, 90 Ala. 281; Hutton v. Lockridge, 22 W. Va. 159; Pallen v. Agricultural Bank, 1 Freem. (Miss.) 419; Dugger v. Tayloe, 60 Ala. 504; Aiken v. Bruen, 21 Ind. 137; McCullum v. Turpie, 32 Ind. 146; Lock v. Fulford, 52 Ills. 166; Matteson v. Thomas, 41 Ills. 110; State v. Titus, 17 Wisc. 241; Warren v. Foreman, 19 Wisc. 35; Aiken v. Milw. & St. Paul R. R. Co., 37 Wisc. 469; Sibley v. Baker, 23 Mich. 312; Cooper v. Bigley, 13 Mich. 463; Payne v. Avery 21 Mich. 524.

[3] Welling v. Ryerson, 94 N. Y. 98.

[4] Van Slyke v. Van Loan, 26 Hun (N. Y.), 344; Ellison v. Pecare, 29 Barb. (N. Y.) 333; Edge v. Goulard, 36 N. J. Eq. 43; Horning's Appeal, 90 Penn. St. 388; Miller v. Rogers, 49 Tex. 398.

for his purchase until after other portions of the mortgaged premises had been purchased and paid for by other purchasers.[1] This principle of charging different portions of the mortgaged premises which have been sold at different times after the execution of the mortgage, in the inverse order of their alienation, is not confined to the original alienations of the mortgagor who is personally responsible for the debt.[2] It is equally applicable to several conveyances of separate parcels of the mortgaged premises made at different times by his grantee, who conveys with warranty.[3] The first purchaser with warranty of a portion of an estate, the whole of which is subject to the burden of a mortgage, judgment-lien, or other incumbrance, acquires by his purchase an equitable right to have the payment of the debt which creates the incumbrance cast upon the remaining property;[4] and each subsequent purchaser of other portions of the incumbered estate takes subject to this right in prior purchasers, and acquires the same right against those who purchase other portions subsequently to his purchase.[5] And the subsequent purchasers have sufficient notice of the equitable charge; for when the records disclose an incumbrance upon property of which a party is taking a conveyance, and also show that this incumbrance rests likewise upon other prop-

---

[1] Gouverneur v. Lynch , 2 Paige (N. Y.), 300. And see George v. Kent, 7 Allen (Mass.), 16; Northrup v. Metcalf, 11 Paige (N. Y.), 570.

[2] See Crawford v. Richeson, 101 Ills. 351; Hardin v. Melton, 28 So. Car. 38.

[3] Guion v. Knapp, 6 Paige (N. Y.), 35; Hiles v. Coult, 30 N. J. Eq. 40.

[4] Georgia Pacific R. R. Co. v. Walker, 61 Miss. 481; Beard v. Fitzgerald, 105 Mass. 134; Schryver v. Teller, 9 Paige (N. Y.), 173; Lowry v. McKinney, 68 Penn. St. 294; Bank of Hamburg v. Howard, 1 Strobh. Eq.

(So. Car.) 173; Wallace v. Nichols, 56 Ala. 321; Hunt v. Mansfield, 31 Conn. 488; Gilbert v. Haire, 43 Mich. 283; McClaskey v. O'Brien, 16 W. Va. 791.

[5] Hahn v. Behrman, 73 Ind. 120; Lynch v. Hancock, 14 So. Car. 66; Niles v. Harmon, 80 Ills. 396; McKinney v. Miller, 19 Mich. 142; Middletown Bank v. Middletown Academy, 5 Del. Ch. 596; Miller v. Holland, 84 Va. 652; Rousseau's Succession, 23 La. Ann. 1; Iglehart v. Crane, 42 Ills. 261; Judson v. Dada, 79 N. Y. 373.

erty, and on an examination directed to this other property
disclose the additional fact that a conveyance of this latter
property has been made which gives an equitable right to the
grantee thereof to throw the burden of the incumbrance upon
the first property, the intending purchaser must be presumed
to have made such examination, and accordingly to have had
notice of such equitable right.[1] Successive mortgages, to the
extent of the interest which they create, are regarded like
other conveyances.[2] But this rule has no application to a
case in which successive conveyances of different parcels of
the mortgaged property have been made to the same purchaser;[3] nor will it be extended to cover successive sales of
undivided interests in the same property,[4] nor so as to cover
any case in which its enforcement would be prejudicial to
the creditor.[5] And the request for its application must be
made before the foreclosure is completed.[6] The same rule
has been applied for the protection of a purchaser from the
mortgagor of one of several mortgaged chattels by compelling
the mortgagee to resort for his payment first to the chattels
retained by the mortgagor.[7]

§ 76. **Rule in Iowa and Kentucky.** — But this rule of applying upon the mortgage such portions of the mortgaged property as have been conveyed by the mortgagor in the inverse
order of their alienation has not been followed in Iowa and
Kentucky. In Iowa it is held that where portions of the
mortgaged property have been sold and conveyed subsequently

[1] Hunt v. Mansfield, 31 Conn. 488;
Iglehart v. Crane, 42 Ills. 261.
[2] Schryver v. Fuller, 9 Paige (N. Y.),
173; Thomas v. Moravia Foundry Co.,
43 Hun (N. Y.), 487; Converse v.
Ware Savings Bank, 152 Mass. 407;
Millsaps v. Bond, 64 Mississippi,
453; Fassett v. Mulock, 5 Colorado,
466.
[3] Steere v. Childs, 15 Hun (N. Y.),
51L

[4] Cashman v. Martin, 50 How. Pr.
(N. Y.) 337.
[5] Pancoast v. Duval, 26 N. J. Eq.
445; Cashman v. Martin, 50 How. Pr.
(N. Y.) 337; Francis v. Herren, 101
Nor. Car. 497; Jackson v. Sloan, 76
Nor. Car. 306.
[6] St. Joseph Manufacturing Co. v.
Daggett, 84 Ills. 556.
[7] High v. Brown, 46 Iowa, 259;
Lee v. Buck, 13 So. Car. 178.

to the mortgage, and the mortgagor retains the remaining part, the portion which remains unsold should indeed be first subjected to the payment of the mortgage-debt;[1] for although the mortgage is a lien resting upon all the estate alike, yet the mortgagor, in addition to the legal obligations resulting from the stipulations in his mortgage-deed, and from the covenants in his deed to his grantee, is morally bound to pay the debt and to clear away any incumbrance from the property which he has sold; but that, as between the grantees who have purchased different parcels of the incumbered estate from the mortgagor at different times, there is no greater moral obligation to pay the debt resting upon one than upon the other; and accordingly the subsequent purchasers of the different portions of the mortgaged premises must contribute ratably to the discharge of the incumbrance.[2] The same doctrine is maintained in Kentucky.[3] And it has been held in Georgia that the purchasers of parts of the mortgaged property from the mortgagor cannot compel the mortgagee to resort for the payment of his debt to that part of the mortgaged property which remains in the possession of the mortgagor;[4] though their rights against the debtor and against incumbrancers junior to themselves are recognized.[5]

§ 77. **No Distinction between Mortgage and Judgment-lien or other Incumbrance.** — A distinction has sometimes been made between the lien of a judgment or attachment and that of a mortgage. It was decided in Virginia that where a judgment has been recovered against a debtor which is a lien upon his real estate, and he subsequently conveys his lands

---

[1] Mickley v. Tomlinson, 79 Iowa, 383; Dilger v. Palmer, 60 Iowa, 117; Taylor v. Short, 27 Iowa, 361.

[2] Huff v. Farwell, 67 Iowa, 298; Barney v. Meyers, 28 Iowa, 472; Griffith v. Lovell, 26 Iowa, 226; Massie v. Wilson, 16 Iowa, 390; Bates v. Ruddick, 2 Iowa, 423.

[3] Dickey v. Thompson, 8 B. Mon. (Ky.) 312; Beall v. Barclay, 10 B. Mon. (Ky.) 261; Morrison v. Beckwith, 4 T. B. Mon. (Ky.) 73; Blight v. Banks, 6 *Id.* 192.

[4] Knowles v. Lawton, 18 Ga. 476.

[5] Craigmales v. Gamble, 85 Ga. 439; Manley v. Ayers, 68 Ga. 507.

by separate conveyances made at various times in different
parcels to different grantees, all the debtor's lands in the
hands of these respective grantees are alike liable to the
creditor, and must contribute to satisfy the judgment *pro
rata*, and not in the inverse order of their alienation;[1] but
doubt was speedily thrown upon this decision by the same
court which had rendered it,[2] and it has since been expressly
overruled.[3]   And in Tennessee it has been held that the
several purchasers of different tracts of land from one whose
real estate is all subject to the lien of an execution are mere
strangers to each other; and if some of these purchasers
afterwards lose their lands by having them sold on the execution, they have no right either of indemnity or contribution against the others, and no remedy against the grantor,
if their purchases were by deed and without fraud or warranty.[4]   But the great mass of the cases put the incumbrance
of a judgment upon exactly the same ground as any other
incumbrance, as to its effects upon the rights of subsequent
purchasers of parts of the incumbered premises.[5]   The same
rule will be applied to a devise of lands charged with the
payment of legacies: portions of the lands which have been
conveyed by the devisee at different times will be charged

[1] Beverley *v.* Brooke, 2 Leigh (Va.), 426.

[2] Conrad *v.* Harrison, 3 Leigh (Va.), 532.

[3] McLung *v.* Beirne, 10 Leigh (Va.), 394; Henkle *v.* Allstadt, 4 Gratt. (Va.) 284; Rodgers *v.* Mc-Cluer, 4 Gratt. (Va.) 81; Brengle *v.* Richardson, 78 Va. 406.

[4] Jobe *v.* O'Brien, 2 Humph. (Tenn.) 34.

[5] National Savings Bank *v.* Cress-well, 100 U. S. 630; Hunt *v.* Mans-field, 31 Conn. 488; Pallen *v.* Agri-cultural Bank, 1 Freem. (Miss.) 419; Welch *v.* James, 22 How. Pr. (N. Y.) 474; Clowes *v.* Dickinson, 5 Johns. Ch. (N. Y.) 235; s. c., on appeal, 9 Cow. (N. Y.) 403; Barnes *v.* Mott, 64 N. Y. 397; Ingalls *v.* Morgan, 10 N. Y. 178; Howard Ins. Co. *v.* Halsey, 8 N. Y. 271; James *v.* Hubbard, 1 Paige (N. Y.), 228; Taylor *v.* Maris, 5 Rawle (Penn.) 51; Nailer *v.* Stanley, 10 Serg. & R. (Penn.) 450; Eben-hardt's Appeal, 8 Watts & Serg. (Penn.) 327; Cowden's Estate, 1 Penn. St. 267; Edwards *v.* Applegate, 70 Ind. 325; Russell *v.* Houston, 5 Ind. 180; Fowler *v.* Barksdale, 1 Harp. Eq. (So. Car.) 164; Relfe *v.* Bibb, 43 Ala. 519; Hunt *v.* Ewing, 12 Lea (Tenn.), 519.

for the legacies in the hands of his grantees in the inverse
order of their alienation by him;[1] and the same rule has
been applied to the incumbrance of a widow's right of dower,[2]
and to other liens upon property.[3]

§ 78. **Release of Estate primarily liable discharges pro tanto
that secondarily liable.** — From the foregoing rule as to the
order of charging the different parcels of the incumbered
premises, it follows that if the mortgagee, with notice of
the facts,[4] releases from the lien of his mortgage that portion
of the premises which is primarily liable thereto, he thereby
releases *pro tanto* that portion of the premises which is only
secondarily liable; for he has thereby prevented the subrogation to which the owner of the latter portion would, upon his
payment, be entitled against the former.[5] When, after such
a release, the incumbrance is sought to be enforced against
the latter portion, its owner can claim an abatement of his
liability to the extent of the value of that portion which
should have been made the primary fund for the payment of
the debt.[6] Thus, if the mortgagee of several parcels of land
releases one parcel, he will be held to junior incumbrancers

[1] Elwood v. Deifendorf, 5 Barb. (N. Y.) 398; Jenkins v. Freyer, 4 Paige (N. Y.), 47; Nellons v. Truax, 6 Ohio St. 97.

[2] Raynor v. Raynor, 21 Hun (N. Y.), 36.

[3] Jones v. Phelan, 20 Gratt. (Va.) 229; Whitten v. Saunders, 75 Va. 563; Alabama v. Stanton, 5 Lea (Tenn.), 423; Wright v. Atkinson, 3 Sneed (Tenn.), 585; Blight v. Banks, 6 T. B. Mon. (Ky.) 192; Cone v. Donaldson, 47 Penn. St. 363; Dungan v. Dollman, 64 Ind. 327; Bull v. Griswold, 14 R. I. 22; Thorington v. Montgomery, 82 Ala. 591.

[4] *Postea,* § 81.

[5] Murray v. Fox, 104 N. Y. 382; James v. Hubbard, 1 Paige (N. Y.), 228; Livingston v. Freeland, 3 Barb.

Ch. (N. Y.) 510; Ingalls v. Morgan, 10 N. Y. 178; Guion v. Knapp, 6 Paige (N. Y.), 35; Blair v. Ward, 10 N. J. Eq. 119; Harrison v. Guerin, 27 N. J. Eq. 219; Paxton v. Harrier, 11 Penn. St. 312; Brown v. Simons, 44 N. H. 475; Parkman v. Welch, 19 Pick. (Mass.) 231; Johnson v. Rice, 8 Greenleaf (Me.), 157; Stewart v. McMahan, 94 Ind. 389; Iglehart v. Crane, 42 Ills. 261; Mobile Ins. Co. v. Huder, 35 Ala. 713; Groesbeck v. Matteson, 43 Minn. 547; Shepherd v. Brown, 3 Mackey (D. C.), 266.

[6] Shrack v. Shiner, 100 Penn. St. 451; Hoy v. Bramhall, 19 N. J. Eq. 74, and (on appeal) 563; Gaskill v. Sine, 2 Beas. (13 N. J. Eq.) 400; Lafarge Ins. Co. v. Bell, 22 Barb. (N. Y.) 54; Taylor v. Short, 27 Iowa, 361; Johnson

for its proportionate value;[1] but this would not be so, if it was shown that the mortgagor had no title to the lot released, so that the subsequent grantees of the mortgagor could be in no way prejudiced by the release.[2] Nor will the release of a part of the mortgaged premises from the lien of the mortgage in any manner affect that lien upon the residue of the premises, as between the original parties; so far as their rights are concerned, every part of the mortgaged premises is bound for the payment of the whole debt.[3] The release of the primary fund will exonerate *pro tanto* the secondary fund in the hands of one who has purchased the latter since the creation of the lien,[4] although the release contained an express reservation of all rights against such purchaser.[5] If a mortgagee, having notice of a subsequent mortgage upon a portion of the same land, releases that portion upon which he has an exclusive lien, and which was of sufficient value to have satisfied his whole claim, the court, upon a foreclosure sale of the remainder of the premises, will postpone his claim to that of the subsequent mortgagee.[6] Such a junior incumbrancer has an equitable right to have the property which is not included in his security, but is subject to the prior lien, first applied to the satisfaction of that prior lien to the relief of his security.[7] The purchaser for value and with warranty of incumbered lands and his grantees occupy a position similar to that of sureties for the debtor, and are entitled to the same

---

*v.* Williams, 4 Minn. 260; Carey *v.* Boyle, 53 Wisc. 574; Jones *v.* Maney, 7 Lea (Tenn.), 341; Warner *v.* De Witt County Bank, 4 Ills. App. 305.

[1] Wolf *v.* Smith, 36 Iowa, 454; Birnie *v.* Main, 29 Ark. 591; Stevens *v.* Cooper, 1 Johns. Ch. (N. Y.) 425.

[2] Taylor *v.* Short, 27 Iowa, 361; Van Orden *v.* Johnson, 14 N. J. Eq. 376.

[3] Coutant *v.* Servoss, 3 Barb. (N. Y.) 128.

[4] Martin's Appeal, 97 Penn. St.

85; McVeigh *v.* Sherwood, 47 Mich. 545; Ford *v.* Geauga County, 7 Ohio (part 2), 143; Leffingwell *v.* Freyer, 21 Wisc. 392; Moore *v.* Trimmier, 32 So. Car. 511.

[5] Dugger *v.* Tayloe, 60 Ala. 504.

[6] Deuster *v.* McCamus, 14 Wisc. 307; Alsop *v.* Hutchings, 25 Ind. 347.

[7] Schofield *v.* Cox, 8 Gratt. (Va.) 533; Mickle *v.* Rambo, 1 N. J. Eq. 501; Baring *v.* Moore, 4 Paige (N.Y.), 166.

equities as sureties would be. A release by the creditor without their consent, and with knowledge of their rights, of any security to which they would be entitled on payment of the debt, discharges *pro tanto* the lien on their property.[1]

§ 79. **Release of Estate primarily liable will not exonerate Estate secondarily liable unless in Justice it ought to have that Effect.** — But the rule of charging different parcels of land which are subject to a common incumbrance in the inverse order of their alienation by the debtor being a mere rule of equity,[2] and a release to a subsequent purchaser of one parcel of the land not being a technical discharge of the parcels previously conveyed from the lien of the incumbrance, it will be treated as an equitable release only in those cases in which, according to natural justice and equity, it ought so to operate against the one giving the release.[3] If the full value of what is primarily liable is realized upon the debt, that is all that can be asked by those interested in the other parcels.[4] Thus where a mortgagor, having sold and conveyed a part of the mortgaged premises and received full payment therefor, afterwards sells the remainder of the premises to another purchaser for their full value, with the agreement that all the purchase-money shall be applied upon the mortgage-debt, and the premises thus be relieved from the lien of the mortgage, the mortgagee will not, by receiving the value of this remainder from the second purchaser, and thereupon releasing the land of the latter from the mortgage, discharge

---

[1] Coffin *v.* Parker, 127 N. Y. 117; Barnes *v.* Motte, 64 N. Y. 397; Ingalls *v.* Morgan, 10 N. Y. 178; Hicks *v.* Bingham, 11 Mass. 300.

[2] Francis *v.* Herren, 101 Nor. Car. 497; Aderholt *v.* Henry, 87 Ala. 415; Fleishel *v.* House, 52 Ga. 60; Hawhe *v.* Snydaker, 86 Ills. 197; Worth *v.* Hill, 14 Wisc. 559.

[4] Libby *v.* Tufts, 121 N. Y. 172;

Kendall *v.* Woodruff, 87 N. Y. 1; Kendall *v.* Niebuhr, 58 How. Pr. (N. Y.) 156; s. c. 45 N. Y. Superior Ct. 542; Torrey *v.* Cook, 116 Mass. 163; Clark *v.* Fontain, 135 Mass. 464; Bradley *v.* Fuller, 23 Pick. (Mass.) 1; Williams *v.* Brown, 57 Ga. 304.

[4] Santa Marina *v.* Connolly, 79 Calif. 517.

wholly or in part the portion conveyed to the first purchaser
from the lien of the mortgage for the balance of the debt;
the full value of the second purchase having been applied
upon the mortgage-debt, the first purchaser has enjoyed all
his rights;[1] and the mortgagee has not the equitable right
further to hold the second tract, of which he has thus once
received the full value;[2] if he could hold it, it would be only
upon refunding the amount so paid.[3] It has been held that
if a mortgagor sells a portion of an estate which is incumbered by a mortgage to secure the payment of various debts,
to a purchaser who has only constructive notice of the mortgage, and transfers the notes given by such purchaser for the
purchase-money to one of the mortgage-creditors to be applied upon one of the mortgage-debts, the purchaser's payment of these notes to one of the mortgage-creditors does not
release the land thus purchased from the lien of the mortgage, unless it was so agreed between the purchaser and the
mortgagees.[4] A prior purchaser from the debtor who has
not yet paid all his purchase-money must, to the extent of
the unpaid purchase-money,[5] contribute to the relief of a
subsequent purchaser who has been compelled to pay a common incumbrance, although the latter had agreed with his
grantor, the original debtor, to pay the amount due upon the
common lien out of his purchase-money, if the subsequent
purchaser made this agreement in consequence of fraudulent
misrepresentations of his grantor as to the amount of the
incumbrance.[6] If, after the original incumbrance, the debtor
first gave a mortgage upon part of the incumbered premises,
which has not been foreclosed, and subsequently gave an
absolute deed of the residue to another party, then, the origi-

[1] Patty v. Pease, 8 Paige (N. Y.),
277; Hawke v. Snydaker, 86 Ills. 197.

[2] Pearson v. Carr, 94 Nor. Car.
567.

[3] Browne v. Davis, 109 Nor. Car.
23.

[4] Colby v. Cato, 47 Ala. 247.

[5] Baldwin v. Sager, 70 Ills. 503.

[6] Beddow v. DeWitt, 43 Penn. St.
326.

nal incumbrance should be charged first upon the equity of redemption from the second mortgage, and secondarily upon the parcel sold and conveyed absolutely.[1] And if such second mortgagee, after an absolute sale of the residue of the premises with warranty to a subsequent purchaser, takes from the mortgagor a quitclaim deed of the equity of redemption in the property mortgaged to him, and this interest is equal in value to the sum due upon the first mortgage on the entire premises, then the second mortgagee and his grantees should discharge that first mortgage, without contribution from such subsequent purchaser; and an assignment of the first mortgage to the second mortgagee will exonerate the lands which have been conveyed to the subsequent purchaser.[2]

§ 80. **Release of any Remedy to which the Subsequent Grantee would be subrogated releases the Lien on the Latter's Property.** — Any act of the prior incumbrancer releasing a remedy to which the grantee of the owner of the equity of redemption would, on paying the debt, be entitled to be subrogated, will release the lien of the prior incumbrance on the property in the hands of such grantee.[3] A judgment-creditor's voluntary relinquishment of a levy upon personal property of his debtor sufficient to have satisfied the judgment will release the judgment-lien upon land previously conveyed by the debtor to a *bona fide* purchaser for value.[4] If, after a mortgagor has given a second mortgage of premises which are subject to a prior mortgage, the first mortgagee, with notice of the second mortgage, diminishes the security of the junior incumbrancer by releasing the mortgagor from personal responsibility for the debt, he will thereby postpone his lien upon the property to that of the second mortgagee;[5] if, with notice of the facts, he gives such a release after a

---

[1] Kellogg v. Rand, 11 Paige (N. Y.), 59. See Watson v. Grand Rapids Co., 51 No. W. Rep. 990.

[2] Pike v. Goodnow, 12 Allen (Mass.), 472.

[3] As in the case of sureties: *postea*, § 119 *et seq.*

[4] Voorhes v. Gros, 3 How. Pr. (N. Y.) 262.

[5] Sexton v. Pickett, 24 Wisc. 346.

conveyance by the mortgagor to a purchaser of part of the mortgaged premises, who has acquired by his purchase the right to throw the burden of the incumbrance upon the mortgagor and upon the residue of the mortgaged property in his hands, this will discharge the land of such purchaser from its liability under the mortgage, even though at the time of such release the payment of the mortgage-debt was assumed by another person, the purchaser not having assented to this substitution.[1]

§ 81. **Prior Incumbrancer not affected by Subsequent Alienations of the Premises unless notified of them.** — Before the holder of a mortgage or other incumbrance upon property can be required to act in collecting his demand with reference to the order of subsequent alienations of portions of the incumbered property, he must have notice of what that order is,[2] other than the mere constructive notice derived from the registry of the deeds given subsequently to his mortgage,[3] unless special circumstances have made it his duty to examine the records.[4] He is not bound to take notice of subsequent liens or conveyances, or of litigation which arises concerning them;[5] and subsequent purchasers of portions of the mortgaged premises who desire him to act with reference to the order of subsequent alienations by the mortgagor must notify him of the facts in proper time, and request him to act accordingly.[6] They cannot remain passive until after a fore-

---

[1] Coyle v. Davis, 20 Wisc. 564.

[2] Patty v. Pease, 8 Paige (N. Y.), 277; La Farge Ins. Co. v. Bell, 22 Barb. (N. Y.) 54; Robinson v. Sherman, 2 Gratt. (Va.) 178; Boone v. Clark, 129 Ills. 466; Sarles v. McGee, 1 Nor. Dak. 365; James v. Brown, 11 Mich. 25.

[3] George v. Wood, 9 Allen (Mass.), 80; Wheelright v. De Peyster, 4 Edw. Ch. (N. Y.) 232; Hoy v. Bramhall, 19 N. J. Eq. 74 and 563; Mark v. Speck, 133 Penn. St. 27; Birnie v.

Main, 29 Ark. 591; Straight v. Harris, 14 Wisc. 509; Hosmer v. Campbell, 98 Ills. 572.

[4] Alexander v. Welch, 10 Ills. Ap. 181.

[5] Lewis v. Hinman, 56 Conn. 55; Uniontown Building Association's Appeal, 92 Penn. St. 200; Stuyvesant v. Hone, 1 Sandf. Ch. (N. Y.) 419; Ward v. Hague, 25 N. J. Eq. 397; Meier v. Meier, 105 Mo. 412.

[6] Snyder v. Crawford, 98 Penn. St. 414; Horning's Appeal, 90 Penn. St.

closure has been completed, and then set up against the mortgagee facts of which the latter had no knowledge.[1] A second mortgagee or a purchaser from the mortgagor can have the benefit of a release given by the first mortgagee only where the first mortgagee gave the release with notice of the second incumbrance or conveyance.[2] If the release was given without notice of the equities of the subsequent incumbrancer or grantee, the first mortgagee who gave it is not responsible for the consequences of his act, nor is the lien of his mortgage upon the unreleased portion of the premises in any wise impaired thereby.[3] But if a mortgagee, before giving a partial release of his mortgage, employs an attorney to examine the title to the mortgaged property, the mortgagee is chargeable with notice of all the conveyances thereof found by such attorney upon record, although they have not been communicated by the attorney to him.[4] Actual notice is not necessary in such cases; knowledge of facts which impose the duty of inquiring before acting is sufficient;[5] but the mere possession of a subsequent grantee is not sufficient,[6] unless the prior mortgagee also knows who has such possession and its character.[7]

§ 82. **The Mortgagor may by Stipulation vary the Order of Liability.** — If the owner of incumbered premises, in conveying different parcels thereof, fixes in his conveyances the order of primary liability for the payment of the whole or a part[8]

388; McIlvain v. Mutual Assurance Co., 93 Penn. St. 30; Iglehart v. Crane, 42 Ills. 261; King v. Mc Vickar, 3 Sandf. Ch. (N. Y.) 192; Lausman v. Drahos, 8 Neb. 457.

[1] Richey v. Merritt, 108 Ind. 347; McAfee v. McAfee, 28 So. Car. 218; Matteson v. Thomas, 41 Ills. 110; Blair v. Ward, 10 N. J. Eq. 119.

[2] McIlvain v. Mutual Assurance Co., 93 Penn. St. 30; Johnson v. Bell, 58 N. H. 395 ; Powell v. Hayes, 31 La. Ann. 789.

[3] Vanorden v. Johnson, 14 N. J. Eq. 376; Taylor v. Maris, 5 Rawle (Penn.), 51; Guion v. Knapp, 6 Paige (N. Y.), 35 ; Holman v. Norfolk Bank, 12 Ala. 369.

[4] Kendall v. Niebuhr, 58 How. Pr. (N. Y.) 156 ; s. c. 45 N. Y. Superior Court, 542.

[5] Hall v. Edwards, 43 Mich. 473.

[6] Coggswell v. Stout, 32 N. J. Eq. 240.

[7] Dewey v. Ingersoll, 42 Mich. 17.

[8] Ellis v. Johnson, 96 Ind. 377.

of the incumbrance, then this order will follow the different
parcels in subsequent conveyances thereof,[1] even if one parcel comes to the hands of the mortgagee himself.[2]  Accordingly, if the owner of mortgaged land conveys a portion
thereof, of more than sufficient value to pay the mortgage-
debt, with a provision in the deed that the purchaser is to
assume and pay the whole of the mortgage, and afterwards
conveys the remainder of the land with the understanding
that the mortgage is to be paid off by the former purchaser,
and the mortgagee subsequently takes another mortgage upon
the portion first conveyed, with notice of the facts, the purchaser of the second lot may maintain a bill in equity to redeem the same without contribution towards the payment of
the debt secured by the first mortgage.  The contract of the
mortgagor is binding upon the land in the hands of any subsequent purchaser who acquires his title with knowledge of
his grantor's agreement.[3]  And a grantee who has in his
deed assumed and agreed to pay a certain amount of a mortgage upon the premises which he has purchased cannot afterwards contest the question of the amount which is due upon
that mortgage, so long as he is not called upon to pay more
than the sum which he has thus assumed.[4]  The prior grantee
of a portion of incumbered premises whose grant is expressly
made subject to the incumbrance must, for the relief of subsequent grantees of the property, contribute ratably with

---

[1] Hoy v. Bramhall, 19 N. J Eq. 74
and 563; Mayo v. Merrick, 127 Mass.
511; Stevens v. Goodenough, 26 Vt.
676; Bowne v. Lynde, 91 N. Y. 92;
Harlem Savings Bank v. Mickles-
burgh, 57 How. Pr. (N. Y.) 106; Za-
briskie v. Salter, 80 N. Y. 555;
Torrey v. Orleans Bank, 9 Paige (N.
Y.), 649; Atwood v. Vincent, 17
Conn. 575; Engle v. Haines, 1 Halst.
(5 N. J. Eq.) 186; s. c., on appeal,
nom. Ross v. Haines, Id. 632; Caruth-
ers v. Hall, 10 Mich. 40; McCloskey
v. O'Brien, 16 W. Va. 791; Moore v.
Shurtleff, 128 Ills. 370; Briscoe v.
Power, 47 Ills. 447.

[2] Sanford v. Van Arsdall, 55 Hun
(N. Y.), 70.

[3] Welch v. Beers, 8 Allen (Mass.),
151; Johnson v. Walter, 60 Iowa,
315; Miller v. Fasler, 42 Minn. 366;
Burger v. Greif, 55 Md. 518.

[4] Ritter v. Phillips, 53 N. Y. 586;
Wilcox v. Campbell, 106 N. Y. 325.

them for the discharge of the lien,[1] and they must in like manner contribute with him.[2] But mere proof of a purchase of land with full covenants of warranty for less than its value is not by itself sufficient proof that the purchaser undertook to discharge a mortgage thereon of the existence of which he does not appear to have had actual notice.[3] As between a mortgagor and his voluntary grantee with full covenants, the latter has a right in equity, in the absence of any disqualifying facts, to cast the burden of an incumbrance existing at the time of the conveyance upon the remaining land of the grantor which is also subject to the incumbrance;[4] but if the covenants were inserted without the knowledge of the grantor in a voluntary conveyance from the mortgagor to his wife, then the burden of the incumbrance would not be shifted; and it may be shown by parol evidence that the voluntary grantee understood that the conveyance was subject to the mortgage: the effect of this will be to rebut the equity which would otherwise arise in favor of the grantee, and to subject the portion of the premises conveyed to her to pay its proportional part of the mortgage-debt.[5] The general rule that the mortgage will be enforced upon the different parcels which have since been conveyed in the inverse order of their alienation applies only where the mortgage is a lien resting upon all the land.[6] Nor can any agreement between the mortgagee and his subsequent grantee of a part of the land diminish the mortgagee's right to hold finally all the mortgaged premises for his security.[7]

§ 83. **Extent of the Right of a Subsequent Purchaser.** — Where lands subject to a judgment-lien are advertised for

---

[1] Hill v. McCarter, 27 N. J. Eq. 41; Haskell v. State, 31 Ark. 91.

[2] Hall v. Morgan, 79 Mo. 47; Brown v. South Boston Savings Bank, 148 Mass. 300.

[3] Kilborn v. Robbins, 8 Allen (Mass.), 466; Vilas v. McBride, 62 Hun (N. Y.), 324; McKinnis v. Estes, 81 Iowa, 749.

[4] See Renick v. Ludington, 20 W. Va. 511.

[5] Harrison v. Guerin, 27 N. J. Eq. 219. See Oliver v. Moore, 23 Ohio St. 473.

[6] Evansville Gas Co. v. State, 73 Ind. 219.

[7] Windsor v. Evans, 72 Iowa, 692.

sale under the judgment, and parts of these lands have previously been sold by the debtor, and there are other lands of
the debtor unsold, but the judgment-lien upon these latter
lands would expire before they could be advertised and sold,
the owner of the judgment will not be bound, at the request
of the purchaser from the debtor, to abandon the sale of the
lands which he has advertised.   The purchaser's remedy
would be to offer to pay the judgment, and then, by his bill
in equity against all parties in interest before the expiration
of the lien of the judgment, to enforce his equitable rights to
contribution and indemnity.[1]  After such a tender, the owner
of the judgment would have no right to proceed with his levy
and sale.[2]  If the purchaser's land is sold upon the judgment,
he can compel one who purchased from the debtor subsequently to himself to indemnify him, to the extent of the
value of the lands of such subsequent purchaser.[3]  The purchaser who has not seasonably enforced his right to the
proper order of sale can protect his rights only by redeeming
from the prior incumbrance, and holding by subrogation the
parcels that are primarily liable.[4]  A purchaser from the
debtor or mortgagor of part of the incumbered premises cannot, against the will of the creditor, redeem his property
alone from the incumbrance; he must pay the whole debt.[5]
But if the mortgagee or holder of the lien himself becomes,
with notice, the owner of the property which is primarily
liable for the payment of the debt, and is of sufficient value
therefor, then such a purchaser may redeem his property
from the incumbrance without paying any portion of the

[1] James v. Hubbard, 1 Paige (N.
Y.), 228. See also Dobbins v. Wilson,
107 Ills. 17.

[2] Welch v. James, 22 How. Pr.
(N. Y.) 474.

[3] Clowes v. Dickinson, 5 Johns.
Ch. (N. Y.) 235; s. c., on appeal, 9
Cow. (N. Y.) 403; James v. Hubbard,
1 Paige (N. Y.), 228.

[4] Case v. O'Brien, 66 Mich. 289;
Long v. Kaiser, 81 Mich. 518; Quackenbush v. O'Hare, 61 Hun (N. Y.),
388.

[5] Andreas v. Hubbard, 50 Conn.
351; Carnes v. Platt, 59 N. Y. 405;
Street v. Beal, 16 Iowa, 68; North
western Co. v. Randolph, 47 Kans.
420.

debt.[1] The purchaser of land at a tax-sale acquires no such equitable right as a grantee with warranty, and cannot compel a mortgagee to resort first to the mortgagor's remaining land.[2]

§ 84. **Instances of the Application of these Rules.** — After three pieces of land had been attached by a creditor of their owner, the debtor sold and conveyed one of the pieces for value, and afterwards mortgaged the two remaining pieces, the grantees in these conveyances having no actual knowledge of the attachment. The attaching creditor then recovered judgment, and the mortgagees purchased this judgment, and levied it upon the piece first conveyed, refusing to levy upon the other pieces, which were sufficient to satisfy their judgment; and it was held that the first grantee acquired by his purchase an equitable right against the debtor to have the other pieces first applied to the satisfaction of the judgment; that the debtor's subsequent mortgagees of the remaining pieces took their mortgage subject to the same equitable burden;[3] and accordingly that their purchase of the judgment did not give them the right to levy their execution on the piece first sold, so long as the other pieces were sufficient to satisfy it.[4] The creditor of a mortgagor levied an execution upon the equity of redemption, and had an undivided share thereof set off to himself in satisfaction of his judgment. The debtor then gave a second mortgage of his interest in the equity of redemption, which was foreclosed. The first mortgagee then obtained a decree of foreclosure against the other creditors, the time limited to the judgment-creditor to redeem being a week later than that limited to the second mortgagee. A stranger, at the instance of the second mortgagee, paid off the first mortgagee, and took for his security

---

[1] Bradley *v.* George, 2 Allen (Mass.), 392; Meacham *v.* Steele, 93 Ills. 135.

[2] Miller *v.* Cook, 135 Ills. 190.

[3] As in Acquackanonk Water Co. *v.* Manhattan Ins. Co., 36 N. J. Eq. 586.

[4] Hunt *v.* Mansfield, 31 Conn. 488.

an assignment of the first mortgage-debt and a conveyance of
all the second mortgagee's interest in the premises.  After
this payment, and before the expiration of the time limited
for the judgment-creditor to redeem, the judgment-creditor
tendered to this stranger the amount so paid by him, and
demanded a release of his interest in the premises, which
was refused.  The court held that the judgment-creditor had
acquired by his levy an indefeasible interest in his share of
the equity of redemption, with the right, as against the rest of
the land, to perfect his title by paying a corresponding share
of the debt secured by the first mortgage; that the second
mortgagee, by the foreclosure of his mortgage, became the
owner of the residue of the equity, with a like right to redeem
his share; and that the judgment-creditor and the second
mortgagee thus became tenants in common of the equity of
redemption, each owning an undivided share thereof, and
each bound to pay a proportionate share of the prior incumbrance; and that the stranger, having, in behalf of one of
them, paid the whole of the prior incumbrance, could now
call upon the other to contribute his proportional share
thereof, or to be foreclosed of his interest in the equity of
redemption.[1]  C. sold fifty acres of land, and took from the
purchaser a mortgage for $870 of the purchase-money, and
afterwards purchased a farm from K., and mortgaged it back
for the purchase-money, and as a further security assigned to
K. the mortgage upon the fifty acres; and both of these mortgages were afterwards assigned by K. to J., in payment of a
debt.  C. then sold and conveyed the farm with warranty;
and the farm subsequently came by mesne conveyances to S.
J. then obtained a decree to foreclose the mortgage upon the
fifty acres; and C. afterwards repurchased the fifty acres, and
agreed with the mortgagor to satisfy this decree of foreclosure, but failed to do so, and afterwards conveyed the fifty

[1] Young v. Williams, 17 Conn. 393.  See also Mallory v. Hitchcock,
29 Conn. 127.

acres to a *bona fide* purchaser for value. It was held that
the mortgage upon the fifty acres was the primary fund for
the payment of the debt to J., and that S., who had obtained
an assignment of both securities, was entitled to enforce the
decree upon that mortgage for the payment of the balance
which was due upon it.[1] The holder of a large tract of land
subject to a vendor's lien sold and conveyed some portions
of it with warranty to different purchasers, and then died,
leaving a will, by which he charged with the payment of his
debts some- of the parcels that remained his property, and
devised the residue to his children. His executor having
sold the parcels charged with the payment of debts, the purchaser of two lots paid the price of one, but failed to pay for
the other, which upon his default was sold again, for less
than the amount which he had agreed to pay. This new purchaser then bought the decree which had in the meantime
been obtained to enforce the original vendor's lien, and at-
tempted to subject the other portions of the land to its satisfaction; and it was held that the lot bought and paid for at
the executor's sale must be first subjected, because its owner
was primarily liable for both lots; and that the new purchaser and the several devisees must contribute ratably to
make up the deficiency according to the present value of
their respective lots, relieving the grantees with warranty of
the testator in his lifetime.[2] A debtor, having given a first
mortgage of a lot of three hundred and sixty acres of land,
and then a second mortgage of all but seventy-five acres of
the lot, and then a third mortgage of the whole parcel, it was
held that the second mortgage might require that the first
mortgage should be enforced first upon the seventy-five acres
not included in his second mortgage, and that the third mortgagee had no right to call upon the second mortgagee to contribute *pro rata* to the satisfaction of the first mortgage-debt.[3]

[1] Skeel *v.* Spraker, 8 Paige (N. Y.), 182.

[2] Aderholt *v.* Henry, 87 Ala. 415.

[3] Conrad *v.* Harrison, 3 Leigh

A railroad company having taken for the construction of its road the title to a portion of a piece of land, upon which there was a prior mortgage, of which it had constructive notice, it was held, upon a foreclosure of the mortgage and a sale in parcels of the whole of the mortgaged premises, that the company was bound to contribute to the payment of the mortgage-debt, if the same were not paid by the sale in the inverse order of alienation of the other property covered by the mortgage, the full value of the land which it had taken as of the time of the taking, with interest to the time of payment; so that the railroad company was in effect allowed to redeem its land from the mortgage-lien by paying a ratable proportion of the mortgage-debt, to the extent of the full value of the land at the time of their taking it with interest.[1]  The owner of two tracts of land, having given a mortgage of both tracts, sold one of the tracts to a purchaser, who, by the terms of his deed, assumed the payment of the whole mortgage-debt, and also gave a mortgage back to his grantor, conditioned to save him harmless from the original mortgage. This purchaser afterwards sold his tract to other vendees, the amount of the debt due upon the original mortgage being deducted from the price.  This tract was held to have become by these conveyances the primary fund for the payment of the mortgage; nor did it cease to be such because the original owner afterwards agreed to discharge his mortgage; for that was a mere personal security to himself.[2]

§ 85. **When the Purchaser of an Equity of Redemption assumes the Payment of the Mortgage.** — It is generally held that an agreement by the purchaser of an equity of redemp-

---

(Va.), 532.  So in Sibley v. Baker, 23 Mich. 312.  See also Bernhardt v. Lymburner, 85 N. Y. 172.

[1] Dows v. Congdon, 16 How. Pr. (N. Y.) 571.  So in Foster v. Union Bank, 34 N. J. Eq. 48.  See also Boraem v. Wood, 27 N. J. Eq. 371; Mutual Ins. Co. v. Easton & Amboy R. R. Co., 38 Id. 132.

[2] State v. Ripley, 32 Conn. 150.

tion with his vendor that he will himself assume and pay the mortgage-debt will render him personally liable, not only to his grantor but also directly to the holder of the mortgage,[1] and that without affecting the liability of the original debtor.[2] The original doctrine, which is still often supported, was that this right of the mortgagee to hold the purchaser of the equity of redemption by reason of the latter's agreement with the mortgagor to assume the payment of the mortgage-debt, does not mean that the mortgagee can maintain an action at law upon this agreement between the mortgagor and the purchaser, but rests on the ground that the contract of the purchaser is a collateral stipulation obtained by the mortgagor, which by equitable subrogation inures to the benefit of the mortgagee.[3] The mortgagee is said to stand on the rights of

[1] Union Ins. Co. v. Hanford. 143 U. S. 187; Twichell v. Mears, 8 Biss. C. C. 211; Bowen v. Beck, 94 N. Y. 86; Ricard v. Sanderson, 41 N. Y. 179; Burr v. Beers, 24 N. Y. 178; Vrooman v. Turner, 8 Hun (N. Y.), 78; Thorp v. Keokuk Coal Co., 48 N. Y. 253; Dunning v. Leavitt, 85 N. Y. 30, reversing Dunning v. Fisher, 20 Hun (N. Y.), 178; Campbell v. Smith, 8 Hun (N. Y.), 6; Lamb v. Tucker, 42 Iowa, 118; Thompson v. Bertram, 14 Iowa, 476; Moses v. Dallas District Court, 12 Iowa, 139; Mechanics' Savings Bank v. Goff, 13 R. I. 516; Urquhart v. Brayton, 12 R. I. 169; Lennig's Estate, 52 Penn. St. 135; Thompson v. Thompson, 4 Ohio St. 333; Society of Friends v. Haines, 47 Ohio St. 423; Daub v. Englebach, 109 Ills. 267; Carnahan v. Tousey, 93 Ind. 561; Jones v. Parks, 78 Ind. 537; Follansbee v. Johnson, 28 Minn. 311; Keedle v. Flack, 27 Neb. 836; Da Costa v. Comfort, 80 Calif. 507; Rickman v. Miller, 39 Kans. 362; Schmucker v. Seibert, 18 Kans. 104; Willson v. Phillips, 27 Tex. 543; Palmeter v. Carey, 63 Wisc. 426; Unger v. Smith, 44 Mich. 22; Crawford v. Edwards, 33 Mich. 354; Carley v. Fox, 38 Mich. 387; Miller v. Thompson, 34 Mich. 10; Fitzgerald v. Barker, 85 Mo. 13 and 70 Mo. 685; Schlatre v. Greaud, 19 La. Ann. 125; Tunnard v. Hill, 10 La. Ann. 247; Hebert v. Doussan, 8 La. Ann. 267.

[2] Conn. Ins. Co. v. Tyler, 8 Biss. C. C. 369; Latiolais v. Citizens' Bank, 33 La. Ann. 1444.

[3] Keller v. Ashford, 133 U. S. 610; Crowell v. Currier, 27 N. J. Eq. 152; s. c., on appeal, nom. Crowell v. St. Barnabas Hospital, 27 N. J. Eq. 650; Klapworth v. Dressler, 2 Beasl. (13 N. J. Eq.) 62; Jarmon v. Wiswall, 9 C. E. Green (24 N. J. Eq.), 68, 267; Wilson v. King, 23 N. J. Eq. 150; Whitcomb v. Whitmore, 57 Vt. 437; Garnsey v. Rogers, 47 N. Y. 233; Trotter v. Hughes, 12 N. Y. 74; King v. Whitely, 10 Paige (N. Y.) 465; Halsey v. Reed, 9 Paige (N. Y.), 446; Curtis v. Tyler, 9 Paige (N. Y.), 432; Blyer v. Monholland, 2 Sandf. Ch. (N. Y.) 478; Scott v. Featherston, 5 La. Ann. 306.

his debtor,[1] and to be entitled to appropriate for his debt any
security held by his debtor for its payment;[2] and his remedy
is restricted to the privilege of subrogation to the rights of
his debtor,[3] and will give him no rights against the purchaser
which could not under the contract of purchase have been
claimed by the original debtor.[4]  Accordingly the mortgagee
has been allowed to enforce the personal liability of such a
purchaser only to the extent of the deficiency upon a foreclosure sale of the mortgaged premises,[5] and only if the party
to whom the purchaser's agreement was given was himself
personally liable for the payment of the mortgage-debt.[6]
The doctrine of equity is that, when the grantee in a deed
assumes the payment of the mortgage-debt, he is to be regarded as the principal debtor, and the mortgagor occupies
the position of a surety;[7] and the mortgagee is permitted to
resort to this grantee to recover the deficiency after applying
the proceeds of a sale of the mortgaged premises, by the
equitable rule that the creditor is entitled to the benefit of
all the collateral securities which his debtor has obtained
to reinforce the principal obligation,[8] though this right is
strictly an equitable one, and its exercise at law has been
refused.[9]  But the broad doctrine has since been laid down,

[1] Berkshire Ins. Co. v. Hutchings,
100 Ind. 496.
[2] As in the case of sureties : *postea*,
§§ 154 *et seq.*
[3] Osborne v. Cabell, 77 Va. 462;
Biddel v. Brizzolara, 64 Calif. 354;
Crowell v. Currier, 27 N. J. Eq. 152
and 650.
[4] Laing v. Byrne, 34 N. J. Eq. 52;
Emley v. Mount, 32 N. J. Eq. 470;
Dunning v. Leavitt, 85 N. Y. 30;
Albany Savings Institution v. Burdick,
87 N. Y. 40; Talburt v. Berkshire
Ius. Co., 80 Ind. 434; Gilbert v. Sanderson, 56 Iowa, 349.
[5] Klapworth v. Dressler, 13 N. J.
Eq. 62; Halsey v. Reed, 9 Paige (N.
Y.), 446.

[6] King v. Whitely, 10 Paige (N.
Y.), 465; Norwood v. De Hart, 30
N. J. Eq. 412; Vreeland v. Van Blar-
com, 35 N. J. Eq. 530; Nelson v.
Rogers, 47 Minn. 103; Brown v. Stillman, 43 Minn. 126.
[7] *Antea,* § 24.  Huyler v. Atwood,
26 N. J. Eq. 504.
[8] Trotter v. Hughes, 12 N. Y. 74;
Curtis v. Tyler, 9 Paige (N. Y.), 432;
Brown v. Winter, 14 Calif. 31; Pru-
den v. Williams, 26 N. J. Eq. 210;
William & Mary College v. Powell, 12
Gratt. (Va.) 372; Hicks v. McGarry,
38 Mich. 667.
[9] Coffin v. Adams, 131 Mass. 133;
Gable v. Scarlett, 56 Md. 169.

that one for whose benefit a promise is made to another may maintain an action upon the promise, though he was not a party to the agreement or privy to the consideration thereof;[1] and it was then held in unqualified terms that whoever has for a valuable consideration assumed and agreed to pay another's debt may be sued directly by the creditor,[2] and that a mortgagee or other incumbrancer may maintain a personal action against a purchaser from the owner of the equity of redemption who has agreed with his grantor to assume and pay off the incumbrance, if the party with whom the agreement was made was himself personally liable upon the mortgage-debt,[3] and that a purchaser who has made such an agreement cannot afterwards be released therefrom by his grantor, to whom it was made, without the consent of the creditor, to whose benefit it inures,[4] if the latter has accepted it.[5] The same rule will be applied to the case of any other incumbrance.[6] But the mortgagee can simply hold such a purchaser to the performance of his agreement; he will not

[1] Lawrence v. Fox, 20 N. Y. 268; Fischer v. Hope Ins. Co., 69 N. Y. 161; Hand v. Kennedy, 83 N. Y. 149; Farley v. Cleveland, 4 Cow. (N. Y.) 432; s. c., on error, nom. Cleveland v. Farley, 9 Cow. (N. Y.)639; Delp v. Bartholomay Brewing Co., 123 Penn. St. 42; Ayers's Appeal, 28 Penn. St. 179; Lewis v. Sawyer, 44 Maine, 332; Cross v. Truesdale, 28 Ind. 44; Lamb v. Donovan, 19 Ind. 40; Nelson v. First National Bank, 48 Ills. 36; O'Conner v. O'Conner, 88 Tenn. 76; Travellers' Ins. Co. v. California Ins. Co., 1 Nor. Dak. 151; Shamp v. Meyer, 20 Neb. 223; Flint v. Cadenasso, 64 Calif. 83.

[2] Wood v. Moriarty, 15 R. I. 518; Paducah Lumber Co. v. Paducah Water Supply Co., 12 So. W. Rep. 554; Redelsheimer v. Miller, 107 Ind. 485; Pulliam v. Adamson, 43 Minn. 511; Mumper v. Kelly, 43 Kans. 256;

Piano Manufacturing Co. v. Burrows, 40 Kans. 361; Ringo v. Wing, 49 Ark. 457.

[3] Antea, n. 2, p. 94.

[4] N. Y. Life Ins. Co. v. Aitkin, 125 N. Y. 660; Gifford v. Corrigan, 117 N. Y. 257; Whitting v. Gearty, 14 Hun (N. Y.), 498; Ranney v. McMullen, 5 Abbott New Cas. (N. Y.) 246; Douglass v. Wells, 18 Hun (N. Y.), 88 (overruling Stephens v. Casbacker, 8 Hun (N. Y.), 116, and disapproving Crowell v. St. Barnabas Hospital, 27 N. J. Eq. 650); Fleischauer v. Doellner, 58 How. Pr. (N. Y.) 190; Willard v. Worsham, 76 Va. 392; Bay v. Williams, 112 Ills. 91; Raum v. Kaltwasser, 4 Mo. App. 573, 574. See School Trustees v. Anderson, 30 N. J. Eq. 366; Young v. School Trustees, 31 N. J. Eq. 290.

[5] Jones v. Higgins, 80 Ky. 409.

[6] Haverly v. Becker, 4 N. Y. 169.

be subrogated to any other right against the purchaser.[1] The
development of this doctrine, though doubtless an outgrowth
of the law of substitution, scarcely comes within the scope
of this investigation. It is sufficient to say that it has also
been emphatically denied;[2] and the court which laid down
this proposition in its broadest terms has refused to apply it
to other somewhat similar cases,[3] and has said that the rule
is one which ought not to be extended.[4]

[1] Duncan v. Baker, 72 Mo. 469.

[2] Malcolm v. Scott, 5 Exch. 601,
610; Meech v. Ensign, 49 Conn. 191;
Prentice v. Brimhall, 123 Mass. 291;
Colt, J., in Pettee v. Peppard, 120
Mass. 522; Exchange Bank v. Rice,
107 Mass. 37; Dow v. Clark, 7 Gray
(Mass.), 198; Field v. Crawford, 6 Id.
116; Millard v. Baldwin, 3 Gray
(Mass.), 484; Mellen v. Whipple, 1
Gray, 317; Mason v. Barnard, 36 Mo.
384; Peacock v. Williams, 98 Nor.
Car. 324; Edwards v. Clement, 81
Mich. 513; Booth v. Conn. Ins. Co.,
43 Mich. 299; Goodenow v. Jones,
75 Ills. 48; Gautgert v. Hoge, 73 Ills.
30.

[3] Merrill v. Green, 55 N. Y. 270;
Metropolitan Trust Co. v. N. Y. R. R.
Co., 45 Hun (N. Y.), 84.

[4] Pardee v. Treat, 82 N. Y. 385.
And see Garnsey v. Rogers, 47 N. Y.
233; Durnherr v. Rau, 60 Hun (N. Y.),
358; Beveridge v. N. Y. Elevated R.
R. Co., 112 N. Y. 1; Biddel v.
Brizzolara, 64 Calif. 354.

# CHAPTER III.

## SUBROGATION IN CASES OF SURETYSHIP.

§ 86. **Surety's Right of Subrogation.** — A surety, on paying
the debt for his principal, is entitled to be subrogated to all
the securities, funds, liens, and equities, which the creditor
holds against the principal debtor, or as a means of enforcing
payment from him.[1]  This right will be enforced whether the

---

[1] Lake v. Brutton, 8 De G., M. &
G. 440; Goddard v. Whyte, 2 Giff.
449; Wooldridge v. Norris, L. R. 6
Eq. 410; Heyman v. Dubois, L. R.
13 Eq. 158; Union Trust Co. v. Morrison, 125 U. S. 591; Hunter v.
United States, 5 Peters, 173, 182;
Colvin v. Owens, 22 Ala. 782; Faw-
cetts v. Kimmey, 33 Ala. 261; Talbot
v. Wilkins, 31 Ark. 411; Belcher v.
Hartford Bank, 15 Conn. 381; Mc-
Dowell v. Wilmington Bank, 1 Harringt. (Del.) 369; Billings v. Sprague,
49 Ills. 509; Pence v. Armstrong, 95

Ind. 191; Rooker v. Benson, 83 Ind.
250; Zook v. Clemmer, 44 Ind. 15;
Jones v. Tincher, 15 Ind. 308; Bryson v. Close, 60 Iowa, 357; Keokuk
v. Love, 31 Iowa, 119; Sears v. La-
force, 17 Iowa, 473; Fields v. Sherrill,
18 Kans. 365; Burk v. Chrisman, 3
B. Mon. (Ky.) 50; Lumpkin v. Mills,
4 Ga. 343; Davidson v. Carroll, 20
La. Ann. 199; Scott v. Featherston,
5 La. Ann. 306; Tuck v. Calvert, 33
Md. 209; Winder v. Diffenderffer, 2
Bland Ch. (Md.) 166, 199; Johnson
v. Bartlett, 17 Pick. (Mass.) 477;

surety is bound in one instrument with the principal or not;[1] and it will be transmitted to the surety's assignees, and to his creditors, when the principal demand has been so used as to destroy their subordinate liens upon his property,[2] and to his heirs when necessary for their protection,[3] and to his grantees, who have lost the property conveyed by him to them in consequence of its being taken upon the principal obligation.[4] And the creditor must do nothing to defeat this right of subrogation on the part of the surety, or to vary the position of the surety;[5] if he takes from the principal debtor a pledge or security for the debt, he must hold the same fairly and impartially, for the benefit of the surety, as well as for his own protection;[6] and if he parts with such property without the knowledge and consent of the surety, he will lose his claim against the latter to the extent of the value of the property so

Dick v. Moon, 26 Minn. 309; Dozier v. Lewis, 27 Miss. 679; Allison v. Sutherlin, 50 Mo. 274; Arnot v. Woodburn, 35 Mo. 99; Wilson v. Burney, 8 Nebraska, 39; Low v. Blodgett, 21 N. H. 121; Dearborn v. Taylor, 18 N. H. 153; Young v. Vough, 23 N. J. Eq. 325; Irick v. Black, 17 N. J. Eq. 189; Lewis v. Palmer, 28 N. Y. 271; King v. Baldwin, 2 Johns. Ch. (N. Y.) 554; Chatham Bank v. Shipman, 20 Hun (N. Y.), 543; Ottman v. Moak, 3 Sandf. Ch. (N. Y.) 431; Towe v. Newbold, 4 Jones Eq. (Nor. Car.) 212; Smith v. McLeod, 3 Ired. Eq. (Nor. Car.) 390; Cochran v. Shields, 2 Grant's Cas. (Penn.) 437; Ware, ex parte, 5 Rich. Eq. (So. Car.) 473; Bittick v. Wilkins, 7 Heisk. (Tenn.) 307; Wade v. Green, 3 Humph. (Tenn.) 547; Carpenter v. Minter, 72 Tex. 370; Willson v. Phillips, 27 Tex. 543; James v. Jacques, 26 Tex. 320; Leake v. Ferguson, 2 Gratt. (Va.) 419; Miller v. Pendleton, 4 Hen. & Munf. (Va.) 436; Highland v. Highland, 5 W. Va. 63.

[1] Enders v. Brune, 4 Randolph (Va.), 438; Havens v. Willis, 100 N. Y. 482.

[2] Moore v. Bray, 10 Penn. St. 519; Holt v. Bodey, 18 Penn. St. 207; Neff v. Miller, 8 Penn. St. 347; Neff's Appeal, 9 Watts & Serg. (Penn.) 36; Ebenhardt's Appeal, 8 Watts & Serg. (Penn.) 327; Huston's Appeal, 69 Penn. St. 485 (overruling Harrisburg Bank v. German, 3 Penn. St. 300); Skinner v. Terhune, 45 N. J. Eq. 565; Davenport v. Hardeman, 5 Ga. 580; Morris v. Evans, 2 B. Mon. (Ky.) 84; Neimcewicz v. Gahn, 3 Paige (N. Y.), 614; York v. Landis, 65 Nor. Car. 535; Watts v. Kinney, 3 Leigh (Va.), 272; McDaniels v. Flower Brook Manufg. Co., 22 Vt. 274.

[3] Meador v. Meador, 88 Ky. 217.

[4] Beaver v. Slanker, 94 Ills. 175; Wilson v. Murray, 90 Ind. 477; State Bank v. Davis, 4 Ind. 653.

[5] Pearl v. Deacon, 24 Beav. 186.

[6] Forbes v. Jackson, 19 Ch. D. 615.

surrendered.[1] The surety is discharged, at least *pro tanto*, whenever by reason of the affirmative act of the creditor, the surety can no longer be substituted to the rights and securities of the creditor.[2] "The rule is undoubted, and it is one founded on the plainest principles of natural reason and justice, that the surety paying off a debt shall stand in the place of the creditor, and have all the rights which he has, for the purpose of obtaining his reimbursement. It is hardly possible to put this right of substitution too high; ,and the right results more from equity than from contract or *quasi* contract, unless in so far as the known equity may be supposed to be imported into any transaction, and so to raise a contract by implication. A surety will be entitled to every remedy which the creditor has against the principal debtor; to enforce every security and all means of payment; to stand in the place of the creditor, not only through the medium of contract, but even by means of securities entered into without the knowledge of the surety, having a right to have those securities transferred to him, though there was no stipulation for that, and to avail himself of all those securities against the debtor."[3] But the surety

---

[1] Guild *v.* Butler, 127 Mass. 386; Baker *v.* Briggs, 8 Pick. (Mass.) 122; Cummings *v.* Little, 45 Maine, 183; New Hampshire Savings Bank *v.* Colcord, 15 N. H. 119; Everly *v.* Rice, 20 Penn. St. 297; Ashby *v.* Smith, 9 Leigh (Va.), 164; Stallings *v.* Americus Bank, 59 Ga. 701; Perrine *v.* Mobile Ins. Co., 22 Ala. 575; McMullen *v.* Hinkle, 39 Miss. 142; Pratt's Succession, 16 La. Ann. 357; Philbrooks *v.* McEwen, 29 Ind. 347; Stewart *v.* Davis, 18 Ind. 74; Kirkpatrick *v.* Howk, 80 Ills. 122; Morley *v.* Dickinson, 12 Calif. 561.

[2] Kinnaird *v.* Webster, 10 Ch. Div. 139; American Bank *v.* Baker, 4 Met. (Mass.) 164; City Bank *v.* Young, 43 N. H. 457; Hurd *v.* Spencer, 40 Vt.

581; Black River Bank *v.* Page, 44 N. Y. 453; Commonwealth *v.* Miller, 8 Serg. & R. (Penn.) 452; Kennedy *v.* Brossiere, 16 La. Ann. 445; Jenkins *v.* McNeese, 34 Tex. 189; Cooper *v.* Wilcox, 2 Dev. & Bat. Eq. (No. Car.) 90; Turner *v.* McCarter, 42 Ga. 491; Winston *v.* Yeargin, 50 Ala. 340; Hall *v.* Hoxsey, 84 Ills. 616; Rogers *v.* School Trustees, 46 Ills. 428; Payne *v.* Commercial Bank, 6 Sm. & M. (Miss.) 24; Middleton *v.* Marshalltown Bank, 40 Iowa, 29; Saline County *v.* Buie, 65 Mo. 63.

[3] Lord Brougham, in Hodgson *v.* Shaw, 3 Myl. & K. 183; Hill *v.* Voorhies, 22 Penn. St. 68.

cannot acquire by subrogation any greater rights than the creditor himself enjoyed.[1]

§ 87. **It is an Equitable Assignment to the Surety.** — Although the surety's right of subrogation has been sometimes limited to securities in the hands of the creditor at the inception of the suretyship,[2] yet it is now settled that no such limitation exists.[3] So soon as the surety pays the debt of his principal, there arises in his favor an equity to have all the securities held by the creditor for the demand turned over to him, and to avail himself of them as fully as the creditor could have done.[4] For the purposes of his indemnification he is entitled to be subrogated to all the rights, remedies, and securities of the creditor, and is allowed to enforce all the creditor's rights and remedies and means of payment against the principal.[5] Although the surety's payment discharges the debt and extinguishes all the securities, so far as it concerns the creditor, it does not have that effect as between the principal and the

---

[1] Schur v. Schwartz, 140 Penn. St. 53; Miller v. Stout, 5 Del. Ch. 259; Walsh v. M'Bride, 72 Md. 45; Morsell v. Caroline, 22 Md. 391; Barton v. Brent, 87 Va. 385; Perkins v. Nolan, 79 Ga. 295, 300; Benneson v. Savage, 130 Ills. 352; Wynne v. Willis, 76 Tex. 589; Kilpatrick v. Dean, 15 Daly (N. Y.), 182.

[2] Wade v. Coope, 2 Sim. 155; Newton v. Chorlton, 10 Hare, 646; Lake v. Brutton, 8 De G., M. & G. 440.

[3] Alexander v. Ellison, 79 Ky. 148; Ruble v. Norman, 7 Bush (Ky.), 582; Lochenmeyer v. Fogarty, 112 Ills. 572; Fegley v. McDonald, 89 Penn. St. 128; Commonwealth v. Miller, 8 Serg. & R. (Penn) 452; Hubbell v. Carpenter, 5 Barb. (N. Y.) 520; Springer v. Toothaker, 43 Maine, 381; Pearl St. Society v. Imlay, 23 Conn. 10; Pierce v. Holzer, 65 Mich. 263; Nelson v. Williams, 2 Dev. & Bat. Eq. (No. Car.) 118; Shattuck v. Cox, 128 Ind. 293; Monroe Bank v. Gifford, 79 Iowa, 300; May v. White, 40 Iowa, 246.

[4] Barger v. Buckland, 28 Gratt. (Va.) 850; Sassoer v. Young, 6 Gill & J. (Md.) 243; Lowndes v. Chisolm, 2 McCord Eq. (So. Car.) 455; Klopp v. Lebanon Bank, 46 Penn. St. 88; Murray v. Catlett, 4 Green (Iowa), 108; Jacques v. Fackney, 64 Ills. 87; Holliday v. Brown, 50 N. W. Rep. 1042; Smith v. Schneider, 23 Mo. 447; Loughridge v. Bowland, 52 Miss. 546.

[5] Ward's Appeal, 100 Penn. St. 289; May v. Burke, 80 Mo. 675; Darst v. Bates, 95 Ills. 493; Conway v. Strong, 24 Miss. 665; Chrisman v. Harman, 29 Gratt. (Va.) 494; Cullum v. Emanuel, 1 Ala. 23; Storms v. Storms, 3 Bush (Ky.), 77; Ghiselin v. Fergusson, 4 Harr. & Johns. (Md.) 522; Cottrell's Appeal, 23 Penn. St. 294.

surety;[1] as to these, it is in the nature of a purchase by the
surety from the creditor, and does not exonerate the principal
debtor.[2] It operates in equity as an assignment of the debt
and the securities to the surety.[3] The right of subrogation
and the equitable assignment relate back to the time of entering into the contract of suretyship, as against the principal
and those claiming under him.[4] If a question is made whether
the acts of the surety have been such as to keep the security
on foot, the court, in the absence of evidence to the contrary,
will presume that they were done with that intention which is
most for the benefit of the party doing them.[5] Thus, the
guarantor of a promissory note or other debt will be subrogated to the rights of the creditor to whom he has made payment.[6] And since the surety is entitled to the benefit of all
the securities for the debt, all persons taking any of them,
either from the principal debtor or from the creditor with notice of the facts and of the surety's responsibilities, are bound
in equity to hold them for his benefit.[7] Nor will it make any
difference that the surety, in entering upon the obligation, did
not rely upon the security, or even know of its existence.[8]

[1] *Postea,* §§ 135 *et seq.,*

[2] Bendey *v.* Townsend, 109 U. S.
665; Strong *v.* Blanchard, 4 Allen
(Mass.), 538; Thornton *v.* McKewan,
1 Hem. & M. 525; Torp *v.* Gulseth,
37 Minn. 135.

[3] Magee *v.* Leggett, 48 Miss. 139;
Dinkins *v.* Bailey, 23 Miss. 284; Mc-
Cormick *v.* Irwin, 35 Penn. St. 111;
Jones *v.* Tincher, 15 Ind. 308; *Dead-
erick, J.,* in Bittick *v.* Wilkins, 7 Heisk.
(Tenn.) 307; Hauser *v.* King, 76 Va.
731.

[4] McArthur *v.* Martin, 23 Minn.
74; Conner *v.* Howe, 35 Minn. 518;
Lewis *v.* Faber, 65 Ala. 460; Wood *v.*
Lake, 62 Ala. 489; Rice *v.* Southgate,
16 Gray (Mass.), 142.

[5] McArthur *v.* Martin, 23 Minn.

74; Dempsey *v.* Bush, 18 Ohio St.
376; Gossin *v.* Brown, 11 Penn. St.
527; Rittenhouse *v.* Levering, 6 Watts
& Serg. (Penn.) 190; Kleiser *v.* Scott,
6 Dana (Ky.), 137.

[6] Pennsylvania R. R. Co. *v.* Pemberton R. R. Co., 28 N. J. Eq. 338;
Babcock *v.* Blanchard, 86 Ills. 165.

[7] Atwood *v.* Vincent, 17 Conn. 575;
Norton *v.* Soule, 2 Greenl. (Me.) 341;
Greene *v.* Ferrie, 1 Desaus. Eq. (So.
Car.) 164; Drew *v.* Lockett, 32 Beav.
499.

[8] Forbes *v.* Jackson, 19 Ch. D.
615; Lake *v.* Brutton, 8 De G., M. &
G. 440; Mayhew *v.* Crickett, 2 Swanst.
185; Hevener *v.* Berry, 17 W. Va.
474.

Any collateral security received by the creditor from the principal debtor will inure to the benefit of the surety.[1]

§ 88. **Surety subrogated to Priority of Creditor.** — Accordingly, where the government is entitled to priority in the payment of a debt, a surety for the debtor will, upon paying the debt to the government, be subrogated to its priority;[2] and he can enforce this right in a court of equity.[3] This doctrine has been applied to the case of a surety upon a custom-house bond for the payment of duties to the United States,[4] even in cases in which there was no statutory provision for such substitution, the owner of the goods not having been a party to the bond;[5] and also in favor of some of the sureties of a United States collector who had made default and died insolvent, after their payment of his indebtedness to the United States, as against their co-sureties,[6] and also to protect such sureties against the principal debtor.[7] But where the principal debtor is still further indebted to the government, the surety, although he has paid all for which he was bound, cannot be subrogated to this right of priority in competition with the government,[8] nor will the surety necessarily be subrogated to all the prerogative rights of the government.[9] And the claim of sureties upon bonds given to the United States for the payment of duties upon imported goods, which they have since paid, is superior to the claim of a purchaser of these

[1] Kirkman v. Bank of America, 2 Coldw. (Tenn.) 397; Newton v. Chorlton, 10 Hare, 646.

[2] United States v. Herron, 20 Wallace, 251; Hunter v. United States, 5 Peters, 173, 182, 183; Richeson v. Crawford, 94 Ill. 165; Jackson v. Davis, 4 Mackey (D. C.), 194; Regina v. Salter, 1 Hurlstone & Norman, 274.

[3] Churchill, in re, 39 Ch. D. 174; Boltz's Estate, 133 Penn. St. 77; Orem v. Wrightson, 51 Md. 34; Miller v. Woodward, 8 Mo. 169.

[4] United States v. Preston, 4 Wash.

C. C. 446; Dias v. Bouchaud, 10 Paige (N. Y.), 445; West v. Creditors, 3 La. Ann. 529.

[5] Enders v. Brune, 4 Rand. (Va.) 438. And see Prather v. Johnson, 3 Harr. & Johns. (Md.) 487.

[6] Robertson v. Triggs, 32 Gratt. (Va.) 76.

[7] Livingston v. Anderson, 80 Ga. 175; Irby v. Livingston, 81 Ga. 281.

[8] Queen v. O'Callaghan, 1 Irish Eq. 439; Heth v. Lewis, 114 Ind. 508.

[9] Kerr v. Hamilton, 1 Cranch, C. C. 546; Jones v. Gibson, 82 Ky. 561.

goods from the importer, although such purchaser has lost the goods by reason of an unlawful sale of them for the same duties by the collector.[1]

§ 89. **Sureties of a Trustee subrogated to the Rights of the Trustee and of the Cestuis que Trustent.** — Where the sureties of a trustee have been compelled to answer for his breach of trust, they are subrogated to the remedies of the trustee[2] and to the rights of both the trustee and the *cestui que trust* against those who have participated in his wrongful acts.[3] The guardian of an infant having wrongfully assigned a bond payable to him in his official capacity, and the sureties upon his official bond having made up the loss, they were allowed to recover from the assignee of the bond, just as the ward could have done.[4] The sureties of a deceased guardian who have satisfied the ward for his default will be subrogated to the rights and remedies of the ward against the guardian's estate,[5] and against all parties whose liability was primary to that of the sureties.[6] The sureties upon the official bond of an insolvent clerk of court will in equity be entitled, upon a breach of trust by their principal, to all the remedies and securities that were in the power of the *cestuis que trustent* or the creditors against one who participated in the breach of trust.[7] If an administrator, being about to leave the State, deposits the

[1] Dias *v.* Bouchaud, 10 Paige (N. Y.), 445.

[2] Boyd *v.* Myers, 12 Lea (Tenn.), 175; Bushong *v.* Taylor, 82 Mo. 660; Wheeler *v.* Hawkins, 116 Ind. 515; Schoonover *v.* Allen, 40 Ark. 132.

[3] Blake *v.* Traders' Bank, 145 Mass. 13; Edmunds *v.* Venable, 1 Patton & H. (Va.) 121; Adams *v.* Gleaves, 10 Lea (Tenn.), 367; Wilson *v.* Doster, 7 Ired. Eq. (Nor. Car.) 231; Rhame *v.* Lewis, 13 Rich. Eq. (So. Car.) 270; McNeil *v.* Morrow, Rich. Eq. Cas. (So. Car.) 172.

[4] Powell *v.* Jones, 1 Ired. Eq. (No. Car.) 337; Fox *v.* Alexander,

1 Ired. Eq. (Nor. Car.) 340; Cowgill *v.* Linville, 20 Mo. Ap. 138.

[5] McClelland *v.* Davis, 4 Lea (Tenn.), 97; Walker *v.* Crowder, 2 Ired. Eq. (Nor. Car.) 478; State *v.* Atkins, 53 Ark. 303; Gilbert *v.* Neely, 35 Ark. 24.

[6] Blake *v.* Traders' Bank, 145 Mass. 13; Thompson *v.* Humphrey, 83 Nor. Car. 416; Shields *v.* Whittaker, 82 Nor. Car. 516; Harris *v.* Harrison, 78 Nor. Car. 202; Morley *v.* Metamora, 78 Ills. 394; Muldoon *v.* Crawford, 14 Bush (Ky.), 195.

[7] Bunting *v.* Ricks, 2 Dev. & Bat. Eq. (Nor. Car.) 130.

assets of the estate with a stranger, in trust for the next
of kin of the intestate, the sureties of the administrator,
against whom recoveries have been had by any of the next of
kin, have a right to call upon this stranger for an account of
the assets so received by him, and to be subrogated against
him to the rights of such of the next of kin as have held the
sureties to responsibility.[1]   And although it has been decided
in Massachusetts that a surety upon an administrator's probate bond, who has been obliged to pay a judgment recovered
by the heirs-at-law upon the bond, and has taken an assignment of all their rights in the estate and all claims of theirs
therefor, cannot maintain a suit against an agent of the administrator having in his hands moneys belonging to the
estate, yet this decision was put upon the ground that the
heirs could not themselves have maintained such an action,
but were restricted to their remedy upon the administrator's
bond.[2]   A surety upon an administrator's bond who has paid
one-half of a judgment recovered by a creditor of the intestate against the administrator will not be subrogated to the
rights of the creditor whom he has partly paid, but to those
of the administrator for whom he has made the payment;[3]
for a surety's subrogation to the remedies of the creditor is
allowed only when the creditor has been fully satisfied.[4]

§ 90. **Sureties of a Sheriff subrogated to Rights which they
have satisfied for him.** — The sureties of a sheriff, who have
been compelled to pay a judgment recovered against him by
the owner of property which he had taken on an execution
against a third party, and had turned over to the judgment-
creditor, have been allowed to recover the value of such property against that plaintiff; the sureties who had satisfied the
owner were substituted to his cause of action against the

[1] Kennedy v. Pickens, 3 Ired. Eq. (Nor. Car.) 147.

[2] Winslow v. Otis, 5 Gray (Mass.), 360, as in Adams v. Gleaves, 10 Lea (Tenn.), 367.  And see Stetson v. Moulton, 140 Mass. 597.

[3] Clark v. Williams, 70 Nor. Car. 679.

[4] Antea, § 88; postea, § 127.

creditor.[1] So if the sureties of a sheriff have to pay money
for the default of his deputy in failing to take a bail-bond
from the defendant in a writ, they may in equity be subrogated
to the rights of the sheriff against such deputy, and may also
resort to a fund which the deputy had obtained from such defendant to indemnify himself against the consequences of the
same default.[2] They could also resort to the sureties in a
bond given by the deputy to the sheriff to secure the latter
against the deputy's delinquencies in office.[3] The sureties of
a sheriff who have been compelled, by reason of his default,
to pay to the owners of land the amount for which he had
sold the land in partition proceedings, will be subrogated to
the rights of the sheriff in a note which he took for the price
of the land from the purchaser at his sale.[4] The sureties of a
sheriff who have been compelled, through his neglect to serve
an execution committed to him, to pay the amount of such
execution to the creditor therein, will be subrogated to the
rights of the creditor against the original defendants in the
execution,[5] just as the sheriff would have been if he had himself made the payment.[6]

§ 91. **Subrogation of a Debtor's Surety against a Sheriff.** —
Where a plaintiff recovered judgment and issued execution
against both principal and surety, and the sheriff collected the
amount of the judgment from the principal debtor, but paid
over only a part thereof to the plaintiff, and the surety paid
the balance of the judgment to the plaintiff, neither of them
then knowing that the sheriff had the funds in his hands, the
surety was subrogated to the plaintiff's claim against the

[1] Skiff v. Cross, 21 Iowa, 459;
Philbrick v. Shaw, 61 N. H. 356.

[2] Blalock v. Peak, 3 Jones Eq.
(Nor. Car.) 323; Philbrick v. Shaw,
61 N. H. 356.

[3] Brinson v. Thomas, 2 Jones Eq.
(Nor. Car.) 414; Nebergall v. Tyree,
2 W. Va. 474.

[4] Sweet v. Jeffries, 48 Mo. 279.

[5] Bittick v. Wilkins, 7 Heisk.
(Tenn.) 307; Saint v. Ledyard, 14
Ala. 244. But not in Mississippi,
Dillon v. Cook, 5 Sm. & M. (Miss.)
773.

[6] Antea, § 7.

sheriff for such funds.[1] A surety who has been obliged to satisfy an execution against his principal in consequence of the sheriff's having wrongfully applied the proceeds of the principal's property to the payment of a junior execution for which the surety was not liable, will be subrogated to the prior creditor's remedy against the sheriff,[2] as he will be if the opportunity of obtaining satisfaction from the principal has been lost by the fault of the sheriff.[3] But if the liability of the sheriff had been for mere negligence, in not collecting and returning the execution, under such circumstances that the sheriff himself, upon making compensation for his default, would have been entitled to be subrogated to the rights of the creditor against all the defendants in the execution,[4] then a payment by the surety would not have entitled him to any redress against the sheriff,[5] unless the sheriff's neglect had resulted in a loss to the surety for which he could not obtain satisfaction from his principal.[6] And the surety cannot be subrogated to the principal debtor's remedies against the sheriff, until the surety shall have satisfied the judgment.[7] In a suit at law on a constable's bond for an escape, if, since the bringing of the action, the original judgment has been satisfied by a surety for the debtor, no more than nominal damages will be allowed, even though the suit, after this satisfaction, was prosecuted for the benefit of the surety.[8]

§ 92. **Surety subrogated to Corporation's Lien upon the Stock of its Shareholders.** — When corporations have a lien upon the

[1] Merryman v. State, 5 Harr. & Johns. (Md.) 423; Bellows v. Allen, 23 Vt. 169.

[2] Commonwealth v. Straton, 7 J. J. Marsh. (Ky.) 90. See Straton v. Commonwealth, 2 Dana (Ky.), 397.

[3] Rowe v. Williams, 7 B. Mon. (Ky.) 202; Miller v. Dyer, 1 Duv. (Ky.) 263. Contra, in Massachusetts, at law, in Harrington v. Ward, 9 Mass. 251.

[4] Antea, § 7.

[5] Bellows v. Allen, 23 Vt. 169; O'Hara v. Schwab, 26 La. Ann. 78.

[6] Pennsylvania Bank v. Potius, 10 Watts (Penn.), 148, 152. See Boughton v. Orleans Bank, 2 Barb. Ch. (N. Y.) 458; Gary v. Bank of the State, 11 Ala. 771; Hill v. Sewell, 27 Ark. 15.

[7] Griff v. Steamboat Stacy, 12 La. Ann. 8.

[8] State v. Miller, 5 Blackf. (Ind.) 381.

stock of their shareholders for the payment of debts due from the latter to the corporations, a surety paying such indebtedness will be subrogated to this lien,[1] and if the corporation abandons this lien, it puts itself in the place of the debtor.[2] The surety's equitable right attaches the instant the lien of the corporation commences, and is consummated by his payment of the indebtedness for which he is bound as surety.[3] If, however, the corporation, though having the power to create such a lien, has never exercised its option to do so, then no lien exists, and there is nothing to which the surety can be subrogated.[4]

§ 93. **Surety entitled to be subrogated though not in Privity with his Principal.** — The surety will be subrogated to the rights of the creditor against the principal, though there is no privity of contract between the principal and the surety.[5] A. owed a debt to B., who was indebted to C. At the request of B., and in pursuance of an arrangement between B. and C., A. gave a bond and mortgage for his debt directly to C. A third party then, at the solicitation of B., but without any request from the mortgagor, guaranteed the payment of the bond, and was compelled to pay it upon his guaranty : and he was subrogated to the benefit of the mortgage for his reimbursement, although he had no remedy at law against the principal debtor ;[6] for the surety's right of subrogation does not rest upon contract or privity, but upon principles of natural justice and equity ;[7] and it would have been no defence to the surety, in an action against him by the creditor, that he became surety without the privity of the principal,[8] though

[1] Klopp v. Lebanon Bank, 46 Penn. St. 88; Young v. Vough, 23 N. J. Eq. 325.

[2] Houston & Texas Ry. Co. v. Bremond, 66 Tex. 159.

[3] Klopp v. Lebanon Bank, 46 Penn. St. 88 ; Petersburg Savings Co. v. Lumsden, 75 Va. 327.

[4] Perrine v. Mobile Ins. Co., 22

Ala. 575 ; Dunlop, in re, 21 Ch. D. 583.

[5] Burns v. Huntington Bank, 1 Pen. & W. (Penn.) 395 ; Matthews v. Aikin, 1 N. Y. 595.

[6] Matthews v. Aikin, 1 N. Y. 595.

[7] Miller v. Stout, 5 Del. Ch. 259.

[8] Hughes v. Littlefield, 18 Maine, 400. And see Wright v. Garlinghouse, 27 Barb. (N. Y.) 474.

he might not have been able to obtain indemnity from his principal by an action at law.[1] So a surety for a part of the debt, as he cannot be subrogated to the creditor's securities until the whole debt is paid,[2] may pay the whole debt, including the part for which he is not liable, and enforce the creditor's securities to reimburse him for his full payment.[3]

§ 94. **Surety upon a Bond entitled to the Benefit of a Prior Bond for the same Debt.** — Where a bond has been given by two debtors for the payment of a debt, and after the death of one of them the other gives a new bond with a surety for a part of the demand due upon the first bond, such surety, after paying the amount of the second bond, and taking an assignment of the first bond, may enforce it against the estate of the deceased debtor.[4] The surety will be subrogated under any other bonds held for the same debt.[5]

§ 95. **Surety subrogated to the Benefit of an Agreement made by his Creditor.** — A surety has an equity to be substituted to the benefits obtained by the creditor under an agreement made with other creditors of the same debtor, allowing him to share in the proceeds of property of the debtor upon which he would otherwise have had no claim.[6] If a vendor of land has authorized his vendee to bring suit against an adverse occupant of the premises, agreeing to allow as a part payment of the purchase-money the vendee's expenses in prosecuting the suit, sureties on a bond given by the vendee for the prosecution of the suit will, upon being held on their bond, be subrogated to the rights of their principal, the vendee, against the vendor under this agreement.[7]

§ 96. **Surety of a Purchaser subrogated to Vendor's Right of Rescission.** — Where the seller of property has the right to

---

[1] McPherson v. Meek, 30 Mo. 345; Carter v. Black, 4 Dev. & Bat. Law (Nor. Car.) 425.

[2] Postea, § 118.

[3] Gerber v. Sharp, 72 Ind. 553.

[4] Hodgson v. Shaw, 3 Mylne & K.

[5] Dodd v. Wilson, 4 Del. Ch. 108, 399.

[6] Person v. Perry, 70 Nor. Car. 697.

[7] American Land Co. v. Grady, 33 Ark. 550.

183.

rescind the sale for the non-payment of the price, a surety of the purchaser, upon being compelled to pay the price, will be subrogated to this right.[1] After the sureties have been compelled to pay the debt, and have established their claim against their principal, they will be subrogated to all the creditor's rights in equity, and may set aside any conveyance which the creditor could have avoided.[2] But the indorser of a note given by the master of a steamboat for stores and supplies furnished to the boat does not, by paying the note, become subrogated to the right of the party furnishing the supplies to have a lien on the boat.[3] The object of the note was to prevent the lien; and the indorser's remedy is on the note itself. He may be subrogated to the rights of the payee of the note,[4] but not to those which were waived by the taking of the note, for he cannot claim by subrogation any greater rights than belonged to the original creditor.[5]

§ 97. **Surety of a Purchaser subrogated to a Title or Lien retained by the Vendor.** — A surety for the price of property purchased, the title to the property being retained by the vendor as additional security for the payment of the price, has an equity, if he is compelled to pay the purchase-money, or a balance thereof after a partial payment by the purchaser, to resort to the property for his reimbursement.[6] The vendors still holding the legal title, and having the power to sell the property for the payment of the purchase-money, the surety, on being held liable for the purchase-money, may be subrogated to this right.[7] And this right will not be de-

[1] Groves v. Steel, 2 La. Ann. 480; Torregano v. Seguira, 2 Mart. N. s. (La.) 158.
[2] Tatum v. Tatum, 1 Ired. Eq. (Nor. Car.) 113.
[3] Hays v. Steamboat Columbus, 23 Mo. 232.
[4] Postea, § 181.
[5] Antea, §§ 6, 86.
[6] Smith v. Schneider, 23 Mo. 447;

Arnold v. Hicks, 3 Ired. Eq. (Nor. Car.) 17; Barnes v. Morris, 4 Ired. Eq. (Nor. Car.) 22; Tuck v. Calvert, 33 Md. 209.
[7] Ghiselin v. Fergusson, 4 Harr. & J. (Md.) 522; Hatcher v. Hatcher, 1 Rand. (Va.) 53; Uzzell v. Mack, 4 Humph. (Tenn.) 319; Beattie v. Dickinson, 39 Ark. 205.

stroyed by the purchaser's sale and conveyance of his interest in the property.[1] Whenever the vendor of property, real or personal, retains a lien thereon for the payment of the purchase-money, a surety for the purchaser, who is held liable for the purchase-money, is entitled to be subrogated to this lien,[2] except such a lien as is merely personal and unassignable.[3] So, if property is sold under a decree of court, the title being retained or a lien reserved upon the property for the purchase-money, the purchaser's surety for the price may be substituted to this lien upon the default of the purchaser, and may have the property sold for his relief, even before he has himself paid the price,[4] and although the principal debtor has himself transferred his interest in the property to other persons.[5] Though the surety cannot ordinarily be subrogated to the rights of the creditor against the principal debtor until he has actually paid the debt,[6] yet, under such circumstances, the surety has been allowed to have the property resold for his own protection,[7] because the surety's right to hold for his indemnity the property thus purchased is superior to that of the purchaser, the principal debtor.[8]

§ 98. **Surety for Vendor subrogated to Equitable Rights of Vendee.** — A surety for the vendor to the vendee of property will, upon answering for the default of his principal, be sub-

[1] Fulkerson v. Brownlee, 69 Mo. 371; Myres v. Yaple, 60 Mich. 339; Kleiser v. Scott, 6 Dana (Ky.), 137; Smith v. Schneider, 23 Mo. 447; Ghiselin v. Fergusson, 4 Harr. & J. (Md.) 522; Egerton v. Alley, 6 Ired. Eq. (Nor. Car.) 188; Shoffner v. Fogleman, Winston Eq. (Nor. Car.) 12.

[2] Ballew v. Roler, 124 Ind. 557; Wernecke v. Kenyon, 66 Mo. 275; Ellis v. Roscoe, 4 Baxter (Tenn.), 418; Riddle v. Coburn, 8 Gray (Mass), 241; Carter v. Sims, 2 Heisk. (Tenn.) 166; Burk v. Chrisman, 3 B. Mon. (Ky.) 50.

[3] McNeill v. McNeill, 36 Ala. 109. Postea, § 185.

[4] Henry v. Compton, 2 Head (Tenn.), 549.

[5] Green v. Crockett, 2 Dev. & Bat. Eq. (Nor. Car.) 390; Polk v. Gallant, 2 Dev. & Bat. Eq. (Nor. Car.) 395.

[6] Postea, §§ 118, 127.

[7] Bradford v. Marvin, 2 Fla. 463; Pettillo, in re, 80 Nor. Car. 50; Stenhouse v. Davis, 82 Nor. Car. 432; Ferrer v. Barrett, 4 Jones Eq. (Nor. Car.) 455.

[8] Spring v. Chipman, 6 Vermont, 662; Keith v. Hudson, 74 Ind. 333.

rogated in like manner to the equitable rights of the vendee against the vendor. Thus, where the vendor of land gave a bond with surety to the vendee, conditioned to make a title to the land upon payment of the purchase-money, and before the money was all paid the land was sold on an execution against the vendor, who became insolvent, and thereupon the vendee sued the surety upon the bond, and recovered judgment against him for the money that had been paid, it was held that the surety could follow the land, and have remuneration out of it in the hands of the purchasers at the sheriff's sale for the amount that he had thus been compelled to pay,[1] being subrogated to the purchaser's equitable lien[2] upon the land for the reimbursement of partial payments of the price.

§ 99. **Right of Vendor who becomes Surety for Vendee.** — A vendor of land took the purchaser's note for the price thereof, and gave a bond for title when the purchase-money should be paid. When half the purchase-money had been paid the vendee sold the land, giving a warranty deed thereof to a *bona fide* purchaser for value, who had no knowledge that the title was still in the original vendor. Afterwards, the vendor knowing of this conveyance, the original vendor and vendee made a verbal agreement that the vendee should pay the balance of his purchase-money by paying a debt of the vendor, giving his own note therefor with the vendor as a surety, and that, if the vendor as such surety should be compelled to pay this note, the purchase-money should again become due from the vendee to the vendor, and the vendor should still hold the legal title to the land as security therefor. The vendor was compelled to pay this note, and then evicted the new purchaser from the land, and held it himself under his legal title. The vendor then claimed the balance of the

---

[1] Freeman v. Mebane, 2 Jones Eq. (Nor. Car.) 44.

[2] Clark v. Jacobs, 56 How. Pr. (N. Y.) 519; Payne v. Atterbury, Harr. (Mich.) 414; Shirley v. Shirley, 7 Blackf. (Ind.) 452; Wickerman v. Robinson, 14 Wisc. 493; Brown v. East, 5 T. B. Mon. (Ky.) 405; Griffith v. Depew, 3 A. K. Marsh. (Ky.) 177.

purchase-money from the vendee; and the vendee's purchaser
claimed damages for the breach of the vendee's warranty.
It was held that the original price was paid by the making
of the verbal agreement between the vendor and the vendee,
and that the indebtedness for this price was not revived by
reason of the contract of suretyship; but that the original
vendor having elected to rescind his contract of sale by
resorting to his legal title and evicting his vendee's purchaser, and having thus made his vendee liable in damages
to such purchaser, he must refund to his vendee the half of
the purchase-money which he had received.[1]

§ 100. **Surety entitled to Funds held for the Debt in the
Hands of his Principal.** — Where sureties are held to pay the
debt of their principal, they are entitled in equity to the benefit of all funds and assets, so far as these can be specifically
reached, which their principal held as specifically applicable to the debt which they have paid, and to have these funds
and assets made available for their protection.[2] A person
taking any of such securities from the principal debtor, with
notice of his responsibilities, is bound in equity to hold them
for the indemnification of the sureties.[3] So the surety may
enforce the principal's right to indemnity or repayment from
others.[4] Where one who held a mortgage as administrator
took a deed of the equity of redemption from the mortgagor to
himself individually, it was held, since this deed only made
absolute the defeasible estate already vested in him as administrator, that an agreement by the legatees of the estate
that he should hold the land in his own right, leaving his
sureties liable for the balance due upon his account, could
not be supported against the sureties, but that the latter
could resort for their indemnity to the land, both in the

[1] Davis v. Smith, 5 Ga. 274.
[2] Hobson v. Bass, L. R. 6 Ch. 792;
Gee v. Pack, 33 L. J. Q. B. 49;
Shaw, C. J., in Johnson v. Bartlett,
17 Pick. (Mass.) 477, 488; Lingle v.
Cook, 32 Gratt. (Va.) 262.

[3] Atwood v. Vincent, 17 Conn.
575.
[4] Rodenbarger v. Bramblett, 78
Ind. 213; Josselyn v. Edwards, 57
Ind. 212.

hands of the administrator and of his grantee.[1] Where one became surety upon the principal debtor's promise that certain stock should be pledged for the payment of the debt, but the principal died before the transfer could be made, the execution of this agreement was enforced against his executor, although his estate was insolvent.[2] Executors who have paid a debt for which their testator was liable merely as a surety for a residuary legatee will have a lien upon the legacy for their reimbursement superior to that of a mortgagee of the legacy.[3] Where the note of one who had died indebted to a bank was renewed by his executor as such with a surety, the surety, having paid the note, was substituted to the claim of the executor as well as of the bank against the assets of the estate; and the executor being in advance to the estate by reason of the note which the surety had paid, the amount thus due from the estate to the executor was ordered to be paid to the surety in preference to a subsequent assignee from the executor.[4] But in Alabama under similar circumstances it was held that as the claim of the creditor against the estate of the deceased principal was barred by the taking of the new note,[5] and only the parties to the new note were liable upon it in their individual capacity, the surety upon the new note, when he was compelled to pay it, had no equity against the estate of the deceased principal, except to hold the interest therein of the parties to the new note,[6] the executor having no power to bind his testator's estate by a new contract.[7]

§ 101. **Surety may avail Himself of his Principal's Right of**

[1] Johnson v. Bartlett, 17 Pick. (Mass.) 477.

[2] McCoy v. Wilson, 58 Ind. 447. See accordingly Tucker v. Daley, 7 Gratt. (Va.) 330. But the surety's negligence defeated a similar claim in De Meza's Succession, 26 La. Ann. 35.

[3] Willes v. Greenhill, 29 Beav. 376.

[4] Heart v. Bryan, 2 Dev. Eq. (Nor. Car.) 147.

[5] As in Kingman v. Soule, 132 Mass. 285.

[6] Brown v. Lang, 4 Ala. 50.

[7] Kingman v. Soule, *supra*; Brown v. Lang, *supra*.

**Set-off or Defence.** — A surety, when sued upon his contract, may avail himself of his principal's right of set-off growing out of the same transaction.[1] Thus, it is a good equitable defence to the surety, as to part of the amount claimed of him, that a dispute as to the consideration of the contract having arisen between the plaintiff and the defendant's principal, and the dispute having been referred to arbitration in accordance with the original agreement, this amount had been awarded to the defendant's principal, which the principal had offered before suit brought to set off against the present claim.[2] So, when the payee of a note sued a surety thereon, and it appeared that the note was given for a tract of land sold by the payee of the note to the principal maker, and that at the time of the sale there was an incumbrance upon the land, which the principal had since discharged with the consent of the plaintiff, and upon the latter's promise to allow it as a credit upon the note, it was held that this promise to the principal inured also to the benefit of the surety, and operated a satisfaction of the note *pro tanto*.[3] The surety may in general set up against the claim of the creditor any legal or equitable defence which would have been open to the principal,[4] such as the estoppel of a previous judgment between the creditor and the principal.[5] But the surety's equity to avail himself of his principal's right of set-off against the creditor does not extend to distinct demands of the principal, not in themselves available by way of set-off,[6]

---

[1] Bechervaise v. Lewis, L. R. 7 C. P. 372; Hauser v. King, 76 Va. 731; McDonald Manufacturing Co. v. Moran, 52 Wisc. 203; Hiner v. Newton, 30 Wisc. 640; Myers v. State, 45 Ind. 160; Waterman v. Clark, 76 Ills. 428; Ellis v. Fisher, 10 La. Ann. 479.

[2] Murphy v. Glass, L. R. 2 P. C. 408.

[3] Cole v. Justice, 8 Ala. 793.

[4] Baines v. Barnes, 64 Ala. 375; Smokey v. Peters-Calhoun Co., 66 Miss. 471; State v. Cordon, 8 Ired. Law (Nor. Car.) 179; Jarratt v. Martin, 70 Nor. Car. 459; Huntress v. Patten, 20 Maine, 28; Ames v. Maclay, 14 Iowa, 281; First National Bank v. Rogers, 13 Minn. 407; Adams v. Cuny, 15 La. Ann. 485.

[5] Gill v. Morris, 11 Heisk. (Tenn.) 614; Bank of Commerce v. Porter, 1 Baxter (Tenn.), 447.

[6] People v. Brandreth, 3 Abbott,

and not growing out of the same transaction,[1] unless the principal is insolvent,[2] or the principal has taken advantage of the set-off in a joint action against principal and surety.[3] And this right of set-off is reciprocal to the creditor and the sureties as against the principal.[4] But the surety cannot without the authority of the principal set up against the creditor the failure of the title to the property for the price of which he became surety; the principal may bind his surety as well as himself by waiving the defence of a defective title or a breach of warranty in the conveyance by which the debt was created.[5] The surety is bound in the same manner and to the same extent as his principal;[6] and if the latter is satisfied with his purchase, it cannot be rescinded by the surety for a defect in the title which is given.[7] And the surety may prosecute an appeal or a writ of error to reverse a judg-

Pr. n. s., (N. Y.) 224; La Farge v. Halsey, 1 Bosw. (N. Y.) 171; Thalheimer v. Crow, 13 Color. 397.

[1] Morgan v. Smith, 70 N. Y. 537; s. c. 7 Hun (N. Y.), 244; Lasher v. Williamson, 55 N. Y. 619; Springer v. Dwyer, 50 N. Y. 19; Lewis v. McMillen, 41 Barb. (N. Y.) 420; Emory v. Baltz, 22 Hun (N. Y.), 434; Henry v. Daley, 17 Hun (N. Y.), 210; Putnam v. Schuyler, 4 Hun (N. Y.), 166; East River Bank v. Rogers, 7 Bosw. (N. Y.) 493; Baltimore & Ohio R. R. Co. v. Bitner, 15 W. Va. 455; Dart v. Sherwood, 7 Wisc. 523; Woodruff v. State, 7 Ark. 333; Stewart v. Levis, 42 La. Ann. 37; Vastine v. Dinan, 42 Mo. 269.

[2] Coffin v. McLean, 80 N. Y. 560; Morgan v. Smith, supra; Gillespie v. Torrance, 25 N. Y. 306; Hazard v. Irwin, 18 Pick. (Mass.) 95; Edmunds v. Harper, 31 Gratt. (Va.) 637; Patterson v. Gibson, 81 Ga. 802; Marchman v. Robertson, 77 Ga. 40; Sharon v. Sharon, 84 Calif. 433; Becker v. Northway, 44 Minn. 61.

[3] Himrod v. Baugh, 85 Ills. 435; Springer v. Dwyer, 50 N. Y. 19; Bathgate v. Haskin, 59 N. Y. 533; O'Blenis v. Karing, 57 N. Y. 649; Concord v. Pillsbury, 33 N. H. 310; Harris v. Rivers, 53 Ind. 216; Wartman v. Yost, 22 Gratt. (Va.) 595; Mahurin v. Pearson, 8 N. H. 539; Crist v. Brindle, 2 Rawle (Penn.), 121; Guggenheim v. Rosenfeld, 9 Baxter (Tenn.), 533; Lynch v. Bragg, 13 Ala. 773; Harrison v. Henderson, 4 Ga. 198; Bourne v. Bennett, 4 Bing. 423.

[4] Andrews v. Varrell, 46 N. H. 17.

[5] Ross v. Woodville, 4 Munf. (Va.) 324; Henry v. Daley, 17 Hun (N. Y.), 210.

[6] Chilson v. Adams, 6 Gray (Mass.), 364; Evans v. Kneeland, 9 Ala. 42; Moulton v. Beauchamp, 10 La. Ann. 666.

[7] Osborn v. Bryce, 23 Fed. Rep. 171; Lyon v. Leavitt, 3 Ala. 430; Lillard v. Puckett, 9 Baxter (Tenn.), 568; Walker v. Gilbert, 7 Sm. & M. (Miss.) 456.

ment recovered against the principal which would have been conclusive upon the surety.[1]

§ 102. **The Surety is a Creditor of the Principal.** — When the principal debtor is bankrupt, the sureties, in respect of their liability, are regarded in equity as his creditors,[2] and may retain any funds of the principal in their hands,[3] even against a *bona fide* purchaser thereof for value without notice of their rights.[4]  The surety is regarded in equity as a creditor of his principal and has all the privileges of a creditor,[5] from the time of his signing the obligation by which he is bound,[6] just as he is liable to the creditor from that time;[7] though his right of action against his principal[8] and his equity to be subrogated to the securities held by the creditor do not become complete until his payment of the debt.[9] Though the principal's liability to indemnify his surety is, previous to payment by the latter, merely contingent, it is nevertheless a debt, and will be embraced within the terms of a will made by the principal charging his real estate with the payment of his debts.[10] But when a surety is liable as such for several different debts of the same principal, the

---

[1] Farrar v. Parker, 3 Allen (Mass.), 556; Lyon v. Tallmadge, 14 Johns. (N. Y.) 501.

[2] Mace v. Wells, 7 How. 272, reversing Wells v. Mace, 17 Vt. 503; Crafts v. Mott, 5 Barb. (N. Y.) 305; Moorhead's Appeal, 32 Penn. St. 297; Walker v. Dicks, 80 Nor. Car. 263; Reitz v. People, 72 Ills. 435; Davis v. McCurdy, 50 Wisc. 569.

[3] Beaver v. Beaver, 23 Penn. St. 167; Mattingly v. Sutton, 19 W. Va. 19; McKnight v. Bradley, 10 Rich. Eq. (So. Car.) 551.

[4] Reynolds, in re, 16 N. B. R. 158; McKnight v. Bradley, 10 Rich. Eq. (So. Car.) 557; Abbey v. Van Campen, 1 Freem. Ch. (Miss.) 273; Battle v. Hart, 2 Dev. Eq. (Nor. Car.) 31.

[5] McKee u. Scobee, 80 Ky. 124;

Bragg v. Patterson, 85 Ala. 233; Lane v. Spiller, 18 N. H. 209; Williams v. Washington, 1 Dev. Eq. (Nor. Car.) 137.

[6] Scott v. Timberlake, 83 Nor. Car. 382; Keel v. Larkin, 72 Ala. 493; Sargent v. Salmon, 27 Maine, 539; Watson v. Dickens, 12 Sm. & M. (Miss.) 608; State v. Hemingway, 10 So. Rep. 575.

[7] McMillan v. Bull's Head Bank, 32 Ind. 11; Danforth v. Robinson, 80 Maine, 466; Pulsifer v. Waterman, 73 Me. 233, 238.

[8] Adams v. Tator, 57 Hun (N. Y.), 302; Huse v. Ames, 104 Mo. 91.

[9] Loughridge v. Bowland, 52 Miss. 546; Choteau v. Jones, 11 Ills. 300.

[10] Elwood v. Deifendorf, 5 Barb. (N. Y.) 398.

latter may assign a debt due to him from the surety for the security of any one of these debts that he may choose.[1] And if the surety is privy to a deed of trust which assigns a demand due from him to his principal, the assignor, and, the deed being otherwise to his advantage, makes no objection at the time to the assignment, he is taken to have waived for a compensation any equity he may have had against his debt being thus included in the trust fund so assigned.[2]

§ 103. **Surety does not lose this Right by agreeing to exonerate his Co-sureties.** — One of the sureties upon the note of a corporation, which was signed by several sureties, and was also secured to the creditor by a mortgage upon the property of the corporation, does not cease to be a surety, or lose his right of subrogation, as against the corporation, by agreeing for value with his co-sureties that he will himself pay such note; and, upon its payment by him, he will be subrogated to the rights of the mortgagee as fully as if no such agreement had been made, and may enforce the mortgage, both against the corporation and also against other creditors of the corporation holding liens junior to the mortgage.[3] No private arrangement among the co-sureties, for the distribution of the burden of their joint liability among themselves, will affect their rights against their principal.[4]

§ 104. **One who has pledged his Property for the Debt of another entitled to Subrogation.** — One who secures the payment of another's debt by a charge or mortgage upon his own property is a surety,[5] and is, upon his payment of the debt, entitled like any other surety to be subrogated to the benefit of the securities held by the creditor from the principal

---

[1] Miller v. Cherry, 4 Jones, Eq. (Nor. Car.) 197; Walker v. McKay, 2 Met. (Ky.) 294.

[2] Miller v. Cherry, supra.

[3] McDaniels v. Flower Brook Manufg. Co., 22 Vt. 274.

[4] Hook v. Richeson, 115 Ills. 431; Water Power Co. v. Brown, 23 Kans. 676.

[5] Bolton v. Salmon, 2 Ch. D. (1891) 48; Price v. Dime Savings Bank, 124 Ills. 317; Lazarus v. Henrietta Bank, 72 Tex. 354.

debtor;[1] nor will this right be affected by the fact that the charge upon the property of the surety was created by the same instrument by which the property of the principal was mortgaged to the creditor, and that this instrument provided that, upon payment by either principal or surety, the creditor should reconvey both the charge of the surety and the mortgaged lands of the principal, to be held upon the same uses as before the execution of the instrument.[2] If a wife becomes a surety for her husband by the creation of a valid lien upon her own estate for the payment of his debt, she will be entitled to the same equitable rights as would be enjoyed by any other surety,[3] and will be subrogated to the rights of the creditor against her husband's property, even against her husband's assignee in insolvency,[4] and even though the property has come to the hands of a *bona fide* purchaser from her husband, if such purchaser, but for his own negligence, would have been aware of her rights.[5] And the creditor's lien upon the property of such a surety will be discharged by any interference on his part with her right of subrogation.[6] As against her husband, she is entitled in equity to have his property first applied to the payment of the

---

[1] Lewis v. Palmer, 28 N. Y. 271; Bowker v. Bull, 1 Sim. N. s. 29; McNeale v. Reed, 7 Irish Ch. 251; Sheidle v. Weishlee, 16 Penn. St. 134; *Woodward, J.,* in Denny v. Lyon, 38 Penn. St. 98; Christner v. Brown, 16 Iowa, 130; Keel v. Levy, 19 Oreg. 450.

[2] McNeale v. Reed, 7 Irish Ch. 251; Vartie v. Underwood, 18 Barb. (N. Y.) 561.

[3] Neimcewicz v. Gahn, 3 Paige (N. Y.), 614; Gahn v. Neimcewicz, 11 Wend. (N. Y.) 312; Fitch v. Cotheal, 2 Sandf. (N. Y.) Ch. 29; Vartie v. Underwood, 18 Barb. (N. Y.) 561; Albion Bank v. Burns, 46 N. Y. 170; Smith v. Townsend, 25 N. Y. 479; Wolfe v. Banning, 3 Minn. 202; Van

Horne v. Everson, 13 Barb. (N. Y.) 526; Savage v. Winchester, 15 Gray (Mass.), 453; Gore v. Townsend, 105 Nor. Car. 228; Purvis v. Carstaphan, 73 Nor. Car. 575; Moffitt v. Roche, 77 Ind. 48; Barrett v. Davis, 104 Mo. 549; Wilcox v. Todd, 64 Mo. 388; Hubbard v. Ogden, 22 Kans. 363; Spear v. Ward, 20 Calif. 659, 674; Hassey v. Wilke, 55 Calif. 525.

[4] Aquilar v. Aquilar, 5 Madd. 414.

[5] Carley v. Fox, 38 Mich. 387.

[6] Eisenberg v. Albert, 40 Ohio St. 631; Union Ins. Co. v. Slee, 123 Ill. 57; Hubbard v. Ogden, 22 Kans. 363.

debt;[1] and this right will pass to her grantees,[2] and to her creditors and heirs.[3]

§ 105. **Extent to which Subrogation will be carried.** — The subrogation of a surety will not be carried further than is necessary for his indemnity;[4] if he buys up the security at a discount, or makes his payment in a depreciated currency, he can enforce it only for what it cost him.[5] He cannot speculate at the expense of his principal;[6] his only right is to be repaid.[7] Nor will he be subrogated for payments which, when made, were made as gifts to the principal.[8] The extent to which the remedy will be carried for the surety's indemnity will be governed by equitable considerations. A surety who had been subrogated to the rights of a landowner to whom he had been compelled to pay the debt of his principal for land which his principal, a railroad company, had taken under the right of eminent domain, was not allowed to stop the running of trains over the land as the creditor might have done, until he was repaid, because the court saw that

---

[1] Graham v. Londonderry, 3 Atk. 393; Hudson v. Carmichael, 23 L. J. Ch. 893; McFillin v. Hoffman, 42 N. J. Eq. 144; Harrall's Case, 31 N. J. Eq. 101; Shippen's Appeal, 80 Penn. St. 391; Johns v. Reardon, 11 Md. 465; Wilcox v. Todd, 64 Mo. 388; Allis v. Ware, 28 Minn. 166. *Postea*, § 114.

[2] Erie Savings Bank v. Roop, 80 N. Y. 591; Medsker v. Parker, 70 Ind. 509.

[3] Lancaster v. Evors, 10 Beav. 154; Hanford v. Bockee, 20 N. J. Eq. 101.

[4] Blake v. Traders' Bank, 149 Mass. 250; Borland's Appeal, 66 Penn. St. 470; Southall v. Farish, 85 Va. 403; Blow v. Maynard, 2 Leigh (Va.), 29.

[5] Dinkgrave's Succession, 31 La. Ann. 703; Kendrick v. Forney, 22 Gratt. (Va.) 748; Eaton v. Lambert, 1 Nebraska, 339; Martindale v. Brock, 41 Md. 571; Hall v. Cresswell, 12 Gill & J. (Md.) 36; Butler v. Butler, 8 W. Va. 674; Feamster v. Withrow, 9 W. Va. 296; Jordan v. Adams, 2 English (Ark.), 348; Crozier v. Grayson, 4 J. J. Marsh. (Ky.) 514; Miles v. Bacon, 4 J. J. Marsh. (Ky.) 457; Owings v. Owings, 3 *Id.* 590; Bonney v. Seely, 2 Wend. (N. Y.) 481.

[6] Reed v. Norris, 2 My. & Cr. 361; Gillespie v. Creswell, 12 Gill & J. (Md.) 36; Robinson v. Sherman, 2 Gratt. (Va.) 178; Coggeshall v. Ruggles, 62 Ills. 40; Hicks v. Bailey, 16 Tex. 229.

[7] Boltz's Estate, 133 Penn. St. 77; Stanford v. Connery, 84 Ga. 732; Batsell v. Richards, 80 Tex. 505; Waldrip v. Black, 74 Calif. 409.

[8] Scott v. Scott, 83 Va. 251.

this could be of no benefit to him, the company being insolvent and in the hands of a receiver, and the road being operated by a trustee merely for the accommodation of the public, and with a view to a more advantageous sale on foreclosure;[1] for equity will not do that which would be of no benefit to the party asking it, but merely a hardship to the party sought to be coerced.[2] A surety in a bond given in admiralty proceedings who has been compelled to pay the amount of a decree will be subrogated to the rights of the libellant against his principal, but not to the maritime lien which was destroyed by the bond.[3] And a surety who has paid the joint note of his principal and himself cannot reissue it, so as to bind any one but himself, without the consent of his principal.[4]

§ 106. **Surety of Surety may be subrogated, how far.** — A surety of a surety, who has paid and discharged the principal obligation, has the same equity of subrogation to the securities and remedies of the creditor as belonged to the surety for whom he was bound;[5] but he can have no greater rights than his immediate principal would have had.[6] A joint judgment having been recovered against several, one of them, who was originally only a surety, was taken on the execution, and gave a bond with a new surety to obtain his release; and it was held that this new surety, having been compelled to pay the debt, was entitled to be subrogated to the creditor's remedies against the land of the original principal,[7] although this land had been sold by the principal, and had come into the hands of a *bona fide* purchaser for value without notice of the cir-

---

[1] Hewitt, *in re*, 25 N. J. Eq. 210.

[2] Joliet & Chicago R. R. Co. *v.* Healy, 94 Ills. 416.

[3] The Robertson, 8 Biss. C. C. 180; Roberts *v.* The Huntsville, 3 Woods C. C. 386; Carroll *v.* The T. P. Leathers, 1 Newb. (Adm.) 432.

[4] Hopkins *v.* Farwell, 32 N. H. 425.

[5] Hall *v.* Smith, 5 How. 96; Rittenhouse *v.* Levering, 6 Watts & Serg. (Penn.) 190; McDaniels *v.* Flower Brook Manufg. Co., 22 Vt. 274; Elwood *v.* Deifendorf, 5 Barb. (N. Y.) 398.

[6] Putnam *v.* Tash, 12 Gray (Mass.), 121.

[7] Dodd *v.* Wilson, 4 Del. Ch. 399.

cumstances, before the service of the execution upon the original surety.[1] But the surety of a surety who has been compelled to pay the creditor cannot be subrogated to the place of the creditor for the purpose of enforcing payment from the principal if the latter has already paid his immediate surety.[2] The immediate surety can recover of the principal where the debt has been paid by his own surety, treating the payment as made by himself through the latter as his agent, where the latter holds the immediate surety for his reimbursement.[3] One who has agreed to indemnify a surety from loss will, upon carrying out his agreement, be subrogated against the principal debtor as the original surety would have been.[4]

§ 107. **How far Creditors of the Surety may be subrogated.** — Where the lands of a surety have been taken for the debt of the principal, though the subsequent judgment-creditors of the surety, who have thus lost the benefit of their lien upon his lands, have an equity to be subrogated to the lien of the judgment against the principal to the extent to which they have been deprived of the proceeds of the surety's lands by reason of the prior judgment against principal and surety,[5] yet this equity depends entirely upon the rights of the surety against the principal, and is limited to the balance of general accounts between the principal and the surety.[6] And if the surety was in form and apparently a mere joint-debtor, his creditors cannot by subrogation claim his rights as a surety so as to prejudice junior liens against the principal debtor.[7] The claim of a creditor of the surety, such creditor having been deprived of the opportunity to secure the pay-

---

[1] Leake v. Ferguson, 2 Gratt. (Va.) 419.

[2] New York Bank v. Fletcher, 5 Wend. (N. Y.) 85.

[3] Hoyt v. Wilkinson, 10 Pick. (Mass.) 31.

[4] Labeaume v. Sweeny, 17 Mo. 153.

[5] Huston's Appeal, 69 Penn. St. 485.

[6] Neff v. Miller, 8 Penn. St. 347.

[7] Indiana County Bank's Appeal, 95 Penn. St. 500.

ment of his demand by the surety's property having been taken to pay the principal's debt, will be preferred to that of an assignee of the surety, whose assignment was made after the right of the creditor had accrued.[1]

§ 108. **Creditor cannot discharge Security for his own Benefit after Payment by Surety.** — An indorser of a note which is also secured by a mortgage is entitled to look to the proceeds of the mortgaged premises for his relief;[2] and if in such a case the creditor, after receiving payment from the surety, cancels the mortgage without the surety's consent, so as to leave the land subject to a junior lien for another debt which the creditor holds against the principal debtor, the claim of the surety to have reimbursement out of the land will have priority over the creditor's junior lien.[3] The surety's right of subrogation is superior to the creditor's claim to hold the security for another debt, not covered by the agreement.[4] And one who, as surety for the second indorser of a negotiable note, has been compelled to pay the note, is entitled to a recourse against the first indorser to recover the amount which he has thus paid.[5]

§ 109. **Instances of the Application of the Doctrine of Subrogation for the Protection of Sureties.** — Several parties having united in the purchase of land and given their joint bonds for each one's share of the purchase-money to one of their number, in whom the legal title to the land was vested as their trustee, and one of them having failed to pay his share of the purchase-money, the sureties on his bond, who were his associates in the original purchase, paid it for him; and thereupon it was held that they acquired an equitable title to his share in the land, and that, until they were fully reimbursed

[1] Erb's Appeal, 2 Penrose & Watts (Penn.), 296.

[2] Fowler v. Scully, 72 Penn. St. 456; Woods v. Pittsburg Bank, 83 Penn. St. 57.

[3] Ottawa Bank v. Dudgeon, 65 Ills. 11.

[4] Perry v. Miller, 54 Iowa, 277; Simmons v. Cates, 56 Ga. 609.

[5] Chrisman v. Harman, 29 Gratt. (Va.) 494.

for their payment of his share of the purchase-money, neither
he nor those claiming under him could demand of the trustee
a conveyance of his share or a declaration of trust in his
favor.[1] A trustee appointed by a court of chancery to sell
certain land sold the same, and took the purchaser's bond
with a surety for the payment of the purchase-money, the
land not to be conveyed until the purchase-money was paid.
This purchaser soon after sold the land for the same sum
that he had agreed to pay to the trustee for it, to a sub-purchaser, who, knowing that the trustee had not been satisfied,
paid to his own grantor the whole price of the land, and received from the latter an assignment of a claim of his against
the owner of the land, which it was thought would be more
than sufficient to pay for the land. But the estate turned out
to be insolvent; and the dividend upon this claim was not sufficient to pay the purchase-money to the trustee, who accordingly withheld the conveyance from the sub-purchaser, to
whom he was ordered by the court to convey the property
upon the purchase-money being paid, and sued the surety on
the bond of the original purchaser, and recovered a judgment
for the unpaid portion of the purchase-money. The surety
then claimed that what he was thus compelled to pay should
be charged for his reimbursement upon the land in the hands
of the sub-purchaser; and it was held that unless this sub-
purchaser should pay to the surety the amount of his payment, the land, or so much of it as might be necessary,
should be sold to raise that amount; for the sub-purchaser
could not by his purchase put the surety for the original
purchase-money in a worse position than the latter would
otherwise have occupied.[2] A tract of land was sold three
times by the successive purchasers thereof, the original vendor retaining the title, and reserving a lien on the land, as
well as taking a bond with sureties for the payment of the

[1] Deitzler v. Mishler, 37 Penn. St.     [2] Ghiselin v. Fergusson, 4 Harr.
82.                                          & Johns. (Md.) 522.

purchase-money. Under these circumstances, one of these sureties advised a party to buy the land, but gave him no intimation as to the lien. The court held, that, although this advice and concealment might estop that surety from asserting any equity for his own benefit, to the prejudice of the party who purchased it upon his advice, it could not affect the rights of the first vendor, and, the purchase-money having remained unpaid upon each successive sale, that the land might be sold under the first lien, to which the sureties, who had paid the debt secured thereby, were subrogated.[1] But where the vendor had given a full title to the land sold, taking the vendee's bond with two sureties for the payment of the purchase-money, it was held, upon the insolvency and death of the vendee and one of the sureties, and after a sale of the land by a devisee of the vendee to a purchaser with notice of the circumstances, that there was no lien upon which the other surety could hold the land for his indemnification upon the bond.[2]

§ 110. **Surety's Right of Subrogation may be lost by his Waiver.** — The right of a surety to be subrogated to the benefit of the securities and remedies held by the creditor against the principal debtor may be lost by the surety's waiver.[3] If one who claims to be a surety has for a long time allowed himself to be held out as the principal debtor, and other rights have in the mean time accrued against the real principal, it is then too late for him to claim to be subrogated as a surety to the prejudice of those rights.[4] A year's delay in a similar case has been fatal to the rights of the surety, other liens having in the mean time attached upon the estate which the surety desired to hold,[5] and the delay having been

[1] Kleiser v. Scott, 6 Dana (Ky.), 137.

[2] Miller v. Miller, Phillips Eq. (Nor. Car.) 85.

[3] Midland Banking Co. v. Chambers, L. R. 4 Ch. 398, and L. R. 7 Eq. 179; Douglass's Appeal, 48 Penn. St. 223; Harbeck v. Vanderbilt, 20 N. Y. 395.

[4] Smith v. Herbin, 124 Ind. 434; Thomas v. Stewart, 117 Ind. 50; Goswiler's Estate, 3 Pen. & Watts (Penn.), 200.

[5] Gring's Appeal, 89 Penn. St. 336.

made with knowledge of the facts.[1]  Where a bill in equity
*quia timet* was filed for subrogation against persons who
might be ultimately liable, the ground of action being for
bonds given more than twenty years before the suit was
brought, it was held that the complainants had lost their
right to relief in equity by their laches in negligently lying
by until, by reason of the lapse of time, there could be no
safe determination of the matters in controversy.[2]  And just
as the surety could not recover from his principal upon his
voluntary payment of a debt barred by the statute of limitations,[3] so he will be taken to have waived his privilege of
subrogation, unless he claims it before his remedy at law
against his principal is barred by lapse of time.[4]  The right
of subrogation will be barred by the statutory period of limitation like any other right.[5]  But the mere lapse of a shorter
time is not of itself a bar to the right,[6] though the surety's
bare delay, if protracted, is evidence against him of a waiver
of his right.[7]  The surety's right of subrogation accrues upon
his payment; and as to his principal the statute then begins
to run against him,[8] and he should then call at once for the
securities if he desires to be subrogated to them.[9]  The surety

[1] See Blake *v.* Traders' Bank, 145 Mass. 13.

[2] Smith *v.* Thompson, 7 Gratt. (Va.) 112.

[3] Randolph *v.* Randolph, 3 Rand. (Va.) 490; Hatchett *v.* Pegram, 21 La. Ann. 722.

[4] Rittenhouse *v.* Levering, 6 Watts & Serg. (Penn.) 190; Fink *v.* Mahaffy, 8 Watts (Penn.), 384; Joyce *v.* Joyce, 1 Bush (Ky.), 474.  See Rucks *v.* Taylor, 49 Miss. 552.

[5] Kreider *v.* Isenbice, 123 Ind. 10; Arbogast *v.* Hays, 98 Ind. 26; Bledso *v.* Nixon, 68 Nor. Car. 521; Mitchell *v.* Mitchell, 8 Humph. (Tenn.) 359; Walker *v.* Vaudry, 4 Rob. (La.) 395; Simpson *v.* McPhail, 17 Ills. Ap. 499.

[6] Bird *v.* Louisiana Bank, 93 U. S. 96; Robertson *v.* Mowell, 66 Md. 530; Conner *v.* Howe, 35 Minn. 518.

[7] Noble *v.* Turner, 69 Md. 519.

[8] McDonald *v.* Magruder, 3 Peters, 470; Blake *v.* Traders' Bank, 145 Mass. 13; Thayer *v.* Daniels, 110 Mass. 345; Bennett *v.* Cook, 45 N. Y. 268; Samuel *v.* Zackerey, 4 Ired. Law (Nor. Car.), 377; Lowndes *v.* Pinckney, 1 Rich. Eq. (So. Car.) 155; Burton *v.* Rutherford, 49 Mo. 255; Barnsback *v.* Reiner, 8 Minn. 59; Scott *v.* Nichols, 27 Miss. 94; Reeves *v.* Pulliam, 7 Baxter (Tenn.), 119; Garrett *v.* Garrett, 27 Ala. 687; Hammond *v.* Myers, 30 Tex. 375; Junker *v.* Rush, 26 N. E. Rep. 499.

[9] Barton *v.* Moore, 45 Minn. 98.

11

has an election to seek his reimbursement either by subrogation to the remedies of the creditor or by an action against his principal upon the latter's implied promise of indemnity.[1] His failure, upon paying a debt secured by mortgage from the principal debtor, to take either a discharge or an assignment thereof has been held to bar his right to a decree for foreclosure of the mortgage by right of subrogation.[2] Indemnity received by the surety from a stranger will be regarded as cumulative to the rights which the surety already possesses.[3] One who is manifestly a surety will not be deprived of the benefit of subrogation to a mortgage-security held by the creditor, merely because he took other security from the principal,[4] which he afterwards released, and did not ask for an assignment of the mortgage immediately upon his payment of the debt which it secured.[5] But he cannot disregard the rights of other parties which have accrued in the mean time. Thus, if the vendor of land has a lien thereon for the price, a surety of the vendee who pays the price will not be subrogated to this lien, if he has taken other security from the vendee for his protection, and has without objection allowed the vendee to sell the land to another purchaser, although this security afterwards turns out to be insufficient.[6] The election of the surety to claim greater rights under an express agreement than he would acquire by subrogation is a waiver of his right to subrogation.[7] If he refuses to accept the security when offered to him by the creditor, he waives his right to demand it afterwards.[8] And if, after a surety

[1] Bowers v. Cobb, 31 Fed. Rep. 678; Hill v. Voorhies, 22 Penn. St. 68; Wernecke v. Kenyon, 66 Mo. 275.

[2] Lynn v. Richardson, 78 Maine, 367.

[3] Wesley Church v. Moore, 10 Penn. St. 273; Cornwall v. Gould, 4 Pick. (Mass.) 444; West v. Rutland Bank, 19 Vt. 403.

[4] Ballew v. Roler, 124 Ind. 557; Hancock v. Holbrook, 40 La. Ann. 54.

[5] Crawford v. Richeson, 101 Ills. 351; Gossin v. Brown, 11 Penn. St. 527.

[6] Henley v. Stemmons, 4 B. Mon. (Ky.) 131.

[7] Whitehouse v. Edwards, 37 Ch. D. 683; Gorton, in re, 40 Ch. D. 536.

[8] Hubbell v. Carpenter, 5 N. Y. 171, reversing s. c., 5 Barb. 520, and 2 Barb. 484.

for two principals has paid the debt, he takes from one of the principals a security for his reimbursement, he has been held to waive his right to the benefit of a security which had previously been given by the other principal to the creditor.[1]  If he has the means of reimbursement in his own hands, and refuses or neglects to make due application thereof, he cannot come upon another fund by way of subrogation.[2]  But a surety who has unsuccessfully attacked for alleged fraud an assignment made by his principal, the benefits of which have been accepted by the creditor, is not thereby estopped from asserting his right of subrogation to the creditor as to these benefits.[3]  Nor is it necessary to the surety's subrogation that his payment should have been coerced by an execution; his payment, though voluntarily made, will be regarded as compulsory whenever it could have been enforced.[4]

§ 111. **Surety's Right of Subrogation subject to Creditor's Rights.** — It has been held that the surety's right of subrogation to the securities held by the creditor cannot be enforced to the prejudice of an intervening charge taken by the creditor from the principal debtor in ignorance of the suretyship. Thus, where A. and B. had given to a creditor their joint and several note, secured by a mortgage of their respective estates, and then A. gave a separate mortgage of his own estate to a creditor of his own, who afterwards took an assignment of the prior mortgage, and it then appeared that B. had joined in the first note and mortgage merely as the surety of A., and B. claimed that upon paying the first debt he was entitled to be subrogated to the rights of the mortgagee, and to hold the entire mortgaged premises for his indemnity, it was held that, before B. could claim the rights of a surety against A.'s cred-

---

[1] Cornwell's Appeal, 7 Watts & Serg. (Penn.) 305.  And see Watts v. Eufaula Bank, 76 Ala. 474.

[2] *Bell, J.*, in Neff v. Miller, 8 Penn. St. 347, 351; Sharp v. Caldwell, 7 Humph. (Tenn.) 415.

[3] Motley v. Harris, 1 Lea (Tenn.), 577.

[4] McNeilly v. Cooksey, 2 Lea (Tenn.), 39; State v. Blakemore, 7 Heisk. (Tenn.) 638.

itor, he must show that the latter knew, or had the means of
knowing of the suretyship; and the court said that though a
creditor cannot tack to an existing mortgage-debt a demand
not secured by the mortgage, nor a subsequent mortgage to a
prior one as against an intervening incumbrancer, yet a mortgagee may take another mortgage, which will be valid against
an intervening incumbrance implied by equity, of which the
mortgagee had neither actual nor constructive notice.[1] But
if the creditor had known that B. was merely a surety, though
it did not appear upon the face of the papers, that would have
been sufficient.[2] Nor will a surety's subrogation to the rights
and liens of the creditor be allowed to defeat an interest acquired and held by a third person, when that interest, though
subordinate to the creditor's lien, is prior in date to the
surety's undertaking.[3] Thus, when a debtor sells property
which he had mortgaged for a debt, and then a judgment for
the debt having been obtained against him, gives a surety for
the judgment, who is afterwards compelled to pay it, this
surety cannot be subrogated to the mortgage so as to defeat
the purchaser's title, which accrued before the contract of
suretyship was entered into;[4] for the subrogation of the
surety to the creditor's means of payment rests solely upon
principles of justice and equity.[5] But the surety's subrogation will overreach all rights that have accrued since the contract of suretyship was entered into.[6]

§ 112. Surety indebted to his Principal not entitled to Subrogation against him. — The equitable right of subrogation will
not be allowed to a surety who is himself indebted to his
principal, against whom he asks to be subrogated, without

---

[1] Orvis v. Newell, 17 Conn. 97;
Budd v. Oliver, 23 Atl. Rep. 1105.

[2] Rogers v. School Trustees, 46
Ills. 428.

[3] Farmers' Bank v. Sherley, 12
Bush (Ky.), 304; Fishback v. Bodman, 14 Bush (Ky.), 117; Johnson

v. Morrison, 5 B. Mon. (Ky.) 106.
See postea, § 131 et seq.

[4] Patterson v. Pope, 5 Dana (Ky.),
241; Fishback v. Bodman, 14 Bush
(Ky.), 117.

[5] Eaton v. Hasty, 6 Nebraska, 419.

[6] Pierce v. Higgins, 101 Ind. 178.

his first satisfying such debt.[1]  A judgment against principal
and surety having been satisfied out of a sale of the surety's
lands, the surplus proceeds in court were claimed by the
principal debtor, who held the next judgment-lien on the
surety's lands, and by subsequent judgment-creditors of the
surety, who claimed, by virtue of the surety's payment, to
be subrogated to the lien of the first judgment-creditor.[2]  The
surety being also indebted on another account to the principal, and being insolvent, it was held that the payment made
out of the surety's estate could not be set off against the
principal's judgment, and that the principal had accordingly
the first right to the surplus proceeds.[3]  And if, as between
principal and surety, the payment of the debt has been assumed by the original surety, the latter cannot in equity insist
that the property of the former principal is primarily liable
for the debt,[4] any more than he could recover against his
principal at law after paying the debt;[5] nor will he have
any right of subrogation against his principal upon paying
the debt;[6] he has become the real debtor, and so cannot be
subrogated.[7]  But the surety's right of subrogation will not
be destroyed by the fact that the principal has himself become a surety upon another obligation upon which the surety
has raised the money to pay the original debt.[8]

**§ 113.  Surety's Right confined to the Contract for which he
was Surety.** — As the surety's liability is limited to the express
terms of his contract,[9] so his right of subrogation is confined

[1] Dwight v. Scranton Lumber Co.,
82 Mich. 624; Coates's Appeal, 7
Watts & Serg. (Penn.) 99.  But see
Barney v. Grover, 28 Vt. 391.

[2] See *antea*, § 107.

[3] Coates's Appeal, *supra.*

[4] Wright v. Crump, 25 Ind. 339;
Laboyteaux v. Swigart, 103 Ind. 596.

[5] Lewis v. Lewis, 92 Ills. 237.

[6] Shipley v. Fox, 69 Md. 572;
Washington, Ohio & Western R. R.

Co. v. Lewis, 83 Va. 246; Boulware
v. Hartsook, 83 Va. 679; Chaplin v.
Baker, 124 Ind. 385; Crim v. Fleming, 123 Ind. 438.

[7] *Antea*, § 46.

[8] Owen's Appeal, 11 W. N. C. 488.

[9] Ward v. Stahl, 81 N. Y. 406;
Chelmsford Co. v. Demarest, 7 Gray
(Mass.), 1; Stull v. Hance, 62 Ills. 52;
Parham v. Cobb, 9 La. Ann. 423;
Glassell v. Coleman, 94 Calif. 260.

to the rights and securities of the contract for which he was surety.[1] One who has guaranteed the payment of a promissory note by an indorser thereof will, upon paying the same, have no greater rights against the maker than the indorser himself had.[2] The bail of a defendant cannot look for reimbursement to one who was jointly liable for the original debt.[3] The surety upon a note will not by paying it acquire any rights against the parties to a former note which had been paid by the note upon which he was surety.[4] If one partner; though for the benefit of the partnership, executes a bond with a surety, this surety, on being compelled to pay the bond, acquires thereby no right of action against the other partners.[5] One who is surety both for a firm and for an individual member of the firm has no right to apply upon the individual debt funds of the firm which may come into his hands ; but if, having done so, he afterwards applies his own money to the payment of the firm debt, his rights will be the same as if he had paid the latter debt out of the partnership funds.[6] If one who has bound himself as bail for the defendant, in an action against a shipmaster for the value of property lost through the neglect of the officers and crew, is compelled to pay the amount of the judgment against the

[1] Wagner v. Elliott, 95 Penn. St. 487; Carlton v. Simonton, 94 Nor. Car. 401; McMullen v. Cathcart, 4 Rich. Eq. (So. Car.) 117; Matthews v Colburn, 1 Strobh. (So. Car.) 258; Duncan v. Lewis, 1 Duv. (Ky.) 183; Bank of England v. Tarleton, 23 Miss. 173; Gerdone v. Gerdone, 70 Ind. 62; Noble v. Murphy, 52 No. W. Rep. 148; Gunn v. Geary, 44 Mich. 615; Old v. Chambliss, 3 La. Ann. 205; Trent v. Calderwood, 2 La. Ann. 942.

[2] Dewey v. Living, 3 Allen (Mass.), 22; Putnam v. Tash, 12 Gray (Mass.), 121; Nelson v. Harrington, 16 Gray, 139.

[3] Cunningham v. Clarkson, Wright (Ohio), 217.

[4] Barnett v. Reed, 51 Penn. St. 190; Merriman v. Social Manufacturing Co., 12 R. I. 175.

[5] Leggett v. Humphreys, 21 How. 66; Tom v. Goodrich, 2 Johns. (N. Y.) 213; Bowman v. Blodgett, 2 Met. (Mass.) 308; Osborn v. Cunningham, 4 Dev. & Bat. Law (Nor. Car.), 423; Foley v. Robards, 3 Ired. Law (Nor. Car.), 177; Krafts v. Creighton, 3 Rich. Law (So. Car.), 273; Adair v. Campbell, 4 Bibb (Ky.), 13.

[6] Downing v. Linville, 3 Bush (Ky.), 472.

master, though he will be subrogated to the benefit of the
judgment so obtained, and will have the right of recourse
against the owners of the ship which the master would have
acquired by payment of the judgment, yet he will not be
subrogated to the original cause of action against both the
master and the owners of the ship.[1]  Where the accommodation acceptors of two bills of exchange received a deed of
trust as security from the drawer, and one of these bills was
taken up by giving a new note with a new surety, the surety
upon this new note, after paying it, was not allowed to share
in the benefit of the original security.[2]  If the note of a principal, with three sureties, is discharged at maturity by giving
another note with only two of the sureties, the third surety
having died before the first note fell due, the estate of the
latter will not be liable to contribute upon the insolvency of
the principal and the payment of the new note by the sureties
thereon, although when they executed the new note they
supposed that the estate of the third surety would be liable
thereon.[3]  If two executors have given a joint and several
bond for their faithful administration, and after the death of
one of them the survivor has wasted the estate, the sureties,
after satisfying a judgment recovered upon the bond against
the survivor and themselves for such waste, will have no
right of action against the estate of the deceased executor,
either for indemnity or contribution,[4] though if this executor
had lived their rights upon the bond would have been complete against him.[5]

§ 114. **Surety's Right to marshal Securities given to the same
Creditor for Separate Debts.** — Where a debtor gives to his
creditor collateral securities for the payment of the debt, and
afterwards borrows of the same creditor a further sum of

---

[1] Tardy v. Allen, 3 La. Ann. 66.
[2] Houston v. Huntsville Bank, 25 Ala. 250.
[3] Hutchings v. McCauley, 2 Dev. & Bat. Eq. (Nor. Car.) 399.

[4] Brazer v. Clark, 5 Pick. (Mass.) 96; Towne v. Ammidown, 20 Pick. (Mass.) 535.
[5] McCoun v. Sperb, 53 Hun (N. Y.), 165. *Postea,* § 202.

money, for the payment of which he gives a surety, the surety, if called upon to pay the second debt, is entitled to the surplus of the securities over the amount needed to satisfy the first debt.[1] The surety for only one loan, if he has been obliged to pay that loan, has a right, against the principal debtor or his representatives, to marshal the securities given by the principal to the creditor for several successive loans, so as to obtain reimbursement for himself out of the balance of the several securities, after the creditor is satisfied.[2] The purchaser of several lots of land having given his separate note for each lot with the same indorser, and the lots having been afterwards resold for his default in the payment of these notes, and some of the lots having brought more and some less than the first contract price, this indorser was allowed to marshal the proceeds of these sales, so as to make good the deficiency of one set by the surplus of the other.[3] So where husband and wife have given security for the husband's debt upon the property of each, she may require the creditor to sell her husband's property before resorting to hers.[4]

§ 115. **Surety cannot require the Creditor to resort first to Security.** — The right of the surety does not extend to requiring the creditor to exhaust the security given to him by the principal debtor for the payment of the debt before coming upon the surety.[5] The subrogation of the surety will never be allowed to the prejudice of the creditor's right to collect his debt;[6] the latter may proceed against the surety person-

---

[1] Praed v. Gardiner, 2 Cox Ch. Cas. 86.

[2] Heyman v. Dubois, L. R. 13 Eq. 158.

[3] Smith v. Arden, 5 Cranch, C. C. 485.

[4] Erie Savings Bank v. Roop, 80 N. Y. 591; Payne v. Burnham, 62 N. Y. 74; Neimcewicz v. Gahn, 3 Paige (N. Y.), 614; Shinn v. Smith, 79 Nor. Car. 310. *Antea*, § 104.

[5] Koehler v. Farmers' Bank, 51 Hun (N. Y.), 418; Gary v. Cannon, 3 Ired. Eq. (Nor. Car.) 64; Miller v. White, 25 So. Car. 235; Armstrong v. Poole, 30 W. Va. 666; Hardy v. Overman, 36 Ind. 549; Sayre v. McEwen, 41 Ind. 109; Roberts v. Jeffries, 80 Mo. 115; Dougherty v. Mackenzie, 34 Mo. 462; Speight v. Porter, 26 Miss. 286.

[6] New Bedford Savings Bank v.

ally, and at the same time subject the collateral security to
the payment of his debt until he has obtained full satisfaction.[1]
The creditor may proceed against the surety in the first in·
stance, or against the principal and the surety jointly, for the
satisfaction of his demand.[2]  The payee of a note may maintain an action thereon without first exhausting a mortgage-
security given by the principal.[3]  A guarantor will not be
released by the mere fact that the creditor has entered upon
the land of the principal debtor under a mortgage given to
him by the latter to secure the debt.[4]  The existence of a
judgment which is a lien upon the lands of the principal,
and on which the money might be made by issuing an execution, is no reason for refusing the creditor a recovery against
the surety.[5]  An indorser of a promissory note given as collateral security for the payment of a sum of money directed
by the order of a court of chancery to be paid by the maker
of the note on pain of attachment, has no right to require the
creditor to enforce the attachment previous to calling on him
for payment.[6]  The surety must first pay the debt, and can
then himself enforce the securities.[7]  One who in giving a
lease of land takes notes with a surety for the payment of
the rent, and also reserves in his lease the right of distress,
is not bound to resort to the right of distress, but may collect

Union Mill, 128 Mass. 27; Brough's
Estate, 71 Penn. St. 460; Anderson
v. Sharp, 44 Ohio St. 260; Fox v.
Hudson, 20 Kans. 247.

[1] Harlan v. Sweeney, 1 Lea (Tenn.),
682; Lincoln v. Bassett, 23 Pick.
(Mass.) 154; Brown v. Brown, 17
Ind. 475.

[2] Muscatine v. Miss. R. R. Co., 1
Dillon, C. C. 536; Storrs v. Engel, 3
Hughes, C. C. 414; Domestic Sewing
Machine Co. v. Saylor, 86 Penn. St.
287; Fuller v. Loring, 42 Maine, 481;
Gary v. Hignutt, 32 Md. 552.

[3] Allen v. Woodard, 125 Mass.
400; Buffalo Bank v. Wood, 71 N. Y.

405; New Orleans Canal Co. v.
Escoffie, 2 La. Ann. 830; Walker v.
Collins, 22 Tex. 189.

[4] Crocker v. Gilbert, 9 Cush.(Mass.)
131.

[5] Geddis v. Hawk, 1 Watts(Penn.),
280, reversing Hawk v. Geddis, 16
Serg. & R. (Penn.) 23; Neff's Appeal, 9 Watts & Serg. (Penn.) 36.

[6] Beardsley v. Warner, 6 Wend.
(N. Y.) 610.

[7] Buffalo Bank v. Wood, 71 N. Y.
405; Brick v. Freehold Banking Co.,
37 N. J. Law, 307; Geddis v. Hawk,
1 Watts (Penn.), 280; Hall v. Hoxsey, 84 Ills. 616.

the notes from the surety.[1]  Indeed, the right of distress has
been held to be the mere personal privilege of the landlord,
and not to pass by subrogation to the surety.[2]

§ 116. **Right of Subrogation destroyed by Application of the
Security upon the Debt.** — Although the surety is entitled to
the benefit of a security held by the creditor for the payment
of the debt, yet if the whole security has been applied upon
the debt without paying it in full, and the surety has been
compelled to make up the deficiency, he cannot then resort to
the security for subrogation or contribution;[3] for this would
so far defeat the very object, the payment of the debt, for
which the security was taken.[4]  And if the debt is paid by
the principal debtor, a mortgage held by the creditor to secure
its payment is thereby extinguished;[5] and an assignment of
it by the surety to secure money borrowed by him on his
individual account is invalid, especially if the lender knew
before such assignment that the original debt had been paid.[6]

§ 117. **Creditor's Right to apply Security as needed for his own
Protection.** — A creditor who holds against the same debtor
several securities for different debts, on which there are distinct sureties, may obtain security or satisfaction, by attachment and judgment or otherwise, of one debt in full, and yet
retain his entire claim upon the surety for the others.  Neither
law nor equity requires that such a payment shall be considered to have been made for the benefit of all the sureties
ratably.[7]  The holder of one security for different demands

[1] Hall v. Hoxsey, 84 Ills. 616; Brooks v. Carter, 36 Ala. 682.

[2] Russell, in re, 29 Ch. D. 254; Newman v. Greenville Bank, 66 Miss. 323; Wohner v. Handy, 68 Miss. 153.

[3] Sawyers v. Baker, 72 Ala. 49; Marshall v. Dixon, 82 Ga. 435; Schaeffer v. Bond, 72 Md. 501.

[4] Marchand v. Frellsen, 105 U. S. 423; Stafford v. New Bedford Savings Bank, 132 Mass. 315; Belcher v. Hartford Bank, 15 Conn. 381; Stire-walt v. Martin, 84 Nor. Car. 4; Landry v. Victor, 30 La. Ann., pt. II., 1041; Whan v. Irwin, 27 id. 706.

[5] Tarbell v. Parker, 101 Mass. 165; Shackleford v. Stockton, 6 B. Mon. (Ky.) 390.

[6] Kinley v. Hill, 4 Watts & Serg. (Penn.) 426.

[7] Shaw, C. J., in Dalton v. Wo-

may apply the security upon whichever debt he chooses, and still hold a surety upon the others.[1] And where a debtor gave to one creditor a mortgage of two funds and also a covenant by a surety, and then gave a second mortgage of one of the funds to another creditor, and, the second creditor's fund having been exhausted by part payment of the first creditor's debt, the surety paid the balance due to the first creditor and took a transfer of the first mortgage, it was held that the second creditor had a right to marshal the securities against the surety, and that the second creditor's right to be subrogated to the first fund was superior to the surety's equity.[2] Where the creditor, holding a surety for the payment of his debt, took from the debtor a mortgage to secure both this and an additional indebtedness, it was held that the surety would have no right of subrogation to this mortgage until both debts had been paid to the creditor; and the creditor was allowed to apply all the proceeds of the security upon the second indebtedness, and still to hold the surety for the first.[3] A surety upon an appeal-bond whose liability has become fixed, cannot require the creditor to apply towards the satisfaction of the bond a partial payment obtained from the property of the principal defendant, but is responsible for the unsatisfied damages arising on the appeal to the full amount of the bond.[4] If a mortgage runs jointly to the creditor and the surety, and is conditioned for the payment both of a note given by the mortgagor to the creditor and of another note given by the mortgagor and the

burn Association, 24 Pick. (Mass.) 257; Harding v. Tifft, 75 N. Y. 461; Hansen v. Rounsavell, 74 Ills. 238. But see Bridenbecker v. Lowell, 32 Barb. (N. Y.) 9.

[1] Hanson v. Manley, 72 Iowa, 48; Bryan v. Henderson, 88 Tenn. 23, 28; Mathews v. Switzler, 46 Mo. 301; s. p. in Mosher v. Hotchkiss, 3 Abbott (N. Y.), App. Dec. 326.

[2] South v. Bloxam, 2 Hem. & Mill. 457. So in Hanford v. Robertson, 47 Mich. 100. But the surety's right is not usually so much restricted. Antea, §§ 86, 111.

[3] Stamford Bank v. Benedict, 15 Conn. 437.

[4] Sessions v. Pintard, 18 How. 106; Ives v. Merchants' Bank, 12 How. 159.

surety to the creditor, the surety cannot, upon paying the
note for which he is liable, assert any rights under this mortgage against the creditor, until the creditor's other note is
paid; if the surety wishes to avail himself of the mortgage,
he must, on default of the debtor, pay the latter note also.[1]
But if several debts are secured by a mortgage given by the
principal debtor, and for some of the debts there are sureties
who are not parties to the mortgage, the mortgagee is sometimes regarded as a trustee of the sureties for the security
thus provided for their indemnity, and bound to apply a just
proportion of its proceeds upon the debts for which the sureties
are liable, operating a payment of these debts *pro tanto*, and
discharging the sureties to that extent.[2] If property is deposited with the creditor by the principal debtor, to be applied
upon an indebtedness on which there is a surety, the creditor
has no right against the surety to apply this upon another
debt on which the principal alone is liable.[3] And the proper
application, once made, cannot be afterwards changed, so as
to revive the obligation of the surety.[4]

§ 118. **Surety for Part of a Debt cannot be subrogated, while
the other Part remains unpaid.** — A surety for part of the debt
is not entitled to the benefit of a security given by the debtor
to the creditor at a different time for another part of the
debt.[5] A vendor of land took the notes of the vendee without
any other security for the payment of the purchase-money,
retaining only a lien upon the land to secure the payment of
the notes. Regarding the land as an insufficient security
he brought an action upon the first one of these notes, and
attached property of the vendee of the value of one thousand

[1] Root v. Stow, 13 Metcalf (Mass.)
5.

[2] Fielder v. Varner, 45 Ala. 429;
Cory v. Leonard, 56 N. Y. 494.

[3] Rosborough v. McAliley, 10 So.
Car. 235; Wetherell v. Joy, 40 Maine,
325, 328.

[4] Miller v. Montgomery, 31 Ills.
350.

[5] Wade v. Coope, 2 Sim. 155. See
also Grubbs v. Wysors, 32 Gratt. (Va.)
127; Parker v. Mercer, 6 How. (Miss.)
320; Welch v. Parran, 2 Gill (Md.)
320.

dollars. To secure the release of this property, the vendee gave to the vendor a bond with sureties in the sum of a thousand dollars, as security to that amount for the note upon which the suit was brought. Judgment was then rendered for the amount due upon the note. Afterwards the vendor obtained a judgment upon the third note, and sold the land upon these judgments. He applied the proceeds of this sale first upon the last judgment, and only the balance of these proceeds upon the first judgment, leaving due thereon an amount exceeding the bond. The sureties upon the bond contended that, as the first judgment was a lien upon the land sold, they had a right to be substituted as to this lien to the place of the judgment-creditor, and that as he had discharged this lien by selling the land on the executions, he had thereby discharged their liability. But it was held that they had no such right; that the doctrine of subrogation did not apply to the case; that it was not the case of a surety asking to be substituted to the place of a creditor who had collateral security for the debt, but of a surety for one part of the debt asking to be substituted for the creditor in relation to a security which the creditor had the right to apply upon another part of his debt, when the effect would be to deprive the creditor of his resources, and cause him a partial loss of his demand.[1] But this rule means only that the surety's creditor must be satisfied: if a mortgage is made to two different mortgagees to secure their respective demands against the same debtor, a surety to one of the mortgagees for his demand who pays the same, being the whole amount due to this creditor, will be subrogated to the same *pro rata* interest in the mortgage which was possessed by the creditor whom he has paid.[2]

§ 119. **Surety discharged by Creditor's giving up Security to which he would be subrogated.** — As the surety has an interest

---

[1] Crump *v.* McMurtry, 8 Mo. 408; Vance *v.* Monroe, 4 Gratt. (Va.) 52.

[2] Lynch *v.* Hancock, 14 So. Car. 66.

in every security which the creditor holds against the principal debtor, whether the surety has known of its existence or
not, so, if the creditor interferes with the surety's right of
subrogation by parting with any such security without the
consent of the surety, the surety is thereby discharged to the
extent of the value of such security.[1] Not only an actual
parting with the security, but any dealing with it such that the
surety cannot have the benefit of it in the same condition in
which it existed in the creditor's hands, will have this effect.[2]
The surety is entitled to the benefit of all the securities in
the hands of the creditor; and if any of these are lost by the
creditor's acts or neglect, the surety is discharged to the
extent to which the acts of the creditor may have prejudiced
his recourse for the reimbursement of what he may be obliged
to pay under his contract of suretyship,[3] but only to this extent.[4] The surety will not be discharged by what cannot
injure him.[5] Accordingly, the creditor will not discharge the
surety by making an exchange of securities with the principal
debtor, whereby he obtains a more valuable security than he
gives up.[6] Any affirmative act of the creditor by which a
security of which the surety might have availed himself is

[1] Wulff v. Jay, L. R. 7 Q. B. 756,
762; Bechervaise v. Lewis, L. R. 7
C. P. 372, 377; Fitchburg Savings
Bank v. Torrey, 134 Mass. 239; Grow
v. Garlock, 97 N. Y. 81; Griswold v.
Jackson, 2 Edw. Ch. (N. Y.) 461;
Fegley v. McDonald, 89 Penn. St.
128; Smith v. McLeod, 3 Ired. Eq.
(Nor. Car.) 390; Ruble v. Norman,
7 Bush (Ky.), 582; Dillon v. Russell,
5 Nebraska, 484; Burr v. Boyer, 2
Nebraska, 265; Allen v. Henley, 2
Lea (Tenn.), 141.

[2] Pledge v. Buss, Johns. (Eng.
Ch.) 663; Hutchinson v. Woodwell,
107 Penn. St. 509; Mellendy v. Austin, 69 Ills. 15; Foss v. Chicago, 34
Ills. 488; Johnson v. Young, 20 W.

Va. 614; Roberson v. Tonn, 76 Tex.
535; Hubbard v. Pace, 34 Ark. 80;
Lafayette County v. Hixon, 69 Mo.
581; Cordaman v. Malone, 63 Ala.
556.

[3] Nichols v. Burch, 128 Ind. 324;
Armor v. Amis, 4 La. Ann. 192;
Pratt's Succession, 16 La. Ann. 357;
Chaffe v. Taliaferro, 58 Miss. 544.

[4] Blydenburgh v. Bingham, 38 N.
Y. 371; Dobson v. Chambers, 79 Nor.
Car. 142; Barrow v. Shields, 13 La.
Ann. 57.

[5] Cambridge Savings Bank v.
Hyde, 131 Mass. 77; Heath v. Griswold, 18 Blatchf. C. C. 555.

[6] Thomas v. Cleveland, 33 Mo.
126.

put out of the latter's reach operates as a discharge of the surety *pro tanto*,[1] but only *pro tanto*.[2] And this principle is now generally extended to securities taken by the creditor after the contract of suretyship has been made,[3] although it has been determined in England, contrary to the usual doctrine,[4] that the creditor is not bound to retain for the protection of the surety securities for the debt which he may have acquired from the principal debtor subsequently to the contract of suretyship, and which, while the creditor holds them, the surety does not call upon him to enforce; and that a creditor who, having taken a further security from the principal after the contract of suretyship was made, afterwards parts with that security, does not thereby discharge the surety, either wholly or *pro tanto*.[5]

§ 120. **Creditor held to Responsibilities of Trustee for Surety.** — The creditor who, holding the engagement of a surety, takes also from the principal debtor collateral security for the payment of the debt, is bound to hold the property which he so takes in trust, not only for his own benefit, but also for the protection of the surety.[6] He must act with good faith towards the surety as his *cestui que trust*, and hold the fund fairly and impartially for the benefit of the surety as well as of himself. He must account to the surety for the value of the property, not only if he parts with it, or surrenders it without the consent of the surety, or does any affirma-

---

[1] Allen *v.* O'Donald, 23 Fed. Rep. 573; Philbrook *v.* McEwen, 29 Ind. 347; Guild *v.* Butler, 127 Mass. 386; Marbury *v.* Ehlen, 72 Md. 206; Watson *v.* Reed, 4 Baxter (Tenn.), 49; Cullum *v.* Emanuel, 1 Ala. 23.

[2] Allen *v.* O'Donald, 28 Fed. Rep. 17; Bedwell *v.* Gephart, 67 Iowa, 44.

[3] Scanland *v.* Settle, Meigs (Tenn.), 169; Pearl St. Society *v.* Imlay, 23 Conn. 10; May *v.* White, 40 Iowa, 246; Springer *v.* Toothaker, 43 Maine,

391; Sherradeen *v.* Parker, 24 Iowa, 28; Nelson *v.* Williams, 2 Dev. & Bat. Eq. (Nor. Car.) 118.

[4] *Antea*, §§ 86, 87.

[5] Newton *v.* Chorlton, 10 Hare, 646.

[6] Kesler *v.* Linker, 82 Nor. Car. 456; Pipkin *v.* Bond, 5 Ired. Eq. (Nor. Car.) 91; Holland *v.* Johnson, 51 Ind. 346; Willis *v.* Davis, 3 Minn. 17; McMullen *v.* Hinkle, 39 Miss. 142; Hardin *v.* Eames, 5 Ills. App. 153.

tive act in violation of the trust upon which he holds it,[1] but also for his negligence, or omission to perform any act, whereby the surety's recourse to the fund is prejudiced.[2] Though mere non-action by the creditor will not ordinarily release the surety,[3] yet, if it is such non-action as to render unproductive some collateral security, such as a mortgage, held for the payment of the debt, this will be an available defence for the surety, at least *pro tanto*.[4] If he waives his security by proving his claim as an unsecured one against the estate of the principal debtor, in bankruptcy, this will discharge the surety to the extent of the value of the security thus released,[5] though it has been held that the creditor is none the less entitled to exercise his option of surrendering the security and proving in full against the principal's estate because he holds a surety, and that the surety will not be discharged by such proof.[6] The right of the creditor against

[1] Otis v. Von Storch, 15 R. I. 41; Humphrey v. Hayes, 94 N. Y. 594; Wharton v. Duncan, 83 Penn. St. 40; Sample v. Cochran, 84 Ind. 594, and 82 *Id.* 260; Nelson v. Munch, 28 Minn. 314.

[2] Strange v. Fooks, 4 Giff. 408; Watts v. Shuttleworth, 5 Hurl. & Nor. 235; s. c., on error, 7 Hurl. & Nor. 353; Taylor v. Scott, 62 Ga. 39; Payne v. Commercial Bank, 6 Sm. & M. (Miss.) 24; Phares v. Barbour, 49 Ills. 370; Brockman v. Sieverling, 6 Ills. App. 512; Sherradeen v. Parker, 24 Iowa, 28; Saulet v. Trepagnier, 2 La. Ann. 427.

[3] Trent Navigation Co. v. Hurley, 10 East, 34; Allen v. Brown, 124 Mass. 77; Watertown Ins. Co. v. Simmons, 131 Mass. 85; Chapin v. Livermore, 13 Gray (Mass.), 561; Taylor v. State, 73 Md. 208; Kelser v. Linker, 82 Nor. Car. 456; Cherry v. Miller, 7 Lea (Tenn.), 305; Grisard v. Hinson, 50 Ark. 229; McKecknie v. Ward, 58 N. Y. 541; Clark v. Sickler, 64 N. Y.

231; Schroeppell v. Shaw, 3 N. Y. 446; Deck v. Works, 18 Hun (N. Y.), 266; Canton Bank v. Reynolds, 13 Ohio, 84; Kirby v. Studebaker, 15 Ind. 45; Vason v. Beall, 58 Ga. 500; Pickens v. Finney, 12 Sm. & M. (Miss.) 468; Clopton v. Spratt, 52 Miss. 251; Buckalew v. Smith, 44 Ala. 638; Humphreys v. Crane, 5 Calif. 173; Parker v. Alexander, 2 La. Ann. 188; Murrell v. Scott, 51 Tex. 520; Hunter v. Clark, 28 Tex. 159; Terrel v. Townsend, 6 Tex. 149.

[4] Lumsden v. Leonard, 55 Ga. 374; City Bank v. Young, 43 N. H. 457; Russell v. Weinberg, 2 Abbott, New Cas. (N. Y.) 422; Ramsey v. Westmoreland Bank, 2 Pen. & Watts (Penn.), 203; Gillespie v. Darwin, 6 Heisk. (Tenn.) 21; Merchants' Bank v. Cordeviolle, 4 Rob. (La.) 506.

[5] Jones v. Hawkins, 60 Ga. 52. See Phoenix Manufg. Co. v. Fuller, 3 Allen (Mass.), 441.

[6] Rainbow v. Juggins, 5 Q. B. Div. 138; s. c. affirmed on appeal, 5 Q. B.

the surety will be destroyed by making such a compromise with the principal debtor that the surety cannot for his reimbursement be subrogated to the creditor's rights;[1] but a compromise which preserves the privileges of the surety will not have this effect.[2]

§ 121. **Laches of Creditor resulting in Loss of Security may discharge Surety.** — Accordingly it has been held that the creditor's failure to record a mortgage or conveyance of property which has been given to him by the principal debtor as a security for the debt, whereby the benefit of the security is lost both to the creditor and the surety, will discharge the surety to the extent of the value of the property;[3] for the loss must be borne by the person to whose neglect it was due.[4] This has, however, been sometimes denied on the ground that the creditor's liability is for positive acts only, not for mere passive negligence;[5] but it is generally considered that the creditor should be held responsible for the loss of any security arising from his wrongful acts, whether of omission or of commission.[6] If, however, the creditor's neglect has not

---

Div. 422. And see St. Albans Bank. v. Wood, 53 Vt. 491.

[1] Hopkirk v. McConico, 1 Brock. C. C. 220; Morris Canal Co. v. Van Vorst, 21 N. J. Law, 100; Renick v. Ludington, 14 W. Va. 367

[2] Mueller v. Dobschuetz, 89 Ills. 176; Kenworthy v. Sawyer, 125 Mass. 28; Tobey v. Ellis, 114 Mass. 120; Hutchins v. Nichols, 10 Cush. (Mass.) 299; Sohier v. Loring, 6 Id. 537.

[3] Capel v. Butler, 2 Sim. & Stu. 457; Wulff v. Jay, L. R. 7 Q. B. 756; Teaff v. Ross, 1 Ohio St. 469; Burr v. Boyer, 2 Nebraska, 265; Atlanta National Bank v. Douglass, 51 Ga. 205; Toomer v. Dickerson, 37 Ga. 428.

[4] Ducker v. Rapp, 67 N. Y. 464; Muirhead v. Kirkpatrick, 21 Penn. St. 237; Beale v. The Bank, 5 Watts

(Penn.), 529; Harper v. Kean, 11 Serg. & R. (Penn.)280; Simmons v. Tongue, 3 Bland Ch. (Md.) 341; Curry v. Mack, 90 Ills. 606; Lyon v. Huntingdon Bank, 12 Serg. & R. (Penn.) 61; Russell v. Hester, 10 Ala. 536.

[5] Wasson v. Hodshire, 108 Ind. 26; N. Y. Exchange Bank v. Jones, 9 Daly (N. Y.), 248; Philbrooks v. McEwen, 29 Ind. 347; Hampton v. Levy, 1 McCord Eq. (So. Car.) 107.

[6] Douglass v. Reynolds, 7 Peters, 113; Gettysburg Bank v. Thompson, 3 Grant (Pa. Cas.), 114; Shippen v. Clapp, 36 Penn. St. 89; Kemmerer v. Wilson, 31 Penn. St. 110; Sellers v. Jones, 22 Penn. St. 423; Lang v. Brevard, 3 Strobh. Eq. (So. Car. 59; Smith v. McKean, 99 Ind. 101; Wendell v. Highstone, 52 Mich. 552; Jennison v. Parker, 7 Mich. 355; Slevin

12

resulted in the loss of any means of payment to which the
surety, on discharging the debt, would have the right to be
subrogated, the creditor's claim upon him will not be affected.[1]   And as laches cannot be imputed to the government,[2] the failure of a county court to take a mortgage on
unincumbered real estate, as was required by statute, to
secure the payment of school-money loaned, will not discharge a surety for the loan.[3]   And though a rule of court
requires that a recognizance should be taken and recorded
for the payment of the rent of property in charge of the
court, a failure of the clerk of the court to record such a
recognizance, whereby a lien for the rent upon the property
of the lessee is lost, will not discharge a surety for the payment of the rent from his liability.[4]   So, where an order of
court, made in pursuance of a statute, provided that a mortgage should be taken for the purchase-money of property sold
at an administrator's sale, a surety for the purchase-money was
not released by the fact that, contrary to his expectation, no
such mortgage was taken, no misrepresentation having been
made to him.[5]   But the creditor is not required to do more
for the protection of the surety than to preserve the force
and validity of the security furnished by the debtor; it is
enough if he is able to produce the security in as good condition as he received it.[6]

v. Morrow, 4 Ind. 425; Lamberton v.
Windom, 18 Minn. 506; *Crounse, J.*,
in Burr v. Boyer, 2 Nebraska, 265;
Chichester v. Mason, 7 Leigh (Va.),
244; Lee v. Baldwin, 10 Ga. 208;
Pickens v. Yarborough, 26 Ala. 417;
Noland v. Clark, 10 B. Mon. (Ky.)
239; Wood v. Morgan, 5 Sneed
(Tenn.). 79; Hill v. Bourcier, 29 La.
Ann. 841; Watson v. Allcock, 1 Sm.
& Giff. 319; s. c., on appeal, 4 De G.,
M. & G. 242.

[1] Pottawattamie Co. v. Taylor, 47
Iowa, 520.

[2] Osborne v. United States, 19
Wall. 577, 581; Ganssen v. United
States, 97 U. S. 584.

[3] Marion County v. Moffett, 15
Mo. 604.

[4] Jephson v. Maunsell, 10 Irish Eq.
38, and (on appeal) 132.

[5] Wornell v. Williams, 19 Tex.
180. See Reynolds v. Dechaums, 24
Tex. 174.

[6] Clark v. Young, 1 Cranch, 181;
Ormsby v. Fortune, 16 Serg. & R.
(Penn.) 302; Trotter v. Crockett, 2
Porter (Ala.), 401.

§ 122. **Creditor's Discharge of Levy or Attachment on the Property of the Principal, how far a Discharge of the Surety.** — If the creditor releases the levy of an execution for the debt upon property of the principal sufficient to satisfy the debt, this will discharge the surety;[1] for this is a security which the surety can require the creditor to preserve.[2] Much less can the creditor, to the injury of the surety, discharge the levy, so as to let in another debt due to himself,[3] or by assigning his judgment to another person enable the latter, by discharging the levy, to save another debt out of the property, to the loss of the surety.[4] A release of property upon which the judgment is a lien will have the same effect as if the property had been actually levied upon.[5] If the lien of the judgment upon the land of the principal debtor has been lost by the creditor's having proved it as an unsecured debt against the estate of the principal in bankruptcy, this will discharge the surety to the extent of the injury thereby resulting to him, but only to this extent.[6] And it has been held that after a levy upon property of the principal, a delivery of such property by the sheriff to the principal debtor will discharge the surety to the extent of the value of this property; for if the creditor was not in fault, the sheriff will be liable to him, and the surety should be released; if the

---

[1] Spangler v. Sheffer, 69 Penn. St. 255; McKenzie v. Wiley, 27 W. Va. 658; Farmers' Bank v Kingsley, 2 Doug. (Mich.) 379; Hutton v. Campbell, 10 Lea (Tenn.), 170; Stockard v. Granberry, 3 Id. 668; Holt v. Manier, 1 Id. 488; Winston v. Yeargin, 50 Ala. 340; Mulford v. Estudillo, 23 Calif. 94.

[2] Stephens v. Monongahela Bank, 88 Penn. St. 157; Shutts v. Fingar, 100 N. Y. 539, 546; Spring v. George, 50 Hun (N. Y.). 227; Day v. Ramey, 40 Ohio St. 446; Moorman v. Wood, 117 Ind. 144; Cooper v. Wilcox, 2 Dev. & Bat. Eq. (Nor. Car.) 90; Winston v. Yeargin, 50 Ala. 340;

Curan v. Colbert, 3 Ga. 239; Brown v. Riggins, 3 Ga. 405; Morley v. Dickinson, 12 Calif. 561; Moss v. Pettingill, 3 Minn. 217; Harrison Machine Works v. Templeton, 82 Tex. 443; Jenkins v. McNeese, 34 Tex. 189.

[3] McMullen v. Hinkle, 39 Miss. 142.

[4] Nelson v. Williams, 2 Dev. & Bat. Eq. (Nor. Car.) 118.

[5] Holt v. Bodey, 18 Penn. St. 207; Hollingsworth v. Tanner, 44 Ga. 11; McMullen v. Hinkle, 39 Miss. 142; Robeson v. Roberts, 20 Ind. 155.

[6] Jones v. Hawkins, 60 Ga. 52.

creditor was in fault, then *a fortiori* the surety should be released,[1] though the doctrine is not commonly carried to this
extent.[2]  But the mere failure of the officer through negligence to make the money out of the property of the principal
will not discharge the surety.[3]  If the delay or dismissal of
the levy does not annul the lien of the judgment upon the
property, then, as the rights of the surety are not thereby
affected, he will not be discharged from his liability;[4] a
mere suspension of execution will not discharge the surety,[5]
unless it is the result of an agreement of the creditor with
the principal debtor not to issue execution, or not to attempt
collection from him.[6]  Some act of interference with the
surety's right of subrogation to a security or a remedy must
be shown to operate his discharge by reason of the creditor's
neglect in pursuing the principal or his property.[7]  The lien
of an attachment for the debt obtained by the creditor upon
the property of the principal debtor is a security for the
debt[8] which will inure to the benefit of the surety; and its
discharge will release the surety, at least *pro tanto.*[9]  Some
courts have indeed held that the release by the creditor of an
attachment upon the property of the principal will not dis-

[1] Lumsden v. Leonard, 55 Ga. 374;
Ramsey v. Westmoreland Bank, 2 Pen.
& W. (Penn.) 203; Lackey v. Steere,
121 Ills. 598.

[2] Raddy  v.  Whitney, 4 E. D.
Smith (N. Y ), 378.

[3] Kindt's Appeal, 102 Penn. St.
441; Moss v. Craft, 10 Mo. 720;
Bank of Alabama v. Godden, 15 Ala.
616; Grieff v. Steamboat Stacy, 12
La. Ann. 8.

[4] Wyley v. Stanford, 22 Ga. 385;
Summerhill v. Tapp, 52 Ala. 227;
Ambler v. Leach, 15 W. Va. 677.

[5] Wilson v. Eads, Hempst. 284;
Brown v. Chambers, 63 Tex. 131;
Hetherington v. Mobile Bank, 14 Ala.
68; Crawford v. Gaulden, 33 Ga. 173;
Jerauld v. Trippett, 62 Ind. 122;

Manice v. Duncan, 12 La. Ann. 715;
Humphrey v. Hitt, 6 Gratt. (Va.)
509; Sharp v. Fagan, 3 Sneed (Tenn.),
541.

[6] Evans v. Raper, 74 Nor. Car.
639; Sterne v. Vincennes Bank, 79
Ind. 549; Blaser v. Bundy, 15 Ohio
St. 57; Storms v. Thorn, 3 Barb.
(N. Y.) 314.

[7] Jackson v. Patrick, 10 So. Car.
197; Dills v. Cecil, 4 Bush (Ky.),
579.

[8] Cook, *in re*. 2 Story, C. C. 376.

[9] Templeton v. Shakley, 107 Penn.
St. 370; Springer v. Toothaker, 43
Maine, 381; Maquoketa v. Willey,
35 Iowa, 323; Ashby v. Smith, 9
Leigh (Va.), 164; Missouri Bank
v. Matson, 24 Mo. 333.

charge a surety for the debt, because the creditor is not bound to prosecute a suit or to use any active diligence to obtain payment from the principal;[1] but no satisfactory reason has ever been given why the release of an attachment lien upon the property of the principal should be distinguished from that of any other lien.[2] The mere failure, however, of the creditor to take out and levy an execution[3] or to prosecute a suit which he has commenced against the principal for the debt, no security having been obtained therein, will not release the surety.[4] It has been held that this doctrine of the release of the surety will not be applied in favor of one of the joint makers of an obligation who was in fact a surety for the other makers; for that they were all principal debtors as to the creditor, and that the relation of suretyship existed only as between themselves:[5] but elsewhere it is held to be immaterial whether or not the creditor at the time that he releases the property, knows of the relation of his debtors among themselves as principal and surety; if he in fact releases the property of the principal, he does so at his peril.[6]

§ 128. **Creditor bound to retain Money or Property of the Principal rightfully in his Hands.** — Whenever the creditor has

---

[1] Somersworth Savings Bank v. Worcester, 76 Maine, 327; Herrick v. Orange County Bank, 27 Vt. 584; Baker v. Marshall, 16 Vt. 522; Montpelier Bank v. Dixon, 4 Vt. 587; Carr v. Sterling, 114 N. Y. 558; Morrison v. Citizens' Bank, 65 N. H. 253; Barney v. Clark, 46 N. H. 514; Bellows v. Lovell, 5 Pick. (Mass.) 307.

[2] See Green v. Mann, 76 Ga. 246; Hollingsworth v. Tanner, 44 Ga. 11; Freanor v. Yingling, 37 Md. 491; State Bank v. Edwards, 20 Ala. 512; Dixon v. Ewing, 3 Hammond (Ohio), 280; Hurd v. Spencer, 40 Vt. 581.

[3] Knight v. Charter, 22 W. Va. 422; Charlotte Bank v. Homesley, 99 Nor. Car. 531; Anderson v. Lith-

go, 5 Baxter (Tenn.), 603; Fox v. Hudson, 20 Kans. 247; Thompson v. Robinson, 34 Ark. 44.

[4] Somerville v. Marbury, 7 Gill & Johns. (Md.) 275; Richards v. Commonwealth, 40 Penn. St. 146; Manchester Bank v. Bartlett, 13 Vt. 315; Creath v. Sims, 5 Howard, 192.

[5] Patterson v. Brock, 14 Mo. 473; Shriver v. Lovejoy, 32 Calif. 574. And see Pintard v. Davis, 21 N. J. Law, 632; McCall v. Evans, 2 Brev.. (So. Car.) 3.

[6] Artcher v. Douglass, 5 Denio (N. Y.), 509; Gipson v. Ogden, 100 Ind. 20; Cates v. Thayer, 93 Ind. 156; Holt v. Bodey, 18 Penn. St. 207.

in his hands money or property of the principal debtor, which
he may rightfully retain and apply to the payment of the
debt, without violating any duty or subjecting himself to any
action, the surety may require it to be so applied;[1] and if
the creditor, instead of retaining it, suffers it to pass into
the possession of the principal, the surety is thereby to that
extent discharged;[2] but this must be property on which the
creditor has a lien, to which the surety, on payment by him,
can be subrogated.[3] Thus, a corporation which has the
option to prevent the transfer of stock by its shareholders
who are indebted to it, but has never exercised that option,
will not lose its right to hold a surety for an indebtedness of
one of its stockholders by allowing the latter to transfer his
stock, the surety never having called upon the corporation to
enforce its possible lien.[4] A creditor who holds a judgment
against principal and surety does not release the surety by
employing the principal to do work for him, and then paying
the principal for such work in accordance with an agreement
to do so, instead of setting it off against his judgment.[5]
Nor will he discharge the surety by purchasing property of
the principal and paying him for it, before the debt for
which the surety is liable becomes due and payable.[6]  Where,

[1] Redman v. Turner, 65 Nor. Car.
445; Allen v. Smitherman, 6 Ired.
Eq. (Nor. Car.) 341; Henderson v.
Huey, 45 Ala. 275.

[2] Law v. East India Co., 4 Vesey,
824; Kinnaird v. Webster, 10 Ch.
Div. 139; Bixby v. Barklie, 26 Hun
(N Y.), 275; Brown v. Rathburn,
10 Oreg. 158; Jones v. Findley, 84
Ga. 52; Crim v. Fleming, 101 Ind.
154; Kiessig v. Allspaugh, 91 Calif.
231; Spalding v. Bank of Susque-
hanna, 9 Penn. St. 28; Richards v.
Commonwealth, 40 Penn. St. 146.

[3] Tenant v. Tenant, 110 Penn. St.
478; Clow v. Derby Coal Co., 98

Penn. St. 432; McShane v. Howard
Bank, 73 Md. 135; Street v. Old
Town Bank, 67 Md. 421; Coombs v.
Parker, 17 Ohio, 289; Foster v. Gas-
ton, 123 Ind. 96; Ætna Bank v.
Hollister, 55 Conn. 188; Glazier v.
Douglass, 32 Conn. 393; Beaubien
v. Stoney, Speers Eq. (So. Car.) 508;
Taylor v. Jeter, 23 Mo. 244; Good-
acre v Skinner, 47 Kans. 575.

[4] Perrine v. Mobile Ins. Co., 22
Ala. 575.

[5] Hollingsworth v. Tanner, 44 Ga.
11.

[6] Echols o. Head, 68 Ga. 152;
Higdon v. Bailey, 26 Ga. 426.

after the contract of suretyship had been made, the principal
debtor gave to the creditor, as new security, a mortgage of real
estate, under an agreement that the creditor should surrender this mortgage when the debtor should furnish other sufficient security in its place, and afterwards, on the debtor's
furnishing the indorsement of a responsible person, the creditor gave up this mortgage, it was held that this surrender of
a security did not release the original surety, because the
creditor, under the agreement by which he acquired it, had
no right to retain it after other sufficient security had been
furnished.[1] So, where principal and surety were indebted
to a bank on a note which was overdue, and the principal
deposited more than the amount of the note with the bank,
on the express agreement that this deposit should be applied
to meet certain checks which were to be drawn against it,
the bank's application of this deposit to the payment of such
checks would not release the surety.[2] And the surrender by
the creditor of a forged or fraudulent bond or other similar
security given to him by the principal debtor, which could
not have been enforced against the obligor therein, will not
release the surety.[3] In all these cases, if the creditor had
preserved the · property or means of payment in his own
hands, and then collected the debt from the surety, the latter
would have had no right of subrogation to these resources;
and therefore he was not released by their surrender. Even
a payment made to the creditor by the principal debtor, if
afterwards avoided and recovered back as a fraudulent preference, has been held not to operate a discharge of the surety.[4]
But since, if the principal debtor were insolvent, his set-off
against the creditor would be available to the surety,[5] it has
been held that an insurance company holding the note of a

---

[1] Pearl St. Society v. Imlay, 23
Conn. 10. So in Adams v. Dutton,
57 Vt. 515; Phœnix Ins. Co. v. Hol-
loway, 51 Conn. 310.

[2] Wilson v. Dawson, 52 Ind. 513.

[3] Loomis v. Fay, 24 Vt. 240.

[4] Petty v. Cook, L. R. 6 Q. B.
790.

[5] Antea, § 101; Walsh v. Colquitt,
64 Ga. 740.

deceased policy-holder for money lent to him, and knowing that his estate is insolvent, is bound to retain the money due on the note out of the amount payable to the administrator of the deceased upon the policy; and its neglect so to do will discharge a surety upon the note.[1]

§ 124. **Neglect of a Bank to apply Deposits of the Principal upon his Note, how far a Release of the Surety.** — It has been held that the neglect of a bank to apply the funds of the principal debtor deposited with itself to the payment of his note due to the bank will discharge the sureties and indorsers upon such note, on the ground that the bank had a lien upon these funds for the payment of the note, which it might have enforced, and which therefore the surety could require it to exercise for his protection.[2] This has, however, been denied on the ground that such appropriation is purely optional with the bank,[3] which cannot be compelled to violate the terms upon which the money was obviously placed in the bank, for the payment to the depositor's checks.[4] The bank being the absolute owner of the money deposited, and being a mere debtor to the depositor for the balance of his account, holds no property in which the depositor has any title or right of which a surety on an independent debt of the depositor to the bank can avail himself by subrogation.[5] The true principle is laid down in an English case,[6] that if the circumstances show that a bond given by a depositor to a bank was intended

---

[1] White v. Life Association of America, 63 Ala. 419.

[2] Kinnaird v. Webster, 10 Ch. Div. 139; German Bank v. Foreman, 138 Penn. St. 474; Commercial Bank v. Henninger, 105 Penn. St. 496; McDowell v. Wilmington Bank, 1 Harringt. (Del.) 369; Dawson v. Real Estate Bank, 5 Pike (Ark.), 283.

[3] Antea, §§ 92, 123.

[4] Newburg Bank v. Smith, 66 N. Y.

271; Fishkill Bank v. Speight, 47 N. Y. 668; Steiner v. Erie Savings Co., 98 Penn. St. 591; Grissom v. Commercial Bank, 87 Tenn. 350; Martin v. Mechanics' Bank, 6 Harr. & Johns. (Md.) 235; Voss v. German Bank, 83 Ills. 599.

[5] Mahaiwe Bank v. Peck, 127 Mass. 298, 301; Lafayette Bank v. Hill, 76 Ind. 223.

[6] Henniker v. Wigg, 4 Q. B. (Ad. & El. N. s.) 792.

to be a continuing security, the sureties are bound by that intention, and cannot insist upon such an application. Nor can the principal debtor require a bank holding deposi   of the surety to apply them upon the debt.[1]

§ 125. **Rights of a Surety who has paid the Debt in Ignorance of the Creditor's Discharge of a Security.** — When a creditor makes an agreement whereby a security is made valueless to a surety who is entitled to be subrogated thereto, and the surety, in ignorance of such agreement, pays the debt to the creditor after judgment recovered against him by the latter, the surety may appropriate any security taken by the creditor in lieu of that so abandoned,[2] or he may recover from the creditor the value of the security which the creditor has thus made valueless to him. This doctrine was laid down under the following circumstances: The Kingston Bank discontinued a suit which it had brought against the maker and indorsers of a promissory note, upon the execution of a bond by three of the parties to the note, for the payment of the amount due thereon in eight months; and this bond was delivered on a secret agreement that the bank would endeavor to collect the amount of the note from those parties who were only liable as sureties thereon, though the primary obligation was upon the obligors in the bond and the other parties to the note. The sureties upon the note, being ignorant of this condition, afterwards paid a judgment recovered against them by the bank for the same debt, and the bank transferred the bond to them; and it was held that the bond having, by reason of the condition made when it was delivered, become satisfied when the bank received payment from the sureties, the latter were in equity entitled to recover back from the bank whatever they had paid on the judgment.[3] But if after the surety has paid the debt to the creditor the latter col-

---

[1] Citizens' Bank v. Carson, 32 Mo. 191.

[2] Corey v. Leonard, 56 N. Y. 494.

[3] Chester v. Kingston Bank, 16 N. Y. 336.

lects it again of the principal debtor, the surety cannot then
recover back his payment, because this, when made, was
rightfully received by the creditor.[1]

§ 126. **Instances where Surety discharged by Creditor's Interference with his Right of Subrogation.** — The vendor of slaves
sold in a lump for a round sum, received from the purchaser
a note for the price, indorsed by a third person as surety for
the payment thereof, and subsequently repurchased some of
the slaves from his vendee; and it was held that as the vendor's right of rescission, or lien upon the property for the
price, was indivisible, and could not be exercised upon merely
a part of the property which had been sold in a lump for a
round sum, he had, by his repurchase, destroyed the surety's
right of subrogation to this privilege, and so released the
latter from his liability.[2]  The creditor, having recovered a
judgment for the debt against the principal debtor, assigned
the same to a third party, together with certain property
which had already been sold on the execution and bid in
by the creditor, reserving, however, the right to enforce a
judgment which he had also obtained against a surety for a
part of the same debt.   At the same time he gave to the principal a receipt, in which he agreed not to enforce against the
latter any claims on the judgment or on the original debt.
It was held that by this arrangement the creditor had in
effect released the principal debtor from all further obligation to pay that part of the debt for which the surety was
liable, and accordingly had exonerated the surety also.[3]  A
builder agreed to erect a building, for which he was to receive
specified sums during the progress of the work, and the
balance of the agreed price sixty days after the completion
of the building, and gave a surety for the proper performance

[1] Dalton v. Woburn Agricultural
Association, 24 Pick. (Mass.) 257.
[2] Hereford v. Chase, 1 Rob. (La.)
212.

[3] Hubbell v. Carpenter, 5 Barb.
(N. Y.) 520.

of his contract. The building having been completed, the owner, although he had received notice of various mechanics' liens, paid the builder the balance of the contract-price before it was due under the contract. He afterwards had to pay the amount of the liens, and sued the builder's surety therefor; but it was held that he had exonerated the surety by failing to retain the sums that fell due after he had received notice of the liens.[1] But the mere fact that an agent employed to sell machines on a commission is paid some of his commissions before they are due under his contract will not of itself release a surety upon a bond given by him for the faithful performance of his obligations.[2] A debtor gave to several banks to which he was indebted collateral security of two classes; the first class consisting of notes given for debts due to himself, and the second class consisting of notes made, indorsed, or guaranteed by a surety for his accommodation. By an indenture, to which the surety and the banks were parties, he then assigned all his property, including choses in action, to a trustee to pay the debts due to the banks. By the terms of the indenture, the banks were authorized to use their discretion in collecting the notes of the first class, and were to apply their proceeds, when collected, to the payment of his debts due to the banks. The banks were to hold the notes of the second class as collateral security, and not collect them, until the trustee should have disposed of the property assigned to him, and have distributed the proceeds among the banks. The banks, with the consent of the debtor and of the trustee, but not of the surety, made in good faith a compromise with several of the makers of the notes of the first class, so that a balance remained due

---

[1] Taylor *v.* Jeter, 23 Mo. 244; Lucas County *v.* Roberts, 49 Iowa, 159. So in Fenaille *v.* Coudert, 44 N. J. Law, 286; Ryan *v.* Morton, 65 Tex. 258; Carson Opera House Association *v.* Miller, 16 Nevada, 327. *Antea,* § 123.

[2] Howe Machine Co. *v.* Woolley, 50 Iowa, 549.

to the banks, after the proceeds of the property assigned to the trustee had been paid to them, whereas, if these notes had been collected in full, the banks would have been fully paid. It was held that the banks had discharged the surety, to the extent of the sums given up by their compromise, from his liability on the notes of the second class.[1] The surrender of a leasehold estate by a tenant and its acceptance by the landlord were held to exonerate a third party from the burden of a mortgage which he had given to the landlord as security for the performance by the tenant of his covenants in the lease, on the ground that the term was a security to which he might have resorted for his indemnity, and which could not have been taken from the defendant without freeing him from his liability;[2] but the same rule would not be applied to a transfer of the lease made by the tenant to the lessor as collateral security merely for a debt, or to a surrender which, though made by the tenant, had not been actually accepted by the landlord.[3] And it has been held in New York that the surrender of a lease and the release of the rent thereafter to accrue will not discharge one who has guaranteed the payment of the rent reserved in a lease, from his liability for the rent which is overdue at the time of such surrender.[4] A creditor who held a mortgage from the principal debtor, and also a mortgage from the principal's wife as his surety, bought of the principal the premises mortgaged by him for a price exceeding the amount of his debt, but did not apply the price in payment of his debt; and it was held that he thereby discharged the mortgage which he had from the surety; for he had rendered unavailing the mortgage given by the prin-

---

[1] American Bank v. Baker, 4 Met. (Mass.) 164.
[2] Haberton v. Bennett, 1 Beatty (Ir. Ch.), 386. See also Nichols v. Palmer, 48 Wisc. 110; Farrar v. Kramer, 5 Mo. App. 167.
[3] Breese v. Bange, 2 E. D. Smith (N. Y.), 474; McKensie v. Farrell, 4 Bosw. (N. Y.) 192.
[4] Kingsbury v. Westfall, 61 N. Y. 356.

cipal, to which the surety had a right to be subrogated.[1] So if the purchaser of land which is subject to the lien of a judgment against different persons, one of whom is a mere surety, purchases and takes an assignment of the judgment, he thereby destroys the surety's right of subrogation to such lien, and so discharges the surety *pro tanto*.[2] But a creditor who holds both the liability of a surety and the security of a mortgage from the principal debtor will not discharge the surety by simply purchasing the equity of redemption from the principal, allowing its full value upon the debt,[3] especially if he makes the purchase in good faith with the purpose of giving the surety the benefit of the mortgage, and of appropriating the rents and profits in aid of his liability; for this will not operate a merger of the mortgage,[4] and the surety's right of subrogation will not be impaired.[5] The surety will not be discharged, unless his right of subrogation to the securities and remedies of the creditor has been impaired.[6] If the creditor does any act which destroys or impairs the surety's right of subrogation to his mortgages or privileges,[7] or to his remedies against the principal,[8] he thereby releases the

---

[1] Loomer v. Wheelright, 3 Sandf. Ch. (N. Y.) 135; Wheelwright v. De Peyster, 4 Edw. Ch. (N. Y.) 232.

[2] Wright v. Kuepper, 1 Penn. St. 361.

[3] Marshall v. Dixon, 82 Ga. 435.

[4] *Antea,* § 57 *et seq.*

[5] Cullum v. Emanuel, 1 Ala. 23; Croso v. Allen, 141 U. S. 528.

[6] Tiernan v. Woodruff, 5 McLean, C. C. 350; Agricultural Bank v. Bishop, 6 Gray (Mass.), 317; Payne v. Commercial Bank, 6 Sm. & M. (Miss.) 24; Muller v. Wadlington, 5 So. Car. 342; Rawlings v. Barham, 12 La. Ann. 630; Claiborne v. Birge, 42 Tex. 98.

[7] Thayer v. Finnegan, 134 Mass.

62; Port v. Robbins, 35 Iowa, 208; Smith v. Clopton, 48 Miss. 66; New England Ins. Co. v. Randall, 42 La. Ann. 260; Daigle's Succession, 15 La. Ann. 594; *Morphy, J.,* in Hereford v. Chase, 1 Rob. (La.) 212; St. Joseph's Ins. Co. v. Hauck, 71 Mo. 464.

[8] *Blackburn, J.,* in Swire v. Redman, 1 Q. B. D. 541; *Best, C. J.,* in Philpot v. Briant, 4 Bing. 717, 719; Kemmerer's Appeal, 125 Penn. St. 283; Boschert v. Brown, 72 Penn. St. 372; Boyd v. McDonough, 39 How. Pr. (N. Y.) 389; Bangs v. Strong, 10 Paige (N. Y.), 11; Calloway v. Snapp, 78 Ky. 561; Wheaton v. Wheeler, 27 Minn. 464.

surety, even though he has already recovered judgment against the latter.[1]

§ 126 *a.* **Surety on Bond not to be discharged by Release of Security caused by Act against which Bond taken.** — A surety on a guardian's bond cannot claim that he is discharged from liability by reason of his having given up security that he held, in reliance upon acts of the ward induced by the fraudulent actions of the guardian against which the bond was intended to be a security.[2] Where such a surety had taken a mortgage from the guardian as a protection against his liability, and then discharged this mortgage in reliance upon a receipt in full given by the ward after coming of age to the guardian, but it appeared that the guardian had fraudulently obtained this receipt from the ward, who was of feeble mind, by misrepresentations of its character, it was held that the ward could still hold the surety upon the bond; for the ward owed no duty to the surety, but the surety had undertaken for the fidelity and honesty of the guardian towards the ward,[3] and so could not avail himself of the receipt obtained from the ward by the mere fraud and circumvention of the guardian, even though by means of the same receipt the guardian had procured his discharge from the court to which he was accountable.[4] The surety on a bond given by a contractor to a city to pay laborers employed by the contractor on the city's work cannot complain that money earned upon the contract was paid according to its provision by the city to the contractor.[5]

§ 127. **Surety not entitled to Subrogation until the whole Debt is paid.** — The right of subrogation does not arise in favor of a surety until he has actually paid the debt for

[1] Allison *v.* Thomas, 29 La. Ann. 732.

[2] Bank *v.* Buchanan, 87 Tenn. 32; Douglass *v.* Ferris, 63 Hun (N. Y.), 413.

[3] So in the case of a bank-cashier: McShane *v.* Howard Bank, 73 Md. 135.

[4] Gillett *v.* Wiley, 126 Ills. 310.

[5] Duluth *v.* Heney, 43 Minn. 155.

which he is liable as surety;[1] the right does not accrue upon a partial payment by the surety, until the creditor is wholly satisfied.[2] Even if a surety is liable only for a part of the debt, and pays that part for which he is liable, he cannot be subrogated to the securities held by the creditor until the whole demand of the creditor is satisfied.[3] Where the surety is allowed by bill in equity after the debt has become due to compel the creditor to enforce his demand against the principal debtor,[4] yet he cannot be subrogated to the creditor's liens, securities, and equities for the debt until he has actually paid it.[5] So, the indorser of a promissory note which is payable on time and secured by a mortgage of the principal's real estate, who has been compelled by the mortgagee to pay the interest which has become due thereon, cannot enforce the mortgage for his indemnity, while the note remains the property of another holder and the principal sum is still due thereon.[6] The payment need not be in one sum, but may be made at different times;[7] nor need it be wholly

---

[1] Ewart v. Latta, 4 McQu. H. L. 983; Church, Petitioner, 16 R. I. 231; Kemmerer's Appeal, 125 Penn. St. 283; Glass v. Pullen, 6 Bush (Ky.), 346; Pennsylvania Bank v. Potius, 10 Watts (Penn.), 148, 152; Conwell v. McCowan, 53 Ills. 363; Darst v. Bates, 51 Ills. 439; Gilliam v. Esselman, 5 Sneed (Tenn.), 86; McConnell v. Beattie, 34 Ark. 113; Rushforth, ex parte, 10 Ves. 409.

[2] Bridges v. Nicholson, 20 Ga. 90; Magee v. Leggett, 48 Miss. 139; Commonwealth v. Chesapeake & Ohio Canal Co., 32 Md. 501; Kyner v. Kyner, 6 Watts (Penn.), 221; Brough's Estate, 71 Penn. St. 460; Cox v. N. J. Midland R. R. Co., 31 N. J. Eq. 106; Barton v. Brent, 87 Va. 385; Stamford Bank v. Benedict, 15 Conn. 437; Field v. Hamilton, 45 Vt. 35; Vert v. Voss, 74 Ind. 566;

Harlan v. Sweeny, 1 Lea (Tenn.), 682.

[3] Neptune Ins. Co. v. Dorsey, 3 Md. Ch. Dec. 334; s. c. nom. Swan v. Patterson, 7 Md. 164; Union Bank v. Edwards, 1 Gill & J. (Md.) 346; Wilcox v. Fairhaven Bank, 7 Allen (Mass.), 270; Hopkinsville Bank v. Rudy, 2 Bush (Ky.), 326; Rice v. Morris, 82 Ind. 204; Cooper v. Jenkins, 32 Beav. 337; Farebrother v. Wodehouse, 23 Beav. 18.

[4] Postea, § 130

[5] Covey v. Neff, 63 Ind. 391; Rice v. Downing, 12 B. Mon. (Ky.) 44; Lee v. Griffin, 31 Miss. 632; Delaney v. Tipton, 3 Hayw. (Tenn.) 14.

[6] Gannett v. Blodgett, 39 N. H. 150.

[7] Davies v. Humphreys, 6 M. & W. 153; Bullock v. Campbell, 9 Gill (Md.), 182; Williams v. Williams, 5

or at all in money, if the creditor accepts something else; though, as has been already stated, if it be not in money, the surety's right will extend only to his reimbursement for the real value of what he has paid.[1] It has been held in Missouri that a surety for part of the indebtedness of his principal becomes entitled, by paying the part for which he is liable, to a *pro rata* or proportionate share of the proceeds arising from a sale of the debtor's property, and may be subrogated accordingly to the rights of the other creditors, so as to have the benefit of all their securities;[2] but this is contrary to the general doctrine.[3] But if the effect of the surety's subrogation would be to give him a lien upon the property of the creditor himself, so that he would be entitled to immediate repayment from the creditor's property, then, to avoid circuity of action, the right may be enforced in the creditor's suit against the surety, without waiting for actual payment.[4]

§ 128. **Satisfaction is Creditor's Right; it need not come wholly from Surety.** — It is the creditor who is entitled to satisfaction; and neither the debtor nor any other creditors can object to any arrangement between the surety and the creditor for the subrogation of the surety, whether the latter has or has not completely satisfied the debt.[5] If the creditor accedes to the request of the surety for the enforcement of the collateral security, this will be ordered.[6] If the surety has satisfied the creditor partly by a set-off of the creditor's own obligations, or otherwise, and only partly in money, his right of subrogation will yet extend to the whole of the indebtedness which he has satisfied.[7] If the principal debtor has himself paid part of the indebtedness, and the surety only

Ohio, 444; Hall v. Hall, 10 Humph. (Tenn.) 352; Pickett v. Bates, 3 La. Ann. 627.

[1] *Antea*, § 105.

[2] Allison v. Sutherlin, 50 Mo. 274.

[3] Child v. New York & New England R. R. Co., 129 Mass. 170.

[4] State v. Atkins, 53 Ark. 303.

[5] Motley v. Harris, 1 Lea (Tenn.), 577; Spaulding v. Crane, 46 Vt. 292; Gedye v. Matson, 25 Beav. 310.

[6] Lusk v. Hopper, 3 Bush (Ky.), 179.

[7] Keokuk v. Love, 31 Iowa, 119; Bausman v. Credit Guarantee Co., 47 Minn. 378.

the balance, yet, when once the creditor is wholly satisfied, the same principle of equity which substitutes the surety who has paid the whole debt to the place of the creditor will equally protect the surety paying a part thereof, to the extent of his payment.[1] A partial payment is sufficient to establish the surety's right as against the principal,[2] or any one standing in the place of the principal;[3] it is only the creditor who can insist that the debt must be paid in full. Nor need the surety's payment be made in money; whatever is accepted by the creditor as a payment, so as to discharge the principal debtor from his liability, will operate as a payment in favor of the surety.[4] But until the creditor has been paid in full, the surety cannot, against the will of the creditor, in any manner interfere with the latter's rights or securities, so as to put him to any embarrassment in collecting the remainder of his demand.[5] If the surety has made partial payments upon a debt secured by a mortgage from the principal debtor, then upon foreclosure any surplus proceeds over the amount needed to pay the creditor in full must be applied to repay the surety.[6]

§ 129. **Creditor's Right to apply Security held for Several Debts until all are satisfied.** — A creditor who holds security without special stipulations as to its application, for various sums due to him from his debtor, for some of which he also holds sureties, may, in case of the insolvency of the principal and of some of the sureties, apply the proceeds of the security upon such of the debts as may be necessary for his own protection; and solvent sureties upon others of the debts cannot in any

---

[1] Hess's Estate, 69 Penn. St. 272; Magee v. Leggett, 48 Miss. 139; Hardcastle v. Commercial Bank, 1 Harringt. (Del.) 374, *note*.

[2] Gedye v. Matson, 25 Beav. 310; Comins v. Culver, 35 N. J. Eq. 94.

[3] Rooker v. Benson, 83 Ind. 250.

[4] Knighton v. Curry, 62 Ala. 404; *antea*, §§ 105, 127.

[5] New Jersey Midland R. R. Co. v. Wortendyke, 27 N. J. Eq. 658; Hollingsworth v. Floyd, 2 Harr. & Gill (Md.), 87; Cason v. Westfall. 18 So. W. Rep. 668.

[6] Bowen v. Barksdale, 33 So. Car. 142.

way avail themselves of such security in equity, without paying or offering to pay the whole of the debts for which the
security was given.[1]   So, where a debtor mortgaged two
estates to a creditor as security for the payment of two distinct sums, with a surety for the payment of one of the sums
only, the right of the creditor to retain both securities until
the payment of both debts will override the right of the
surety, upon his payment of the debt for which he is surety,
to have the benefit of the security pledged for that debt.[2]
And where the principal debtor gave to his creditor both a
mortgage and a covenant by a surety to secure the payment
of the debt, and then gave the creditor a further charge upon
the mortgaged property to secure a further loan, it was held
that the surety was not entitled to the benefit of the first
mortgage without paying the second loan as well as the debt
for which he was surety;[3] but this decision has since been
overruled, on the ground that the creditor could not thus
derogate from the rights of the surety,[4] being aware of the
facts which create those rights.[5]   As the doctrine of subrogation is founded upon reason and justice, and not upon any
contract or stipulation between the parties, it follows as a
necessary consequence that the surety is not to be substituted to the place of the creditor, unless upon the circumstances of the case it is shown to be just and proper that
he should be.   To become entitled to such substitution he
must first pay the whole of the debt or debts for which the
property is held by the creditor; for it would be manifestly
unjust, and a plain violation of the creditor's rights, to com-

[1] Wilcox v. Fairhaven Bank, 7
Allen (Mass.), 270; Richardson v.
Washington Bank, 3 Met. (Mass.)
536; Allen v. Culver, 3 Denio (N.Y.),
285; Stone v. Seymour, 15 Wend.
(N. Y.) 19; Union Bank v. Edwards,
1 Gill & J. (Md.) 346; Noble v
Murphy, 52 N. W. Rep. 148.
[2] Farebrother v. Wodehouse, 23
Beav. 18.

[3] Williams v. Owen, 13 Sim. 597.
[4] Forbes v. Jackson, 19 Ch. D.
616; Green v. Wynn, L. R. 4 Ch.
204.
[5] National Exchange Bank v. Silliman, 65 N. Y. 475; Ottawa Bank v.
Dudgeon, 65 Ills. 11; Perry v. Miller,
54 Iowa, 277; Simmons v. Cates, 56
Ga. 609.

pel him to relinquish any portion of the property before the obligation for the performance of which it had been conveyed to him has been fully complied with.[1] If a creditor, holding a claim for which he has both collateral security from the principal debtor and also the engagement of a surety, acquires an additional claim against the same principal, to which the agreement upon which the security was taken does not extend, the surety will be entitled to the benefit of such security on payment of the first indebtedness alone, and can require the proceeds of such security, when realized by the creditor, to be applied upon the first indebtedness; for the surety's right of subrogation, when once vested, cannot be interfered with by the act of the creditor alone.[2]

§ 130. **Surety may come into Equity to compel Payment of the Debt by the Principal.** — A surety, after the debt has become due, although he has not paid it, may, if the creditor refuses or neglects to enforce his demand against the principal debtor by proper legal proceedings, come into equity, bringing both the debtor and the creditor before the court, and have a decree compelling the debtor to make payment, and thus to exonerate the surety from liability;[3] and the creditor, being

---

[1] *Merrick, J.,* in Wilcox v. Fairhaven Bank, 7 Allen (Mass.), 270, 272, citing Richardson v. Washington Bank, 3 Met. (Mass.) 536; Copis v. Middleton, Turn. & Russ. 224; Hodgson v. Shaw, 3 Myl. & K. 183.

[2] National Exchange Bank v. Silliman, 65 N. Y. 475; Holliday v. Brown, 50 N. W. Rep. 1042; Forbes v. Jackson, 19 Ch. D. 616.

[3] Antrobus v. Davidson, 3 Meriv. 569, 579; Barbour v. Exchange Bank, 45 Ohio St. 133; Norton v. Reid, 11 So. Car. 593; Towe v. Newbold, 4 Jones Eq. (Nor. Car.) 212; Croone v. Bivens, 2 Head (Tenn.), 339; Washington v. Tait, 3 Humph. (Tenn.) 543; Howell v. Cobb, 2 Coldw. (Tenn.) 104; Gilliam v. Esselman, 5 Sneed (Tenn.), 86; Hannay v. Pell, 3 E. D. Smith (N. Y.), 432; Hayes v. Ward, 4 Johns. Ch. (N. Y.) 123; Irick v. Black, 17 N. J. Eq. 189; Pride v. Boyce, Rice Eq. (So. Car.) 275, 287; Tankersly v. Anderson, 4 Desaus. Eq. (So. Car.) 44; McConnell v. Scott, 15 Ohio, 401; Purviance v. Sutherland, 2 Ohio St. 478; Stump v. Rogers, 1 Hammond (Ohio), 533; Ritenour v. Matthews, 42 Ind. 7; Bishop v. Day, 13 Vt. 81; Wetzel v. Sponsler, 18 Penn. St. 460; Ruddell v. Childress, 31 Ark. 511; Stephenson v. Taveners, 9 Gratt. (Va.) 398; Whitridge v. Durkee, 2 Md. Ch. Dec. 442.

first fully indemnified, subjected to no delay, and exposed to
no risk of loss, may, upon such a bill, be compelled to resort
to the property of the principal for the satisfaction of his
claim before coming upon the surety;[1] and the surety may
have any property which has been specifically appropriated
for the payment of the debt by or for the principal debtor
applied thereto for his indemnity,[2] but this is strictly the
right of the surety, and is not for the benefit of the principal.[3] So the surety may for his relief have the debt proved
against the estate of the principal in bankruptcy.[4] But the
surety cannot ask for the use of the securities and remedies
held by the creditor to enforce payment from the principal,
without indemnifying the creditor against any costs and expenses.[5] Nor has the surety any implied authority to sue
the principal in the name of the creditor.[6] And when sureties who are claiming in a court of equity the benefit of subrogation have not yet paid the creditor, though a judgment
has been recovered against them, it has been held that the
court may, in the exercise of its equitable jurisdiction to
declare future rights and duties, order that the sureties be
subrogated to the rights of the creditor when they shall have
paid the debt,[7] and may in the mean time protect the surety.[8]

§ 130 a. **Equitable Relief given to the Surety.** — In equity,
relief may also be given to a surety for his protection out of
the property of his principal, so far as the surety's equitable
rights can be maintained without injury to the creditor,
either by granting an injunction against the sale of the

---

[1] Thompson v. Taylor, 72 N. Y.
32; Hayes v. Ward, 4 Johns. Ch. (N.
Y.) 123; Irick v. Black, 17 N. J. Eq.
189; Huey v. Pinney, 5 Minn. 310.

[2] Wooldridge v. Norris, L. R. 6
Eq. 410.

[3] White v. Schurer, 4 Baxter
(Tenn.), 23.

[4] Babcock, in re, 3 Story C. C.
393; Wright v. Austin, 56 Barb. (N.

Y.) 13, 17; Rushforth, ex parte, 10
Ves. 409.

[5] Beardsley v. Warner, 6 Wend.
(N. Y.) 610.

[6] Hardware Co. v. Deere, 53 Ark.
140.

[7] Keokuk v. Love, 31 Iowa, 119;
Moore v. Topliff, 107 Ills. 241.

[8] Moore v. Topliff, 107 Ills. 241,
249.

surety's property until property pledged by the principal for the debt shall first have been applied for its payment, or by subrogating the surety to the creditor's rights against the principal, or by marshalling the securities available and applying them to the satisfaction of the debt in the order in which they are equitably chargeable, according to the circumstances of the particular case.[1] Even after a judgment at law against principal and surety, equity will still protect the surety so far as this may be done without prejudice to the paramount rights of the creditor,[2] but no farther.[3] If upon a writ of error the principal gives new sureties and supersedes the judgment against himself, the creditor may be restrained from taking out execution against the surety, pending proceedings upon the writ of error.[4] The property of both husband and wife being mortgaged to secure the debt of the husband, she was allowed on foreclosure to have the husband's property first sold and applied on the debt.[5] And if the creditor, having taken out execution against both principal and surety, levies upon the surety's land, and this is purchased at the execution-sale by the principal, then, by reason of the duty incumbent upon the principal himself to pay the judgment, his purchase will inure to the surety's benefit, and he cannot hold the land against the surety.[6]

§ 131. **Rights of Successive Sureties to Subrogation against each other.** — The mere fact that two or more persons are sureties for the same debt will not give them equal rights against each other, unless their liability is the same in kind and degree; "not separate and successive, but joint and coordinate, so that all stand *in æquali jure* in regard to the

---

[1] Skinner v. Terhune, 45 N. J. Eq. 565; Phila. & Reading R. R. Co. v. Little, 41 N. J. Eq. 519; Pettillo, *ex parte*, 80 Nor. Car. 50; Allis v. Ware, 28 Minn. 166.

[2] Stafford v. Montgomery, 85 Tenn. 329.

[3] West v. Brison, 99 Mo. 684.

[4] Wren v. Peel, 64 Tex. 374.

[5] Hoppes v. Hoppes, 123 Ind. 397; Trentman v. Eldridge, 98 Ind. 525.

[6] Greer v. Wintersmith, 85 Ky. 516.

payment of the debt for which they are respectively liable."[1]
A surety who first becomes such in an obligation incidental
to the prosecution of a legal remedy against the principal,
will, upon paying the debt, be allowed to stand in the creditor's
place only as to his remedies against the person or property
of the principal;[2] as to any prior surety, or any prior interest
in property which may be pledged to the creditor for the
debt, he must occupy the position of the debtor;[3] he cannot
claim to be subrogated to the rights of the creditor against
any prior sureties;[4] on the contrary, the prior surety, if compelled to pay the debt, will be subrogated against the subsequent surety.[5] Those who last become sureties do so, not
only for the benefit of the creditor, but in exoneration of the
former sureties, and will be liable to indemnify such former
sureties.[6] Accordingly, if, after a judgment against two,
one of whom appears by the record to be a surety only, a
third party intervenes, solely at the request of the principal,
and becomes bail for the stay of execution, taking indemnity
from the principal therefor, and at the expiration of the stay
the original surety is compelled to pay the judgment, he
may, by subrogation thereto, recover the amount thereof from
such bail.[7] One who becomes surety for the principal in the

---

[1] Bigelow, C. J., in Stout v. Fenno, 6 Allen (Mass.), 579, 580; Adams v. Flanagan, 36 Vt. 400; Schur v. Schwartz, 140 Penn. St. 53; Tracy v. Pomeroy, 120 Penn. St. 14; Semmes v. Naylor, 12 Gill & J. (Md.) 358; Dillon v. Scofield, 11 Neb. 419.

[2] Riemer v. Schlitz, 49 Wisc. 273; Burgett v. Patton, 99 Ills. 288, 302.

[3] Armstrong's Appeal, 5 Watts & Serg. (Penn.) 352; Hopkinsville Bank v. Rudy, 2 Bush (Ky.), 326; Crow v. Murphy, 12 B. Mon. (Ky.) 444; Bohannon v. Coombs, 12 B. Mon. (Ky.) 563; Patterson v. Pope, 5 Dana (Ky.), 241; Yoder v. Briggs, 3 Bibb (Ky.), 228.

[4] Hammock v. Baker, 3 Bush (Ky.), 208; Smith v. Bing, 3 Ohio, 33; Fitzpatrick v. Hill, 9 Ala. 783.

[5] Kellar v. Williams, 10 Bush (Ky.), 216; Friberg v. Donovan, 23 Ills. App. 58.

[6] Chrisman v. Jones, 34 Ark. 73; Bently v. Harris, 2 Gratt. (Va.) 357; Higgs v. Landrum, 1 Coldw. (Tenn.) 81.

[7] Schnitzel's Appeal, 49 Penn. St. 23; Burns v. Huntingdon Bank, 1 Pen. & W. (Penn.) 395; Pott v. Nathans, 1 Watts & Serg. (Penn.) 155; Winchester v. Beardin, 10 Humph. (Tenn.) 247; Hanner v. Douglass, 4 Jones Eq. (Nor. Car.) 262.

course of legal proceedings against him has no right of contribution against a prior surety for the debt;[1] but, on the
contrary, the latter is entitled to be subrogated to the creditor's rights against him as in the case of bail.[2] The rights
of a surety on a second appeal must yield to those of a
surety on the first appeal of the same case, both being sureties for the same principal.[3] And one who, by becoming a
surety on a judgment-bond, has prevented a sale of the
debtor's property will not be substituted to the lien of
the creditor, so as to overreach a junior lien created before
the surety became liable;[4] nor can such a subsequent surety,
after having paid the judgment, claim by subrogation the
benefit of a mortgage given by the principal debtor to the
original surety for the latter's indemnity.[5] But after
the subsequent sureties who are primarily liable have been
held for the full amount for which they became bound, the
earlier sureties will be liable on their obligation for any
deficiency; their right is merely to be preferred to the subsequent sureties.[6]

§ 132. **Rights of one who becomes Surety for the Payment
of a Judgment.** — Where the payee of a promissory note commenced a suit against the three makers thereof, and pending
the suit made an agreement with A., one of these makers,
by which A. was to pay a certain sum upon the note, and the
creditor should take judgment for the balance against the
three, but should not enforce his judgment against A., and
A. made the payment accordingly, and the creditor subse-

---

[1] Daniel v. Joyner, 3 Ired. Eq.
(Nor. Car.) 513; Dent v. Wait, 9
W. Va. 41; Hammock v. Baker, 3
Bush (Ky.), 208.

[2] Bender v. George, 92 Penn. St.
36; Hanby v. Henritze, 85 Va. 177;
Denier v. Myers, 20 Ohio St. 336;
Chaffin v. Campbell, 4 Sneed (Tenn.),
184; Brandenburg v. Flynn, 12 B.
Mon. (Ky.), 397.

[3] Hinckley v. Kreitz, 58 N. Y.
583; Moore v. Larriter, 16 Lea
(Tenn.), 630.

[4] Fishback v. Bodman, 14 Bush
(Ky.), 117.

[5] Havens v. Foudry, 4 Met. (Ky.)
247.

[6] Chester v. Broderick, 131 N. Y.
549; s. c., 60 Hun (N. Y.), 562.

quently collected his judgment from the bail of another of
the defendants, and in pursuance of an order of the county
court the bail took an assignment of the judgment from the
creditor, and subsequently collected the amount of this judgment from A.,[1] it was held that the creditor was not responsible for this act of the bail after the assignment of the
judgment had been made by order of the court, and that A
could not maintain an action against the creditor upon the
agreement not to enforce payment from him; and *Redfield,
J.*, said that the county court had no power to order such
subrogation of the bail to the rights of the creditor, and that
at most the bail by such subrogation could acquire only
those rights which the creditor had, and must take the judgment subject to the creditor's agreement not to enforce collection thereof against A., though A.'s only remedy to
enforce compliance by the bail with this agreement would
be in equity.[2]  Where the original principal in the debt
prosecuted a writ of error, which was overruled, and the
surety or indorser of the note afterwards paid the debt, he
was subrogated to the judgment rendered on the writ of error
against the orginal defendants and the sureties on the *supersedeas* bond, upon the general principle that the surety is
entitled to all collaterals, and that the second sureties may,
by becoming such, have put him in a worse condition; and
the court said that the latter sureties, having, at the instance
of the principal, stipulated to pay the debt, suffered no injustice in being called upon to do so, since they were obliged
to do no more than they undertook, and had no right to complain that they were not allowed to use as a payment by themselves the money which proceeded from another person, whom
their principal was previously bound to save harmless.  If
the interposition of the second sureties may have been the
means of involving the first surety in the necessity of paying

---

[1] See Pierson *v.* Catlin, 3 Vt. 272.      [2] Pierson *v.* Catlin, 18 Vt. 77.

the debt, the equity of the first surety will decidedly preponderate.[1] If the interposition of the bail or the surety for the judgment is the means of hindering or delaying the payment of the debt, such second surety has less equity than a prior surety.[2] The coming in of the bail, by delaying execution, may have prevented a payment by the debtor or out of his funds. As between the bail and the principal debtor, or those whose rights have accrued under him, the former may be subrogated to the rights of the judgment-creditor;[3] but regard must always be had for third persons whose rights might be affected by such subrogation.[4]

§ 133. **Where Later Surety is Surety for Original Sureties as well as for Principal.** — If, however, the subsequent surety can fairly be regarded as a surety for the original sureties, as well as for the principal, then he may be subrogated against the original sureties as well as against the principal.[5] Thus, where, after the recovery of a judgment against both principal and sureties, a third person becomes surety for the payment of the debt, upon the creditor's promise to give him the benefit of the judgment for his satisfaction and indemnity, such new surety has a superior equity over the old sureties, and may after payment enforce the judgment against them for his own protection; his agreement made him the conditional assignee of the judgment.[6] The same principle has been applied to the sureties upon bonds and notes.[7] So, if a judgment against two is affirmed on their

[1] Opp v. Ward, 125 Ind. 241; Mitchell v. De Witt, 25 Tex. Sup. 180.

[2] Burns v. Huntington Bank, 1 Pen. & W. (Penn.) 395; Pott v. Nathans, 1 Watts & Serg. (Penn.) 155; Fletcher v. Menken, 37 Ark. 206.

[3] LaGrange v. Merrill, 3 Barb. Ch. (N. Y.) 625; Brewer's Appeal, 7 Penn. St. 333; Peirce v. Higgins, 101 Ind. 178; Black v. Epperson, 40 Tex. 162.

[4] Armstrong's Appeal, 5 Watts & Serg. (Penn.) 352; United States Bank v. Winston, 2 Brock. (C. C.) 252; Barlow v. Deibert, 39 Ind. 16.

[5] Coffman v. Hopkins, 75 Va. 645; Dessar v. King, 110 Ind. 69; Stinnett v. Crookshank, 1 Heisk. (Tenn.) 496; Chase v. Welty, 57 Iowa, 230; Dillon v. Scofield, 11 Nebraska, 419.

[6] La Grange v. Merrill, 3 Barb. Ch. (N. Y.) 625.

[7] Whiting v. Burke, L. R. 6 Ch.

appeal against them and their surety on the appeal, and on
further appeal is again affirmed against the three and their
surety on the second appeal, the first and second surety are
related to each other, not as co-sureties, but as principal and
surety; and if the first surety pays the final judgment he
has no recourse against the second.[1]  And if a judgment
against a principal debtor and his sureties is superseded by
the defendants with two others as their sureties, all the defendants in the original judgment are principals as to the
sureties in the *supersedeas* judgment.[2]

§ 134. **Exceptions to Usual Rule of Subrogation between Successive Sureties.** — In Louisiana it has been held, contrary to
the general rule, that the second surety is entitled to subrogation against the first surety, on the presumption that the
second surety was induced to bind himself in consequence of
the responsibility of the principal having been guaranteed by
the first surety; and accordingly the surety in an appeal-
bond, after paying the amount of a judgment against his
principal, was allowed to enforce the judgment against the
original bail in the suit for the whole amount so paid by
him.[3]  A like decision was rendered, under special circumstances, in Missouri.[4]  In Virginia a surety who becomes
such in the course of judicial proceedings for the collection of the debt from the principal is subrogated like any
other surety for the debt to all the remedies of the creditor,
even against third persons, whose rights, though subject to
the creditor's lien, have accrued before the obligation of the
surety was entered into; he will be subrogated to the creditor's judgment-lien upon lands alienated by the debtor

342; Harrison *v.* Lane, 5 Leigh (Va.),
414; Adams *v.* Flanagan, 36 Vt. 400;
Harris *v.* Warner, 13 Wend. (N. Y.)
400.

[1] Cowan *v.* Duncan, Meigs (Tenn.),
470.

[2] Yeager's Appeal, 8 Atl. Rep. 225;
Smith *v.* Anderson, 18 Md. 520;

Hartwell *v.* Smith, 15 Ohio St. 200;
Bradford *v.* Mooney, 2 Cincin. (Ohio)
468.  See Monson *v.* Drakeley, 40
Conn. 552.

[3] Howe *v.* Frazer, 2 Rob. (La.)
424.

[4] State *v.* Farrar, 77 Mo. 175.

after the judgment, but before the surety became such.[1]
Where, on an appeal from a judgment, a new judgment was
rendered for a much larger sum, and was paid by the surety
in the appeal-bond, this surety was subrogated to the creditor's judgment-lien against mesne purchasers of the debtor's
real estate, not only for the amount of the original judgment,
but also for the increased amount which the surety had been
compelled to pay,[2] and the original surety cannot have contribution from sureties given in the course of subsequent litigation.[3]    But a judgment-surety for the principal debtor will
not be subrogated to the creditor's lien upon the property of
one who stands in the position of a prior surety for the judgment-debtor.[4]    In Maine and Massachusetts it has been held
that the doctrine of subrogation is not applied at all as
between successive sureties taken in the course of judicial
proceedings against the principal debtor; and neither the
prior nor the subsequent surety is allowed any remedy at law
against the other.[5]    And in Maryland the principles of contribution between co-sureties are not to be applied to such
successive sureties.[6]

§ 135. **Whether Original Obligation extinguished by Surety's
Payment thereof; Rule in England.** — Although it is a general
rule that in equity a surety is subrogated to the benefit of all
the securities for the debt which the creditor holds against
the principal, yet it was finally settled in England that this
subrogation must be limited to such securities only as continue to exist and are not *ipso facto* extinguished by the act
of payment,[7] and that payment of a bond or other specialty

---

[1] Hill *v.* Manser, 11 Gratt. (Va.)
522; Rodgers *v.* McCluer, 4 Gratt.
(Va.) 81; Leake *v.* Ferguson, 2
Gratt. (Va.) 419.

[2] McLung *v.* Beirne, 10 Leigh
(Va.), 394.

[3] Rosenbaum *v.* Goodman, 78 Va.
121.

[4] Douglass *v.* Fagg, 8 Leigh (Va.),
588.

[5] Holmes *v.* Day, 108 Mass. 563;
Morse *v.* Williams, 22 Maine, 17.

[6] Semmes *v.* Naylor, 12 Gill & J.
(Md.) 358.

[7] Copis *v.* Middleton, Turn. &
Russ. 224.

or of a judgment executed by or recovered against both principal and surety, or the principal alone, extinguished the obligation, so as to prevent any subrogation of the surety thereto.[1] But the technical reasoning of these decisions, never entirely satisfactory, has now been done away with in England by a statutory provision that "every person who, being surety for the debt or duty of another, or being liable with another for any debt or duty, shall pay such debt or perform such duty, shall be entitled to have assigned to him or to a trustee for him every judgment, specialty, or other security, which shall be held by the creditor in respect of such debt or duty, whether such specialty, judgment, or other security shall or shall not be deemed at law to have been satisfied by the payment of the debt or performance of the duty; and such person shall be entitled to stand in the place of the creditor, and to use all the remedies, and if need be, and upon a proper indemnity, to use the name of the creditor in any action or other proceeding at law or in equity, in order to obtain from the principal debtor, or from any co-surety, co-contractor, or co-debtor, as the case may be, indemnification for the loss sustained and advances made by the person who shall have so paid such debt or performed such duty; and such payment or performance so made by such surety shall not be pleadable in bar of any such action or other proceeding by him; provided always that no co-surety, co-contractor, or co-debtor shall be entitled to recover from any other co-surety, co-contractor, or co-debtor, by the means aforesaid, more than the just proportion to which, as between the parties themselves, such last-mentioned parties shall be justly liable."[2] This statute will be applied to protect a co-surety or co-debtor from whom the creditor has

---

[1] Jones v. Davids, 4 Russ. 277; Copis v. Middleton, Turn. & Russ. 224; Armitage v. Baldwin, 5 Beav. 278; Dowbiggen v. Bourne, 2 Yo. & Co. Exch. 462; Hodgson v. Shaw, 3 Mylne & K. 183.

[2] Mercantile Law Amendment Act, 19 & 20 Vic., c. 97, § 5.

coerced payment on execution,[1] and is held to be applicable
to a contract made before the passage of the statute, where
the breach of the contract has taken place and the payment
by the surety or co-debtor has been made after its passage,[2]
and the right of a surety who has paid a judgment obtained
by the creditor against the principal debtor and all the sureties to stand in the place of the judgment-creditor, will not
be diminished by the fact that he has not himself paid the
whole judgment.[3]

§ 186. **Present English Rule generally adopted in the United
States.** — With more or less aid from legislation, the rule
laid down in this statute has been pretty generally adopted
in the United States;[4] and the distinction that equity will
not subrogate the sureties in those cases in which payment
discharges or extinguishes the security at law, such as bonds
and judgments which bind the principal and the surety
jointly, or bonds or judgments which constitute or merge the
debt, although the surety be not bound by them, has been
generally denied in this country.[5] As was said by *Nisbet,
J.*, in deciding that a surety who had paid a bond debt of his
principal was, by subrogation to the rights of the creditor,
entitled to rank as a specialty creditor of his principal,
"the substitution of the surety is not for the creditor as he
stands related to the debtor after the payment, but as he
stood related to him before the payment. He is subrogated to
such rights as the creditor then had against the principal, one
of which unquestionably was to enforce his bond against the
principal, and, if he was insolvent, to be let in as a bond-
creditor. What difference is there between permitting the

---

[1] Batchellor *v.* Lawrence, 9 C. B.
N. S. 543.

[2] De Wolf *v.* Lindsell, *in re*
Cochran's Estate, L. R. 5 Eq. 209;
Lockhart *v.* Reilly, 1 De Gex &
Jones, 464.

[3] McMyn, *in re*, Lightbrown *v.*
McMyn, 33 Ch. D. 575.

[4] Lidderdale *v.* Robinson, 12
Wheat. 594; s. c., 2 Brock. 159;
Brown *v.* Decatur, 4 Cranch, C. C. 477;
Miller *v.* O'Kain, 13 Hun (N. Y.), 594.
*Postea*, § 137.

[5] Am. note to Dering *v.* Winchelsea, 1 Lead. Cas. Eq. 434.

surety to reimburse himself out of a mortgage-lien held by the
creditor, and permitting him to take out of the estate generally of the debtor the amount that he has paid? If he realizes upon the mortgage, he abstracts the amount which he has
paid from the estate of the principal; if he realizes on the
bond, the mortgaged property goes back into the common fund,
and the result to him and the other creditors is the same. The
very fact that the surety could not enforce the bond at law is
a reason in equity why he should be allowed to come into the
distribution as a bond-creditor."[1] But the recovery of a judgment in one State upon a judgment previously recovered in
another State or in another court has been held so far to extinguish the first judgment that a surety cannot, upon paying
the later, be subrogated to the earlier judgment.[2]

§ 137. **Right of Surety to be substituted to the Benefit of the
Original Obligation maintained.** — In the following States this
right of the surety has been more or less distinctly affirmed.

In *New Hampshire*, it is held that though payment of a
joint debt by either of the debtors is a discharge of the debt[3]
and of any action, judgment, or execution, founded upon it,[4]
yet, if the debt is paid by a surety, and the creditor upon his
payment assigns to him any collateral security, the debt will
be regarded as still subsisting and undischarged, so far as is
necessary to protect the security. And an attachment of the
property of the principal in an action pending for the recovery of the debt is such a collateral security; and accordingly the surety, after his payment, may take an assignment
of such an action, prosecute it to judgment, and take out
execution thereon for his own use.[5] And if a joint and

---

[1] *Nisbet*, J., in Lumpkin *v.* Mills, 4 Ga. 343, 349.

[2] United States Bank *v.* Patton, 5 How. (Miss.) 200; Frazier *v.* Mc-Queen, 20 Ark. 68; Whiting *v.* Beebe, 12 *Id.* 421, 549; Gould *v.* Hayden, 63 Ind. 443; Denegre *v.* Ham, 13 Iowa,
240; Hanna *v.* Guy, 3 Bush (Ky.), 91; Cook *v.* Armstrong, 25 Miss. 63; Purdy *v.* Doyle, 1 Paige (N. Y.), 558.

[3] Davis *v.* Stevens, 10 N. H. 186.

[4] Stanley *v.* Nutter, 16 N. H. 22.

[5] Brewer *v.* Franklin Mills, 42 N.

several promissory note is taken up by one of the signers thereof who is merely a surety, not with the intention to pay and discharge it, but to purchase it, this will not be a discharge of the debt, and an action may still be maintained upon the note in the name of the payee for the benefit of the real plaintiff.[1]

*Nebraska.* — The New Hampshire rule as to an attachment pending against the principal when payment is made by a surety has been followed in Nebraska.[2]  The surety may, upon proving his suretyship in the original action, but not otherwise, have a judgment against his principal and himself assigned to himself on his payment, and enforce it against the principal for his own indemnity.[3]

In *New York*, a surety upon the performance of his contract is entitled to the original evidences of indebtedness held by the creditor, and to any judgment in which the debt has been merged; the surety has not only a right of subrogation pure and simple, but may also demand an assignment from the creditor; and though the obligation is discharged so far as the creditor has any interest therein, yet the original debt is kept alive for the benefit of the surety, against the principal debtor.[4]  A surety paying a judgment against himself and his principal has the right to have it assigned to himself, and may then enforce it against the principal or his estate.[5]  This rule, originally restricted to equity,[6] is now applied also at law.[7]

H. 292; Edgerly *v.* Emerson, 23 N. H. 555; Low *v.* Blodgett, 21 N. H. 121.

[1] Rockingham Bank *v.* Claggett, 29 N. H. 292.

[2] Wilson *v.* Burney, 8 Nebraska, 39.

[3] Potvin *v.* Myers, 27 Neb. 749.

[4] Townsend *v.* Whitney, 75 N. Y. 425; Fielding *v.* Waterhouse, 8 Jones & Spencer (N. Y.), 424; Cuyler *v.* Ensworth, 6 Paige (N. Y.), 32;

Clason *v.* Morris, 10 Johns. (N. Y.) 524.

[5] Goodyear *v.* Watson, 14 Barb. (N. Y.) 481; Townsend *v.* Whitney, 15 Hun (N. Y.), 93; s. c. 75 N. Y. 425; Waller *v.* Harris, 7 Paige (N. Y.), 167.

[6] Ontario Bank *v.* Walker, 1 Hill (N. Y.), 652, and reporter's note citing New York Bank *v.* Fletcher, 5 Wend. (N. Y.) 85, 89.

[7] Alden *v.* Clark, 11 How. Pr. (N.

In *Pennsylvania*, a surety who has paid a debt secured by a judgment against his principal, and who is in other respects entitled to subrogation, may revive the judgment without first obtaining a decree of substitution, and may have his rights tried on a *scire facias*,[1] even though an entry of satisfaction has been made upon the judgment, if this was not done at the instance of the surety.[2] Actual payment discharges a judgment or other incumbrance at law, but, where justice requires it, it is still kept on foot for the protection of the surety who has paid it.[3] He will be subrogated to all the creditor's rights in the original obligation which he has paid,[4] not only against his principal for indemnity, but against his co-sureties for contribution,[5] and not only to the benefit of a direct obligation, such as a judgment or pending action, but of such an incidental remedy as a distress for rent.[6] The surety will need no formal assignment.[7]

In *New Jersey*, a co-defendant who has been compelled to pay a judgment upon which the other defendant was primarily liable may have the benefit and control of the judgment and execution for his reimbursement against his co-defendant, the primary debtor. The rights of the parties are settled by statute.[8]

In *Delaware*, the surety upon a bond may, on tender of the debt, demand an assignment of the bond, that he may

---

Y.) 209; Dunford *v.* Weaver, 84 N. Y. 445.

[1] Cottrell's Appeal, 23 Penn. St. 294; Richter *v.* Cummings, 60 Penn. St. 441; Cochran *v.* Shields, 2 Grant (Penn. Cas.), 437.

[2] Baily *v.* Brownfield, 20 Penn. St. 41.

[3] *Woodward. J.*, in Cottrell's Appeal, 23 Penn. St. 294, 295; Fleming *v.* Beaver, 2 Rawle (Penn.), 128; Himes *v.* Keller, 3 W. & S. 401; Erb's Appeal, 2 Pen. & W. 296.

[4] Wright *v.* Grover & Baker S. M. Co., 82 Penn. St. 80; Brown *v.* Black, 96 Penn. St. 482; Bank *v.* Harper, 8 Penn. St. 249.

[5] Springer *v.* Springer, 43 Penn. St. 518.

[6] King *v.* Blackmore, 72 Penn. St. 347, distinguishing Quinn *v.* Wallace, 6 Wheat. 452.

[7] Duffield *v.* Cooper, 87 Penn. St. 443.

[8] Durand *v.* Trusdell, 44 N. J. L. 597; White *v.* Brown, 29 *Id.* 307.

enforce it against the principal.[1]   He is entitled to the original evidences of debt and to any judgment in which the debt has been merged,[2] as well as to all collateral securities held by the creditor.[3]

In *Maryland*, a surety, upon paying a judgment-debt of the principal, may in equity compel the creditor to assign to him the judgment, with all liens given by the principal debtor to secure its payment.[4]   The payment in full by the surety will of itself operate, if not at law, yet in equity,[5] as an assignment, so as to enable him to use the name of the creditor for the recovery of the money from the principal,[6] or to levy the execution for his own use upon the property of the principal;[7] and though a partial payment by the surety will not operate as an assignment *pro tanto*,[8] so as to give him any control over the judgment or execution, yet it will not discharge the principal, to the prejudice of the rights of the surety, without the latter's consent, and will give the surety, to the extent of his payment, an equitable interest in the judgment, which he may release or transfer.[9]   But to entitle a surety to an assignment as against his co-sureties, he must not only satisfy the original judgment, but must himself pay the whole amount of it.[10]

In *Virginia*, the surety's payment of a judgment against himself and his principal does not extinguish the judgment, as between the principal and the surety, but the surety will be subrogated to all the liens and remedies which the creditor had by reason of his judgment,[11] and which have not been

---

[1] Merriken *v.* Godwin, 2 Del. Ch. 236.

[2] Dodd *v.* Wilson, 4 Del. Ch. 399.

[3] Miller *v.* Stout, 5 Del. Ch. 259.

[4] Creager *v.* Brengle, 5 Harr. & J. (Md.) 234.

[5] Crisfield *v.* State, 55 Md. 192.

[6] Hollingsworth *v.* Floyd, 2 Harr. & Gill (Md.), 87, 91. Cf. Morgan *v.* Davis, 2 Harr. & McH. 9.

[7] Sotheren *v.* Reed, 4 Harr. & J. (Md.) 307.

[8] *Antea*, § 127; Hollingsworth *v.* Floyd, 2 Harr. & Gill (Md.), 87, 91.

[9] Grove *v.* Brien, 1 Md. 438.

[10] Wilson *v.* Ridgely, 46 Md. 235.

[11] Coffman *v.* Hopkins, 75 Va. 645; Bank *v.* Allen, 76 Va. 200; Leake *v.* Ferguson, 2 Gratt. (Va.) 419; Hill *v.* Manser, 11 Gratt. (Va.) 522; Watts *v.*

already lost;[1] and the same rule is applied to specialties or other obligations.[2] Nor will the surety lose this right by having taken other security from his principal.[3]

In *North Carolina* a surety who pays a judgment for the debt recovered against his principal may have the judgment assigned to a trustee for his reimbursement, and may pursue the bail of his principal,[4] even though a receipt be given by the creditor to the principal.[5] But the surety, to protect his rights, must take such an assignment; if he does not, the debt will be extinguished, both as to his principal and himself.[6] And the assignment must not be made to himself, but to one who was not a party to the record.[7] Such an assignment will preserve the original obligation, and enable the surety to enforce all the remedies which the creditor might have used against the principal;[8] and the surety may control the judgment even against the nominal assignee.[9] The surety upon a specialty debt, who has paid it, will be deemed a specialty creditor, both of his principal and of his co-sureties.[10] But the surety's right, if contested, can be enforced only in an independent action.[11] A mere joint debtor has not the same equity of subrogation against his associates that a surety enjoys against his principal.[12]

Kinney, 3 Leigh (Va.), 272; Rodgers v. McCluer, 4 Gratt. (Va.) 81; McLung v. Beirne, 10 Leigh (Va.), 394.

[1] Carr v. Glasscock, 3 Gratt. (Va.) 343.

[2] Lidderdale v. Robinson, 12 Wheaton, 594; Tinsley v. Oliver, 5 Munf. (Va.) 419; Powell v. White, 11 Leigh (Va.), 309; Eppes v. Randolph, 2 Call (Va.), 125.

[3] Miller v. Pendleton, 4 Hen. & Munf. (Va.) 436.

[4] Hanner v. Douglass, 4 Jones. Eq. (Nor. Car.) 262.

[5] Newbern v. Dawson, 10 Ired. Law (Nor. Car.), 436.

[6] Bledsoe v. Nixon, 68 Nor. Car. 521; Sherwood v. Collier, 3 Dev. Law (Nor. Car.), 380.

[7] Briley v. Sugg, 1 Dev. & Bat. Eq. (Nor. Car.) 366.

[8] Hodges v. Armstrong, 3 Dev. Law (Nor. Car.), 253; Brown v. Long, 1 Ired. Eq. (Nor. Car.) 190.

[9] Rice v. Hearn, 109 Nor. Car. 150.

[10] Howell v. Reams, 73 Nor. Car. 391; Drake v. Coltrane, 1 Busbee (Nor. Car.), 300; Stat. Nor. Car. 1828, c. 110, § 4.

[11] Calvert v. Peebles, 82 Nor. Car. 334.

[12] Jones v. McKinnon, 87 Nor. Car. 294; Towe v. Felton, 7 Jones Law, 216.

In *South Carolina*, a surety who pays a judgment recovered against himself and his principal, or a specialty executed by himself and his principal, does not thereby extinguish it, but may in equity enforce it against his principal's estate,[1] though this privilege has been denied as between co-sureties.[2] But the lien of a judgment which has been paid by one surety has been kept alive for his protection against the insolvent estate of his co-surety.[3] Where after separate judgments against principal and surety for the same debt, the latter paid the judgment against himself, and thereupon the sheriff entered satisfaction upon both judgments, the surety was allowed to vacate this entry upon the judgment against the principal, and to set it up as a lien upon his estate.[4] The same right of subrogation has been allowed to a son who, at the request of his father, has paid a judgment against the latter.[5]

In *Georgia*, a surety who has paid the debt of his principal is, in equity, subrogated to all the remedies of the creditor, and is entitled to occupy the place of and be substituted for the creditor upon the original evidence of the debt;[6] and the surety upon his payment of the debt may require an assignment thereof from the creditor.[7] If a surety pays a judgment rendered against himself and his principal, he is entitled to control such judgment and the execution thereon,[8] and this right will pass upon his decease to his personal representa-

[1] Garvin v. Garvin, 27 So. Car. 472; Kinard v. Baird, 20 So. Car. 377; Thompson v. Palmer, 3 Rich. Eq. (So. Car.) 139; King v. Aughtrey, 3 Strobh. Eq. (So. Car.) 149; Ware, *ex parte*, 5 Rich. Eq. (So. Car.) 473; Smith v. Swain, 7 Rich. Eq. (So. Car.) 112; Schultz v. Carter, Speers Eq. (So. Car.) 534; Le Noir v. Winn, 4 Desaus. 65.

[2] So. Car. Bank v. Adger, 2 Hill Eq. (So. Car.) 262; Cunningham v. Smith, Harp. Eq. (So. Car.) 90.

[3] Burrows v. McWhann, 1 Desaus. Eq. (So. Car.) 409.

[4] Perkins v. Kershaw, 1 Hill, Eq. (So. Car.) 344.

[5] Sutton v. Sutton, 26 So. Car. 33.

[6] Lumpkin v. Mills, 4 Ga. 343.

[7] McDougald v. Dougherty, 14 Ga. 674.

[8] Burke v. Lee, 59 Ga. 165; Davenport v. Hardeman, 5 Ga. 580.

tives.[1] But this right is in equity, not at law;[2] and where, pending a suit brought jointly against the maker and the indorser of a promissory note, the indorser paid the note, it was held that this payment, made before judgment, barred the further prosecution of the suit, even at the instance and for the benefit of the indorser; his remedy was by action in his own name.[3] And this right of subrogation to the original indebtedness is allowed only to a surety; it will not be extended to a mere joint debtor.[4] This right of subrogation is affirmed and regulated by statute.[5]

In *Ohio*, a surety who pays a judgment rendered against himself and his principal will be subrogated to the rights therein of the creditor;[6] this payment will not operate as an extinguishment of the judgment for the benefit of the principal.[7] If one of several co-sureties pays a judgment against them, with the intention of saving his right to be subrogated to the remedies of the judgment-creditor, he may afterwards be subrogated to the judgment, notwithstanding its legal extinction; and such intention on his part will be presumed from the bare fact of payment until the contrary is shown.[8] The remedy against the co-surety is limited to six years, like a simple contract;[9] that against the principal is extended to ten years.[10]

In *Kentucky*, a surety advancing to the creditor the amount of a judgment against his principal may stipulate for substitution and the control of the judgment and execution against his principal for his reimbursement; and a court of law will protect him therein.[11] And under the statutes a surety, upon

[1] Harris v. Wynne, 4 Ga. 521.
[2] Knight v. Morrison, 79 Ga. 55; Elam v. Rawson, 21 Ga. 139.
[3] Griffin v. Hampton, 21 Ga. 198.
[4] Adams v. Keeler, 30 Ga. 86.
[5] Code, §§ 2167, 2171. Thomason v. Wade, 72 Ga. 160.
[6] Ohio Civil Code, § 449. Peters v. McWilliams, 36 Ohio St. 155.
[7] Neal v. Nash, 23 Ohio St. 483; Dempsey v. Bush, 18 Ohio St. 376.
[8] Neilson v. Fry, 16 Ohio St. 552.
[9] Neilson v. Fry, *supra*.
[10] Neal v. Nash, 23 Ohio St. 483.
[11] Morris v. Evans, 2 B. Mon. (Ky.) 84; Roberts v. Bruce, 15 So. W. Rep. 872.

paying the amount of a judgment against himself and his principal, may compel the creditor to assign the judgment to himself.[1] So, if the surety has paid a preferred debt of the principal, he is entitled to the benefit of the preference.[2] But the surety of an intestate who has paid a judgment or specialty debt of his, does not thereby become, *ipso facto* and without an assignment, a judgment or specialty creditor of the estate; he is *prima facie* a simple-contract creditor merely.[3]

In *Tennessee*, though payment by a mere joint debtor discharges the original obligation,[4] a surety who pays a judgment against his principal is subrogated to the judgment lien and to all the rights of the creditor against the principal.[5] Even a partial payment by the surety will give him *pro tanto* the rights of a judgment-creditor as against his principal.[6] The payment by the surety, though it may destroy the remedy or extinguish the security so far as the creditor is concerned, has not that effect between the principal and the surety. As to the surety, it operates in equity as an assignment of the debt and of all legal remedies upon it; and in his favor the debt and all its legal obligations are regarded as subsisting. The surety is not so far subrogated to the rights of the judgment-creditor that an execution can be issued on the original judgment in his favor as an assignee of the judgment; but he may be substituted to the lien which the judgment-creditor had upon the property of the principal and to all the remedies of the creditor,[7] and by contract with the creditor the surety may after paying the judgment cause the execution to be enforced against the principal debtor.[8]

---

[1] Veach *v.* Wickersham, 11 Bush (Ky.), 261; Alexander *v.* Lewis, 1 Met. (Ky.) 407.

[2] Schoolfield *v.* Rudd, 9 B. Mon. (Ky.) 291.

[3] Buckner *v.* Morris, 2 J. J. Marsh. (Ky.) 121.

[4] Baldwin *v.* Merrill, 8 Humph. 132.

[5] McNairy *v.* Eastland, 10 Yerg. (Tenn.) 310; Rhode *v.* Crockett, 2 Yerg. 346.

[6] Williams *v.* Tipton, 5 Humph. (Tenn.) 66.

[7] *Deaderick, J.*, in Bittick *v.* Wilkins, 7 Heisk. (Tenn.) 307 *et seq.*

[8] Floyd *v.* Goodwin, 8 Yerg. 484.

In *Mississippi*, under the former statutes, a surety who had paid a judgment for his principal was in equity entitled to be subrogated to all the rights of the creditor in the judgment; but at law his payment extinguished the judgment, and he became merely a simple-contract creditor of the principal.[1] The present statute[2] protects the rights of the surety at law;[3] and he is subrogated to the judgment-lien, and to all the rights of the judgment-creditor, and may take out execution upon the original judgment. This subrogation takes place. by operation of law upon the surety's payment, without any entry upon the judgment-roll or elsewhere. Nor will the surety's judgment-lien upon the lands of the principal debtor, even in the hands of *bona fide* purchasers thereof, be affected by the fact that upon his payment the judgment was marked settled by the plaintiff's attorney upon the judgment-roll and execution-docket, if the entry was made without the surety's authority or consent.[4]

In *Alabama*, though it was first held that an execution against the principal might be enforced for the benefit of a surety who had paid the judgment,[5] it was afterwards considered that the surety could not after his payment keep the judgment alive against either his principal or his co-sureties;[6] that even though he took an assignment of the judgment he would have no remedy at law except as a simple-contract creditor of the principal;[7] that he could assert no lien by virtue of the instrument upon which he had been surety, as that became *functus officio* by payment of the debt which it secured.[8] But it is now provided by statute[9] that the surety upon paying such a judgment may have it assigned to him-

[1] Dinkins v. Bailey, 23 Miss. 284; Conway v. Strong, 24 Miss. 665.

[2] Code, 1871, § 2258.

[3] Swan v. Smith, 57 Miss. 548.

[4] Yates v. Mead, 68 Miss. 787.

[5] Clemens v. Prout, 3 Stew. & P. 345.

[6] Morrison v. Marvin, 6 Ala. 797; Preslar v. Stallworth, 37 Ala. 402.

[7] Sanders v. Watson, 14 Ala. 198; Smith v. Harrison, 33 Ala. 706.

[8] Foster v. Athenæum, 3 Ala. 302.

[9] Alabama Civil Code, § 3157.

self, and may enforce it for his indemnity, against the principal debtor, at law or in equity, as fully as the creditor himself might have done.[1]

In *Michigan*, the payment of a judgment by a surety with the intent to avail himself, by subrogation, of the lien of the judgment, will not in equity extinguish the debt or destroy the force of a levy upon the execution. Equity will enforce the right of subrogation by keeping the debt alive and preserving the force of the levy for the protection of the surety.[2]

In *Iowa*, the surety on his payment is in equity subrogated to the rights of the creditor in the original obligation,[3] and may enforce the same as of the class to which it originally belonged;[4] but at law his payment of a judgment extinguishes it,[5] and his right of subrogation is not available until enforced by proper legal proceedings seasonably brought.[6] He may take an assignment of the original obligation, and then enforce the creditor's right.[7]

In *Indiana*, though the surety may enforce all the rights of the creditor in the original obligation by having it properly assigned to himself,[8] yet, when a judgment is rendered jointly against two, they are both to be regarded as principals, until one of them is shown to be a surety for the other;[9] and when one of such defendants, claiming to be merely a surety, but without any judicial determination as to his suretyship, pays the judgment, he cannot have execution thereon for his own use.[10] The surety should establish his right by proper proceedings in the original suit or by subsequent proceedings;[11]

---

[1] Bragg v. Patterson, 85 Ala. 233; Blackman v. Joiner, 81 Ala. 344; Vanderveer v. Ware, 65 Ala. 606.

[2] Smith v. Rumsey, 33 Mich. 183.

[3] Hollingsworth v. Pearson, 53 Iowa, 53.

[4] Searing v. Berry, 58 Iowa, 20; Braught v. Griffith, 16 Iowa, 26.

[5] Drefahl v. Tuttle, 42 Iowa, 177; Bones v. Aiken, 35 Iowa, 534.

[6] Johnston v. Belden, 49 Iowa, 301.

[7] Schleissman v. Kallenberg, 72 Iowa, 338.

[8] Manford v. Firth, 68 Ind. 83.

[9] Klippel v. Shields, 90 Ind. 81. So in the case of bail. Kane v. State, 78 Ind. 103.

[10] Laval v. Rowley, 17 Ind. 36; Evans v. Moore, 84 Ind. 440.

[11] Scherer v. Schutz, 83 Ind. 543.

then he may be subrogated to the creditor's rights, after paying the debt.[1]

In *Wisconsin*, a surety upon paying a judgment against himself, his principal, and his co-sureties, may be subrogated to the creditor's rights therein, — against the principal, for the full amount of the debt, and against the sureties for their proportions thereof.[2] The judgment-lien may be kept alive against the other judgment-debtors, either for reimbursement or for contribution.[3]

In *Minnesota*, a surety who has paid a judgment against his principal and himself may not only maintain an action at law against his principal in his own name, but may also enforce the creditor's original judgment-lien against the principal debtor.[4]

In *Kansas*, by statute, sureties who have paid a judgment rendered against their principals and themselves may take an assignment from the judgment-creditor, and enforce the execution against their principals.[5]

In *Illinois*, the surety, upon paying a judgment against his principal, may take an assignment of it, and have it kept alive for his benefit,[6] and may enforce all the securities held by the judgment-creditor.[7] He has an election to keep the judgment alive against his principal, or to treat it as extinguished and sue his principal for reimbursement.[8] If he takes an assignment to a third person he must, before enforcing execution against a co-defendant, procure and file an assignment to himself.[9]

In *Missouri*, a surety who pays the debt of his principal is entitled to an assignment of the instrument paid. Though

[1] Johnson v. Amano Lodge, 92 Ind. 150.

[2] German American Savings Bank v. Fritz, 68 Wisc. 390.

[3] Mason v. Pierron, 69 Wisc. 585. Wisc. Rev. Stats., § 3021.

[4] Kimmel v. Lowe, 28 Minn. 265.

[5] Harris v. Frank, 29 Kans. 200.

[6] Allen v. Powell, 108 Ills. 584.

[7] Rice v. Rice, 108 Ills. 199.

[8] Katz v. Moessinger, 110 Ills. 372; Chandler v. Higgins, 109 Ills. 602.

[9] Farwell v. Becker, 129 Ills. 261.

his payment extinguishes the obligation so far as the creditor is concerned, this will not affect the rights which the surety has acquired by his payment. It still subsists for his benefit as against his principal.[1] But the fact of suretyship must be judicially etablished; his remedy is not a matter of course.[2] So the lien of a judgment, though satisfied by one surety, will in equity be kept alive as between co-sureties.[3]

In *Arkansas*, when a surety pays a judgment rendered jointly against his principal and himself, it is extinguished at law; and the surety can avail himself of it against his principal only in equity.[4] Nor can it be kept alive against a co-surety.[5]

In *Texas*, the surety, upon his payment of the debt of the principal, is entitled, not only to the benefit of all the securities, both legal and equitable, which the creditor holds in pledge for the debt, but to be substituted for the creditor as to the very debt itself, and to have this assigned to him; and equity will regard that which ought to be done as done already, where this is necessary to sustain an action.[6] If the creditor had a first attachment on the principal's property, the surety after payment is entitled to this.[7] But the issue of suretyship must be made and settled in the original suit.[8]

In *Louisiana*, though it is considered that at the common law a surety would not be subrogated to the rights of the creditor upon his paying a joint judgment against himself and his principal, but that the judgment would be extinguished by such payment,[9] yet under their code a surety who

[1] Benne v. Schnecko, 100 Mo. 250; Campbell v. Pope, 96 Mo. 468; Berthold v. Berthold, 46 Mo. 557.

[2] Hull v. Sherwood, 59 Mo. 172; McDaniels v. Lee, 37 Mo. 204.

[3] Furnold v. Missouri Bank, 44 Mo. 336.

[4] Newton v. Field, 16 Ark. 216.

[5] Chollar v. Temple, 39 Ark. 238.

[6] Sublett v. McKinney, 19 Tex. 438; Jordan v. Hudson, 11 Tex. 82.

[7] Krall v. Campbell Printing Press Co., 79 Tex. 556.

[8] Fort Worth Bank v. Daugherty, 81 Tex. 301.

[9] McKee v. Amonett, 6 La. Ann. 207.

pays a judgment recovered against the principal debtor is thereby subrogated to the rights of the creditor, and may issue an execution on the judgment in the name of the creditor for the recovery of the amount which as surety he has paid;[1] and since the surety has an equitable interest in the payment of the demand by the principal, the creditor may permit an execution to issue at the instance of the surety.[2]

In *California*, one of two co-defendants paying the whole of a judgment against them is entitled to be subrogated to the rights of the plaintiff in the judgment to the extent to which his payment accrues to the benefit of his co-defendant;[3] but this right does not arise until he has fully satisfied the judgment.[4] An assignment, however, though made before maturity, of a joint and several promissory note to one of its makers from the payee thereof, constitutes a payment and discharge of the obligation.[5]

§ 138. **Right of the Surety to be subrogated to the Benefit of the Original Obligation denied.** — On the other hand, it has been maintained in some jurisdictions that, although the surety is entitled, upon his payment of the debt, to take by subrogation all the securities which the creditor held for the debt, this does not mean that the original obligation, which is discharged by the payment, shall be assigned to or vested in the surety, but refers only to such securities as are collateral to the principal obligation.[6] A judgment against principal and surety is taken to merge that relation between the debtors,[7] and cannot, after a payment by the surety, be kept alive against the principal, for the benefit of the surety.[8] This rule is followed in

[1] Connely v. Bourg, 16 La. Ann. 108; Tardy v. Allen, 3 La. Ann. 66.

[2] Fluker v. Bobo, 11 La. Ann. 609.

[3] Coffee v. Tevis, 17 Calif. 239.

[4] McDermott v. Mitchell, 53 Calif. 616.

[5] Gordan v. Wansey, 21 Calif. 77.

[6] Dennis v. Rider, 2 McLean, C. C. 451; United States v. Preston, 4 Wash. C. C. 446.

[7] Findlay v. United States Bank, 2 McLean, C. C. 44.

[8] McLean v. Lafayette Bank, 3 McLean, C. C. 587.

*Vermont,* where it is held that when a debt is paid, though by a surety, all liens and securities taken or obtained in legal proceedings to enforce its collection are also extinguished.[1] The original obligation is extinguished as to all the debtors by one debtor's payment thereof.[2]

In *Massachusetts,* a debtor, whether principal or surety, who pays a debt for which others are bound with him, thereby extinguishes its obligation, and can obtain indemnity or contribution from the other debtors only by an independent action against them.[3] The original debt is extinguished, and no further action can be maintained upon it, though the transaction be in form a purchase and an assignment be made of the debt.[4]

In *Maine,* the same rule prevails as that adopted in Massachusetts.[5]

In *Nevada,* a surety who has paid a note and had it assigned to himself, though he may maintain an action against the principal debtor for his payment, has no remedy upon the note itself.[6]

But the rule generally adopted, except in these States, is that a payment by a surety does not necessarily in equity extinguish the original obligation, as between the surety and his principal, but only so far as the rights of the creditor are concerned.[7]

§ 139. **Indemnity held by a Surety discharged by his Release from Liability.** — A mortgage given to the surety for his indemnity by the principal debtor is extinguished by the

---

[1] Moore *v.* Campbell, 36 Vt. 361.
[2] Dana *v.* Conant, 30 Vt. 246; Allen *v.* Ogden, 12 Vt. 9; Porter *v.* Gile, 44 Vt. 520.
[3] Adams *v.* Drake, 11 Cush. (Mass.) 504; Brackett *v.* Winslow, 17 Mass. 153; Hammatt *v.* Wyman, 9 Mass. 138.
[4] Slade *v.* Mutrie, 156 Mass. 19; New Bedford Savings Institution *v.*

Hathaway, 134 Mass. 69; Gardner *v.* Way, 5 Allen, 452; Chapman *v.* Collins, 12 Cush. 163; Bryant *v.* Smith, 10 Cush. 169; Pray *v.* Maine, 7 Cush. 253.
[5] Whittier *v.* Heminway, 22 Me. 238; Morse *v.* Williams, 22 Maine 17.
[6] Frevert *v.* Henry, 14 Nev. 191.
[7] *Antea,* §§ 135, 136, 137.

surety's discharge from liability.[1] If the original debt is
paid, and the surety accordingly discharged, by the execution
of a new note with a new surety, such a mortgage is extinguished;[2] and it cannot be kept alive by an assignment
thereof to the new surety;[3] though a contemporaneous verbal
agreement between the mortgagor, the mortgagee, and the
new surety that a mortgage of personal property should
stand as security to the new surety, might of itself, as between
the parties, constitute a valid mortgage of the property.[4] If
a surety who holds such a security becomes indebted to his
principal upon a different transaction, and in consideration
thereof assumes the payment of the debt for which he was a
surety, this arrangement will release the security in his hands.[5]
But a mortgage given to a surety for his indemnity was
allowed to pass to a third person who paid the money for the
surety on the faith of an agreement that the mortgage should
be assigned to him.[6] And if the note which constituted the
original indebtedness is, after protest for non-payment, paid
out of the proceeds of a new note made by the mortgagor
and indorsed by the mortgagee for that express purpose, the
mortgage will not thereby be discharged, but will continue
in force as a protection to the mortgagee against his liability
upon the second note.[7] The mere change in the form of the
debt does not discharge the security.[8]

§ 140. **Right of Subrogation among Co-sureties.** — One of two
or more co-sureties who has paid the debt to their common
creditor may be subrogated to the rights of that creditor
against his co-sureties, to enable him to recover contribution

[1] Newsam v. Finch, 25 Barb. (N.
Y.) 175; Yelverton v. Shelden, 2
Sandf. Ch. (N. Y.) 481; Hunter v.
Richardson, 1 Duv. (Ky.) 247.

[2] Albert v. Upton, 19 Pick. (Mass.)
434.

[3] Bonham v. Galloway, 13 Ills. 68;
Brooks v. Ruff, 1 Ala. Sel. Cas. 409.

[4] Brooks v. Ruff, *supra*.

[5] United States Bank v. Stewart, 4
Dana (Ky.), 27.

[6] Brien v. Smith, 9 Watts & Serg.
(Penn.) 78; Haven v. Foley, 18 Mo.
136.

[7] Chapman v. Jenkins, 31. Barb.
(N. Y.) 164.

[8] Bobbitt v. Flowers, 1 Swan
(Tenn.), 511.

from them.[1] He will be subrogated as against his co-sureties
in most of the States, as in England under the Mercantile
Law Amendment Act,[2] to all the rights of the creditor, and
entitled to enforce all the creditor's liens, priorities, and
remedies, as well against his co-sureties as against the principal debtor.[3] This right will pass to the creditors of a
co-surety whose means of obtaining their demand have been
lost by their debtor's property, upon which they had a subordinate lien, having been taken to pay the whole obligation of
which his co-sureties should have paid a part;[4] and to a
grantee of one of the co-sureties, who, to save the property
which he has purchased, has been obliged to pay a judgment
which was a lien upon the property of all the sureties, against
both the co-sureties themselves and their grantees of the
other property upon which the judgment was also a lien.[5]
One surety in a joint and several obligation in which there
was a warrant to confess judgment, having paid the whole
indebtedness, may enter judgment upon the obligation to his
own use, and have execution against his co-surety for the
latter's proportion.[6] One of two co-sureties who has paid the
full amount of a civil recognizance will be allowed to use
the recognizance for the purpose of recovering out of the estate
of his co-surety one half of the sum so paid by him.[7] If one
surety has received property or security for or to be applied
upon the debt, and another surety is then compelled to pay the
whole debt, the latter can follow this property in equity and

[1] Hess's Estate, 69 Penn. St. 272;
Croft v. Moore, 9 Watts (Penn.), 451;
Crisfield v. Murdock, 127 N. Y. 315;
Cuyler v. Ensworth, 6 Paige (N. Y.),
32; Felton v. Bissel, 25 Minn. 15.

[2] St. 19 & 20 Vic., c. 97, § 5.

[3] Stokes, Ex parte, De G. (Bnkcy.)
68; Burrows v. McWhann, 1 Desaus.
Eq. (So. Car.) 409; Smith v. Rumsey,
33 Mich. 183; Hess's Estate, 69
Penn. St. 272; Fleming v. Beaver,

[2] Rawle (Penn.), 128; Howell v.
Reams, 73 Nor. Car. 391.

[4] Moore v. Bray, 10 Penn. St. 519.

[5] Furnold v. Missouri Bank, 44
Mo. 336.

[6] Wright v. Grover & Baker S. M.
Co., 82 Penn. St. 80.

[7] Swan's Estate, Irish R. 4 Eq.
209, overruling Salkeld v. Abbott,
Hayes & Jones Irish Eq. 110, and
Onge v. Truelock, 2 Molloy, 42.

have the benefit of it,[1] or he may at law recover its value from the surety who has received it.[2] In Massachusetts the enforcement of this rule has been refused at law,[3] but it is fully recognized as a doctrine of equity.[4]

§ 141. **Co-sureties entitled to the Benefit of Securities held by each other.** — A fund deposited by the principal debtor with one of his sureties as a security against the latter's liability will inure proportionally to the benefit of all the co-sureties.[5] In the absence of special circumstances all the sureties are entitled to share in the benefit of any indemnity which their co-surety may have taken from the principal debtor,[6] even though such indemnity may have been intended by the principal for the benefit of the latter surety alone.[7] Any security given to one surety and conditioned for the payment of the common indebtedness will inure to the benefit of all the co-sureties.[8] Persons who are subject to a common burden stand to each other upon a common ground of interest and of right; and whatever indemnity is furnished to one of them by him for whom the burden is assumed must be applied equally for the relief of all the associates.[9] If one surety

---

[1] Hinsdill v. Murray, 6 Vt. 136.

[2] Parham v. Green, 64 Nor. Car. 436.

[3] Bowditch v. Green, 3 Met. (Mass.) 360.

[4] New Bedford Savings Institution v. Hathaway, 134 Mass. 69, 72, per Devens, J.

[5] Berridge v. Berridge, 44 Ch. D. 168; Scribner v. Adams, 73 Maine, 541; Shaeffer v. Clendenin, 100 Penn. St. 565; Smith v. Conrad, 15 La. Ann. 579; Hall v. Robinson, 8 Ired. Law (Nor. Car.), 56; Hayden v. Cornelius, 12 Mo. 321; Aldrich v. Hapgood, 39 Vt. 617; Fishback v. Weaver, 34 Ark. 569.

[6] Brown v. Ray, 18 N. H. 102; Whiteman v. Harriman, 85 Ind. 49;

Comegys v. State Bank, 6 Ind. 357; Fagan v. Jacocks, 4 Dev. Law (Nor. Car.), 263; Gregory v. Murrell, 2 Ired. Eq. (Nor. Car.) 233; Bobbitt v. Flowers, 1 Swan (Tenn.), 511; McMahon v. Fawcett, 2 Rand. (Va.) 514; Elwood v. Deifendorff, 5 Barb. (N. Y.) 398.

[7] Steel v. Dixon, 17 Ch. Div. 825; Cannon v. Connaway, 5 Del. Ch. 559; Hartwell v. Whitman, 36 Ala. 712.

[8] Logan v. Talbot, 59 Calif. 652; Paul v. Berry, 78 Ills. 158; State v. Berning, 74 Mo. 87, 98; Dye v. Mann, 10 Mich. 291; Bell v. Lamkin, 1 Stew. & P. (Ala.) 460; Low v. Smart, 5 N. H. 353; Lane v. Stacey, 8 Allen (Mass.), 41.

[9] Nally v. Long, 56 Md. 567;

gets possession of a fund belonging to the principal, he may
not take the entire benefit of it, but must share it with
his co-sureties.[1] If one who is a surety for the same principal on various liabilities, on some of which he has co-sureties,
takes from his principal security generally for his protection,
this is, for the benefit of his co-sureties, to be apportioned
among all the demands *pro rata*.[2] But if one surety takes
from his principal a mortgage for his protection against a
particular debt, this will inure to the benefit of his co-sureties
on that debt, and the mortgagee will have no right to apply
the proceeds of the security to the payment of any other
debt, to the prejudice of his co-surety.[3] To prevent circuity
of action and attain the ends of natural justice, a court of
equity will completely indemnify one of the sureties upon a
bond by means of a lien upon the property of the principal
existing in favor of another surety, notwithstanding the
former surety has himself relinquished another lien upon
the same property, originally created for his indemnification.[4]
A mortgage executed to one or more of the sureties upon the
official bond of an officer will inure to the benefit of all the
sureties, as well those who subsequently become such under
a proper and lawful order of court requiring additional sureties upon the bond, as those who were sureties at the date
of the mortgage.[5] The same rule will be applied to property
or securities deposited by one co-surety with another for
their joint benefit, as to securities furnished by the principal;

Neely *v.* Bee, 32 W. Va. 519; Mc-
Lewis *v.* Furgerson, 59 Ga. 644;
Reinhart *v.* Johnson, 62 Iowa, 155;
Miller *v.* Sawyer, 30 Vermont 412;
Agnew *v.* Bell, 4 Watts (Pennsylva-
nia), 31.

[1] Leary *v.* Cheshire, 3 Jones, Eq.
(Nor. Car.) 170; Whipple *v.* Briggs,
28 Vt. 65; Boughner *v.* Hall, 24 W.
Va. 249; Robinson *v.* Brooks 32 Ala.

222; Pinkston *v.* Taliaferro, 9 Ala.
547.

[2] Brown *v.* Ray, 18 N. H. 102;
Goodloe *v.* Clay, 6 B. Mon. (Ky.)
236.

[3] Steele *v.* Mealing, 24 Ala. 285.

[4] West *v.* Belches, 5 Munf. (Va.)
187.

[5] Farmers' Bank *v.* Teeters, 31
Ohio St. 36.

each is entitled to his proportion, and only to his proportion thereof.[1]

§ 142. **A Surety cannot have Contribution from his Co-sureties without accounting for such Security.** — A surety who, being indebted to his principal or having received property or security from the principal, has paid the whole debt, cannot require contribution from his co-sureties without showing that this indebtedness or security has been properly disposed of, and is insufficient to satisfy the debt for which contribution is demanded.[2] If he has appropriated the security to himself by means of a collusive sale, he must account for it at a fair value.[3] If the security has not yet been disposed of, his remedy is in equity.[4] But if the surety who has paid the debt has received only a partial indemnity from his principal, he may recover from his co-surety the latter's proportionate share of the balance.[5] And if indemnity other than money has been provided by the principal for his sureties, but no satisfaction has been realized therefrom, this will not prevent the surety who has paid the debt from recovering contribution from his co-sureties.[6] The principal debtor having mortgaged to one of his sureties as security against his suretyship land worth less than half of the debt, and then become insolvent, the unsecured surety gave to the mortgagee half the amount of the debt, and the mortgagee agreed to pay the debt, and to give to the other surety half of all that he might receive from the principal debtor; and it was held that this promise included whatever he might realize upon the mortgage previously given to him by the principal.[7] But a mere indebtedness

[1] Mitchell v. Bass, 24 Tex. 392.

[2] Davis v. Toulmin, 77 N. Y. 280; Neely v. Bee, 32 W. Va. 519; Morrison v. Poyntz, 7 Dana (Ky.), 307; Chilton v. Chapman, 13 Mo. 470.

[3] Sanders v. Weelburg, 107 Ind. 266; Owen v McGehee, 61 Ala. 440; Hall v. Robinson, 8 Ired. Law (Nor. Car.), 56.

[4] Morrison v. Poyntz, 7 Dana (Ky.), 307.

[5] Bachelder v. Fiske, 17 Mass. 464.

[6] Anthony v. Percifull, 8 Ark. (3 English), 494; Johnson v. Vaughn, 65 Ills. 425.

[7] Sheldon v. Welles, 4 Pick. (Mass.) 60.

of the surety who seeks contribution to the principal is not available to the co-sureties;[1] and where lands of the principal debtor are sold under an execution against him, and are purchased by one surety with money belonging to himself and a second co-surety, as this is not a fund coming from the principal, a third co-surety cannot maintain a claim to participate in the benefit of the purchase as indemnity against his liability with the other sureties.[2]

§ 143. A Surety holding Security regarded as a Trustee thereof for his Co-sureties. — A security obtained by one co-surety for the payment of the debt is held by him for the benefit of all the sureties; he is a trustee for his co-sureties as to such security,[3] and is subject to the duties which arise from that relation,[4] and must refrain from any act or voluntary omission, by which such security will be depreciated or lost, but must faithfully apply it to the payment of the debt; or he will be chargeable to his co-sureties with the amount of the security, in the adjustment of their proportions of the debt.[5] He must use reasonable diligence to secure the application of the property to the payment of the debt.[6] All the co-sureties are liable among themselves for contribution to the extent of any balance that may remain due after such application.[7] If one surety takes from the principal a mortgage or other security to indemnify him for becoming such surety, and afterwards discharges the same, it being of sufficient value to have paid the debt, he will by that act be prevented from calling

[1] Davis v. Toulmin, 77 N. Y. 280.

[2] Crompton v. Vasser, 19 Ala. 259.

[3] Hall v. Robinson, 8 Ired. Law (Nor. Car.), 56; Sayles v. Sims, 73 N. Y. 551; Hilton v. Crist, 5 Dana (Ky.), 384; Leggett v. McClelland, 39 Ohio St. 624; Carpenter v. Kelly, 9 Ohio, 106.

[4] Taylor v. Morrison, 26 Ala. 728; Ramsey v. Lewis, 30 Barb. (N. Y.) 403.

[5] Simmons v. Camp, 71 Ga. 54; Mandigo v. Mandigo, 26 Mich. 349; Schmidt v. Coulter, 6 Minn. 492; Roberts v. Sayer, 6 T. B. Mon. (Ky.) 188; Fielding v. Waterhouse, 8 Jones & Spencer (N. Y.), 424.

[6] Goodloe v. Clay, 6 B. Mon. (Ky.) 236; Kerns v. Chambers, 3 Ired. Eq. (Nor. Car.) 576.

[7] John v. Jones, 16 Ala. 454.

on his co-sureties for contribution.[1] But if the security discharged is of unascertained value, it has been said that the only remedy of the co-sureties is in equity; they will still be liable for contribution at law.[2] Where one co-surety, having received security from the principal debtor, caused the same to be sold for enough to pay the debt, but never collected the money, it was held that he could not, upon afterwards paying the debt, recover any contribution thereto from his co-surety;[3] nor if, having collected the money, he had then procured the original debt to be assigned to a third person for his benefit, would such assignee be allowed in equity to collect anything from the co-surety.[4]

§ 144. **His Rights and Liabilities towards his Co-sureties.** — The surety who holds securities from his principal will be protected from loss if he manages them with prudence, good faith, and integrity; a mere change of the security, made in good faith, and not resulting in loss, will not discharge his co-sureties from liability for contribution.[5] If his security is a chattel mortgage, he is not bound to take possession of the property until he has paid the debt, or has reason to apprehend that he will be called upon to pay it, and that the property will be squandered; then, if he fails to take the proper steps to preserve the security, he may be charged by his co-sureties with the value of the property which by the exercise of due diligence he might have secured.[6] If he has taken a mortgage as security, with an agreement that it shall not be recorded, he cannot be charged by his co-sureties for failing to have it recorded.[7] He may, as against his co-sureties, be allowed for his necessary and reasonable expenses incurred

[1] Taylor v. Morrison, 26 Ala. 728; Ramsey v. Lewis, 30 Barb. (N. Y.) 403.

[2] Paulin v. Kaighn, 27 N. J. Law, 503; Johnson v. Vaughn, 65 Ills. 425; Anthony v. Percifull, 8 Ark. (3 English) 494.

[3] Chilton v. Chapman, 13 Mo. 470.

[4] Silvey v. Dowell, 53 Ills. 260.

[5] Carpenter v. Kelly, 9 Ohio, 106.

[6] Tester v. Pierce, 11 B. Mon. (Ky.) 399.

[7] White v. Carlton, 52 Ind. 371

in protecting the security,[1] but not for any expenses unnecessarily incurred without the consent of the co-sureties.[2] Where one of two sureties received from the principal debtor the latter's note for one-half of the debt, payable on demand, by which he might secure himself whenever he pleased, and afterwards took another note from the principal for goods sold to him, and then recovered judgment upon both notes, and collected on the execution enough to pay the whole of the first note and part of the second, and then, the principal having become insolvent, the sureties paid each one-half of the debt for which they were bound, the second surety being ignorant that the first had received any indemnity from the principal, it was held, on a bill in equity brought by the second surety against the first, that the first surety must account to the second for one-half of the amount of the indemnifying note that he had thus received from the principal.[3] Where one surety promised the principal debtor, if the latter would consent to the sale of certain property mortgaged by him to the creditor for the payment of the debt, the creditor being unwilling to sell it without such consent, to buy it if it should be sold for less than its value, and hold it for the common indemnity of himself and his co-sureties, it was decided, on the purchase being made in accordance with the agreement, that a trust immediately arose in favor of the co-sureties, which could be enforced at their instance; that the surety so purchasing would be responsible for the property with its proceeds and profits, and for all losses that could be prevented by the care and diligence which trustees are bound to exercise, and should be allowed the price which he paid for the property.[4]

§ 145. Surety may in Equity prevent Discharge of Security held by his Co-surety. — One surety has no right to discharge

[1] Livingston v. Van Rensselaer, 6 Wend. (N. Y.) 63; Comegys v. State Bank, 6 Ind. 357.

[2] John v. Jones, 16 Ala. 457; Comegys v. State Bank, 6 Ind. 357.

[3] Miller v. Sawyer, 30 Vt. 412.

[4] Steele v. Brown, 18 Ala. 700.

to the prejudice of his co-surety a security taken for the indemnity of both.[1] In a case in Massachusetts, it appeared that A. sold goods to B., who mortgaged them to C., to secure the latter against liability upon a promissory note signed by B. as principal and by C. and D. as sureties. The mortgaged goods were levied upon in a suit against A., as having been sold by him in fraud of his creditors. C. then brought a suit against the attaching officer for a conversion of the goods, but afterwards agreed with the officer to discontinue the suit and discharge his mortgage, upon the officer's agreeing to pay part of the note and to collect the balance thereof from D.; and it was held that D. could maintain a bill in equity against the officer and C., to restrain the discontinuance of the suit and the discharge of the mortgage, and for leave to prosecute the action in his own behalf.[2]

§ 146. **Security held by one who is both a Creditor and a Surety.** — If one who is both a creditor and a surety takes security for the debt due to himself, as well as to indemnify himself from his liability upon his suretyship, he is entitled to appropriate so much of it as is necessary for the payment of his own claim in full.[3] But he cannot hold it against his co-sureties on account of demands against the debtor which he has obtained after taking the security, unless it was agreed when he took the security that he should obtain the other demands and hold the security for them also.[4] Though it is settled in equity that if one surety takes a security from the common principal for his own indemnity, this will inure to the benefit of all his co-sureties, yet, if he has a security for individual claims of his own against the same principal, he may hold this for his own benefit.[5]

---

[1] Hayes v. Davis, 18 N. H. 600.
[2] Sheehan v. Taft, 110 Mass. 331.
[3] Wallace v. Greenlaw, 9 Lea (Tenn.), 115.
[4] Brown v. Ray, 18 N. H. 102.

In Miller v. Sawyer, 30 Vt. 412, the second note was for an indebtedness incurred after the taking of the security.
[5] McCune v. Belt, 45 Mo. 174.

§ 147. **Surety must contribute to Cost of Security of which he seeks the Benefit. Waiver.** — One surety cannot claim the benefit of indemnity obtained by his co-surety from the principal without paying his proportion of the consideration therefor; and if an offer of indemnity is made to the sureties by the principal, on the condition that they shall give him a release, which offer is accepted by the one and refused by the other, though the latter could insist that the proceeds of the securities thus obtained by the former should be applied in reduction of the common debt, yet these securities could in no other way inure to his benefit; and this application would discharge the former surety from contribution to the latter, if it amounted to his proportion of the common debt.[1] The complainants and the defendant being co-sureties for a debtor to whom the defendant was also indebted, the principal proposed to relieve the defendant from his liability as surety by giving a new note with other sureties, if the defendant would give him a sight draft for the amount of his indebtedness, or, if he failed to procure the defendant's release from his suretyship, that he would then place the defendant's notes in the hands of a third person, for the indemnity of the defendant alone: the complainants' assent to this arrangement was held to be a waiver of the right which they would otherwise have enjoyed to participate in the indemnity thus given to the defendant. But the facts that the complainants objected to the principal's making an assignment for the benefit of his sureties, because this would injure his credit, and agreed that he might procure the release of the defendant from his suretyship, if the latter would pay him the amount of his indebtedness, and that the defendant then said in their hearing that if the principal failed to carry out the arrangement for his relief he should take measures to protect himself, are not sufficient to establish a waiver on the part of the complainants of their

[1] White *v.* Banks, 21 Ala. 705.

legal right to share in any indemnity or security which the
defendant might afterwards obtain from the principal.[1]

§ 148. **Right of one Surety to stipulate, on becoming such, for
a Separate Indemnity to himself.** — But if one surety on becoming such stipulates for and receives from his principal a separate indemnity, this is his exclusively; and his co-sureties can
claim from him only the surplus of the proceeds thereof over
what is necessary for his indemnification;[2] so also, if the
co-surety obtains indemnity from a third party.[3] He has the
right so to stipulate for a separate indemnity to himself, and
to apply that indemnity upon his portion of the common liability to his own relief; and such an indemnity can be
reached by his co-sureties only when it was taken in fraud of
their rights or for their common benefit.[4] And one surety is
not entitled to the benefit of a mortgage which was given and
is conditioned merely to indemnify his co-surety after the co-
sureties had adjusted their loss by each of them paying one-
half of the sum for which they were bound.[5] Though whatever
payment one surety may receive from the principal must in
general inure to the benefit of all, yet, where payment of the
debt for which all were liable has been made by one, and the
claim against each for contribution has become fixed, each
may on his separate account look to the principal for the
reimbursement of his own share.[6] And one of two sureties
who has actually paid the whole debt for which both were
liable may recover from the other surety half of the amount
thereof, although, since such payment, he may have received
from the principal the other half expressly for his separate
indemnity.[7]

[1] Tyus *v.* De Jarnette, 26 Ala.
280.

[2] Titcomb *v.* McAllister, 81 Maine,
399; Moore *v.* Moore, 4 Hawks (Nor.
Car.), 358.

[3] Leggett *v.* McClelland, 39 Ohio
St. 624.

[4] Thompson *v.* Adams, 1 Freem.
(Miss.) 225.

[5] Hall *v.* Cushman, 16 N. H. 462.

[6] Gould *v.* Fuller, 18 Maine, 364;
Messer *v.* Swan, 4 N. H. 481.

[7] Gould *v.* Fuller, *supra*; Paulin
*v.* Kaighn, 27 N. J. Law, 503.

§ 149. **A Co-surety called upon for Contribution becomes thereby entitled to Subrogation.** — If one surety calls upon his co-surety for contribution, he must at the same time permit the latter to share in all the rights to which he has himself been subrogated by his payment.[1] So one surety for the payment of a judgment, if he is held to contribute for the benefit of a co-surety who has paid the judgment, will thereupon be subrogated to the lien of the judgment upon the land of the judgment-debtor.[2] And if the surety who has paid the debt has discharged the principal from liability therefor, then, as this would prevent the subrogation of the co-sureties against the principal, they cannot be compelled to contribute for the relief of the surety who has made the payment.[3]

§ 150. **Subsequent Sureties not entitled to Indemnity provided for Prior Sureties.** — Although the rights of co-sureties against each other are not affected by the fact that they became sureties at different times,[4] by different instruments,[5] or even without each other's knowledge,[6] if only they are as among themselves co-sureties,[7] yet sureties who bind themselves after the liability of the original sureties has become fixed are not entitled to share in the benefit of an indemnity provided for the original sureties.[8] Parties to a promissory note

---

[1] Arcedeckne, *in re*, 24 Ch. D. 709 : Stanwood *v.* Clampitt, 23 Miss. 372.

[2] Green *v.* Milbank, 56 How. Pr. (N. Y.) 382.

[3] Fletcher *v.* Jackson, 23 Vermont, 581.

[4] Warner *v.* Morrison, 3 Allen (Mass.), 566; Powell *v.* Powell, 48 Calif. 235; Monson *v.* Drakeley, 40 Conn. 552; Bosley *v.* Taylor, 5 Dana (Ky.), 157.

[5] Armitage *v.* Pulver, 37 N. Y. 494; Bell *v.* Jasper, 2 Ired. Eq. (Nor. Car.) 597; Jones *v.* Blanton, 6 *Id.* 115; Loring *v.* Bacon, 3 Cush. (Mass.)

465; Young *v.* Shunk, 30 Minn. 503.

[6] Norton *v.* Coons, 3 Denio (N. Y.), 130; Chaffee *v.* Jones, 19 Pick. (Mass.) 260; Craythorne *v.* Swinburne, 14 Ves. 160.

[7] Blake *v.* Cole, 22 Pick. (Mass.) 97; Taylor *v.* Savage, 12 Mass. 98; Wells *v.* Miller, 66 N. Y. 255; McPherson *v.* Talbot, 10 Gill & J. (Md.) 499; Robertson *v.* Deatherage, 82 Ills. 511; Salyers *v.* Ross, 15 Ind. 130.

[8] *Antea,* § 131 *et seq;* Harnsberger *v.* Yancey, 33 Gratt. (Va.) 527.

are *prima facie* liable successively in the order fixed by the note. Accordingly, the accommodation-maker of a note cannot treat a mortgage given to the subsequent accommodation indorser thereof by the party for whose benefit the note was made, conditioned for the indemnity of the indorser, as a security taken by the indorser for the benefit of both of them, even though the indorser has since purchased the equity of redemption in the mortgaged property; the maker is liable to the indorser on the latter's taking up the note, for the amount thereof, less only the actual value of the security.[1] If, however, there are two successive accommodation indorsers of a note, and the second indorser, having been furnished by the maker with means to pay the note, promises the first indorser to apply these means for that purpose, and thereby lulls the first indorser into inaction which would result in his injury if held to pay the note, this promise creates an equity in favor of the latter which will support an action by him against the second indorser.[2] The principal in a bond assigned a claim to a trustee for the indemnity of his sureties, in trust to collect the claim and apply its proceeds to the payment of the bond. Before the claim was collected, a suit was brought upon the bond; and the sureties contributed ratably to its payment. One of the sureties having obtained a decree against the principal for what he had paid, took the principal in execution, and obtained from him a bond with sureties, which was afterwards forfeited, and the new sureties paid the amount of the decree. The trustee having afterwards collected the claim assigned to him, it was held that the new sureties could not participate in this trust fund, by subrogation to the rights of the original surety whom they had satisfied; that the surety who had obtained the new bond was bound to proceed thereon against the sureties therein, and could come upon the trust-fund only for any deficiency in

[1] Post *v.* Tradesmen's Bank, 28 Conn. 420.

[2] Rice *v.* Truesdell, 28 N. J. Eq. 200.

his recovery from them; and that the sureties in the new bond could not resort to the trust-fund for their reimbursement except to the extent of any surplus that might remain after the full indemnification of the original sureties.[1] But the original sureties would not lose their rights by afterwards becoming sureties for the payment of a judgment recovered for the original debt; if they were then compelled to pay the judgment, they would be subrogated as if they had been held on their original obligation, so far as their interposition had not resulted injuriously to their co-sureties.[2]

§ 151. **Extent of the Right of Subrogation among Co-sureties. Creditor's Interference with the Right.** — The subrogation of a surety against his co-sureties is the equitable right of the surety himself, and is not affected by the relations existing between the principal debtor and the co-sureties against whom the right is sought to be exercised.[3] It will be carried only to the extent of recovering from them their reasonable proportions of what he has paid,[4] not exceeding, however, the amount of the obligation;[5] for whenever two persons are compelled to contribute to a common burden all the advantages acquired by one in dealing with the common creditor will be made to inure equally to the benefit of all.[6] A surety who has paid the principal obligation by a conveyance of real estate can recover contribution from his co-surety only upon the basis of the real value of the land,[7] though the price at

[1] Givens v. Nelson, 10 Leigh (Va.), 382; Langford v. Perrin, 5 Leigh (Va.), 552.

[2] Preston v. Preston, 4 Gratt. (Va.) 88.

[3] Himes v. Keller, 3 Watts & Serg. (Penn.) 401; Broughton v. Robinson, 11 Ala. 922.

[4] See Snowdon, ex parte, Snowdon, in re, 17 Ch. Div. 44; New Bedford Savings Institution v. Hathaway, 134 Mass. 69; Apperson v. Wilbourn, 58 Miss. 439; Rutherford v. Branch Bank, 14 Ala. 92.

[5] Fuselier v. Babineau, 14 La. Ann. 764; Sinclair v. Redington, 56 N. H. 146; Edmonds v. Sheahan, 47 Tex. 443; Jordan v. Adams, 7 Ark. (2 English) 348.

[6] Steel v. Dixon, 17 Ch. Div. 825; Owen v. McGehee, 61 Ala. 440.

[7] Hickman v. McCurdy, 7 J. J.

which it was taken by the creditor may be evidence of this
value.[1] One of the sureties of an administrator who has
bought up at a discount legacies, for the payment of which
the sureties were bound, will be allowed to charge his co-
surety only with his proportion of the expense actually incurred therefor.[2] A surety cannot by means of an assignment of the creditor's remedies recover from his co-sureties
more than their reasonable proportions of what he has himself paid.[3] Nor will sureties upon one obligation have any
equitable right to securities given by the same debtor to his
sureties upon a different obligation.[4] A surety will not, as
against his co-sureties, be subrogated to any remedies for a
debt which his co-sureties had the right to require him to
discharge.[5] The doctrine of contribution between co-sureties
is not founded upon contract, but is the result of general
equity.[6] And any interference by the creditor with the sureties' right of subrogation against each other will, to the extent of the injury received thereby, discharge the sureties who
are so injured,[7] just as a similar interference with their right
of subrogation against their principal would have discharged

---

Marsh. (Ky.) 555; Edmonds v. Sheahan, 47 Tex. 443; Jordan v. Adams, 7
Ark. (2 English) 348.

[1] Jones v. Bradford, 25 Ind. 305.

[2] Tarr v. Ravenscroft, 12 Gratt.
(Va.) 642.

[3] New Bedford Savings Institution
v. Hathaway, 134 Mass. 69; Kelly v.
Page, 7 Gray (Mass.), 213.

[4] Lacy v. Rollins, 74 Tex. 566.

[5] McCrory v. Parks, 18 Ohio St. 1.

[6] Dering v. Winchelsea, 1 Cox,
Ch. Cas. 318; Dennis v. Gillespie, 24
Miss. 581; Brindle v. Page, 21 Vt.
94; Fletcher v. Grover, 11 N. H.
368.

[7] Stirling v. Forrester, 3 Bligh,
575; Hodgson v. Hodgson, 2 Keen,
704; Evans v. Bremridge, 2 Kay &

Johns. 174; McKim v. Demmon, 130
Mass. 404; Greenfield Savings Bank
v. Stowell, 123 Mass. 196; Howe v.
Peabody, 2 Gray (Mass.), 556; Smith
v. United States, 2 Wallace, 219;
Shock v. Miller, 10 Penn. St. 401;
Klingensmith v. Klingensmith, 31
Penn. St. 460; Ide v. Churchill, 14
Ohio St. 372; State v. Van Pelt, 1
Smith (Ind.), 118; Martin v. Taylor,
8 Bush (Ky.), 384; Mitchell v. Bur-
ton, 2 Head (Tenn.), 613; Jemison
v. Governor, 47 Ala. 390; Lower v.
Buchanan Bank, 78 Mo. 67; State v.
Matson, 44 Mo. 305; Dodd v. Winn,
27 Mo. 501; Rice v. Morton, 19 Mo.
263. Contra, where the sureties were
under a several liability, Teutonia
Bank v. Wagner, 37 La. Ann. 732.

them.[1] The same right exists between co-sureties to be relieved to the extent of the share of each in the debt by the acts of the creditor as exists between them and their principal to be relieved of the whole debt by similar acts of the creditor with their principal ;[2] and when the creditor by his acts discharges one surety, or abandons a lien upon his property for the debt, he can hold the other surety only for a *pro rata* share of the debt.[3] This doctrine is to be limited in the same manner, and with similar diversities of the decisions, as is the case with the similar doctrine of the release of the sureties by the creditor's interference with their rights against their principal.[4]

§ 152. **One Surety holding Security from the Principal holds it for the Whole Debt.** — As one of several sureties who holds security from the principal debtor to secure him against his suretyship holds it *prima facie* for the benefit of his co-sureties as well as of himself, so he has a valid lien upon it, as against his principal, for the whole debt.[5] Accordingly, where the principal maker of a note which was also signed by three others as his sureties made a mortgage of personal property to one of his sureties conditioned to indemnify him against his liability for the debt, the mortgagee was allowed, in an

[1] *Antea*, § 119 *et seq.*

[2] Lewis v. Armstrong, 80 Ga. 402 ; Waggoner v. Walrath, 24 Hun (N. Y.), 443.

[3] *Ex parte* Gifford, 6 Vesey, 805 ; Stirling v. Forrester, 3 Bligh, 575 ; Rice v. Morton, 19 Mo. 263 ; People v. Buster, 11 Calif. 215 ; Gordon v. Moore, 44 Ark. 349 ; North American Ins. Co. v. Handy, 2 Sandf. Ch. (N. Y.) 492. And see Smith v. State, 46 Md. 617 ; State v. Atherton, 40 Mo. 209 ; Alexander v. Byrd, 85 Va. 690.

[4] *Antea*, § 119 *et seq.* And see Ward v. New Zealand Bank, 8 App. Cas. 755 ; Clarke v. Birley, 41 Ch. D. 422 ; Collins v. Prosser, 1 Barn. &

Cress. 682 ; s. c., 3 Dowl. & Ry. 112 ; Thompson v. Lack, 3 Man., Gr. &. Sc. 540 ; Hood v. Hayward, 26 Abbott New Cas. (N. Y.) 271, affirming s. c., 48 Hun, 330 ; Wilbur v. Williams, 16 R. I. 242 ; Chipman v. Todd, 60 Maine, 282 ; Frederick v. Moore, 13 B. Mon. (Ky.) 470 ; Hewitt v. Adams, 1 Patton & Heath (Va.), 34 ; Ide v. Churchill, 14 Ohio St. 372.

[5] McWhorter v. Wright, 5 Ga. 555 ; Bellune v. Wallace, 2 Rich. Law (So. Car.), 80 ; Pringle v. Sizer, 2 Rich. N. S. (So. Car.) 59 ; Tunnell v. Jefferson, 5 Harringt. (Del.) 206 ; Miller v. Howry, 3 Pen. & Watts (Penn.), 374.

action against the mortgagor's assignee in insolvency, who had sold the property, to recover the proceeds of this property to the extent of his legal liability upon the note, although he had paid no part of the amount due thereon, and his co-sureties were equally liable with himself for the payment thereof, and although the consideration named in the mortgage was only one-third of the amount of the note; and parol evidence was held to be inadmissible to show that the principal debtor had intended in giving the mortgage to secure the mortgagee only to the extent of one-third of what was due upon the note, under the belief that this would be a full indemnity for his liability.[1]

§ 153. **Co-sureties' Right of Subrogation subject to Legal Rights of Third Parties.** — The equitable right of one surety upon his payment of the debt to be subrogated to the benefit of securities or property of the principal in the hands of a co-surety must yield to rights which have accrued to others upon the strength of the apparent legal title to such property. Accordingly, where an absolute deed of land was made to three persons, for the real purpose of securing them against their liability as sureties for a debt of the grantor, and they agreed to reconvey the land to him upon his payment of the debt, and then two of the sureties were compelled to pay the debt, the grantor and the other surety having become insolvent, it was held that the levy of an execution by a creditor of the insolvent surety upon the latter's undivided portion of the land vested in such creditor the title to that portion, unaffected by any equitable claims of the sureties who had paid the debt.[2]

§ 154. **The Creditor may be substituted to the Benefit of Security for the Debt held by a Surety.** — A creditor has also an equitable right to be substituted to the benefit of any collateral security for the debt which the principal debtor has

---

[1] Barker v. Buel, 5 Cush. (Mass.) 519.

[2] Jewett v. Bailey, 5 Greenl. (Me.) 87.

given to his surety;[1] and where property has been conveyed in trust for such a purpose, the creditor, although he was no party to the conveyance, may by a bill in equity have the property applied to the payment of his demand.[2] The creditor will be entitled to the benefit of a mortgage assigned by the principal debtor to a trustee for the protection of his surety, with authority, on default in the payment of the debt, to collect the mortgage-notes and pay the debt out of the proceeds.[3] And a trustee who holds property which has been assigned to him by the principal debtor, with authority at the request of the surety on the latter's being threatened with loss by reason of his suretyship, to sell enough of the property to save the surety harmless, is not bound to wait until the surety shall have been actually compelled to pay the money, but should relieve the surety from responsibility, whenever he has the funds in hand for that purpose.[4] The creditor is in equity entitled to the benefit of collateral security for the payment of the debt taken by a surety from the principal debtor, although he did not originally rely upon such security,[5] or even know of its existence.[6] The creditor and the surety have correlative rights; each is entitled to the benefit of the securities held by the other for the payment of the debt.[7] The creditor may, if necessary, compel the

[1] Maure v. Harrison, 1 Eq. Cas. Ab. 97; Owens v. Miller, 29 Md. 144; Roberts v. Colvin, 3 Gratt. (Va.) 358; Loehr v. Colborn, 92 Ind. 24; Alabama Ins. Co. v. Anderson, 67 Ala. 425; Saffold v. Wade, 51 Ala. 214; Troy v. Smith, 33 Ala. 469; Seibert v. True, 8 Kans. 52.

[2] United States Bank v. Stewart, 4 Dana (Ky.), 27; Ray v. Proffett, 15 Lea (Tenn.), 517; Kinsey v. McDearmon, 5 Coldw. (Tenn.) 392; Miller v. Lancaster, 5 Coldw. (Tenn.) 514; King v. Harman, 6 La. 607.

[3] Cullum v. Mobile Bank, 23 Ala. 797.

[4] Daniel v. Joyner, 3 Ired. Eq. (Nor. Car.) 513; Morton v. Lowell, 56 Tex. 643.

[5] Cooper v. Middleton, 94 Nor. Car. 86; Daniel v. Hunt, 77 Ala. 567.

[6] Higgins v. Wright, 43 Barb. (N. Y.) 461; Morehead v. Duncan, 82 Penn. St. 488; Rice's Appeal, 79 Penn. St. 168; Kinsey v. McDearmon, 5 Coldw. (Tenn.) 392; Carpenter v. Bowen, 42 Miss. 28.

[7] United States v. Sturges, 1 Paine, 525; Saylors v. Saylors, 3 Heisk. (Tenn.) 525; Osborn v. Noble, 46 Miss. 449.

surety to surrender to him any peculiar means which have
been intrusted by the principal debtor to the surety for
the purpose of securing the payment of the debt, such as a
mortgage on real or personal property, or any other collateral
security held by the surety.[1]

§ 155. **Security held by a Surety regarded as a Trust for the
Payment of the Debt.** — The security for the debt, in whoseso-
ever hands it may be, is treated as a fund held in trust for
the payment of the debt:[2] if in the hands of the creditor, the
surety, upon paying the debt, will be subrogated to it for his
indemnity; if in the hands of a surety, the creditor may resort to it to secure the payment of his demand.[3]  Accordingly, such a security may by agreement of the parties be
passed to a stranger, upon his paying the original debt at the
request of the debtor, and will be enforceable in the hands of
such stranger.[4]  All demands received by the surety from
the principal debtor for the purpose of discharging the debt,
either by their transfer to the creditor or by the payment of
their proceeds to the creditor, are held by the surety in trust
for the creditor.[5]  Equity, regarding the security as a trust
fund created for the payment of the debt, will compel the
surety to apply it for that purpose,[6] and a voluntary transfer
of such a security by the surety to the creditor will be upheld
as if it had been made under a decree of the court.[7]  The

[1] *Redfield, Ch.,* in McCollum *v.*
Hinckley, 9 Vt. 143, 149; Varney *v.*
Hawes, 68 Maine, 442; Matthews *v.*
Joyce, 85 Nor. Car. 258; Cannon *v.*
McDaniel, 46 Tex. 304.

[2] Pratt *v.* Thornton, 28 Maine, 355;
Clark *v.* Ely, 2 Sandf. Ch. (N. Y.)
166; Price *v.* Trusdell, 28 N. J. Eq.
200; Daniel *v.* Joyner, 3 Ired. Eq.
(Nor. Car.) 513; Montgomery's Succession, 2 La. Ann. 469.

[3] New London Bank *v.* Lee, 11
Conn. 112; Holmes *v.* Bacon, 28 Miss.
607; Heid *v.* Vreeland, 30 N. J. Eq.
591.

[4] First National Bank of Madison
*v.* Schlusser, 2 S. W. Rep. 145.

[5] Barton *v.* Croydon, 63 N. H.
417; Holt *v* Penacook Savings Bank,
62 N. H. 551; Kunkel *v.* Fitzhugh,
22 Md. 567; Mast *v.* Raper, 81
Nor. Car. 330; Green *v.* Dodge, 6
Ohio, 80.

[6] United States *v.* Sturges, 1 Paine,
C. C. 525; Paris *v.* Hulett, 26 Vt.
308; Vail *v.* Foster, 4 N. Y. 312;
Ross *v.* Wilson, 7 Sm. & M. (Miss.)
753.

[7] Paris *v.* Hulett, 26 Vt. 308;
Carlisle *v.* Wilkins, 51 Ala. 371.

effect of a mortgage or other security given by the principal debtor to his surety, conditioned that the principal will himself pay the debt and hold the surety harmless therefrom, is to create a trust and an equitable lien for the creditor;[1] and the surety will hold the property subject to such trust, even though his own liability may have been defeated by his decease or by the operation of the Statute of Limitations,[2] or by the creditor's indulgence given to the principal debtor.[3] The surety cannot defeat this trust by a conveyance of the property, except it be to a *bona fide* purchaser for value without notice;[4] and the record of such a mortgage of real estate will be constructive notice of the trust,[5] so that creditors of the surety, or purchasers from him, even after his foreclosure of the mortgage, cannot, by means of an attachment or conveyance of the property, take it discharged of the trust;[6] nor will it be defeated by the subsequent insolvency or bankruptcy of the principal and the surety, or either of them.[7] By such a mortgage the property is pledged to the surety for the payment of the mortgagor's debt; and the pledge is not redeemed, nor the equitable lien discharged, until the debt is actually paid.[8] The surety cannot himself discharge the trust or relieve the property from the burden to the prejudice of the creditor.[9] He may obtain security for the creditor, but he cannot discharge it.[10]

[1] Markell *v.* Eichelberger, 12 Md. 79 ; McMullen *v.* Neal, 60 Ala. 552 ; Richards *v.* Yoder, 10 Neb. 429.

[2] Crosby *v.* Crafts, 5 Hun (N. Y.), 327 ; Eastman *v.* Foster, 8 Met. (Mass.) 19 ; Cowan *v.* Telford 5 Lea (Tenn.), 449.

[3] Helm *v.* Young, 9 B. Mon. (Ky.) 394.

[4] McRady *v.* Thomas, 16 Lea (Tenn.), 173 ; Carpenter *v.* Bowen, 42 Miss. 28 ; Ross *v.* Wilson, 7 Sm. & M. (Miss.) 753 ; Seibert *v.* Thompson, 8 Kans. 65.

[5] Ijames *v.* Gaither, 93 Nor. Car. 358 ; Blackwood *v.* Jones. 4 Jones Eq. (Nor. Car.) 54.

[6] Eastman *v.* Foster, 8 Met. (Mass.) 19 ; Vail *v.* Foster, 4 N. Y. 312.

[7] Carlisle *v.* Wilkins, 51 Ala. 371 ; Eastman *v.* Foster, 8 Met. (Mass.) 19.

[8] Aldrich *v.* Blake, 134 Mass. 582 ; *Shaw, C. J.,* in Eastman *v.* Foster, *supra ;* Graydon *v.* Church, 7 Mich. 36.

[9] Osborn *v.* Noble, 46 Miss. 449 ; McMullen *v.* Neal, 60 Ala. 552.

[10] Simson *v.* Brown, 6 Hun (N. Y.), 251.

**§ 156. Creditor's Right to Security held by a Surety who is also a Creditor of the Principal.** — It has sometimes been held in Kentucky and in Mississippi that a mortgage given by a principal debtor to his sureties, both to protect them against the debt for which they are sureties and to secure a debt due to them from himself, will be applied to the payment of both debts *pro rata*.[1] The rule has been laid down that since the sureties are *quasi* trustees for the creditor in respect to such security, they are bound to pay over the first proceeds thereof to the common creditor, instead of applying them upon their own demand or paying them to their own general creditors.[2] If the circumstances of the case are such as to show what was intended to be the priority of the respective parties, that intent will be carried out.[3] Neither the creditor nor the surety can destroy the rights of the other in such a security; each will be protected from injury by the acts of the other.[4] The right of the surety to apply the security to the payment of his own demand before meeting that upon which he is liable as surety, has also been maintained.[5] The claim of the principal creditor to the benefit of such a security must be seasonably asserted.[6] The principal debtor on a promissory note gave to the surety a mortgage conditioned that the principal should pay the note to the promisee thereof and hold the surety harmless therefrom, and should also pay a debt due from himself to the mortgagee; but the payee of the note did not make his loan under the inducement of the mortgage; nor was the mortgage made for his benefit or at his request. The principal paid the interest on the loan for

[1] Willis v. Caldwell, 10 B. Mon. (Ky.) 199; Helm v. Young, 9 B. Mon. (Ky.) 394; Moore v. Moberly, 7 B. Mon. (Ky.) 299, 301; Ross v. Wilson, 7 Sm. & M. (Miss.) 753.

[2] Fourth National Bank's Appeal, 123 Penn. St. 473; Skillman v. Teeple, 1 N. J. Eq. 232; Ten Eyck v. Holmes, 3 Sandf. Ch. (N. Y.) 428.

[3] Parsons v. Clark, 132 Mass. 569; Waller v. Oglesby, 85 Tenn. 321; Cannon v. McDaniel, 46 Tex. 304.

[4] Edwards v. Helm, 4 Scam. (Ills.) 142.

[5] First Congregational Society v. Snow, 1 Cush. (Mass.) 510; *antea*, § 146.

[6] Waller v. Oglesby, 85 Tenn. 321.

several years, but no part of the principal sum, or of his debt to the surety, and afterwards died intestate and insolvent, and his estate was never administered upon. The mortgagee was never called upon to pay, and never paid, either the interest or any part of the principal of the note; and his liability upon the note became barred by the Statute of Limitations. The mortgagee afterwards sold and conveyed his interest under the mortgage for a valuable consideration without notice to the purchaser that the payee of the note claimed any interest in the mortgage by way of trust or equitable lien or otherwise; and subsequent dispositions of the mortgaged premises were made without notice of any such claim. The payee of the note then brought a bill in equity against the mortgagee and the purchaser from him, praying that the mortgagee might be directed to turn over to him, as equitably entitled thereto, the proceeds of the sale to such purchaser, and that the purchaser might be decreed to hold the premises as a trustee for the plaintiff, subject to an equitable lien for the payment of his note, and to pay to the plaintiff the balance due from such purchaser to the mortgagee on his purchase; and it was held that he was not entitled to such relief.[1]

§ 157. **Creditors' Right to Security held by Surety measured by that of Surety.** — It is generally considered that while the creditor may be substituted to the place of the surety in a case in which the creditor has given security to the surety,[2] yet the creditor's right must be measured by that of the surety; and the surety's right, to which the creditor will be substituted, must be determined by the instrument which creates it.[3] Accordingly the creditor may usually hold security given by the principal debtor to the surety, but not

---

[1] First Congregational Society v. Snow, 1 Cush. (Mass.) 510.
[2] Thompson v. White, 43 Conn. 509.
[3] Bush v. Stamps, 26 Miss. 463; Bibb v. Martin, 14 Sm. & M. (Miss.) 87.

a bare indemnity given to the surety by a stranger,[1] or by one co-surety to another.[2] When the surety was secured by a pledge of the rents of certain property, and afterwards became the holder of the legal title to the property, operating a merger of the pledge as between the principal and the surety, it was held that the creditor had no longer any right of substitution to the merged security;[3] but if equity would prevent a merger, then the creditor's right would remain unaffected.[4] If the condition of the surety's indemnity was that the principal should thus save the surety harmless by paying the debt in case he should be required by law to pay it, and it appears that the principal was not legally liable upon the debt and that the surety has not been damnified, the creditor cannot have the benefit of the security.[5] So, if the surety's rights were created by a trust-deed which provided that, upon the recovery of judgment against the surety and the principal's failure to satisfy the same, the trustee should sell the property, the creditor could not subject the trust property to the payment of his claim without first obtaining judgment against the surety.[6] If the liability of the surety is contingent, as is that of an accommodation indorser of a note, the creditor cannot be substituted to the benefit of a security held by the surety for his indemnity until this liability has become fixed; and if the indorser has been discharged by the laches of the creditor, the latter's right of substitution is gone.[7] If the surety holds the property only by a conveyance which is fraudulent as against the general creditors of the principal debtor, the creditor's right can be

[1] Taylor v. Farmers' Bank, 87 Ky. 398.

[2] Hampton v. Phipps, 108 U. S. 260; Morgan v. Francklyn, 55 How. Pr. (N. Y.) 244.

[3] Rankin v. Wilsey, 17 Iowa, 463.

[4] Antea, § 57 et seq. Durham v. Craig, 79 Ind. 117.

[5] Bibb v. Martin, 14 Sm. & M. (Miss.) 87.

[6] Bush v. Stamps, 26 Miss. 463.

[7] Tilford v. James, 7 B. Mon. (Ky.) 336; Hopewell v. Cumberland Bank, 10 Leigh (Va.), 206; Higgins v. Wright, 43 Barb. (N. Y.) 461.

no better than that of the surety, and will not prevail against the principal's general creditors.[1]

§ 158. **Security given merely to indemnify Sureties cannot be enforced after Sureties discharged.** — A security given to sureties merely to indemnify them against their suretyship cannot be enforced after the creditor has discharged the sureties. And where a debtor gave to his sureties such a mortgage to protect them against their suretyship, the mortgage was held to be extinguished by their assigning it to the creditor for his security and taking from him a discharge of their liability; for as it was given merely to protect the sureties from their liability, and as that protection had been obtained by their discharge, the condition of the mortgage was fulfilled.[2] So where the surety, having received from the principal a promissory-note for his indemnity, handed this over to the creditor, and the creditor brought suit upon it against the principal, it was held that if the remedy against the surety upon the original debt was barred by the Statute of Limitations, there was a failure of the consideration of the note, and the creditor could not recover. But if the surety had given this note to the creditor in payment of his liability, then it would be no defence to the principal, when sued upon this substituted note, that the remedy upon the principal obligation had now become barred by the lapse of time.[3]

§ 159. **When the Surety's Transfer of his Indemnity to the Creditor does not extinguish it.** — The transfer by a surety to the creditor of an indemnity received by the former from the principal will not always extinguish the security in equity, if the transfer is made in payment of the debt[4] or in consideration of the release of the surety by the creditor.[5] A judgment given by a principal debtor to his surety as an

[1] Thrall v. Spencer, 16 Conn. 139.

[2] Sumner v. Bachelder, 30 Maine, 35.

[3] Russell v. La Roque, 13 Ala. 149.

[4] Howe v. Freidheim, 27 Minn. 294; Morgan v. Dod, 3 Color. 551; McBeth v. McIntyre, 57 Calif. 49.

[5] Carlisle v. Wilkins, 51 Ala. 371.

indemnity against his suretyship may be available before the
surety is actually damnified; for the surety may use it to
compel the payment of the debt by the principal; and upon
the assignment of such a judgment by the surety to the creditor, the latter may, to the extent of his demand, collect it
from the proceeds of the debtor's real estate upon which it
was a lien.[1] If the principal debtor gives to his surety a
mortgage, conditioned that the principal shall save his surety
from any trouble or expense by reason of his suretyship, and
the surety assigns this mortgage to the creditor in consideration of his release by the latter from any other liability
than the use of his name in the collection of the original
debt, this assignment will not extinguish the security; and
the creditor can hold the mortgaged premises until they are
redeemed by the payment of the debt.[2] The surety has a
right, for his protection, to apply the property to the payment of the debt;[3] and the creditor may require this application.[4] When an agent has undertaken to obtain security
from a debtor of his principal, but has so negligently conducted himself therein as to become himself liable for the
loss to his principal, and thereupon procures from the debtor
a mortgage to himself for his protection against such liability, and subsequently, the debtor having become insolvent,
assigns this mortgage to his principal, this assignment will
not in equity extinguish the mortgage for the benefit of a
subsequent mortgagee of the same premises, but the creditor
will be allowed the full advantage thereof, to the extent of
the agent's liability to him.[5]

§ 160. **Surety's Indemnity not available to the Creditor unless
Insolvency intervenes.** — If the contract upon which a surety

[1] Bank v. Douglass, 4 Watts
(Penn.), 95; Phillips v. Thompson, 2
Johns. Ch. (N. Y.) 418.

[2] Hayden v. Smith, 12 Met. (Mass.)
511.

[3] Simmons v. Goodrich, 68 Ga.
750; Cooley v. Osborne, 50 Iowa,
526.

[4] Hauser v. King, 76 Va. 731.

[5] Grant v. Ludlow, 8 Ohio St. 1.

holds a mortgage or other security from the principal debtor is for the personal benefit of the surety, in contradistinction to the idea of creating security for the debt or of providing means for its payment, the creditor can claim no greater rights or remedies in the security than the surety himself enjoys.[1]  If the surety himself has not been damnified and the conditions of his contract of indemnity have not been broken, as the surety himself could have no remedy, so the creditor, claiming under him and in his stead, can derive no benefit from the security.[2]  And until the creditor's interference the surety may deal with it as he may choose.[3]  Security given by the maker of a note to his accommodation indorser to secure him against his liability on the indorsement, not being an accessory to the principal obligation, but simply a personal indemnity depending on the payment of the note by the indorser, the indorser could not enforce the security until he should actually have been held to make payment on his indorsement; and the holder of the note, claiming through the indorser and merely standing in his place, can accordingly have no benefit of the security.[4]  A mortgage given, not to secure the debt, but simply to indemnify the surety, does not in the first instance attach itself to the debt as an incident to it;[5] but whatever equity arises in favor of the creditor in regard to the security comes into existence only upon the insolvency of the parties holden for the debt; and until this equity arises the surety has a right in equity, as well as at law, to release such security.[6]

[1] *Antea*, § 157; Lewis v. Sawyer, 44 Maine, 332; Stuart v. McDougald, 35 Maine, 398; Denny v. Lincoln, 5 Mass. 385; Blackstone Bank v. Hill, 10 Pick. (Mass.) 129; Greenleaf v. Ludington, 15 Wisc. 558.

[2] Walker, *in re*, Sheffield Banking Co. v. Clayton, 1 Ch. D. (1892) 621; Campbell Printing Press Co. v. Powell, 78 Tex. 53; Pool v. Doster, 59 Miss. 258; Osborn v. Noble, 46 Miss. 449.

[3] Jones v. Quinnipiac Bank, 29 Conn. 25; Hopewell v. Cumberland Bank, 10 Leigh (Va.), 206, 222; Rankin v. Wiley, 17 Iowa, 463.

[4] Homer v. New Haven Savings Bank, 7 Conn. 478; Bowman v. McElroy, 15 La. Ann. 646.

[5] Logan v. Mitchell, 67 Mo. 524.

[6] Jones v. Quinnipiac Bank, 29 Conn. 25; Thrall v. Spencer, 16 Conn. 139.

§ 161. **Application of these Principles in Connecticut.** — A debtor mortgaged certain real estate to B., to secure the latter for accepting his bills to a large amount, the condition of the mortgage being that the debtor should pay all such acceptances at their maturity, and save B. harmless therefrom. Afterwards, the debtor desiring to obtain a loan from a bank, an arrangement was made by which B. mortgaged to the bank all his interest in the premises as security for such loan, and the bank made a loan to the debtor upon this security. Both the debtor and B. were at this time solvent and in good credit; but they both soon afterwards became insolvent, the bank's loan being unpaid, and B.'s acceptances being still outstanding in the hands of parties to whom they had been negotiated. The holders of these acceptances then claimed that the mortgaged premises should be applied to their payment; but it was held that this mortgage was to be regarded as a personal security created for the indemnity of B., and not to secure the payment of the bills; that while the parties were solvent the holders of the bills had no equitable right to the security; and in the meantime, until such equitable right arose upon the insolvency of the debtors, B. had a perfect right to surrender his security, or, with the concurrence of the debtor, to transfer it to the bank as a security for a new loan; and that the rights of the bank to the security were not affected by the equity which afterwards, upon the failure of the debtor and of B., arose in favor of the holders of the bills.[1]

§ 162. **The Creditor is entitled to the Benefit of the Surety's Indemnity when Insolvency intervenes.** — But the creditor will be entitled, upon the insolvency of the principal and the surety, to the benefit of security held by the surety from the principal merely for indemnity,[2] if the creditor has not

---

[1] Jones v. Quinnipiac Bank, *supra.*
[2] Pierce, *in re,* 2 Lowell, 343; Foye, *in re,* 16 N. B. R. 572; Fickett, *in re,* 72 Maine, 266; Kelly v. Herrick, 131 Mass. 373; Thompson v. Taylor, 12 R. I. 109; Keyes v. Brush, 2 Paige

waived this right by proving his demand as an unsecured one against the estates of those who are liable to him thereon.[1] Where an assignment of property was made to secure an indorser against the payment of certain notes indorsed by him, and he sold the property and converted it into money, and then became insolvent, the notes being unpaid, and the maker being also insolvent, it was held that this money, having been kept separate from his other property, did not pass to his assignees in bankruptcy, but that equity would follow the fund, and apply it to the payment of the notes.[2] Where the purchaser of land procured a third person to give his note to the vendor for the price thereof, and to secure the maker of the note gave him a bond and mortgage on the land purchased, and the maker of the note became insolvent before it fell due, the vendor of the land was held to be entitled to the benefit of the bond and mortgage.[3] The same rule has been applied upon the insolvency of the principal and the death of the surety who held the indemnity,[4] and also upon the bare insolvency of the principal.[5] But to give this right of substitution to the creditor, the relation of debtor and creditor must still subsist, both between the creditor and the surety,[6] and also between the creditor and the principal.[7] And if the surety has lost his lien, the creditor's equitable right of substitution thereto is also destroyed.[8]

§ 163.  **Surety's Indemnity sometimes treated as a Trust for the**

(N. Y.), 311; Chaffe *v.* Lisso, 33 La. Ann. 206 ; King *v.* Harman, 6 La. 607.

[1] New Bedford Savings Institution *v.* Fairhaven Bank, 9 Allen (Mass.), 175; Foye, *in re*, Morris, *ex parte*, 16 N. B. R. 572; Loder's Case, L. R. 6 Eq. 491.

[2] Kip *v.* New York Bank, 10 Johns. (N. Y.) 63, 65.

[3] Vail *v.* Foster, 4 N. Y. 312.

[4] Moses *v.* Murgatroyd, 1 Johns. Ch. (N. Y.) 119.

[5] Dick *v.* Truly, 1 Sm. & M. (Miss.) Ch. 557 ; Tilford *v.* James, 7 B. Mon. (Ky.) 336.

[6] Constant *v.* Matteson, 22 Ills. 546 ; Tilford *v.* James, 7 B. Mon. (Ky.) 336 ; Foye, *in re*, 16 N. B. R. 572.

[7] Watson *v.* Rose, 51 Ala. 292. It was upon another point that this case was overruled by Smith *v.* Gillam, 80 Ala. 296.

[8] Foye, *in re*, 2 Lowell, 424; s. c., 16 N. B. R. 572.

**Payment of the Debt.** — The broad doctrine has also been often
asserted that equity will regard security given by a principal
debtor to his surety, though merely for the surety's indemnity, as a trust created for the payment of the debt, and will
see that it is applied for that purpose, by substituting, if
necessary, the creditor to its benefit.[1] So it has been held
that in chancery, on the creditor's application, a fund pledged
by the principal for the indemnity of the surety will be applied directly to the payment of the debt, if the surety is
liable for its immediate payment, and could upon his payment resort at once to this fund for his indemnity.[2] On this
principle an accommodation indorser for a firm, who has
been held to payment upon his indorsement, has been subrogated for his protection to the benefit of bonds given by each
partner to the other upon the dissolution of the firm, to protect each respectively from the debts that were assumed by
the other.[3] Where the creditor recovered judgment against
both the principal and the surety, and, the other property of
the principal being insufficient to satisfy the judgment, the
surety directed the sheriff to levy the execution upon property mortgaged by the principal to him for his indemnity,
which was accordingly done, it was held that the sale of this
property upon the execution was valid and absolute, and
that it extinguished the lien of the surety's indemnifying
mortgage.[4]

§ 164. **Partial Surety not to be harmed by the Substitution
of the Creditor to his Indemnity.** — But a surety who is not
liable for the whole debt [5] is not to be harmed by the creditor's appropriation of his indemnity; it must be applied first

---

[1] Burroughs v. United States, 2
Paine, C. C. 569; Branch v. Macon
R. R. Co., 3 Woods, C. C. 385;
Thornton v. Exchange Bank, 71 Mo.
222; Breedlove v. Stump, 3 Yerg.
(Tenn.) 257; Martin v. Bank, 31
Ala. 115.

[2] Constant v. Matteson, 22 Ills.
546; Baltimore & Ohio R. R. Co. v.
Trimble, 51 Md. 99.

[3] Ingles v. Walker, 37 Ga. 256.

[4] Exline v. Lowery, 46 Iowa, 556.

[5] See Kelly v. Herrick, 131 Mass.
373.

as may be needed for his protection.[1] The mortgagee of a tract of land, which is subsequently sold to a third party, may elect to be substituted to the rights of such third party in a mortgage upon other property which the latter has taken to indemnify himself against the lien of the first mortgage; but in doing so he vacates the lien of his own mortgage upon the land which has been sold to the third party.[2] Where a surety executed a mortgage upon his own land to secure the payment of his principal's notes, with a provision that the surety should not be subjected to any further loss or liability than that which was created by this mortgage, and the surety afterwards took security from his principal to indemnify himself against any loss that he might sustain by reason of this mortgage, it was held that the surety's liability was limited to his own property mortgaged, together with any surplus remaining in his hands out of the security received by him from the principal after fully indemnifying himself therefrom for any loss resulting to him from his mortgage of his own property; and that the holders of the notes could either enforce the mortgage, or abandon the mortgage and resort to the security received by the surety from the principal debtor, or hold the mortgaged lands and any surplus of the security that might remain after fully indemnifying the surety for his loss by their resort to his lands; but that they had no further rights against the surety, either directly or by substitution to his security.[3] A creditor of a firm consisting originally of two partners, one of whom is deceased, will be compelled to proceed against property in the hands of the surviving partner before resorting to property which has been deposited by the deceased partner with his surety to indemnify the latter against his suretyship upon both this

[1] Norton v. Plumb, 14 Conn. 512; Kassing v. International Bank, 74 Ills. 16; Keyes v. Brush, 2 Paige (N. Y.), 311.

[2] Robertson v. Baker, 11 Fla. 192.

[3] Van Orden v. Durham, 35 Calif. 136.

and other obligations.[1] Where a surety upon several promissory notes takes a mortgage from the principal, conditioned that the principal shall pay the notes and so save the surety harmless therefrom, and so holds the mortgage in trust for the holders of the notes, and he remains personally liable on only one of the notes, and the principal debtor is insolvent, the mortgaged property, if sufficient to pay all the notes, will be applied for that purpose, and any surplus will be distributed among the general creditors of the mortgagor; but if the mortgaged property is insufficient to pay all the notes, it will be first applied for the indemnification of the surety, by paying in full, if necessary, the note on which he remains liable, and the surplus will be applied to the payment of the other notes *pro rata*.[2]

§ 165. **Creditor cannot be substituted to a Security not created against his Debt.** — Although a creditor of a mortgagee may, by substitution in equity, avail himself of the rights of the mortgagee under a mortgage made to secure the debt which he is seeking to recover, and which is due to himself, yet he cannot do so unless the mortgage was made to secure that very debt;[3] and the fact that a mortgagee has joined with his mortgagor as the latter's surety in a bond given by him to a second mortgagee of the same premises, gives the second mortgagee no equitable interest in the lien of the prior mortgage; nor in such a case would the insolvency of both the mortgagor and the prior mortgagee entitle the junior mortgagee, in the absence of any fraud practised upon him, to be substituted to the rights of the prior mortgagee.[4] Nor can the plaintiff in an action for the recovery of a debt hold money which has been deposited by a third person with a deputy sheriff as security to the deputy that persons whom

[1] Newson v. McLendon, 6 Ga. 392.

[2] Eastman v. Foster, 8 Met. (Mass.) 19.

[3] Shackleford v. Stockton, 6 B. Mon. (Ky.) 390; Seward v. Hunting-ton, 94 N. Y. 104, reversing s. c. 26 Hun (N. Y.), 217, and distinguishing Lawrence v. Fox. 20 N. Y. 268.

[4] Brant v. Clark, 27 N. J. Eq. 234.

he has accepted as bail of the defendant will justify as such bail.[1]

§ 166. **Cases in which a Creditor has sought to be substituted to Securities held by a Surety or by one under a Secondary Liability.** — The principal debtor and two sureties having joined in an obligation to the creditor, the principal gave to one of the sureties a mortgage to secure its payment and save the sureties from loss. Afterwards the mortgagor and the mortgagee joined to convey an interest in the mortgaged property to a stranger, who retained in his hands a portion of the purchase-money to meet the charges thereon. The holder of the original obligation then claimed that he was entitled to be paid out of the mortgaged property, by substitution to the benefit of the mortgage; and it was held that he had a right to be so paid; and that this equitable right of his was not affected by the mortgagee's having joined in the conveyance to the stranger, especially as the latter had not only had notice of the mortgage, and consequently of the rights of the creditor thereto, but also had actually retained in his hands a portion of the purchase-money for his protection therefrom.[2] A mortgage which recited that the mortgagee had indorsed certain notes for the accommodation of the mortgagor, upon the condition that the mortgage should be given to secure him from any loss that he might sustain in consequence of the maker's non-payment of the notes at their maturity, was conditioned to be void if the mortgagor should pay the notes or should repay the mortgagee upon the latter's paying them, and provided that the proceeds of any sale of the mortgaged premises should be applied to the payment of all claims of the mortgagee under the mortgage, whether then or thereafter payable, was held to constitute not merely an indemnity to the indorser, but a security for the payment of the notes, so that any *bona fide* holder of the

[1] Commercial Warehouse Co. *v.* Graber, 45 N. Y. 393.

[2] Kunkel *v.* Fitzhugh, 22 Md. 567.

notes might maintain a bill to foreclose it, and his rights
would not be affected by a release given by the mortgagee.[1]
But it has been decided in New Jersey that a mortgage given
by a guardian to the sureties upon his guardianship bond,
conditioned to be void if the guardian should comply with
the condition of the bond by paying over all the money in
his hands to his ward upon the latter's arrival at full age,
creates no trust for the benefit of the minor, but the mortgagees are the absolute owners of both the legal and the
beneficial interest in the mortgage, and have the full right to
treat it as their own.[2] The contrary has also been held.[3]

§ 167. **Creditor substituted to the Claim of his Debtor for
Reimbursement upon the Party ultimately liable.** — A creditor
may also be substituted to his debtor's claim for reimbursement upon one who is under no liability for the debt, where
the latter is the party upon whom the burden of the debt
ought ultimately to fall.[4] Thus, where an insurance policy
had been properly assigned by the insured as security for a
loan of money made to him by the assignee, but after a loss
had occurred, the insured having failed and the insurance
company having another claim upon a bottomry bond against
the insured and a surety upon this bond, the company, being
indemnified by the surety, retained the amount of this claim
out of the loss upon the assigned policy instead of collecting
it from the surety, the assignee of the policy was allowed in
equity to be substituted to the claim of the company upon the
surety, to the extent of the amount so retained by the company out of what was due to him upon the policy.[5] So, also,
the placing of notes in the hands of an attorney as collateral
security, to collect them, and to apply the proceeds upon a

[1] Boyd v. Parker, 43 Md. 182.
[2] Miller v. Wack, 1 N. J. Eq. 204.
[3] Morrill v. Morrill, 53 Vt. 74.
[4] Antea, § 85, and cases there cited.
According, Jones v. Johnson, 86 Ky.
530; Miller v. Lancaster, 5 Coldw.
(Tenn.) 514.
[5] Wiggin v. Dorr, 3 Sumner, C. C.
410.

judgment against the person depositing them, creates an
equity in favor of the judgment-creditor which will be enforced upon his application, although the attorney's receipt
for the notes has been transferred to a third person.[1]  Where
a mortgagor, having paid the amount due upon the mortgage
to the mortgagee after the latter had without the knowledge
of the mortgagor assigned his mortgage, took from the mortgagee, after learning the facts, a bond conditioned that the
mortgagee should pay to the assignee of the mortgage the
amount that was due thereon and save the mortgagor harmless therefrom, it was held that the assignee of the mortgage
was entitled to the benefit of this bond, and could enforce it
against one who had guaranteed it to the mortgagor, although
the latter had given an acknowledgment of satisfaction thereof
to the mortgagee, the court saying that the mortgagor could
obtain from the mortgagee (who had become the person ultimately liable in equity to pay the debt) security for the holder
of the mortgage, but could not, as against the creditor, destroy that security when obtained.[2]

§ 167 *a*. **Bondholder substituted to Benefit of Security given
by Party ultimately liable.** — Where, to aid in the construction
of a railroad, a State issued its bonds in exchange for those of
the railroad company, under a statute which created a mortgage for the protection of the State, the holders of the State
bonds were held to be entitled to the benefit of this mortgage,
after the State bonds had been decided to be invalid as having been issued without constitutional authority.[3]  So in the
case of bonds issued by a county to a railroad company, for
which that company gave a mortgage to the county, the bonds
having been sold in the market and the coupons remaining
unpaid, it was held that in equity the railroad company must

---

[1] Dunlap *v.* O'Bannon, 5 B. Mon.
(Ky.) 393.

[2] Simson *v.* Brown, 6 Hun (N. Y.),
251.

[3] North Carolina R. R. Co. *v.*
Drew, 3 Woods, C. C. 691.

be regarded as the principal debtor and the county as the surety, and that the bondholders were entitled to be substituted for the payment of their coupons to the benefit of the mortgage.[1] The security to the State or county was considered to be, not only for its own protection, but for the better securing of the bonds.[2] But where a corporation has conveyed lands to a State as a bare indemnity to the State against loss on the State's bonds issued to the corporation, the bondholders cannot, as against the State, compel the land to be applied to the payment of the bond, and the grantees of the State will take the land free from any claim of the bondholders.[3] The question (apart from any considerations of sovereignty) has been taken to be whether the railroad company or the State should be regarded as the principal debtor,[4] and whether the statutory lien was intended to be available for the benefit of the bondholders.[5] But where a town made a lawful appropriation to a railroad company and issued its bonds therefor to the company, the purchaser of these bonds from the company could not claim to have paid the appropriation by his purchase, and, the bonds being in default and having been held to be void in his suit against the town, was not subrogated to any right of the railroad company to enforce payment of the appropriation by the town: he was not a creditor either of the company or of the town; he had paid no debt of

---

[1] Washington, Ohio & Western R. R. Co. v. Cazenove, 83 Va. 744.

[2] So in Tompkins v. Little Rock R. R. Co., 15 Fed. Rep. 6, 18; Hand v. Savannah & Charleston R. R. Co., 12 So. Car. 314; Gibbes v. Greenville & Columbia R. R. Co., 13 So. Car. 228; Forrest v. Luddington, 68 Ala. 1; Colt v. Barnes, 64 Ala. 108.

[3] Chamberlain v. St. Paul R. R. Co., 92 U. S. 299.

[4] Stevens v. Louisville & Nashville R. R. Co., 2 Flip. C. C. 715. See

Railroad Cos. v. Schutte, 103 U. S. 118; Branch v. Macon R. R. Co., 2 Woods, 385; Young v. Montgomery R. R. Co., 2 Id. 606.

[5] Tompkins v. Little Rock R. R. Co., 125 U. S. 109; s. c., 21 Fed. Rep. 370, 18 Id. 344, and 5 McCrary, 597; Stevens v. Louisville R. R. Co., 3 Fed. Rep. 673; Cunningham v. Macon R. R. Co., 3 Woods, 418; Kelly v. Alabama & Cincinnati R. R. Co., 58 Ala. 489; Clews v. Bondholders, 54 Ga. 315.

either, and had no right of subrogation against either as his debtor.[1]

§ 168. **Substitution to the Securities held by the Sureties in a Criminal Recognizance.** — The substitution of the creditor to the securities held by the sureties does not extend to the case of a recognizance taken in the course of criminal proceedings before the liability of the sureties has been fixed at law. Thus, where the principal in such a recognizance gave a trust-deed to his sureties therein, providing that if the recognizance should be forfeited and the sureties become liable thereon, the trust property should be applied to pay the recognizance so far as it would go, it was held that the State could not maintain a bill in equity to subject this property to the payment of the amount due upon the recognizance before obtaining judgment against the sureties.[2]  The doctrine of subrogation does not apply in favor of sureties or bail to bonds taken in the course of criminal proceedings. [3]

---

[1] Ætna Ins. Co. v. Middleport, 124 U. S. 534.

[2] People v. Skidmore, 17 Calif. 260.

[3] United States v. Ryder, 110 U. S. 729.  An Indiana Case (Kane v. State, 78 Ind. 103) seems to be inconsistent with this, and also with the usual rule as to the rights of successive sureties. *Antea,* § 131 *et seq.*

## CHAPTER IV.

### SUBROGATION AMONG JOINT DEBTORS.

§ 169. **Right of Joint Debtors to Subrogation as against each other.** — The right of subrogation among parties severally bound as principals, has been denied;[1] but the usual rule is that one of several joint debtors will, as against his co-debtors, ordinarily be subrogated to the securities and means of payment of the common creditor whom he has satisfied, so as to enable him to recover from his co-debtors, by means thereof, their proportional shares of the indebtedness which he has discharged;[2] and this, as in other cases of subrogation, arises rather from natural justice than from contract.[3] Each joint debtor is regarded as the principal debtor for that

---

[1] Clark v. Warren, 55 Ga. 575; Engles v. Engles, 4 Ark. 286; Benton v. Bailey, 50 Vt. 137.

[2] Ackerman's Appeal, 106 Penn. St. 1; Dobyns v. Rawley, 76 Va. 537; Baltimore & Ohio R. R. Co. v. Walker, 45 Ohio St. 577; Sumner v. Rhodes, 14 Conn. 135; Smith v. Latimer, 15 B. Mon. (Ky.) 75; Shropshire v. Creditors, 15 La. Ann. 705.

[3] Durbin v. Kuny, 19 Oreg. 71.

part of the debt which he ought to pay, and as a surety for his co-debtors as to that part of the debt which ought to be discharged by them.[1] Thus, if three persons mortgage their joint property to indemnify the drawer of certain bills of exchange drawn for their accommodation, each of the mortgagors agreeing to take up a third part of the bills on their return, and then two of them neglect to take up their two-thirds, so that the other mortgagor is compelled to pay the whole of the bills, in consequence of which he requests the drawer not to release the mortgage, but to hold it for his benefit, an equitable lien is thereby created upon the mortgaged property to the amount of two-thirds of the bills in favor of that mortgagor who took up the bills.[2] Where one of several proprietors of land pays the whole cost of a pavement laid on the requirement of the municipal authorities, for which the property was bound and the proprietors were individually liable, he will be subrogated to the rights of the paver, to enable him to recover their proportions from the other proprietors.[3] Where two joint purchasers of real estate gave to their vendor a mortgage thereof to secure the payment of the purchase-money, and after the death of one of them, the survivor paid the purchase-money, the latter was subrogated to the lien of the mortgage, and allowed to hold the mortgaged property for the excess of the joint debt paid by him above his proportion thereof against the widow and heirs of the deceased purchaser.[4] But the creditor may of

---

[1] Henderson v. McDuffee, 5 N. H. 38; Newton v. Newton, 53 N. H. 537; Hatch v. Norris, 536 Maine, 419; Goodall v. Wentworth, 20 Maine, 322; Seward v. Huntington, 26 Hun (N. Y.), 217; Sterling v. Stewart, 74 Penn. St. 445; Morrow v. Peyton, 8 Leigh (Va.), 54; Boyd v. Boyd, 3 Gratt. (Va.) 113; Moore v. State, 49 Ind. 558; Hall v. Hall, 34 Ind. 314; Collins v. Carlisle, 7 B. Mon. (Ky.) 13; Owen v. McGehee, 61 Ala. 440; Martin v. Baldwin, 7 Ala. 923; Chipman v. Morrill, 20 Calif. 130.

[2] Pratt v. Law, 9 Cranch, 456.

[3] Whitehead's Succession, 3 La. Ann. 396.

[4] Wheatley v. Calhoun, 12 Leigh (Va.), 264; Tompkins v. Mitchell, 2 Rand. (Va.) 428.

course hold all the debtors and all the securities that they have given, until he shall be fully satisfied.[1]

§ 170. **Where one Joint Debtor has assumed the Ultimate Liability.** — If, as between joint debtors, it has become the duty of one of them to pay the entire debt, the others, if they shall be compelled to pay it, will be subrogated to the securities and means of payment held by the creditor against the former, just as if they had been sureties of the former *eo nomine*.[2] Thus, if two of the three principal obligors in a bond put into the hands of the third the means to pay it, but he fails to do so, and a judgment recovered upon the bond against the three is paid by one of the two, the latter will be subrogated to the lien of the judgment upon the lands of the third in the hands of his grantees, to whom he has conveyed them since the judgment.[3] The same principle was applied in a case in which it appeared that the plaintiff and M., being partners, agreed that M. should pay the defendant for property which they had bought of him, and M. accordingly sent his note to the defendant, who declined to receive it as payment, and demanded and received the price of the property from the plaintiff. The plaintiff and the defendant then agreed that the defendant should still hold M.'s note, and conceal the plaintiff's payment, and should turn over to the plaintiff whatever M. might pay on the note. M. having afterwards made a payment on the note to the defendant, in ignorance of the plaintiff's payment, it was held that the plaintiff had by subrogation a right to all the securities held by the defendant, and that, M.'s note being such a security,

[1] Hall v. Howard, 32 Ch. D. 430; Kramer v. Carter, 136 Mass. 504; Frost v. Frost, 3 Sandf. Ch. (N. Y.) 188; Hoye v. Penn, 9 Harr. & G. (Md.) 473; Manning v. Gasharie, 27 Ind. 399; Palmer v. Stacy, 44 Iowa 340; Garden v. Morrow, 8 Ala. 486; Schoenewald v. Dieden, 8 Ills. App. 389.

[2] Shinn v. Shinn, 91 Ills. 477; Wheeler's Estate, 1 Md. Ch. Dec. 80; Crafts v. Mott, 4 N. Y. 603; Cherry v. Monro, 2 Barb. Ch. (N. Y.) 618.

[3] Buchanan v. Clark, 10 Gratt. (Va.) 164.

the payment made thereon belonged to the plaintiff.[1] So if one of two joint debtors has given to their surety for the debt collateral security to protect him against his suretyship, and has then agreed with his co-debtor for a valuable consideration, himself to pay the whole debt, the other joint debtor, if he is afterwards compelled by the creditor to pay the debt, will be subrogated to the benefit of that security in the hands of the surety, whom he has discharged by his payment, in preference to the claims of the judgment-creditors of the debtor who should have paid the debt.[2] The same rules will be applied if the joint debtors are a husband and wife who have been divorced.[3] But the debtors cannot by any arrangement among themselves lessen the rights of the creditor against all or any of them; he may insist upon being paid in full, leaving them to adjust their own equities.[4] And even after full satisfaction of the creditor, as subrogation is an equity to be enforced only where it will benefit a meritorious claim without doing injustice to others,[5] it will be denied if the person claiming it has agreed for value to waive his right, or if he is indebted in a larger amount to the party against whom he seeks it.[6]

§ 171. **In Cases of Partnership.** — A partner who, after the dissolution of the partnership, pays a firm debt out of his private property may in equity enforce contribution therefor from his co-partners,[7] by virtue of the partnership agreement to contribute to losses rather than by way of subrogation;[8] but he cannot claim any lien upon the separate estate of his

---

[1] Field v. Hamilton, 45 Vt. 35.

[2] Butler v. Birkey, 13 Ohio St. 514.

[3] Stevens v. Goodenough, 26 Vt. 676.

[4] Jackson v. Roberts, 83 Ga. 358; Hards v. Burton, 79 Ills. 504; Buettel v. Harmount, 46 Minn. 481.

[5] *Antea*, § 4.

[6] Greenlaw v. Pettit, 87 Tenn. 468.

[7] Downs v. Jackson, 33 Ills. 464; Eakin v. Knox, 6 So. Car. (Rich.) 14.

[8] Phillips v. Blatchford, 137 Mass. 510; Hogan v. Reynolds, 21 Ala. 56; Bartlett v. McRea, 4 Ala. 688. *Contra*, Sells v. Hubbell, 2 Johns. Ch. (N. Y.) 394, 397.

partner in bankruptcy for the balance due to himself upon
settlement of the partnership accounts, by subrogation to the
rights of a firm-creditor who has been paid out of the firm
property;[1] for partnership creditors have themselves no lien
upon the firm property,[2] and can secure its application to
their claims only through the rights of the partners.[3] The
creditors of a partner who is entitled to be subrogated as
against the firm will succeed to his rights;[4] and the legatee
of a partner subject to the payment of his debts will occupy
the same position.[5] If individual property of one of the
partners of a bankrupt firm has been pledged for a firm debt,
the creditor may, and if requested by separate creditors of
that partner must, prove his whole debt against the firm assets, for the relief of that partner's separate estate, thus in
effect subrogating that separate estate to the creditor's right
against the firm.[6] The subrogation of one partner who has
paid a firm debt to the position of the creditor as against his
co-partners cannot ordinarily be enforced without a settlement of the partnership accounts.[7] Nor can the bail of one

[1] *In re* Smith, 16 N. B. R. 113;
Singizer's Appeal, 28 Penn St. 524.

[2] Case *v.* Beauregard, 1 Woods,
C. C. 125; s. c. 99 U. S. 119; Allen
*v.* Centre Valley Co., 21 Conn. 130;
Sigler *v.* Knox County Bank, 8 Ohio
St. 511; Gwin *v.* Selby, 5 Ohio St.
96; Mayer *v.* Clark, 40 Ala. 259;
Reese *v.* Bradford, 13 Ala. 837.

[3] Couchman *v.* Maupin, 78 Ky. 33;
O'Bannon *v.* Miller, 4 Bush (Ky.), 25;
Black *v.* Bush, 7 B. Mon. (Ky.) 210;
Guyton *v.* Flack, 7 Md. 398;
Schmidtapp *v.* Currie, 55 Miss. 597;
Hawk Eye Woollen Mills *v.* Conklin,
26 Iowa, 422; Waterman *v.* Hunt, 2
R. I. 298.

[4] Matter of Swayne, 1 Clark
(Penn.), 57; Foot, *in re*, 12 N. B. R.
337; Royalton Bank *v.* Cushing, 53
Vt. 321.

[5] Hill *v.* Huston, 15 Gratt. (Va.)
350.

[6] Collie, *in re*, 3 Ch. D. 481; Bow-
den, *ex parte*, 1 Deac. & Ch. 135;
Plummer, *in re*, 1 Phillips, 56; Rolfe
*v.* Flower, L. R. 1 P. C. 27; English
& American Bank, *ex parte*, L. R. 4
Ch. 49; Holbrook, *in re*, 2 Lowell,
259; Thomas, *in re*, 8 Biss. 139; May,
*in re*, 17 N. B. R. 192; Beasley *v.*
Lawrence, 11 Paige (N. Y.), 581;
Wilder *v.* Keeler, 3 *Id.* 167.

[7] Bittner *v.* Hartman, 139 Penn.
St. 632; Fessler *v.* Hickernell, 82
Penn. St. 150; Baily *v.* Brownfield, 20
Penn. St. 41; Shattuck *v.* Lawson, 10
Gray (Mass.), 405; Le Page *v.* Mc-
Crea, 1 Wend. (N. Y.) 164; Barhydt
*v.* Perry, 57 Iowa, 416; Lyons *v.*
Murray, 95 Mo. 23; McDonald *v.*
Holmes, 29 Pac. Rep. 735.

partner, who have, as such bail, been compelled to pay a
judgment recovered against that partner for a firm debt, recover at law from the other partners any part of the sum
thus paid by them;[1] nor, after suit brought upon a partnership debt and its satisfaction by one of the partners sued, can
equity preserve or extend the validity of the original security
under the guise of an assignment, so as to charge the bail of
another partner for the former's reimbursement.[2]  But a
partner who has gone out of the firm, and taken for a valuable consideration the agreement of the remaining members
of the firm to indemnify him from the partnership debts, will
in equity be regarded as the surety of the other pàrtners,[3]
and will, if he is compelled to pay a firm debt, be subrogated
to the rights and remedies of the creditor therefor against
the remaining members of the firm.[4]  If one partner buys
the interest of the other in the firm property, and assumes the
firm debts, he will in equity be regarded as the principal
debtor, and the other as merely his surety; and a firm creditor who has notice of the facts has been said to be bound at
his peril to treat the former partners respectively as principal
and surety;[5] though any such limitation of the creditor's
original rights can scarcely be maintained on principle.[6]

§ 171 a.  **Substitution of a Partnership Creditor to Agreement
or Security taken by a Retiring Partner against Firm Debts. —**

[1] Bowman v. Blodgett, 2 Met.
(Mass.) 308 ; Osborn v. Cunningham,
4 Dev. & Bat. Law (Nor. Car.), 423.

[2] Hinton v. Odenheimer, 4 Jones,
Eq. (Nor. Car.) 406.

[3] Olson v. Morrison, 29 Mich. 395 ;
Burnside v. Fetzner, 63 Mo. 107 ;
Williams v. Bush, 1 Hill (N. Y.), 623.

[4] Shamburg v. Abbott, 112 Penn.
St. 6 ; Scott's Appeal, 88 Penn. St.
173 ; Frow's Estate, 73 Penn. St. 459 ;
Merrill v. Green, 55 N. Y. 270 ; Conwell v. McCowan, 81 Ills. 285. *Contra,*
in Florida, Griffin v. Orman, 9 Fla. 22.

[5] Oakeley v. Pasheller, 10 Bligh,
N. S. 548 ; Colgrove v. Tallman, 67
N. Y. 95 ; Morss v. Gleason, 64 N. Y.
204 ; Millerd v. Thorn, 56 N. Y. 402 ;
Savage v. Putnam, 32 N. Y. 501 ;
Dodd v. Dreyfus, 17 Hun (N. Y.), 600;
Williams v. Boyd, 75 Ind. 286 ; Smith
v. Shelden, 35 Mich. 42 ; Conwell v.
McCowan, 81 Ills. 285 ; Burnside v.
Fetzner, 63 Mo. 107 ; Leithauser v.
Baumeister, 47 Minn. 151.

[6] Rawson v. Taylor, 30 Ohio St.
389 ; Gates v. Hughes, 44 Wisc. 332.
*Antea,* § 25.

The Court of Appeals of the State of New York and the Supreme Courts of Pennsylvania and Arkansas have refused to allow the creditor of a partnership to maintain an action upon a bond given to a retiring partner by the remaining members of the firm to secure him against his liability for the partnership debts, upon the manifest ground that the bond was given, not at all for the benefit of the firm creditors, but solely for the protection of the retiring partner;[1] but if the bond is conditioned both for the relief of the retiring partner and for the payment of the outstanding firm debts, it has been considered to be more than a mere contract of indemnity, and both the obligee of the bond and the firm creditors themselves have been allowed to proceed upon it to enforce payment of the firm debts.[2] The remaining partners, by their agreement to appropriate the firm property to the payment of the firm debts, have been held to become trustees for the creditors,[3] and will be held by a court of equity to the proper discharge of the trust.[4] The same principle will be

---

[1] Merrill v. Green, 55 N. Y. 270; Mackintosh v. Fatman, 38 How. Pr. (N. Y.) 145; Serviss v. McDonell, 107 N. Y. 260; Berry v. Brown, 1 Silvernail's N. Y. Ct. Appeals, 542; Campbell v. Lacock, 40 Penn. St. 448; Hicks v. Wyatt, 23 Ark. 55.

[2] Hood v. Spencer, 4 McLean, C. C. 168; Collier, in re, 12 N. B. R. 266; Claflin v. Ostrom, 54 N. Y. 581, 584; Barlow v. Myers, 3 Hun (N. Y.), 720, and 6 Thomp. & C. (N. Y.) 183; Wilson v. Stilwell, 14 Ohio St. 464; Ingles v. Walker, 37 Ga. 256; Dunlap v. McNeil, 35 Ind. 316; Devol v. McIntosh, 23 Ind. 529; Francis v. Smith, 1 Duv. (Ky.) 121; Garvin v. Mobley, 1 Bush (Ky.), 48; Meyer v. Lowell, 44 Mo. 328; Poole v. Hintrager, 60 Iowa, 180; Kimball v. Noyes, 17 Wisc. 695; Sanders v. Clason, 13 Minn. 379. See further

Arnold v. Nichols, 64 N. Y. 117; Floyd v. Ort, 20 Kans. 162. Similar doctrines are maintained in Rice v. Savery, 22 Iowa, 470; Wiggins v. McDonald, 18 Calif. 126; Allen v. Thomas, 3 Met. (Ky.) 198; Hall v. Roberts, 61 Barb. (N. Y.) 33. Most of these decisions were made in States in which the distinction between law and equity has been abolished, and the real party in interest allowed to sue in his own name.

[3] Gorham, in re, 9 Biss. 23; Marsh v. Bennett, 5 McLean, 117; Wildes v. Chapman, 4 Edwards, Ch. (N. Y.) 669.

[4] Sedan v. Williams, 4 McLean, 51; Wilson v. Soper, 13 B. Mon. (Ky.) 411; Phelps v. McNeely, 66 Mo. 554; Baer v. Wilkinson, 35 W. Va. 422; Conroy v. Woods, 13 Calif. 626.

applied to the deposit by the retiring partner of a sum of money with the new firm which, by agreement between him and the members of the new firm, is to be applied to his share of the liabilities of the old firm; it becomes a trust fund for the creditors of the old firm, and their rights will not be affected by any subsequent equities that may arise in favor of the members of the new firm.[1] But a promise by the members of the new firm to the retiring partner, upon their taking merely the assets of the old firm, to pay its debts, though it has been held to give the old creditors a direct right of action against these new members,[2] or others who have made it,[3] under the liberal doctrine that one for whose benefit a promise is made may enforce it, though not a party to it or privy to the consideration,[4] yet gives the retiring partner no lien upon these assets for the enforcement of the promise,[5] and gives the firm creditors no lien upon the assets which can be enforced against third persons to whose hands these assets come without notice of any trust,[6] and no special rights, it is sometimes held, against the remaining partners personally,[7] or against the assets in the hands of the latter,[8] even though the firm and all the partners were insolvent when the promise was made.[9] The right of partnership creditors to hold the partnership property doubtless arises by way of subrogation to the right of the partners to have the firm property applied to the payment of the firm

[1] Fries v. Ennis, 132 Penn. St. 195.

[2] Bellas v. Fagely, 19 Penn. St. 273; Weaver v. White, 19 N. Y. Supt. 616.

[3] Goldman v. Biddle, 118 Ind. 492; Maxfield v. Schwartz, 43 Minn. 221; Lehow v. Simonton, 3 Color. 346.

[4] Antes, § 85.

[5] Griffith v. Buck, 13 Md. 102; Goembel v. Arnett, 100 Ills. 34; Andrews v. Mann, 31 Miss. 322;

Commercial Bank v. Lewis, 13 Sm. & M. (Miss.) 226.

[6] Fulton v. Hughes, 63 Miss. 61; Hapgood v. Cornwell, 48 Ills. 64.

[7] Wild v. Dean, 3 Allen (Mass.), 579; Fowle v. Torrey, 131 Mass. 29.

[8] Robb v. Mudge, 14 Gray (Mass.), 534; Richardson v. Tobey, 3 Allen (Mass.), 81.

[9] Howe v. Lawrence, 9 Cush. (Mass.) 553; Robb v. Mudge, 14 Gray (Mass.), 534.

debts;[1] but these rights are now a part of the law of partnership rather than of subrogation.

§ 172. **Where Securities belonging to Different Owners are held for the Same Debt.** — Where securities belonging to several different persons are held together to secure the payment of a single debt, they should be applied *pari passu* to the satisfaction of the creditor, so that each of the several owners of the securities may contribute his just proportion of the common burden;[2] and if such creditor satisfies the demand out of the securities of only one of the owners, leaving the other securities undisturbed, equity will so dispose of these others as to throw the burden of the debt upon all in reasonable proportions.[3] The one whose property has paid the whole debt will, to the extent of his actual payment, be subrogated to the rights of the creditor against the others, and may hold their securities to enforce the payment by them of such sums as they ought in equity to contribute.[4] If the security is a mortgage, and the whole debt is paid to save the estate of the party paying it, by one of two tenants in common who have, since the giving of the mortgage, acquired the equity of redemption, the assignment of the mortgage to this cotenant will not extinguish its claim in favor of the other, who has paid nothing.[5] That share of the mortgage-debt which it belonged to such an assignee to pay is extinguished;

---

[1] Manchester Bank, *ex parte*, 12 Ch. D. 917; Wiley, *in re*, 4 Biss. C. C. 214; Rice v. Barnard. 20 Vt. 479; Washburn v. Bank of Bellows Falls, 19 Vt. 278; Richardson v. Tobey, 3 Allen (Mass.),81; Howe v. Lawrence, 9 Cush. (Mass.) 553; Waterman v. Hunt, 2 R. I. 298; Fargo v. Ames, 45 Iowa, 491; Schmidlapp v. Curry, 55 Miss. 597; Grabenheimer v. Rindskopf, 64 Tex. 49.

[2] Wright, *in re*, 16 Fed. Rep. 482; Hoyt v. Doughty, 4 Sandf. (N. Y.) 462; Paine v. Bonney, 4 E. D. Smith (N. Y.), 734; s. c., 6 Abbott Pr. (N. Y.) 99, 101; Semmes v. Boykin, 27 Ga. 47. So in admiralty, The Dewthorpe, 2 Notes of Cas. 264; The Constantia, 4 *Id.* 512.

[3] Gould v. Central Trust Co., 6 Abbott New Cas. (N. Y.) 381; McCready v. Van Antwerp, 24 Hun (N. Y.), 322.

[4] Aiken v. Gale, 37 N. H. 501; Dowdy v. Blake, 50 Ark. 205; Beck v. Tarrant, 61 Tex. 402.

[5] Barker v. Flood, 103 Mass. 474; Calkins v. Steinbach, 66 Calif. 117.

his title to his portion of the mortgaged property is perfected; and he is subrogated to the rights of the mortgagee as to the other share, and may call upon his co-tenant to pay him the proportion of that share, or be foreclosed of the right to redeem.[1] If the creditor himself purchases the share or the property of one of the debtors subject to the burden, a corresponding share of the debt is extinguished.[2] As between the purchasers in common of an estate bound by a joint lien, each share is obliged to contribute only its proportion of the common burden, and beyond this amount is to be regarded as the surety of the others;[3] and if the owner of one share is called upon to pay more than its due proportion of the debt, such owner or his creditors will be entitled to stand in the place of the satisfied creditor to the extent of the excess which ought to have been paid out of the other shares.[4] One tenant in common, upon redeeming the estate from a tax-sale, though he will not acquire an absolute title, yet, if his payment were necessary for the protection of his own estate,[5] may hold the estate under his tax-title against his co-tenants until they pay or tender to him their proportion of the taxes.[6] As his redemption will be deemed to have been made for their benefit if they so desire on their payment of their proportionate shares of the indebtedness,[7] so it will be for his own benefit until they shall make such payment.[8]

---

[1] Young v. Williams, 17 Conn. 393; Lyon v. Robbins, 45 Conn. 513; Cornell v. Prescott, 2 Barb. (N. Y.) 16.

[2] Daigle's Succession, 15 La. Ann. 594.

[3] Higham v. Harris, 108 Ind. 246.

[4] Gearhart v. Jordan, 11 Penn. St. 325; Furiman v. McMillian, 2 Lea (Tenn.), 121.

[5] Preston v. Wright, 81 Maine, 306.

[6] Watkins v. Eaton, 30 Maine, 529; Moon v. Jennings, 119 Ind. 130; Weare v. Van Meter, 42 Iowa, 128; Oliver v. Montgomery, 42 Iowa, 36, and 39 Iowa, 601; Harrison v. Harrison, 56 Miss. 174.

[7] Barnes v. Boardman, 152 Mass. 391; Van Horne v. Fonda, 5 Johns. Ch. (N. Y.) 388; Flagg v. Mason, 2 Sumner, 486; Tice v. Derby, 59 Iowa, 312, 314.

[8] Hurley v. Hurley, 148 Mass. 444, and cases there cited.

§ 173. **Where Land of two or more Owners is subject to one Mortgage.** — Where one of the owners of land subject to a mortgage pays off the mortgage-debt by instalments, and upon making the last payment takes an assignment of the mortgage, its lien is not thereby extinguished in favor of the other owners.[1] Either one of such owners, whether they hold distinct parcels of the incumbered estate, or are tenants in common of the whole, is at liberty to redeem for the protection of his estate; and upon so redeeming he becomes subrogated to the rights of the mortgagee, and may hold the land as if the mortgage subsisted,[2] until the other owners reimburse him their proportions of the incumbrance; and in the absence of any agreement their proportions will be according to the proportionate value of their respective interests.[3] The grantee of such an owner will have the same right of subrogation as was possessed by his grantor.[4] Where two purchasers of land gave their joint notes for the purchase-money thereof, secured by a mortgage of the premises, and after a partition of the premises one of them refused to pay his proportion of the last note, so that the other was compelled to redeem the whole mortgage, the latter was allowed to hold the land of the defaulter for the amount which he had thus been compelled to pay above his own share of the note,[5] and to have the same interest as had been agreed to be paid upon the original debt.[6] Upon the same principle, the assignee of a mortgage which covered three estates, having purchased two of these estates, can recover from the third estate only its ratable proportion of the mortgage-debt.[7]

[1] Duncan v. Drury, 9 Penn. St. 332.

[2] Newbold v. Smart, 67 Ala. 326; Lowery v. Byers, 80 Ind. 443; Carter v. Penn, 99 Ills. 390; Brooks v. Harwood, 8 Pick. (Mass.) 497.

[3] Hubbard v. Ascutney Mill Dam Co., 20 Vt. 402; Sawyer v. Lyon, 10 Johns. (N. Y.) 32; Aiken v. Gale, 37 N. H. 501.

[4] Watson's Appeal, 90 Penn. St. 426.

[5] Fisher v. Dillon, 62 Ills. 379.

[6] Simpson v. Gardiner, 97 Ills. 237.

[7] Colton v. Colton, 3 Phila. 24.

§ 174. **This Principle applied against one claiming under a Joint Purchaser.** — One Pierson and four others purchased a lot of land, and gave for the purchase-money their joint note secured by a mortgage upon the lot. They then divided the lot among themselves into four equal parts, one of which was allotted to Pierson, and agreed to give each other quitclaim deeds of their respective parts. Pierson took possession of his part, built a house upon it, and then sold it to one Williams, who paid him therefor in full. The title still remaining in all the purchasers, they joined in conveying to him the parcel purchased by him of Pierson. Pierson paid nothing of the original purchase-money, of which he should have paid one-fourth; the remaining three-fourths were paid by the other purchasers. The mortgagee then filed a bill to foreclose his mortgage for the unpaid fourth part of the purchase-money; and it was decreed that the part of the lot set off to Pierson and conveyed to Williams should be first sold, *Judge Davison* saying, "The several owners of the residue of the lot having each paid one-fourth of the purchase-money, the remaining fourth was in equity the debt of Pierson; and as his debt it was properly chargeable on the property set off to him."[1] It was not pretended in this case that Williams had notice that Pierson had not paid his share of the purchase-money; but, having notice of the mortgage, he was to be regarded as having purchased subject to the equities that arose under it. But under somewhat similar circumstances in Georgia it was held that one purchaser who had been compelled to pay the whole of the purchase-money was not to be subrogated for his reimbursement to the mortgage-lien upon the share of the other purchaser in the hands of a grantee from the latter, although such grantee had constructive notice of the mortgage from the fact of its being recorded.[2]

§ 175. **Applied to Mortgagees whose Estate was subject to a Prior Lien.** — Where three junior mortgagees of land, having

[1] Williams v. Perry, 20 Ind. 437.  [2] Clark v. Warren, 55 Ga. 575.

no priority among themselves, had agreed with the mortgagor, that if it should be necessary to redeem from the prior
mortgage each of these three junior mortgagees should pay
one-third of the amount due thereon, and be indemnified
therefor out of the property, and one of the three paid one-
third of the amount due upon the prior mortgage, and then
advanced the remaining amount and took an assignment of
that mortgage, it was held that as to the remaining two-
thirds he became subrogated to the rights of the prior mortgagee, and might require his co-mortgagees to redeem by
paying to him those two-thirds, or to forfeit all title to the
mortgaged premises.[1]

§ 176. **Not applied where Lien upon one Security extinguished.**
— If two securities are held for the payment of a debt, and
the lien upon one of them has been lost by lapse of time, the
owner of the other security, upon paying the debt, will acquire no right of subrogation to that which has been thus
discharged.[2] A testator devised a tract of land to his two
sons, Benjamin and Thomas. The purchase-money due from
the testator for this land being unpaid, the testator's vendor
brought his bill against the executors, and obtained a decree
charging the land with its payment. By a subsequent decree, the land was ordered to be sold therefor. While these
decrees remained unexecuted, Benjamin sold his portion of
the land; and the purchaser thereof took and held possession
until, by the lapse of time, he acquired a title which was
valid against these decrees. Then the decrees were revived;
and by order of the court the remaining portion of the land,
being the share of Thomas, was sold for the payment of the
testator's indebtedness for the price of the whole tract. On
a bill brought by Thomas against Benjamin for contribution
it was held that, as the vendor's lien upon the whole tract

---

[1] Hubbard v. Ascutney Mill Dam
Co., 20 Vt. 402.
[2] See *antea*, § 110. Doughty v.
Bacot, 2 Desaus. Eq. (So. Car.) 546;
Lovell v. Nelson, 11 Allen (Mass.),
101.

had been lost and ended by the statute of limitations, so that the complainant could not have been subrogated to that lien, his payment of the debt conferred no benefit upon Benjamin, and consequently that Benjamin was not bound to contribute for his relief.[1]  Nor can one joint debtor be subrogated to the benefit of a security which has been otherwise lost as against the other.  Where two purchasers of land gave back a mortgage for the price thereof, which, however, was not recorded, and the interest of one of them was subsequently conveyed to a *bona fide* purchaser for value who had no notice of the unrecorded mortgage, it was held that the mortgagee might yet enforce his mortgage for the whole amount remaining due thereon against the interest of the other debtor, who must then look to his co-debtor personally for the payment of the latter's share.[2]

§ 177. **Where the Ultimate Liability is upon one of Several Owners of Securities held for the Same Debt.** — If the property of two owners is subject to a mortgage, and as between themselves it is the duty of one of them to discharge it, and the other pays the debt on an agreement that the mortgage shall inure to his benefit, or if he takes an assignment of the mortgage, he will be entitled to reimbursement through the lien of the mortgage.[3]  The relation between the debtors or the owners of the incumbered property in such a case is that of principal and surety;[4] the primary and ultimate liability is upon him whose duty it is to pay the debt and upon his property; his payment of the debt will discharge it in favor of his co-debtor;[5] and the grantee of his property incumbered with the debt, who has notice of the incumbrance and of the

---

[1] Screven v. Joyner, 1 Hill, Eq. (So. Car.) 252.

[2] Ohio Ins. Co. v. Ledyard, 8 Ala. 866.

[3] Laylin v. Knox, 41 Mich. 40; Cornell v. Prescott, 2 Barb. (N. Y.) 16.

[4] Swan v. Smith, 57 Miss. 548; Cherry v. Monro, 2 Barb. Ch. (N. Y.) 618; Barnard v. Wilson, 74 Calif. 512; *antea*, Ch. III.

[5] Birdsall v. Cropsey, 29 Neb. 679; Cook v. Hinsdale, 4 Cush. (Mass.) 134.

respective rights of the parties, will be in no better position
than his grantor;[1] he must pay the whole debt, even though
his co-debtors should convey the other incumbered property
to the common creditor.[2]  And in such a case a court of
equity may order the properties or interests which the creditor holds for the security of his debt to be sold in the succession or in the proportion in which they are, among
themselves, liable for its payment;[3] thus, where the joint
purchasers of land, having given back a mortgage for its
price, made partition of it among themselves, and one of
them paid his proportion of the mortgage debt, it was held
that the court might properly order the share of the other
purchaser to be first sold on a foreclosure of the mortgage.[4]
And although, where a bill to redeem from a mortgage is filed
by several persons as owners in different proportions of the
equity of redemption, the proceedings of the mortgagee to
enforce his security will not be delayed until the complainants have settled the proportions in which they are respectively to contribute to the redemption,[5] yet, if they pay into
court the full amount which is due to the mortgagee, the suit
may be delayed for a reasonable time to enable them to proceed against another defendant, who is also interested in the
equity of redemption, for the purpose of compelling him to
contribute his proportion of the mortgage-debt.[6]

§ 178. **These Principles applied to Joint Mortgagors and to the
Grantees of a Mortgagor**. — C. and S. purchased a lot of land,
and gave their joint note and mortgage for the price thereof.
C. afterwards conveyed his undivided half to S., subject to
the mortgage, which S. assumed and agreed to pay, and gave

---

[1] Cherry v. Monro, 2 Barb. Ch.
(N. Y.) 618; Crafts v. Crafts, 13
Gray (Mass.), 360; Cook v. Hinsdale,
4 Cush. (Mass.) 134.

[2] Crafts v. Crafts, 13 Gray (Mass.),
360.

[3] Cornell v. Prescott, 2 Barb. (N.

Y.) 16; Williams v. Perry, 20 Ind.
437.

[4] Roddy's Appeal, 72 Penn. St. 98.

[5] Antea, § 170.  Weihl v. Atlanta
Furniture Co., 15 So. E. Rep. 282.

[6] Brinckerhoff v. Lansing, 4 Johns.
Ch. (N. Y.) 65.

to C. a bond of indemnity against the same. S. subsequently conveyed the lot to a grantee with full covenants of warranty and against incumbrances, and then became insolvent and left the State, having failed to pay the mortgage-debt. The mortgagee having brought a suit against C. on the note, instead of proceeding against the land, C. thereupon tendered to the mortgagee the full amount due, and demanded an assignment of the note and mortgage to a third person for his benefit, so that he might enforce them against the land for his indemnity; but the mortgagee refused to make such an assignment. It was held, on a bill in equity then brought by C. against the mortgagee and the grantee of S., that the arrangement between C. and S. and the conveyance from the former to the latter constituted in equity the relation of principal and surety, not only between themselves personally, but also with reference to their interests in the mortgaged property; that the equitable rights of C. and S. were now the same as if S. had originally owned the whole lot, and had given the mortgage for his own debt, and C. had been merely his surety; that accordingly the land was the primary fund for the payment of the debt, and the surety, if compelled by the mortgagee to pay the debt, would be entitled to be subrogated to the charge of the mortgage upon the land; and that C.'s rights were not affected by the fact that he had taken a bond of indemnity from S., for, as S. was insolvent, his sureties on that bond might well insist that the land should be first resorted to for the payment of the mortgage-debt, instead of its being collected from C., and their liability to him upon the bond thus becoming fixed.[1] The owner of land mortgaged it, and subsequently sold a part of it to a purchaser who assumed the mortgage, but failed to pay it, and conveyed the land he had purchased to B., who had notice of the facts. In the mean time, the mortgagor had conveyed another portion of the mortgaged

[1] Cherry v. Monro, 2 Barb. Ch. (N. Y.) 618.

premises to C., who conveyed it with warranty to another
purchaser; and, the mortgage being still unpaid, this last
purchaser, to relieve his estate, applied to its discharge a
portion of the purchase-money which he would otherwise
have paid to C.  B. being still indebted to his vendor for
the price of his land in a sum greater than had been paid for
the discharge of the mortgage, it was held that C., having in
effect, through the payment made by his grantee, redeemed
from the mortgage, was entitled for his reimbursement to be
subrogated to its lien upon the land of B., which should have
discharged it.[1]  So when the amount due upon a purchase
of two separate lots has been apportioned between the two
purchasers of each lot, and the purchaser of one lot has paid
his share of the debt, the other lot should be sold first upon
foreclosure of the mortgage for the balance due thereon, as
against a subsequent purchaser of that lot whose deed was
made subject to all existing mortgages.[2]

§ 179. **Extent of the Right of Subrogation.** — This right of
subrogation is paramount to any other claim or lien upon the
property against which it is sought to be exercised, if such
other claim or lien was subject to the obligation which has
been discharged by one debtor, or to the satisfaction of which
his property has contributed more than its equitable share;[3]
but it cannot take place beyond the amount actually paid
under a legal liability,[4] or under compulsion,[5] by or from the
property of the one who seeks to enforce it, nor beyond the
proportional share of those who are, either personally or by
a pledge or mortgage of their property, jointly liable with
him.[6]  He cannot be subrogated upon the payment of any-

[1] Rardin v. Walpole, 38 Ind. 146.
[2] Weyant v. Murphy, 78 Calif. 278.
[3] Silk v. Eyre, Irish Rep. 9 Eu.
893; Duncan v. Drury, 9 Penn. St.
332.
[4] Walker v. Municipality No. One,
5 La. Ann. 10.

[5] As where a husband pays his
own debt out of his wife's property.
Greiner v. Greiner, 58 Calif. 115;
Pease v. Egan, 131 N. Y. 262.
[6] Shropshire v. Creditors, 15 La.
Ann. 705.

thing less than his proportion of the debt, although the others have paid nothing.[1] If one of several obligors in a bond, each one of whom is bound for himself alone, overpays the amount due from himself, this overpayment, being made only upon his own liability, gives him no right of subrogation against the others, and does not inure to the benefit of either of the others.[2] Nor can there be any subrogation if nothing more appears than that the joint debt has been paid, without any indication by whom or upon whose credit this was done.[3]

§ 180. **Whether Original Obligation discharged as to all the Debtors upon Payment by one.** — It was at one time held in Pennsylvania that, although a surety who has paid the bond debt of his principal will be subrogated to all the creditor's rights and remedies against the principal, this rule will not be applied to a payment made by a joint debtor in a bond who is not a surety; but his claim against his co-obligors will be treated as merely a simple-contract claim for contribution;[4] but this distinction has not since been followed in that State.[5] The rule in England is now the same in this respect as to both sureties and joint debtors;[6] and in this country the same principles are generally applied between joint debtors or other persons who are, either personally or by a charge upon their property, liable for the same debt, as between principal and surety,[7] though the claim of a mere joint debtor to subrogation has often been less favored than that of a surety,[8] on the assumed ground that the payment of

[1] Garfield v. Foskett, 57 Vt. 290; Sawyer v. Lyon, 10 Johns. (N. Y.) 32.

[2] Pettengill v. Pettengill, 64 Maine, 350.

[3] Brick v. Buel, 73 Tex. 511.

[4] Greiner's Estate, 2 Watts (Penn.), 414.

[5] Sterling v. Stewart, 74 Penn. St. 445; Gearhart v. Jordan, 11 Penn. St. 325; Duncan v. Drury, 9 Penn. St. 332.

[6] Mercantile Law Amendment Act, 19 & 20 Vic., c. 97, § 5.

[7] *Antea*, § 136 *et seq.* See also Neilson v. Fry, 16 Ohio St. 552; O'Bryan v. Neel, 84 Ga. 134; Newsom v. McLendon, 6 Ga. 392; Hendrickson v. Hutchinson, 29 N. J. Law, 180; Hollingsworth v. Pearson, 53 Iowa, 53.

[8] Arnott v. Webb, 1 Dillon, C. C. 362; Stanley v. Nutter, 16 N. H 22; Morley v. Stevens, 47 How. Pr. (N.

18

a debt by one of several joint debtors inures to the benefit of all of them.[1] If the principal obligation is held to be extinguished upon its payment by one of the debtors, it cannot be kept alive by being assigned to a stranger who has paid it with money furnished to him for that purpose by one of the debtors.[2] But if the assignment was made to the stranger by contemporaneous agreement to secure him for advancing money to take up the indebtedness, though at the request of one who is liable for the debt, such an assignment will not extinguish the original obligation.[3]

Y.) 228; Boykin v. Buie, 109 Nor. Car. 501; Adams v. Keeler, 30 Ga. 86; Maxwell v. Owen, 7 Coldw. (Tenn.) 630; Baldwin v. Merrill, 8 Humph. (Tenn.) 132; Tompkins v. Fifth National Bank, 53 Ills. 57; Planters' Bank v. Spencer, 3 Sm. & M. (Miss.) 305.

[1] As in French v. Edwards, 5 Saw-

yer, C. C. 266; Booth v. Farmers' Bank, 11 Hun (N. Y.), 258; Allison v. Pattison, 11 So. Rep. 194; James v. Yaeger, 86 Calif. 184; Fort Worth Bank v. Daugherty, 81 Tex. 301; Boos v. Morgan, 30 No. E. Rep. 141.

[2] Hogan v. Reynolds, 21 Ala. 56.

[3] McIntyre v. Miller, 13 M. & W. 725.

# CHAPTER V.

## SUBROGATION AMONG PARTIES TO BILLS AND NOTES.

**§ 181. An Indorser upon Payment subrogated to Rights of Holder against Prior Parties.** — The payment of a note or bill by an indorser to the holder thereof will not extinguish the instrument; but the indorser, after his payment, whether made voluntarily or upon compulsion, if he was liable for it,

will be subrogated to all the remedies that are available upon
the note or bill against the antecedent parties thereto,[1] including the right of action against a bank which has by its
negligence caused the release of a prior indorser.[2] A partial
payment by an indorser will not extinguish *pro tanto* the liability of antecedent parties, unless it was made in their
behalf and not by reason of the liability of the party making
the payment to the holder;[3] the holder of the note can still
collect the full amount thereof from the parties who are an-
tecedently liable thereon, receiving the amount of such partial payment as a trustee for the indorser who originally
made it,[4] unless the ultimate liability to pay the note rests
upon this indorser as between himself and the other parties to
the note, in which case the payment made by him will accrue to their benefit.[5] So the holder of a note, after receiving payment thereof from the indorser, may maintain an
action thereon at the request and for the benefit of the indorser against the maker; and the latter cannot set up the
indorser's payment as a defence to the action against himself.[6] The indorser of a promissory note, after its maturity
and after his liability upon it has become fixed, does not
cease to be entitled to the rights of a surety and become
a joint principal debtor by joining with the maker of the
note in a bond giving further time for its payment, although
the bond does not describe him as a surety.[7] It has been

[1] Woodward v. Pell, L. R. 4 Q. B.
55; Picquet v. Curtis, 1 Sumner,
478; Rushworth v. Moore, 36 N. H.
188; Parker v. Sanborn, 7 Gray
(Mass.), 191; Cassebeer v. Kalb-
fleisch, 11 Hun (N. Y.), 190; Beckwith v. Webber, 78 Mich. 390; Seixas
v. Gonsoulin, 40 La. Ann. 351; Crawford v. Logan, 97 Ills. 396. See also
Pollard v. Ogden, 2 El. & Bl. 459;
Pacific Bank v. Mitchell, 9 Met.
(Mass.) 297; Dougherty v. Deeny,
45 Iowa, 443.

[2] Bird v. Louisiana Bank, 93 U. S. 96.

[3] Randall v. Moon, 12 C. B. 261;
Jones v. Broadhurst, 9 C. B. 173;
North National Bank v. Hamlin, 125
Mass. 506.

[4] Madison Square Bank v. Pierce,
62 Hun (N. Y.), 493; s. c., 17 N. Y.
Supt. 270.

[5] Cook v. Lister, 13 C. B. N. s.
543.

[6] Williams v. James, 15 Q. B. 498;
Bank of America v. Senior, 11 R. L
376.

[7] Merriken v. Godwin, 2 Del. Ch.
236.

held that the joint indorsers of commercial paper, though liable as co-promisors, have upon payment no right of subrogation against each other;[1] but it is now usually considered that the true relation of all the successive parties to a note or bill to each other may be shown by parol evidence, and that their rights of subrogation will depend upon their true relations as thus established.[2]

§ 182.  **The Maker of a Note not entitled to the Benefit of Payments made by Indorsers thereon.** — The maker of a note is *prima facie* the party ultimately liable thereon, and is not entitled, in an action on the note against himself, to a deduction for a partial payment not made by him or in his behalf, but by an indorser or by a guarantor;[3] for such a payment does not in law inure to his benefit.[4]  An indorser, upon taking up a bill which he has indorsed, is entitled like a surety to receive securities which the holder has received from prior parties to the bill, the debts secured by such securities being first fully paid to the holder;[5] and he is entitled to the benefit of a proof previously made by the holder of the note against the bankrupt estate of the maker.[6]  The holder of a note is entitled to prove it in full against the bankrupt estate of the maker, although he has since the bankruptcy received a partial payment thereon from an indorser on the note.  "The general rule undoubtedly is," said *Lowell*, J., "that the holder of a note may prove against all parties for the full amount, and receive dividends from all until he has

[1] West Branch Bank *v.* Armstrong, 40 Penn. St. 278; Holliman *v.* Rogers, 6 Tex. 91.

[2] McDonald *v.* Whitfield, 8 App. Cas. 733; Goldsmith *v.* Holmes, 13 Sawyer, C. C. 526; Martin *v.* Marshall, 60 Vt. 321; Thompson *v.* Taylor, 12 R. I. 109; Farwell *v.* Ensign, 66 Mich. 600.

[3] Granite Bank *v.* Fitch, 145 Mass. 567.

[4] *Lord, J.*, in North National Bank *v.* Hamlin, 125 Mass. 506, 508; Madison Square Bank *v.* Pierce, 62 Hun (N. Y.), 493; Ward *v.* Tyler, 52 Penn. St. 393; Southern Michigan Bank *v.* Byles, 67 Mich. 296.

[5] Duncan *v.* North & South Wales Bank, 6 App. Cas. 1.

[6] Richardson *v.* City Bank, 11 Gray (Mass.), 261.

obtained the whole of his debt with interest. It is likewise
the general rule, that what he has received from one party,
or from dividends in bankruptcy of one party to the note, are
payments which he must give credit for if he afterwards
proves against others.[1] I am of opinion that this latter rule
must be confined to cases in which the payment has been
made by the person primarily liable on the note or bill. . . .
The better opinion at common law is that payment by a
drawer or indorser does not exonerate the acceptor or maker,
unless the promise of the latter was for the accommodation
of the former, or there is some other equity which makes the
note or bill the debt of the party who has made the payment,
or unless he has made it at the request or for the benefit of
the acceptor or maker.[2] If this be not the rule at law, still
I consider it to be so in bankruptcy. . . . A creditor may
prove the debt, notwithstanding payment in whole or in part
by a surety, because he in fact proves as trustee for the
surety." [3] "On the other hand, a partial payment of a bill
by any party to it inures to the benefit and is a discharge *pro
tanto* of the liability of all subsequent parties.[4] Consequently any payment or dividend received by the holder
from a prior party before proof in bankruptcy against a subsequent party must be deducted from the amount of the
claim provable against the latter." [5]

[1] Sohier *v.* Loring, 6 Cush. (Mass.)
537; Wildman, *ex parte,* 1 Atk. 109;
Royal Bank, *ex parte,* 2 Rose, 197;
Taylor, *ex parte,* 1 De G. & J. 302.

[2] Byles on Bills (10th ed.), 221,
and cases there cited.

[3] Souther, *in re,* Talcott, *ex parte,*
2 Lowell, 320. Professor Ames (1
Cases on Bills & Notes, 880) cites as
agreeing with this case De Tastet, *ex
parte,* 1 Rose, 10; Ellerhorst, *in re,* 5
N. B. R. 144; Harris, *ex parte,* 2
Lowell, 568, and says that Cooper *v.*
Pepys, 1 Atk. 106; Leers, *ex parte,* 6

Ves. 644; Worrall, *ex parte,* 1 Cox,
309; Taylor, *ex parte,* 1 De G. & J.
302; Oriental Bank, *in re,* L. R. 6
Eq. 582; and Howard, *in re,* 4 N. B.
R. 571, *contra,* are not to be supported.

[4] See accordingly Pulsifer, *in re,* 9
Biss. 487; Lowell *v.* French, 54 Vt.
193; Dearth *v.* Hide & Leather Bank,
100 Mass. 540; Nash *v.* Burchard, 87
Mich. 85.

[5] 1 Ames's Cases on Bills & Notes,
880, citing Ryswick, *ex parte,* 2 P.
Wms. 89; Wyldman, *ex parte,* 2 Ves.

§ 182 *a*.  **Indorser or Accommodation Maker of Note regarded as Surety merely.** — An indorser of a note or bill, or one who has to the knowledge of the holder thereof become a party thereto merely for the accommodation of the maker or primary debtor thereon, is to be regarded merely as a surety of the primary debtor;[1] and has all the rights of a surety.[2]  But parties who have exchanged notes with each other cannot claim to be accommodation makers or to have the rights of sureties.[3]  The indorser's right of subrogation will not accrue until he has paid the note;[4] but it has been held that an indorser of notes secured by a deed of trust who has been compelled to pay the interest thereon acquires by his payment an interest in the security which is complete against the debtor, and awaits only the full satisfaction of the creditor to become complete as against all parties; so that upon a subsequent foreclosure by the creditor the indorser may have a decree for the interest so paid against the original debtor.[5]  One who makes a promissory note for the accommodation of another has the same rights against the holder of the note who has notice of the facts as any surety for the debt.[6]  Such a surety has the same right to be subrogated to the benefit of any collateral security held by the creditor or holder of the note,[7] and the same equitable right to be discharged by the creditor's surrender of any collateral security or impairment of the right of recourse against the principal

---

Sen. 115; s. c. 1 Atk. 109; Royal Bank, *ex parte*, 2 Rose, 197; Weeks, *in re*, 13 N. B. R. 263; Sohier *v.* Loring, 6 Cush. (Mass.) 537; Blake *v.* Ames, 8 Allen (Mass.), 318; National Bank *v.* Porter, 122 Mass. 308.

[1] Story on Prom. Notes, § 412 *et seq.*  Okie *v.* Spencer, 2 Wharton (Penn.), 253; Pease *v.* Tilt, 9 Daly (N. Y.), 299.  But a statute increasing the rights of a surety will not necessarily extend to an indorser. Dibrell *v.* Dandridge, 51 Miss. 55, ex-

tended in Yates *v.* Mead, 68 Miss. 787.

[2] Hoffman *v.* Butler, 105 Ind. 371; Gunnis *v.* Weigley, 114 Penn. St. 191.

[3] Smith's Appeal, 125 Penn. St. 404; Stickney *v.* Mohler, 19 Md. 490.

[4] Malone Bank *v.* Shields, 55 Hun (N. Y.), 274.

[5] Telford *v.* Garrels, 132 Ills. 550.

[6] Guild *v.* Butler, 127 Mass. 386.

[7] Hagey *v.* Hill, 75 Penn. St. 108; Mayhew *v.* Boyd, 5 Md. 102.

debtor,[1] as would be possessed by a surety *eo nomine*,[2] though this has been denied in two old cases.[3] Thus, if a mortgagee, when one instalment of the mortgage-debt has become payable, so conducts himself as to operate a release of the mortgage, this will release the indorsers of notes which had been given for subsequent instalments of the mortgage-debt.[4] But, as would be the case with any surety,[5] if the indorser has himself assumed the burden of the debt as his own, then, as he would not be entitled to take the security by subrogation, he cannot complain of its release by the creditor.[6] And the right of an accommodation maker to demand the privileges of a surety against the holder depends upon the holder's knowledge of the relations between the parties to the note.[7] The apparent principal has not the rights of a surety against the creditor unless the real facts were known to the creditor.[8] So an accommodation indorser, on taking up the bill, may hold an accommodation acceptor, but not a subsequent indorser.[9]

§ 183. **Transferee of Bona Fide Holder substituted to his Rights though himself chargeable with Equities.** — One who takes a bill or note from a *bona fide* holder for value thereof will be substituted to all the rights of such holder, although he himself takes it overdue, or with notice of facts which would otherwise constitute a defence to the note or bill in his hands,[10] on

[1] Guild v. Butler, *supra*; Nassau Bank v. Campbell, 63 Hun (N. Y.), 229; Dunn v. Parsons, 40 Hun, 77; Newcomb v. Raynor, 21 Wend. (N. Y.) 108; German Bank v. Fourhaw, 138 Penn. St. 474; Bridgman v. Johnson, 44 Mich. 491; Hillegas v. Stephenson, 75 Mo. 118; Union Bank v. Cooley, 27 La. Ann. 202.

[2] Case v. Hawkins, 53 Miss. 702; Capital Savings Bank v. Reel, 62 Calif. 419.

[3] Hurd v. Little, 12 Mass. 502; Liggett v. Pennsylvania Bank, 7 Serg. & R. (Penn.) 218.

[4] Bridgman v. Johnson, 44 Mich. 491.

[5] *Ante*, § 112.

[6] Sieger v. Second National Bank, 132 Penn. St. 308.

[7] Tyler v. Busey, 3 McArthur (D. C.), 344.

[8] Harrison v. Courtauld, 3 B. & Ad. 36; Auburn Bank v. Marshall, 73 Maine, 79; Goodman v. Litaker, 84 Nor. Car. 8.

[9] Gillespie v. Campbell, 39 Fed. Rep. 724.

[10] Carruthers v. West, 11 Q. B. 143; Fairclough v. Pavia, 9 Exch. 690;

the ground that the purchaser is subrogated to all the rights of his vendor.[1]  So the indorsee of protested drafts on which a direct action was prohibited by statute has been subrogated in New York to his indorser's right of action for the consideration paid for such drafts;[2] and the same rule has been applied to a void certificate of indebtedness.[3]  But an indorser is not always by his payment subrogated to all the rights of the holder from whom, upon his payment, he takes the note, against prior parties thereto.  If the notice of dishonor sent by the holder to the first indorser was wrongly addressed in consequence of erroneous information carelessly given by the second indorser to the holder, though the latter, having used due diligence, might have held the first indorser to pay the note,[4] yet the second indorser, upon taking up the note from the holder, cannot do so; for it was his fault that the notice was not properly sent.[5]  The principle that a notice given by the holder will inure to the benefit of the other parties to a bill or note[6] does not apply to such a case.

May v. Chapman, 16 M. & W. 355; Robinson v. Reynolds, 2 Q. B. 196, 211; Chalmers v. Lanion, 1 Campb. 383; Scotland County v. Hill, 132 U. S. 107; Commissioners v. Clark, 94 U. S. 278; Dillingham v. Blood, 66 Maine, 140; Roberts v. Lane, 64 Maine, 108; Suffolk Savings Bank v. Boston, 149 Mass. 364; Woodman v. Churchill, 52 Maine, 58; Barker v. Parker, 10 Gray (Mass.), 339; Williams v. Matthews, 3 Cow. (N. Y.) 252, 260; Wilson v. Mechanics' Bank, 45 Penn. St. 488, 494; Prentice v. Zane, 2 Gratt. (Va.) 262; Boyd v. McCann, 10 Md. 118; Hogan v. Moore, 48 Ga. 156; Bassett v. Avery, 15 Ohio St. 299; Kost v. Bender, 25 Mich. 515; Woodworth v. Huntoon, 40 Ills. 131; Riley v. Schawacker, 50 Ind. 592; Mornyer v. Cooper, 35 Iowa, 257; Sonoma Bank v. Gove, 63 Calif.

355; Cotton v. Sterling, 20 La. Ann. 282; Cook v. Larkin, 19 La. Ann. 507; Howell v. Crane, 12 La. Ann. 126.

[1] Antea, § 34.

[2] Oneida Bank v. Ontario Bank, 21 N. Y. 490; affirmed in McMahon v. Allen, 35 N. Y. 407, and Thomas v. Richmond, 12 Wallace, 354.  But this subrogation could scarcely have been effected at law except in a code State.

[3] McCormick v. District of Columbia, 7 Mackey (D. C.), 534.

[4] Lambert v. Ghiselin, 9 How. 552.

[5] Beale v. Parish, 20 N. Y. 407, overruling s. c. 24 Barb. (N. Y.) 243.

[6] Palen v. Shurtleff, 9 Met. (Mass.) 581; Stafford v. Yates, 18 Johns. (N. Y.) 327; Mead v. Engs, 5 Cow. (N. Y.) 303; Marr v. Johnson, 9 Yerg. (Tenn.) 1.

§ 184. **Acceptor of Bill supra protest substituted to Rights of Holder from whom he takes it.** — The acceptor of a bill *supra protest.* for the honor of a particular party to the bill succeeds to the rights of the party from whom he takes it, except that he discharges all the parties to the bill subsequent to the one for whose honor he takes it up, and that he cannot indorse it over.[1] Accordingly he can recover on the bill against any prior parties thereto who could have been held by the person from whom he receives it, or by any prior holder of the bill, even though they could not have been held by the one for whose honor such acceptor has taken up the bill.[2] As the acceptor *supra protest* is liable like an indorser,[3] so, when he takes up the bill upon such an acceptance, he is entitled to hold antecedent parties as an indorser could do.[4]

§ 185. **Transferees of Notes or Bills entitled to the Benefit of Security held for their Payment.** — The right to enforce security given for the payment of a note will pass to the indorsees or transferees of the note, even though the security itself has not been formally transferred or delivered to them.[5] A mort-

---

[1] Swan, *ex parte*, Overend, *in re*, L. R. 6 Eq. 344 (overruling Lambert *ex parte*, 13 Ves. 179); Wackerbath, *ex parte*, 5 Ves. 574; Mertens *v.* Winnington, 1 Espinasse, 113; Goodall *v.* Polhill, 1 C. B. 233; Cox *v.* Earle, 3 B. & Ald. 430; Konig *v.* Bayard, 1 Peters, 250.

[2] Swan, *ex parte*, Overend, *in re*, *supra.*

[3] Williams *v.* Germaine, 7 B. & C. 468; Hoare *v.* Cazenove, 16 East, 391; Lenox *v.* Leverett, 10 Mass. 1; Schofield *v.* Bayard, 3 Wend. (N. Y.) 488.

[4] *Antea*, § 181.

[5] Vose *v.* Handy, 2 Greenl. (Me.) 322; Page *v.* Pierce, 26 N. H. 317; Blake *v.* Williams, 36 N. H. 39; Keyes *v.* Wood, 21 Vt. 331; Belding *v.* Manley, 21 Vt. 550; Dudley *v.* Cadwell, 19 Conn. 218; Evertson *v.*

Booth, 19 Johns. (N. Y.) 486; Pattison *v.* Hull, 9 Cow. (N. Y.) 747; West's Appeal, 88 Penn. St. 341; Partridge *v.* Partridge, 38 Penn. St. 78; Phillips *v.* Lewistown Bank, 18 Penn. St. 394; Hyman *v.* Devereux, 63 Nor. Car. 624; Muller *v.* Wadlington, 5 So. Car. 342; Martin *v.* McReynolds, 6 Mich. 70; Union Ins. Co. *v.* Slee, 123 Ills. 57; Mapps *v.* Sharpe, 32 Ills. 13; Pardee *v.* Lindley, 31 Ills. 174; French *v.* Turner, 15 Ind. 59; Martindale *v.* Burch, 57 Iowa, 291; Indiana Bank *v.* Anderson, 14 Iowa, 544; Bange *v.* Flint, 25 Wisc. 544; Exchange Bank *v.* Stone, 80 Ky. 109; Burdett *v.* Clay, 8 B. Mon. (Ky.) 287; Jackson *v.* Rutledge, 3 Lea (Tenn.), 626; Wolffe *v.* Nall, 62 Ala. 24; Graham *v.* Newman, 21 Ala. 497; Hobson *v.* Edwards, 57

gagee's indorsement and delivery of the notes secured by the mortgage will operate as an equitable assignment of the mortgage itself.[1] The holder of the legal title to the security will be considered to hold it as a trustee for the benefit of the indorsees.[2] When the purchaser of a melodeon gave his note for the price thereof, with the agreement that the property should not vest in him until his payment of the note, it was held that the vendors' interest in the melodeon was merely an incident to the note, as in the case of a mortgage or pledge, and that it passed to one to whom they indorsed the note, so that trover for the melodeon could not afterwards be maintained in the name of the vendors.[3] And after a *bona fide* transfer of the note, not overdue, and for value, the holder of the security cannot discharge it to the prejudice of the holder of the note.[4] Such a taker of the note may enforce the security in the hands of the payee of the note, even though this payee could not himself have enforced the security against the maker of the note by reason of the equities

Miss. 128; Dick v. Maury, 9 Sm. & M. (Miss.) 448; Holmes v. McGinty, 44 Miss. 94; McQuie v. Peay, 58 Mo. 56; Potter v. Stevens, 40 Mo. 229; Scott v. Turner, 15 La. Ann. 346; Bennett v. Soloman, 6 Calif. 134; Webb v. Hoselton, 4 Neb. 308; Creaner v. Creaner, 36 Ark. 91; Biscoe v. Royston, 18 Ark. 508.

[1] Converse v. Michigan Dairy Co., 45 Fed. Rep. 18; O'Neil v. Seixas, 85 Ala. 80; Burnett v. Lyford, 93 Calif. 114; Storch v. McCain, 85 Calif. 304; Smith v. Brunk, 14 Color. 75; Farrell v. Lewis, 56 Conn. 280; Holway v. Gilman, 81 Maine, 185; Gabbert v. Wallace, 66 Miss. 618; Patterson v. Booth, 103 Mo. 402; Blair v. White, 61 Vt. 110; Jenkins v. Hawkins, 34 W. Va. 799; Zwickey v. Hainey, 73 Wisc. 464.

[2] Wolcott v. Winchester, 15 Gray

(Mass.), 461; Young v. Miller, 6 Gray (Mass.), 152; Crane v. March, 4 Pick. (Mass.) 131; Nelson v. Ferris, 30 Mich. 497; Hagerman v. Sutton, 91 Mo. 519; Studebaker Mfg. Co. v. McCargur, 20 Neb. 500; Kuhns v. Bankes, 15 Neb. 92; Hamilton v. Lubukee, 51 Ills. 415; Sargent v. Howe, 21 Ills. 148; Gordon v. Mulhare, 13 Wisc. 22; Graham v. Newman, 21 Ala. 497; Colt v. Barnes, 64 Ala. 108; Phelan v. Olney, 6 Calif. 478; Burhans v. Hutcheson, 25 Kans. 625.

[3] Esty v. Graham, 46 N. H. 169. But see Domestic Sewing Machine Co. v. Arthurhultz, 63 Ind. 322.

[4] Gordon v. Mulhare, 13 Wisc. 22; Keohane v. Smith, 97 Ills. 156; McCormick v. Digby, 8 Blackf. (Ind.) 99; Gottschalk v. Neal, 6 Mo. App. 596.

between them,[1] although this has sometimes been denied in the case of a mortgage;[2] but one who takes the note overdue will not be protected by this principle against such equities of the owner of the security.[3] The equitable lien of a vendor of land to secure the payment of a note which he has taken for the purchase-money will not usually pass to an indorsee who cannot hold the vendor for the payment of the note, since the effect of the transfer was to secure to the vendor all the advantages of a payment.[4] Nor will the mortgagee's bare right of action for a mere tort pass by his transfer of the mortgage-note.[5]

§ 186. **Rights of a Stranger upon taking up a Note.** — When,

[1] Carpenter v. Longan, 16 Wallace, 271 (overruling Longan v. Carpenter, 1 Col. Ter. 205); Myers v. Hazard, 50 Fed. Rep. 155; Pierce v. Faunce, 47 Maine, 507; Sprague v. Graham, 29 Maine, 160; Taylor v. Page, 6 Allen (Mass.), 86; Breen v. Seward, 11 Gray (Mass.), 118; Green v. Hart, 1 Johns. (N. Y.) 580; Jackson v. Blodgett, 5 Cow. (N. Y.) 202; Gould v. Marsh, 4 Thomp. & C. (N. Y.) 128; s. c. 1 Hun (N. Y.), 566; Bloomer v. Henderson, 8 Mich. 395; Judge v. Vogel, 38 Mich. 568; Cornell v. Hichens, 11 Wisc. 353; Croft v. Bunster, 9 Wisc. 503.

[2] Hostetter v. Alexander, 22 Minn. 559; Johnson v. Carpenter, 7 Minn. 176; Baily v. Smith, 14 Ohio St. 396; White v. Sutherland, 64 Ills. 181; Sumner v. Waugh, 56 Ills. 531; Walker v. Dement, 42 Ills. 272; Olds v. Cummings, 31 Ills. 188; Foster v. Strong, 5 Ills. App. 223; Grassly v. Reinback, 4 Ills. App. 341; Union College v. Wheeler, 61 N. Y. 88; Briggs v. Langford, 1 Silvernail's N. Y. Ct. of Appeals, 553; Horstman v. Gerker, 49 Penn. St. 282; Bouligny v. Fortier, 17 La. Ann. 121; Jennings v. Vickers, 31 La. Ann. 679.

[3] Fish v. French, 15 Gray (Mass.), 520; Howard v. Gresham, 27 Ga. 347.

[4] Barnett v. Riser, 63 Ala. 347; Bankhead v. Owen, 60 Ala. 457; Hightower v. Rigsby, 56 Ala. 126. See generally as to the somewhat anomalous case of a vendor's lien, which is sometimes held to be merely personal to the vendor, not assignable, and not the subject of subrogation, and sometimes to pass only when manifestly so intended, and sometimes to pass like any other lien, Salem Bank v. Salem Flour Mills, 39 Fed. Rep. 89, and 14 Sawyer, 84; Rogers v. James, 33 Ark. 77; Shall v. Biscoe, 18 Ark. 142; Davis v. Smith, 88 Ala. 596; Avery v. Clarke, 87 Calif. 619; Gruhn v. Richardson, 128 Ills. 178; Dayhuff v. Dayhuff, 81 Ills. 499; Pillow v. Helm, 7 Baxter (Tenn.), 545; Hamblen v. Foltz, 70 Tex. 132. As to subrogation to a statutory crop lien, see St. Peter's Literary Association v. Webb, 31 Ark. 140; Mercer v. Cross, 79 Ga. 432; Benson v. Gottheimer, 75 Ga. 642; Scott v. Pound, 61 Ga. 579.

[5] Gabbert v. Wallace, 66 Miss. 618.

at or after the maturity of a promissory note, one who is not interested in its payment, either as indorser or as surety, takes it up, declining to have it cancelled, but saying nothing about buying it, and not stipulating for a conventional subrogation to the rights of the holder, he is not subrogated to those rights; but the note is paid and satisfied, and the indebtedness of the maker is extinguished;[1] the voluntary payment of the note made by one who was not bound for it and had no interest in discharging it affords no ground for subrogation.[2] But if a stranger has made such a payment without a previous authority from the debtor, and before any ratification of the payment by the debtor the creditor and the stranger undo the transaction, and the creditor returns the money to the stranger, it is then too late for the debtor to ratify the payment, and the creditor can enforce the original obligation against him.[3] Such a payment made by a stranger becomes an efficacious payment only when it is ratified or adopted by the debtor,[4] although such ratification and adoption may be made and shown by the debtor's setting up the payment as a defence in an action against him on the note.[5] A third person who has given to the holder of a note his written agreement to be holden for its payment like an indorser will neither be regarded as a mere stranger nor yet as a party to the note; and if he pays the note upon the default of the parties to it, he is entitled to the note undischarged, and may maintain an action thereon for his reimbursement.[6] And if a stranger takes up a note, this will be deemed a pur-

[1] Burr v. Smith, 21 Barb. (N. Y.) 262; Oliver v. Bragg, 15 La. Ann. 402.

[2] Eastman v. Plumer, 32 N. H. 238; Lancey v. Clark, 64 N. Y. 209; Weil v. Enterprise Ginnery Co., 42 La. Ann. 492.

[3] Walter v. James, L. R. 6 Exch. 124; Mechanics' Bank v. Seitz, 30 W. N. C. 261.

[4] Edgeworth Co. v. Wetherbee, 6 Gray (Mass.), 166.

[5] Simpson v. Eggington, 10 Exch. 845; Martin v. Quinn, 37 Calif. 55. See Dodge v. Freedman's Savings Co., 93 U. S. 379.

[6] Bishop v. Rowe, 71 Maine, 263. See Pacific Bank v. Mitchell, 9 Met. (Mass.) 297; Warner v. Chappell, 32 Barb. (N. Y.) 309.

chase and not an extinguishment thereof, if such was the
intent of the parties.[1]

§ 187. **Holder of Note substituted to Benefit of Security given
by one to another Party to the Note to secure its Payment.** —
Property mortgaged to secure to the mortgagee the payment
of notes indorsed by the mortgagee for the benefit of the
mortgagor will be applied in equity, upon the insolvency of
both maker and indorser, to the payment of such notes,[2] and
may be so appropriated by the creditor upon the insolvency
of only the maker.[3] And such a mortgage, not being given
merely for the indemnity of the mortgagee, cannot be released
by him so as to deprive the holders of the notes of their rights
under the mortgage.[4] And notes issued by the mortgagee to
the mortgagor in consideration of the mortgage and purporting on their face to be secured by the mortgage will be protected by the mortgage in the hands of third persons to whom
they have been negotiated for value, even after a discharge
of the mortgage by the nominal mortgagee.[5] But security
given by one party to a note to another on a secret trust for
the payment of the note will pass free of all equities to a *bona
fide* purchaser for value.[6]

§ 188. **Substitution of the Holder to the Benefit of Indemnity
held by an Indorser.** — Security given by the maker of a note
to his accommodation indorser thereon, to indemnify the latter against his liability, is not an accessory to the principal
obligation, but merely a personal indemnity, ordinarily available only upon payment by the indorser.[7] Such an indem-

[1] Swope *v.* Leffingwell, 72 Mo.
348; Montgomery Bank *v.* Albany
Bank, 7 N. Y. 459.

[2] Rice *v.* Dewey, 13 Gray (Mass.),
47; Harmony Bank's Appeal, 101
Penn. St. 428; DeMott *v.* Stockton
Paperware Co., 32 N. J. Eq. 124;
Ohio Life Ins. Co. *v.* Winn, 4 Md.
Ch. Dec. 253.

[3] DeMott *v.* Stockton Paperware
Co., 32 N. J. Eq. 124.

[4] Boyd *v.* Parker, 43 Md. 182;
Hartford & N. Y. Transportation
Co. *v.* Hartford Bank, 46 Conn.
569.

[5] McCracken *v.* German Ins. Co,
43 Md. 471.

[6] Mifflin County Bank's Appeal, 98
Penn. St. 150.

[7] O'Hara *v.* Baum, 88 Penn. St.
114; Hartford & N. Y. Transp. Co. *v.*
Hartford Bank, 46 Conn. 569; Spiller

nity would not be available to a surety upon the note who
had been compelled to pay it; for the maker, though a
surety, and an accommodation indorser are not co-sureties;[1]
nor has an accommodation maker the rights of a co-surety
against an accommodation indorser.[2]  Nor have successive
accommodation indorsers the rights of co-sureties against
each other, unless they have agreed to become such as among
themselves.[3]  The holder of the note cannot in equity be substituted to the benefit of the indorser's indemnity,[4] when he
has obtained no judgment against either maker or indorser,
and does not aver that either is insolvent,[5] or that the debt
cannot be collected on execution.[6]  If the indorser has been
discharged from his liability upon the note by the neglect
of its holder to give him proper notice upon its dishonor,
the security held for his indemnity is discharged, and neither
the holder nor any other party to the note can claim the
benefit of such security by subrogation to his rights;[7] for an
indorser does not, by taking indemnity against his indorsement, waive his right to notice.[8]  But the holder is entitled
to the benefit of any securities received by an insolvent in-

---

v. Creditors, 16 La. Ann. 292; Peterson v. Willing, 3 Dall. 506.

[1] Dawson v. Pettway, 4 Dev. &
Bat. Law (Nor. Car.), 396; Nurre v.
Chittenden, 56 Ind. 462.

[2] Hillegas v. Stephenson, 75 Mo.
118; Smith v. Smith, 1 Dev. Ch. (Nor.
Car.) 173.

[3] Stillwell v. How, 46 Mo. 589;
McCune v. Belt, 45 Mo. 174; Mc-
Neilly v. Patchin, 23 Mo. 40; Wood-
ward v. Severance, 7 Allen (Mass.),
340; Sweet v. McAllister, 4 Id. 353;
Clapp v. Rice, 13 Gray (Mass.), 403;
Smith v. Morrill, 54 Maine, 48;
Hogue v. Davis, 8 Gratt. (Va.) 4;
Quarrier v. Quarrier, 15 So. E. Rep.
154; Abercrombie v. Connor, 10 Ala.
293; Armstrong v. Cook, 30 Ind. 22.

[4] Post v. Tradesmen's Bank, 28
Conn. 420.

[5] Antea, §§ 160, 161; Nightingale
v. Chaffee, 11 R. I. 609.

[6] Ohio Ins. Co. v. Reeder, 18 Ohio,
35.

[7] Virginia Bank v. Boisseau, 12
Leigh (Va.), 387.

[8] Ray v. Smith, 17 Wallace, 411,
415; Haskell v. Boardman, 8 Allen
(Mass.), 38: Moses v. Ela, 43 N. H.
557; Seacord v. Miller, 13 N. Y. 55;
Kramer v. Sandford, 4 Watts & Serg.
(Penn.) 328; Denny v. Palmer, 5
Ired. Law (Nor. Car.), 610; Wilson
v. Senier, 14 Wisc. 380; Peets v.
Wilson, 19 La. 478.  But see Story
on Prom. Notes, §§ 281, 282, and cases
there cited.

dorser as a surety for prior parties.[1] If all the indorsers of
a bill of exchange have become such for the accommodation
of the drawer, and he gives a deed of trust for the indemnity
of the two last indorsers, the first indorser cannot compel
them to sell the trust property and apply it to the payment
of the bill; he will have no right of subrogation to their
security until he pays the bill.[2]

§ 189. **Bill drawn against a Consignment of Merchandise and
made a Lien upon it.** — The indorsee of a bill which purports
to be drawn against a consignment of merchandise, and has
annexed to it a warehouse receipt for the merchandise and a
certificate by which the drawer declares a lien upon the merchandise in favor of the holder of the bill, reserving to the
consignee upon whom the bill is drawn the right to sell the
merchandise upon its arrival and hold its proceeds in trust
for the holder of the bill, acquires by taking the bill a special
property in the merchandise thus appropriated for its payment, and may enforce the trust by a bill in equity against
the consignee and one to whom the latter has pledged the
property after accepting the bill.[3] The indorsee or transferee
of the bill acquires a special property in the goods described
in the shipping documents which accompany it;[4] and the
shipper is deprived of his property, and has no longer either
possession or title.[5] And one who pays such a draft at the

---

[1] *In re* Jaycox, 8 N. B. R. 241.

[2] Dunlap v. Clements, 7 Ala. 539;
Buffalo Bank v. Wood, 71 N. Y. 405.

[3] Michigan Bank v. Gardiner, 15
Gray (Mass.), 362; Ullman v. Bar-
nard, 7 *Id.* 554; Marine Bank v.
Wright, 48 N. Y. 1.

[4] Dows v. Exchange Bank, 91 U. S.
618; Wells v. Oregon R. & N. Co., 32
Fed. Rep. 51; Hathaway v. Haynes,
124 Mass. 311; Cairo Bank v. Crocker,
111 Mass. 163; Chicago Bank v.
Bailey, 115 Mass. 228; Batavia Bank
v. Ege, 109 N. Y. 120; Commercial

Bank v. Pfeiffer, 22 Hun (N. Y.),
327; Holmes v. Bailey, 92 Penn. St.
57; Holmes v. German Security Bank,
87 Penn. St. 525; West Michigan
Bank v. Howard, 52 Mich. 423; Chester Bank v. Atlanta Ry. Co., 25 So.
Car. 216; Taylor v. Turner, 87 Ills.
296; Halsey v. Warden, 25 Kans.
128; Stackville Bank v. Meyer, 43
La. Ann. 1; Delgado v. Wilbur, 25
La. Ann. 82.

[5] De Wolf v. Gardner, 12 Cush.
(Mass.) 19; Petitt v. First National
Bank, 4 Bush (Ky.), 334.

request of the drawee, and on the latter's agreement that he shall be secured by the property will acquire the same right to the property.[1] If, however, the acceptor on his acceptance was to acquire against the drawer the full control of the property, or if the property had been delivered to the carrier as agent for the purchaser, upon whom the bill was drawn, though the carrier's receipt was annexed to the bill,[2] the case would be different. A Liverpool merchant, wishing to obtain consignments of cotton from a Pernambuco firm, and being called upon for security, obtained from a bank a letter of credit by which the bank authorized the Pernambuco firm to draw upon them for such consignments, and engaged to honor the bills upon receipt of the shipping documents. Some shipping documents were sent, and some bills accepted; and one bill was accepted without any shipping documents being sent; and then, before any of the bills fell due, the bank became bankrupt, and bills arriving immediately afterwards were unaccepted. The agent of the Pernambuco firm claimed to prove against the bank for the full amount of the bills, without bringing into the account the value of the cotton which had been sold, or which remained on hand; but it was held that he had no right to do so; that the holders of the unaccepted bills had no lien upon the cotton in the hands of the bank, so as to enable them to treat the bank as their trustee, and the bank was indebted to the holders of the bills only for the surplus remaining after the goods consigned had been applied to the payment of the bills accepted.[3]

§ 189 a. **Right of Indorsee of Bill of Exchange with fraudulent Bill of Lading attached.** — Since the indorsee of a bill of exchange having a warehouse receipt or bill of lading attached

---

[1] Newcomb v. Boston & Lowell R. R. Co., 115 Mass. 230; Alderman v. Eastern R. R. Co., 115 Mass. 233; Joslyn v. Grand Trunk Ry. Co. 51 Vt. 92; Tiedeman v. Knox, 53 Md. 612.

[2] Wigton v. Bowley, 130 Mass. 252; First Nat'l Bank v. Crabtree, 52 No. W. Rep. 559.

[3] Banner v. Johnston, L. R. 5 Ho. Lds. 157.

to it is ordinarily held to acquire no greater right of property
in the goods thereby represented than belonged to the original shipper under whom he claims,[1] and since a carrier is
not bound by a bill of lading given by his agent for goods
which have not been actually delivered to the carrier,[2] so the
indorsee of a bill of exchange purporting to be secured by
such a bill of lading, though taking it *bona fide* and in reliance upon the apparent security, cannot, it is generally held,
enforce the contract of the bill of lading against the carrier.[3]
Nor can the indorsee compel the carrier to answer for a mis-
description of the goods in the bill of lading caused by the
fraud of the consignor.[4] But it is sometimes considered that
the carrier is estopped, against such a *bona fide* indorsee for
value, to deny his receipt of the goods stated in the bill of lading.[5] And the general rule of law has in England and in
many of our States been similarly modified by statutes.[6] But
if the goods are actually received by the carrier, though after
the bill of lading was given, the rights of such an acceptor or
indorsee are valid,[7] unless the goods were so received upon a
new agreement wholly independent of the old bill of lading.[8]

---

[1] The Idaho, 93 U. S. 575, 583; Maybee v. Tregent, 47 Mich. 495; Moore v. Robinson, 62 Ala. 537.

[2] Brown v. Powell Steam Co., L. R. 10 C. P. 562; Mackay v. Commercial Bank, L. R. 5 P. C. 394; Friedlander v. Texas Ry. Co., 130 U. S 416; Pollard v. Vinton, 105 U. S. 7; Sears v. Wingate, 3 Allen (Mass.), 103; Baltimore & Ohio R. R. Co. v. Wilkins, 44 Md. 11; Dean v. King, 22 Ohio St. 118; Louisiana National Bank v. Laveille, 52 Mo. 380.

[3] Pollard v. Vinton, 105 U. S. 7; Robinson v. Memphis & Charlestown R. R. Co., 9 Fed. Rep. 129; Lehman v. Central R. R. Co, 12 Fed. Rep. 595; Baltimore & Ohio R. R. Co. v. Wilkins, 44 Md. 11; Adone v. Seelig-

son, 54 Tex. 593, 604; Hunt v. Miss. Central R. R. Co., 29 La. Ann. 446.

[4] Miller v. Hannibal & St. Joseph R. R. Co., 90 N. Y. 430, overruling s. c., 24 Hun, 607.

[5] Schooner Freeman v. Bucking-ham, 18 How. 182; Batavia Bank v. N. Y. R. R. Co., 106 N. Y. 195; Armour v. Michigan Central R. R. Co., 65 N. Y. 111; Meyer v. Peck, 28 N. Y. 590; St. Louis R. R. Co. v. Larned, 103 Ills. 293; Sioux City R. R. Co. v. Fremont Bank, 10 Neb. 556.

[6] See Valieri v. Boyland, L. R. 1 C. P. 382.

[7] Rowley v. Bigelow, 12 Pick. (Mass.) 307.

[8] The John K. Shaw, 32 Fed. Rep. 491.

§ 190. **Securities held by a Banker against his Acceptances available to their Holders.** — Securities held by a banker against his acceptances are available to the holders of the bills, through the equity of the banker or his assignees in bankruptcy to have them applied to meet the acceptances;[1] though it has been said[2] that while the rule is perfectly just where the securities are sufficient to pay the bills in full, yet if the case is otherwise it gives the bill-holders an advantage at the expense of the acceptor to which they are not entitled, and that the reasons assigned[3] for the extension of this rule to the case of a deficient security are unsatisfactory, and appear to overlook the fact that when the whole benefit of such a security is given to the bill-holder, the estate of the bankrupt acceptor may lose some part of the indemnity to which he is entitled.   On the same principle, the indorser of a bill of exchange has an equitable claim upon property deposited with the drawee as a security against his acceptance thereof, upon the latter's bankruptcy.[4]  But the application of this principle will not be prevented by the fact that the person who deposited the security was not a party to the bills either as drawer or indorser, provided they were drawn with respect to a transaction in which he was liable.[5]  Where merchants consigned goods to one party, and by arrangement drew bills for their value upon another party, who accepted them, it was held, upon the bankruptcy of both, that remittances made by the consignor to the acceptor on account of the bills should be specifically applied to the payment of the bills.[6]  Nor is this principle limited to the bankruptcy of the parties to the bills; it will be applied upon their mere in-

---

[1] Waring, *ex parte*, 19 Ves. 345; Seligman *v.* Wells, 17 Blatchf. C. C. 410; Sproule *v.* Samuel, 5 Ills. 135.

[2] Royal Bank *v.* Commercial Bank, 7 App. Cas. 366.

[3] By Lord Cranworth in Powles *v.* Hargreaves, 3 De G., M. & G. 453.

[4] Perfect, *ex parte*, Mont. Bnkcy. 25.

[5] Smart, *ex parte*, Richardson, *in re*, L. R. 8 Ch. 220.

[6] Dover, *ex parte*, Suse, *in re*, 14 Q. B. D. 611; Smart, *ex parte*, Richardson, *in re*, *supra*.

solvency.[1] The acceptor has a lien against his acceptances
upon property in his hands belonging to the drawer;[2] and
the holder of the bill may claim the benefit of this lien by
way of substitution, just as a creditor may hold the indemnity of a surety upon the latter's insolvency.[3] A mortgage
given to the acceptor of bills to secure their payment by the
drawer will, upon the insolvency of the drawer and the acceptor, be applied directly to the payment of the bills.[4] So,
where one who has procured bills to be drawn for his accommodation afterwards gives a deed of trust to the acceptors
thereof to secure notes given to the acceptors for the amount
of the acceptances, the holders of the bills may resort to the
trust property for their payment when dishonored, if the
notes have not been negotiated to *bona fide* holders for a
valuable consideration.[5] Where the holders of a judgment
given to secure them for their acceptances made for the benefit of the judgment-debtor assigned it to a prior creditor of
their own, the collection of the judgment by such assignee
was restrained on a bill in equity filed by the judgment-
debtor for whose benefit the acceptances had been made, the
holders of the acceptances were declared to have an equitable
interest in the judgment, and the proceeds of the judgment
were directed to be applied to their payment.[6]

§ 191. **This Principle extends to all Parties to the Bill.** — This
substitution to the benefit of security held for the payment
of negotiable paper will be made for the benefit of all parties
thereto who, by reason of their liability thereon, have paid
the same.[7] One who has accepted a bill of exchange on the ·

[1] Powles v. Hargreaves, 3 De G.
M. & G. 430, 453.
[2] Hammond v. Barclay, 2 East,
227; Madden v. Kempster, 1 Campbell, 12.
[3] *Antea,* § 162.
[4] City Bank v. Luckie, L. R. 5 Ch.
773.
[5] Toulmin v. Hamilton, 7 Ala.
362.
[6] Heath v. Hand, 1 Paige (N. Y.),
329; Auburn Bank v. Throop, 18
Johns. (N. Y.) 505.
[7] Stevenson v. Austin, 3 Met.
(Mass.) 474.

agreement that certain property of the drawer in his hands shall be applied to the payment thereof, is entitled, upon paying the acceptance out of his own funds, to hold this property for his reimbursement against attaching creditors of the drawer.[1] The payee of a promissory note who has transferred it by indorsement, and has afterwards, on the failure of the maker, been compelled to take it up, may enforce a mortgage given by the maker of the note to the indorsee, while it was held by the latter, to secure its payment.[2] If the holder of a promissory note who has proved it against the estate of the first indorser, and has then received payment of it from the second indorser, afterwards obtains a dividend in the bankruptcy proceedings, he must account for this dividend to the second indorser and not to the bankrupt's creditors.[3] If debtors have given acceptances to their creditor for their debt, and have also given to him security for the payment of their indebtedness, and have then gone into bankrupcty, and the holders of the bills have proved them for their full amount under the bankruptcy, the creditor cannot have the full benefit of the security without first himself taking up these bills: the security will be applied first to pay to the creditor any balance due to him over the amount of the bills, and then to relieve him from his liability under the bills.[4] And if the holder of a note surrenders collateral security which he holds therefor from the maker, this will operate the discharge of the indorser to the extent, but only to the extent, of the real value of such security.[5] The indorser will be discharged under such circumstances just as a surety *eo nomine* would be.[6]

§ 192. **Property in Securities deposited by Drawer with Acceptor.** — The property in securities deposited by the drawer

---

[1] Printup *v.* Johnson, 19 Ga. 73.

[2] O'Hara *v.* Haas, 46 Mississippi, 374.

[3] Selfridge *v.* Gill, 4 Mass. 95. *Antea,* §§ 181, 182.

[4] Mann, *ex parte*, Kattengell, *in re*, 5 Ch. D. 367.

[5] Union National Bank *v.* Cooley, 27 La. Ann. 202.

[6] *Antea,* §§ 119 *et seq.*, 182 *a.* Case *v.* Hawkins, 53 Miss. 702.

with the acceptor of bills for their payment remains, subject
to the trust, in the drawer;[1] and so far as not applied for
that purpose they are held by the acceptor for the drawer.
G. in Malaga was in the habit of drawing bills on Y. in London, and of remitting bills to the latter to enable him to
meet his acceptances. Y. rendered to G. half-yearly accounts, charging him with bills accepted, and crediting him
with bills remitted, with a credit of interest to the same
time; if a bill remitted was dishonored, then its amount
was entered on the debit side, thus in effect striking it
out of the account. Y. became insolvent, and compounded
with his creditors. Crediting Y. with the amount he thus
paid on his acceptances, the balance of account was in
favor of G. At the time of suspending payment, Y. had
remittances which had been thus sent to him by G. It
was held that as Y. had been discharged from his liability
on his acceptances by his composition, and as the remittances were specifically appropriated to the payment of the
acceptances, the remainder of the remittances after Y. had
been reimbursed for the amount that he paid on the bills
belonged to G.[2] But if the remittances, being negotiable
paper or current coin, had been passed for value to a *bona
fide* holder without notice of the equities existing in favor
of the drawer, the drawer could not reclaim them from
such a holder.[3] On the same principle, if the acceptor of
bills deposits with one banker money and negotiable securities for the express purpose of taking up his acceptances
payable at another banker's, and the first banker remits the
deposit to the second without notice of the instructions on
which it was received, the acceptor cannot follow the property into the hands of the second banker to the prejudice of
the latter's rights against the first.[4]

[1] Pearl *v.* Clark, 2 Penn. St. 350.    Bank, 8 Ch. D. 160; Broad, *in re,*
[2] Gomez, *ex parte,* Yglesias, *in re,*   Neck, *ex parte,* 13 Q. B. D. 740.
L. R. 10 Ch. 639.                           [4] Johnson *v.* Robarts, L. R. 10
[3] Banco de Lima *v.* Anglo-Peruvian    Ch. 505.

**§ 198. Holder not substituted to Security held by one under no Liability, unless actually appropriated.** — The holder will not, upon the insolvency or bankruptcy of both drawer and drawee, be substituted to the benefit of security deposited by the drawer with the drawee to secure the latter against his intended acceptances, unless the drawee has accepted the bills, or unless the holder has the right to prove his demand against the estate of both the drawer and the drawee.[1] Nor will such substitution be allowed if the security is held by the acceptor, not specifically against the acceptances, but for the payment of any money which should be due from the drawer to the acceptor, even though there may be no indebtedness apart from the bills.[2] But an actual appropriation to the payment of bills of property consigned by the drawer to the drawee will be upheld,[3] although the latter has not accepted the bills.[4] The consignor of coffee drew bills upon the consignees, which bills were negotiated to the plaintiff. The bills did not purport to be drawn against any particular shipment. The consignee refused to accept the bills, and they were protested. The consignor then wrote to one S., asking him to take charge of the consignment, realize on it, and honor the bills. The day before the maturity of the bills, S. wrote to the plaintiff, saying that he expected soon to receive from the consignees the coffee sent by the drawer against the bills, and would then write the plaintiff again. Soon afterwards S. received the warrants for the coffee from the consignees, and wrote to the plaintiff to that effect, referring to his previous letter, and saying he should dispose of the coffee as instructed by the consignor, and would send further particulars in due time. The same day the consignees attached

---

[1] Vaughan v. Halliday, L. R. 9 Ch. 561.

[2] Levi's Case, L. R. 7 Eq. 449; Smith, in re, 15 N. B. R. 459.

[3] Ross v. Saulsbury, 52 Ga. 379; Allen v. Williams, 12 Pick. (Mass.)

297. See Matter of Le Blanc, 4 Abbott, New Cas. (N. Y.) 221.

[4] Frith v. Forbes, 4 De G. F. & J. 409; Marine Bank of Georgia v. Jauncey, 1 Barb. (N. Y.) 486; *antea,* § 189.

the coffee as the property of a firm who they alleged had an
interest in it, but with whom S. had had no dealings; but it
was held, on the plaintiff's bill in equity, that the consignor
had given S. authority to make an equitable charge upon
the property, and S. had acted on that authority, and that
the coffee must be applied to the payment of the bills.[1]

§ 194. **Right of Holders to Securities held by Acceptor not a
paramount one.** — This right of the holders of negotiable paper
to be substituted to the benefit of securities for its payment
given by one of the debtors upon it to another cannot be preferred to the legal rights of prior creditors of both these
debtors in the same transaction. This principle was established in an English case, in which it appeared that two
separate firms, one in Bombay and one in London, were engaged in the joint adventure of buying and selling goods in
England and in India. The Bombay firm drew bills on the
London firm, which they discounted in India; and with the
proceeds they bought cotton, which they consigned to London, specially to meet these acceptances. Both firms being
insolvent, the holders of certain unpaid bills which had been
drawn and accepted in this way claimed to have the proceeds
of the shipments of cotton appropriated to their payment;
and it was held that they were entitled to this appropriation,
but that it must be subject to the right of any creditors of
the joint adventure to have the cotton applied first to their
payment as part of the assets of the joint adventure.[2] And
it has been intimated that the rule that securities held by a
banker against his acceptances are available to the holders
of the bills will not be applied in bankruptcy where the
drawers owe the acceptors on other accounts more than the
amounts of the bills, at least if the acceptors have a general
lien on the securities so deposited with them.[3] If the drawer

---

[1] Ranken v. Alfaro, 5 Ch. D. 786.
[2] Dewhurst, ex parte, L. R. 8 Ch.
965. And see Addison v. Burokmyer,
4 Sandf. Ch. (N. Y.) 498.

[3] Royal Bank v. Commercial Bank,
7 App. Cas. 366; Hickie's Case, L. R.
4 Eq. 226.

of bills has made remittances to the acceptor to cover his acceptances, and the acceptor has become insolvent before the payment of the bills, and the drawer has also become insolvent, owing the acceptor on general account a larger sum than the amount of the bills, but has not gone into bankruptcy, the equity of the holders of the bills to be paid out of these remittances will not prevail over the direction of the drawee to have them applied upon his general indebtedness to the acceptor.[1]  So where the acceptor of a bill paid the amount thereof to his bankers in order to meet it, but the day before the bill matured died indebted to his bankers on general account, and the bankers dishonored the bill, it was held that the drawer, having taken up the bill, could not compel the bankers to reimburse him, as having received the amount of the bill in trust for its payment.[2]

§ 195. **Holder's Right to control Securities given by Drawer to Acceptor no greater than Drawer's.** — The right of the holders of bills to the benefit of property deposited by the drawer with the acceptor thereof will, even upon the bankruptcy of the acceptor, be limited by the right of the drawer against him.[3]  It will not extend to the case of a guaranty given to the acceptor by a third person, no notice having been given by the holder to the guarantor.[4]  The claim of the holder of the bill cannot prevail against one who has in good faith and for value acquired the deposited property from the drawer and the acceptor.[5]  If the drawer could not require the appropriation of the property to the payment of the bills, the holder will have no such right.[6]  Thus, A. in England

---

[1] General South American Co., *ex parte*, Yglesias, *in re*, L. R. 10 Ch. 635.

[2] Hill *v.* Royds, L. R. 8 Eq. 290.

[3] Rindge *v.* Sanford, 117 Mass. 460. See Walker *v.* Birch, 6 T. R. 258; Moore *v.* Robinson, 62 Ala. 537.

[4] Barned's Banking House, *in re*, L. R. 3 Ch. 753.

[5] Hopkins *v.* Beebe, 26 Penn. St. 85.

[6] Dever, *ex parte*, Suse, *in re*, 13 Q. B. D. 766; First National Bank of Marquette *v.* Weed, 89 Mich. 357.

employed B. in South America to purchase goods for him.
The mode adopted was that B. raised money by drawing bills
on A. and selling them, and with the proceeds bought goods,
which he shipped to Liverpool, consigned to A.   In his accounts, B. credited A. with the bills, and charged him with
the cost of the goods and with his commissions; and in his
letters he directed A. to place the price of the goods to his
credit and the bills to his debit.   Both A. and B. became
bankrupt.   When A. became bankrupt, goods were in transit
to Liverpool; and some of the bills out of the proceeds of
which the goods had been bought had been accepted, and
others were presented to A. after his bankruptcy, and were
unaccepted.   The goods having arrived and come into the
possession of A.'s trustees in bankruptcy, it was held that
the holders of the bills had no right to have the goods specifically appropriated to their payment.   The property in the
goods passed to A., subject only to B.'s right of stoppage *in
transitu ;* it did not revest in B. upon A.'s failure to accept
some of the bills; and the facts showed no agreement by
which B. would have a charge on the goods in the hands of
A. and a right to have them applied to take up the bills.[1]   If
the property was purchased originally at the joint risk of the
drawer and the drawee, although the drawee has promised
the drawer to protect the bills, but has afterwards, upon the
insolvency of the drawer, refused to accept them, the right
of the holders of the bills to the property will be limited to
the surplus of its proceeds over the amount due from the
drawer to the drawee.[2]   A mere direction in a bill of exchange to place the amount to the account of a shipment
made by the drawer to the acceptor,[3] or a mere letter of
advice accompanying the bill to the effect that the bill is

[1] Banner, *ex parte*, Tappenbeck, *in
re*, 2 Ch. Div. 278.
[2] Robey *v.* Ollier, L. R. 7 Ch. 695,
limiting and explaining Frith *v.* Forbes,
4 De G., F. & J. 409.

[3] Brown *v.* Kough, 29 Ch. D. 848;
Entwistle, *in re*, Arbuthnot, *ex parte*,
3 Ch. Div. 477.

drawn on account of a specified shipment,[1] will not operate a specific appropriation of that shipment to the payment of the bill, which can be enforced against a purchaser of the goods from the acceptor; just as the mere fact that bills are given in partial payment for property agreed to be sold by the drawer to the acceptor, upon which the seller retains a lien for the unpaid portion of the price, will not, upon the bankruptcy of both parties, give to the persons to whom the bills have been negotiated any lien upon the property for their payment.[2]

§ 196. **Holder's Right to Application of Security perishes with that of its Depositor.** — If the drawer of bills holding security from the acceptor for their payment has, by the substitution of new bills therefor, lost the right, as against the acceptor, to have the security applied for their payment, the holder of the old bills, claiming under the drawer, will also be deprived of such right. Thus, a debtor borrowed money from a corporation, giving it his acceptances, and depositing shares as security therefor. When the bills became due, the corporation presented to him fresh bills for acceptance stating them to be in place of those falling due; and he accepted the new bills accordingly. Both he and the corporation then became insolvent. Both sets of bills being still outstanding, it was held that the holders of the first bills had no equity to have them paid out of the shares; for the letter and the debtor's new acceptances had put an end to the security as to the first set of bills.[3] But it is to be observed that the first set of bills did not purport to be drawn against the security.[4]

---

[1] Phelps v. Comber, 29 Ch. D. 813, affirming s. c., 26 Ch. D. 755, and approving Perseverance Iron Works v. Ollier, L. R. 7 Ch. 695 ; Brown v. Kough, 29 Ch. D. 848, overruling on this point Frith v. Forbes, 4 De G., F. & J. 409.

[2] Lambton, ex parte, Lindsay, in re, L. R. 10 Ch. 405.

[3] General Rolling Stock Co., in re, L. R. 4 Ch. 423.

[4] See McCracken v. German Ins. Co., 43 Md. 471.

**§ 197. Taking Bill on the Credit of the Funds is not enough.**
— Although the drawer of a bill has funds in the hands of
the drawee, and the holder takes it upon the assurance of
the drawer that the funds are specifically appropriated to the
payment of the bill,[1] this assurance will not of itself operate
such an appropriation, unless the bill was so drawn against
that particular fund as to constitute an equitable assignment
thereof;[2] otherwise, the mere drawing and negotiation of the
bill does not pass any right to the fund.[3]  Thus, where the
plaintiffs bought a bill of exchange on the assurance of
the drawer that there were funds in the hands of the drawee
which were specifically appropriated to meet it, but before
any acceptance of the bill the drawer stopped payment,
although it was at first considered, upon the plaintiffs' bill
against both drawer and drawee, that the plaintiffs, having
taken the bill upon the faith of these representations, were
entitled to be paid its amount out of the funds of the drawer
in the hands of the drawee, yet on appeal it was decided that
the plaintiffs had no right to any charge upon these funds.[4]
Where one bank has deposited bonds with another bank as
security against its overdrafts, and has then become insolvent, being indebted to the second bank, the holders of such
bills, drawn by the first bank before its insolvency but presented afterwards, cannot resort to the proceeds of these
bonds to the prejudice of the right of the second bank to
apply them upon its own demand.[5]

[1] Canton Bank v. Dubuque R. R.
Co., 52 Iowa, 378.

[2] See Smith, in re, 16 N. B. R. 399;
Tremont Nail Co., ex parte, Id. 448;
Brill v. Tuttle, 81 N. Y. 454, revers-
ing s. c., 15 Hun, 289; Attorney-
General v. Continental Ins. Co., 71 N.
Y. 325; Kahnweiler v. Anderson,
78 Nor. Car. 133; Wellsburg Bank v.
Kimberlands, 16 W. Va. 555.

[3] Whitney v. Eliot Bank, 137 Mass.
351; Bush v. Foote, 58 Miss. 5; Commerce Bank v. Bogy, 9 Mo. Ap. 335.
But see Cincinnati Bank v. Coates, 3
McCrary, C. C. 9.

[4] Thomson v. Simpson, L. R. 5
Ch. 659; reversing s. c., L. R. 9. Eq.
497.

[5] Garvin v. State Bank, 7 So. Car.
266.

§ 198. **Extent of Holder's Right of Substitution to Acceptor's Securities.** — The substitution of the holder of a bill to securities held by the acceptor will, if the parties to the bill have not become insolvent, be limited to the rights of the acceptor. If the acceptor's security is a mortgage from the drawer, conditioned only to indemnify him for what money he should actually have paid upon his acceptance, then, as the acceptor could not enforce his security until actual payment by him, the holder of the bill cannot require a foreclosure of the mortgage for its payment.[1] The acceptor holding such indemnity may, before the rights of the creditors arise upon his insolvency, release the whole or part of it to the drawer; and the holder of the bills cannot, upon the acceptor's subsequent insolvency, avoid such release against those who have since acquired rights in the released property.[2]

§ 199. **Rights of an Acceptor to Securities held against the Bill by Prior Parties thereto.** — The acceptor of a bill, being the party primarily liable upon it, cannot, upon paying it, be subrogated to the benefit of a security given by the drawer to the payee to secure its payment.[3] Thus, where the purchaser of property gave to the vendor a mortgage on the property to secure the payment of a bill drawn by the purchaser in favor of the vendor upon a third person for the price of the property, the mortgage reciting that a lien was retained on the property in favor of the vendor or any other holder of the bill, but not stipulating that the drawee should have the benefit of the mortgage on paying the bill without having been put in funds therefor by the drawer and without being bound as to the drawer to pay it, if the bill is paid by the drawee at its maturity without any conventional subrogation in his favor at the time of the payment, the debt will be extinguished as to third persons, and the mortgage will be

[1] Planters' Bank *v.* Douglass, 2 Head (Tenn.), 699.
[2] St. Louis Building Association *v.* Clark, 36 Mo. 601.

[3] Fowler *v.* Gate City Bank, 13 So. E. Rep. 831; Trimble *v.* City Bank, 15 So. W. Rep. 853.

extinguished as to the holders of other liens upon the mortgaged property; for the acceptor was the principal debtor
upon the bill, and simply paid his own debt in paying it;
and the mortgage, containing no stipulation in his behalf,
cannot be kept alive for his benefit, or for the benefit of any
other person, unless this results from the terms of the bill
itself.[1]   An indorser and an accommodation acceptor of a
bill are not co-sureties; and the acceptor cannot be subrogated to the benefit of a mortgage given by the drawer to the
indorser to indemnify the latter against his liability, even
though the bill was paid after being protested by giving to
its holder the note of the drawer, with the indorser and the
acceptor as sureties thereon, and the acceptor on paying this
note took an assignment of all the securities in the hands of
the indorser and of the holder, because the mortgage was
given only for the personal indemnity of the indorser and
not for the payment of the bill, so that the acceptor had no
right to it; and on the indorser's being indemnified by the
acceptor's payment of the substituted note, the mortgage
became *functus officio*.[2]   But in New York it has been decided
that although at law the accommodation acceptor of a bill is
regarded in favor of a *bona fide* holder of the bill as the principal debtor thereon, yet as between the drawer and such
acceptor the latter is regarded in equity as merely a surety,
and is entitled upon his payment of the bill to be subrogated
to the benefit of any securities taken by the holder of the bill
from the drawer to secure its payment; and accordingly, in
an action against such an acceptor by a non-resident holder
of the bill, the drawer having become insolvent, the defendant
may, under the code allowing the giving of both legal and
equitable relief in the same action, demand such subrogation
upon payment of the amount due to the plaintiff.[3]

[1] Salaun v. Relf, 4 La. Ann. 575.       [3] Toronto Bank v. Hunter, 4 Bosw.
[2] Gomez v. Lazarus, 1 Dev. Eq.  (N. Y.) 646.
(Nor. Car.) 205.

**§ 200. Acceptor's Securities to be applied upon all Acceptances alike.** — Security in the hands of an acceptor for the payment of his acceptances will, in case of need, be applied to the payment of all the acceptances alike.[1] If the holders of some of the acceptances have established their right by litigation, they will be preferred only to the extent of a fair share of the expenses of their litigation. Thus, a drawer having given to his acceptor a judgment as security for his acceptances, these acceptances were negotiated; and some of them remained unpaid in the hands of three firms. The acceptor assigned a portion of the judgment to two of these firms, as collateral security for the payment of the drafts which they respectively held. They enforced the judgment at their own expense, and claimed to be fully paid out of its proceeds, leaving only a small balance for the benefit of the other firm, which had taken no part in the litigation. But it was held that the security of the judgment attached to all the unpaid acceptances alike, and that the holders were entitled to *pro rata* shares of the money, which had been collected, the litigants receiving in addition to their dividend a fair share of the costs and expenses of their litigation. But the court also said that such third firm would be required to exhaust whatever independent securities they had, and should not be allowed to receive their *pro rata* share until such other securities had been exhausted or shown to be worthless, and that anything which they might receive from such securities should be reckoned as a part of their dividend, so as to increase the share of the two firms which had borne the burden of the litigation and had realized the fund.[2]

**§ 200 a. Subrogation of Holder of Check to Rights of Drawer.** — By analogy to the now widely adopted rule that one for whose benefit a promise is made, though not a party to the

[1] Franklin County Bank v. Greenfield Bank, 138 Mass. 515.

[2] Kramer's Appeal, 37 Penn. St. 71.

contract or privy to the consideration, may maintain an action thereon,[1] it has been occasionally decided that the holder of a check is subrogated to the rights of its drawer, the depositor, and may sue the bank, upon its failure to pay the check, in his own name.[2] But the old rule is still generally maintained, that such an action can be brought only by the depositor.[3] But it has been held that a check drawn against the whole of a specific fund deposited in the bank in the name of the drawer, but belonging in equity to the payee, transfers to the payee on its delivery to him the legal title to the deposit,[4] and that when this payee, in pursuance of his prior parol assignment of the fund made for value, indorses and delivers the check to his assignee, the title to the deposit vests in that assignee, even against subsequently attaching creditors of the depositor,[5] though an ordinary check cannot be treated as an equitable assignment of the money for which it calls,[6] and would not, before its payment or acceptance or certification by the bank, give the payee any rights against a creditor of the depositor making an intervening attachment.[7]

§ 201. **Whether Suits or Judgments extinguished upon Payment by Parties secondarily liable.** — If separate suits have been brought against the maker and the indorser of a promissory note, and the indorser pays the amount due with the agreement that the suit against the maker shall be prosecuted for

---

[1] *Antea*, §§ 85, 171 a.

[2] Fonner v. Smith, 31 Neb. 107, and cases there cited ; Union Bank v. Oceana Bank, 80 Ills. 212 ; Lester v. Given, 8 Bush (Ky.), 357 ; Roberts v. Austin, 26 Iowa, 315 ; Fogarties v. State Bank, 12 Rich. Law (So. Car.), 518.

[3] First Nat'l Bank v. Whitman, 94 U. S. 343 ; Bank of Republic v. Millard, 10 Wallace, 152 ; Essex County Bank v. Bank of Montreal, 7 Biss. C. C. 193 ; Carr v. Security Bank, 107 Mass. 45 ; Magiun v. Dollar Savings Bank, 131 Penn. St. 362.

[4] German Savings Institution v. Adae, 1 McCrary, C. C. 501.

[5] Hemphill v. Yerkes, 132 Penn. St. 545.

[6] Hopkinson v. Forster, L. R. 19 Eq. 74 ; Schroeder v. Central Bank, 24 Weekly Reporter 710 ; s. c., 34 L. T. N. s. 735.

[7] Bank of Commerce v. Russell, 2 Dillon, C. C. 215 ; Ballard v. Randall, 1 Gray (Mass.), 605.

his benefit, the maker cannot avail himself of the indorser's payment as a defence to the further prosecution of the suit against himself;[1] nor, if the indorser's payment was made after judgment against the maker, can the maker's bail set up such a defence in an action upon their recognizance.[2] If separate judgments have been obtained against maker and indorser, the latter may pay the judgment against himself, and take an assignment of that against the maker and enforce it for his own benefit.[3] If the maker and the indorser have been jointly sued under the New York statute, and a judgment has been recovered against them, the indorser, upon paying the judgment, may take an assignment thereof from the creditor, and use it for his indemnification as a subsisting judgment against the maker.[4] If an indorser of a bill of exchange has recovered a judgment thereon against the maker, this judgment will not be extinguished by its assignment to a prior indorser of the bill, upon the latter's paying the amount due thereon.[5] The indorser may be subrogated to the benefit of a judgment against the maker without taking an assignment thereof.[6] But this subrogation of the indorser is to a suit or a judgment against the maker directly upon the original obligation; it does not extend to the prosecution of a merely incidental remedy,[7] such as an

[1] *Antea*, §§ 181, 182.

[2] Mechanics' Bank *v.* Hazard, 13 Johns. (N. Y.) 353.

[3] Folsom *v.* Carli, 5 Minn. 333; State Bank *v.* Wilson, 1 Dev. Law (Nor. Car.) 484.

[4] Yates *v.* Mead, 68 Miss. 787; Davis *v.* Perrine, 4 Edw. Ch. (N. Y.) 62; Corey *v.* White, 3 Barb. (N. Y.) 12, overruling Salina Bank *v.* Abbott, 3 Denio (N. Y.), 181, and explaining Ontario Bank *v.* Walker, 1 Hill (N. Y.), 652. The statement in Davis *v.* Perrine, *supra*, that this rule has not been extended to the case of principal and surety has not since been followed. *Antea*, § 137.

[5] Harger *v.* McCullough, 2 Denio (N. Y.), 119; Stiles *v.* Eastman, 1 Ga. 205; Wilson *v.* Wright, 7 Rich. (Law) So. Car. 399. But see Topp *v.* Branch Bank, 2 Swan (Tenn.), 184.

[6] Ross *v.* Jones, 22 Wallace, 576; Old Dominion Bank *v.* Allen, 76 Va. 200; Yates *v.* Mead, 68 Miss. 787, extending Dibrell *v.* Dandridge, 51 Miss. 55; Lyon *v.* Bolling, 9 Ala. 463. See *antea*, § 135 *et seq.*

[7] Heighe *v.* Farmers' Bank, 5 Harr. & J. (Md.) 68; Dehn *v.* Heckman, 12 Ohio St. 181.

action against a notary for negligence in making a protest of the note, whereby other parties were released.[1] The payment of a note by one of several joint promisors extinguishes it, and it cannot afterwards be kept alive against the other signers.[2] Nor will either the maker or a surety for the maker acquire by paying a judgment on the note any right of action against the indorser.[3]

[1] *Semble* in Warren Bank *v.* Parker, 8 Gray (Mass.), 221.

[2] Stevens *v.* Hannan, 88 Mich. 13; s. c., 86 Mich. 305.

[3] Allegheny R. R. Co. *v.* Dickey, 131 Penn. St. 86.

# CHAPTER VI.

## SUBROGATION IN THE ADMINISTRATION OF ESTATES.

§ 202. **Subrogation of Executor or Administrator to Debts and Legacies which he has paid.** — If an executor or administrator pays debts of the estate out of his own means to the value of the assets in his hands, he may apply these assets to reimburse himself; and by such election these assets become his own property;[1] but his subrogation will be carried to no greater extent than the actual value of his payments.[2] So

---

[1] Livingston *v.* Newkirk, 3 Johns. Ch. (N. Y.) 312; Chesson *v.* Chesson, 8 Ired. Eq. (Nor. Car.) 141; Milam *v.* Ragland, 19 Ala. 85; Buckingham *v.* Wesson, 54 Miss. 526; Hancock *v.* Minot, 8 Pick. (Mass.) 29, 37, 38.

[2] Powell *v.* Powell, 80 Ala. 11; Sorrels *v.* Trantham, 48 Ark. 386; Amos *v.* Heatherby, 7 Dana (Ky.), 45.

upon his payment of his testator's debts, he will be subrogated
to an equitable charge upon property charged by the will with
the payment of debts, but will not become the absolute owner
of such property.[1]   And although an executor ordered to sell
land cannot himself retain it, as he may personal assets, yet,
if the personal estate proves to be insufficient, and he has
paid debts of the estate to the value of the land out of his
own property, he may, upon a sale of the land, retain the
proceeds of the sale for his own indemnity.[2]   His right to be
reimbursed for advances properly made for the benefit of the
estate is paramount to the claims of the distributees.[3]   So, if
he has paid debts of the deceased to an amount exceeding the
available personal assets, he may for his indemnity be subrogated to the rights of the creditors whom he has paid[4] against
the lands of the deceased,[5] and may subject the real estate in
the hands of the heirs for his reimbursement;[6] and a surety
of the administrator upon his payment may be subrogated to
this right of his principal.[7]   Though an administrator acts
at his own peril in paying unpreferred debts of his intestate
before he could lawfully be called upon to pay them, and if
the estate afterwards turns out to be insolvent cannot charge
it with the full amount so paid by him,[8] yet, in the absence
of statute regulations, he may, by subrogation to the rights of
the creditors whom he has thus satisfied, receive the share of

---

[1] Graham v. Jones, 24 So. Car. 241.

[2] Turner v. Shuffler, 108 Nor. Car. 642; Livingston v. Newkirk, *supra*; Clayton v. Somers, 27 N. J. Eq. 230; Wheeler v. Wheeler, 1 Conn. 51.

[3] Pendergrass v. Pendergrass, 26 So. Car. 19; Terrell v. Rowland, 86 Ky. 67.

[4] Gundry v. Henry, 65 Wisc. 559.

[5] Crowley v. Mellon, 52 Ark. 1; Gaw v. Huffman, 12 Gratt. (Va.) 628; Kinney v. Harvey, 2 Leigh (Va.), 70; Smith v. Hoskins, 7 J. J. Marsh. (Ky.) 502.

[6] Collinson v. Owens, 6 Gill & J. (Md.) 4; Gist v. Cockey, 7 H. & J. (Md.) 134; Goodbody v. Goodbody, 95 Ills. 456; Black v. Black, 42 Iowa, 694; McCullough v. Wise, 57 Ala. 623.

[7] Taylor v. Taylor, 8 B. Mon. (Ky.) 419.

[8] Haslett v. Glenn, 7 Harr. & J. (Md.) 17; Rhea v. Greer, 86 Tenn. 59.

the assets to which they would have been entitled;[1] and the same rule will be applied to any other trustee;[2] but if his payments were made for his own relief, they will not give him a right of subrogation to the prejudice of other creditors of the deceased.[3] An administrator who has made voluntary payments to a creditor of the estate will be protected by a subsequent decree in favor of such creditor.[4] If he has employed assets of the estate to pay a debt owed by a legatee, he can hold only such legatee's share of the estate for his reimbursement;[5] but he may be subrogated to the rights of a legatee whom he has, even before the probate of the will,[6] advanced the money to pay.[7] If one of two personal representatives has committed waste by applying the personal estate to the payment of debts which were properly chargeable upon the real estate, the other representative, if compelled to replace the amount so misapplied by his colleague, may hold the real estate in the hands of the heirs for his reimbursement;[8] for co-executors are not at the common law responsible for each other's waste, in which they have not participated,[9] unless it has been made possible through their

---

[1] Pierce v. Allen, 12 R. I. 510; Woolley v. Pemberton, 41 N. J. Eq. 394; Breckenridge's Appeal, 127 Penn. St. 81; Millard v. Harris, 119 Ills. 185; Byrd v. Jones, 84 Ala. 336; McNeill v. McNeill, 36 Ala. 109; Feemster v. Good, 12 So. Car. 573.

[2] Salter v. Creditors, 6 Bush (Ky.), 624; Corcoran v. Allen, 11 R. I. 567.

[3] McNeill v. McNeill, 36 Ala. 109; Ex parte Allen, 89 Ills. 474; Stott's Estate, Myrick's Prob. (Calif.) 168.

[4] Charlton's Appeal, 88 Penn. St. 476; Chamberlin v. McDowell, 42 N. J. Eq. 628.

[5] Johnson v. Henagan, 11 So. Car. 93.

[6] Pinkham v. Grant, 78 Maine, 158.

[7] Stetson v. Moulton, 140 Mass. 597; Stayner v. Bower, 42 Ohio St. 314; Dickie v. Dickie, 80 Ala. 57.

[8] Johnson v. Corbett, 11 Paige (N. Y.), 265.

[9] Peter v. Beverly, 10 Peters, 532; s. c. 1 How. 134; McKim v. Aulbach, 130 Mass. 481; Brazer v. Clark, 5 Pick. (Mass.) 96; Towne v. Ammidown, 20 Pick. (Mass.) 535; Fisher v. Skillman, 18 N. J. Eq. 229; Gaultney v. Nolan, 33 Miss. 569; Gates v. Whetstone, 8 So. Car. 244; Clarke v. Jenkins, 3 Rich. Eq. (So. Car.) 318; Turner v. Wilkins, 56 Ala. 173; Walker v. Walker, 88 Ky. 615; Mosely v. Floyd, 31 Ga. 564; Sparhawk v. Buell, 9 Vt. 41; Nanz v. Oakley, 120 N. Y. 84; Croft v. Williams, 88 N. Y. 384; Sutherland v. Brush, 7 Johns. Ch. (N. Y.) 17; Douglass v. Satterlee, 11 Johns. (N. Y.) 16, 21; Elwell v. Quash, Str. 20; Hargthorpe v. Millforth, Cro. Eliz. 318.

negligence.[1] And one executor who has paid legacies that should have been paid by the other may be subrogated to the benefit of security given by that other for their payment.[2]

§ 203. Such Subrogation must be seasonably claimed. Its Limitations. — The claim of personal representatives to be substituted to the rights of creditors whom they have satisfied must be seasonably made.[3] Though an executor who has, in pursuance of a bond given by his testator, made a deed with covenants of warranty, on which he has been sued and subjected to the payment of damages, is entitled to be subrogated to the rights of the obligee in the bond, and thereby to be reimbursed out of the estate, yet, if the estate was settled in chancery, and the executor, with notice of the claim, failed to have this subrogation provided for in the decree for the settlement of the estate, he cannot afterwards, without explanation of his laches, maintain a bill for his reimbursement against legatees to whom he has paid their legacies.[4] Or, if his course of administration has been irregular and without regard to the rights of creditors, as by paying simple contract debts and leaving specialties unpaid, his claim for reimbursement has no right of priority on a deficiency of assets.[5] He must show that property charged by the will with the payment of debts has been faithfully administered and has proved to be inadequate, before he can be allowed a lien upon the testator's other estate for his indemnity.[6] If an administrator has in his hands the proceeds of property sufficient to pay a preferred mortgage to which it is subject, and instead of paying the mortgage-debt pays

[1] Adair v. Brimmer, 74 N. Y. 539; Smith v. Pettigrew, 34 N. J. Eq. 216; Hays v. Hays, 3 Tenn. Ch. 88.

[2] Miller's Appeal, 127 Penn. St. 95.

[3] Antea, § 110; Donnell v. Cooke, 63 Nor. Car. 227; Loomis's Appeal, 29 Penn. St. 237; Allen, ex parte, 15 Mass. 58.

[4] Lambert v. Hobson, 3 Jones Eq. (Nor. Car.) 424.

[5] Greiner's Estate, 2 Watts (Penn.), 414; Findlay v. Trigg, 83 Va. 539; Moye v. Albritton, 7 Ired. Eq. (Nor. Car.) 62; Evans v. Halleck, 83 Mo. 376.

[6] Frary v. Booth, 37 Vt. 78, 93.

another demand, he cannot recover back the latter payment,
if the fund subsequently, by reason of his own laches, becomes insufficient to pay the mortgage-debt.[1] Though any
trustee who has in good faith paid out his own money for the
protection of the trust estate, by discharging claims against
it, is entitled to relief by subrogation to the rights of the
creditors whom he has thus satisfied,[2] yet this subrogation
to the rights of creditors to whom he has paid more than
their proportion of the assets will not be for his own benefit,
but for the protection of those creditors who have not received
what they were entitled to demand.[3]

§ 204. **Subrogation in Favor of Creditors of Deceased. Marshalling of Assets.** — The equitable rule adopted in the marshalling of assets, that where one creditor may resort to two
funds for the satisfaction of his demand, another creditor
who can hold only one of these funds may compel the former
to take his satisfaction out of that to which the latter has
no resort,[4] is of general application in the settlement of
estates,[5] especially in those cases in which one class of creditors can avail themselves of both the real and the personal
property of the deceased, while another class is restricted to
the personal assets. If the creditors of the former class exhaust the personal estate, those of the latter class will be
subrogated to their rights against the real estate, to the
extent to which the former have appropriated the personal
estate for their satisfaction.[6] If a testator had purchased an
estate in his lifetime, and after his death the purchase-money
is paid out of his personal assets; the right of his simple-
contract creditors, if necessary for their satisfaction, to be

---

[1] Succession of Foster, 4 La. Ann.
479.

[2] Robb's Appeal, 41 Penn. St. 45;
Boyd v. De Ham, 12 Lea (Tenn.),
175; Lewis v. Nichols, 38 Tex. 54.

[3] Ellicott v. Ellicott, 6 Gill & J.
(Md.) 35; State v. McAleer, 5 Ired.

Law (Nor. Car.) 632; Robinson v.
Chairman, 8 Humph. (Tenn.) 374.

[4] *Antea,* § 61 *et seq.*

[5] Rice v. Harbeson, 63 N. Y. 493;
Hill v. Mellon, 55 Ark. 450.

[6] Aldrich v. Cooper, 8 Vesey, 382;
Cralle v. Meem, 8 Gratt. (Va.) 496.

subrogated to the vendor's lien upon this estate against the
devisees thereof, though at first left undecided,[1] has since
been established.[2]   But the creditor of an intestate is not, in
the absence of special circumstances, entitled to be substituted to the rights of the heirs in respect of a debt due to
them as such heirs.[3]   Creditors who have been postponed
because of a belief that all property had been discovered and
exhausted may, upon the discovery of further assets, be subrogated to the rights of those to whom they were postponed.[4]

§ 205. **Creditors subrogated to a Charge upon Property purchased from Funds of the Deceased Debtor.** — If an administrator or other trustee purchases property with the assets of
the trust, the creditors and *cestuis que trustent* may in equity
treat such property as part of the trust estate.[5]   Where a
widow, before the appointment of any administrator upon
the estate of her deceased husband, used his assets in making
a partial payment for land which she purchased, giving her
note for the remainder of the purchase-money with a surety,
and the surety afterwards paid the note, and took a deed of
the land for his indemnity, it was decided that this surety
held the title to the land in trust for the creditors and distributees of the deceased, subject, however, to his own prior
lien for what he had been compelled to pay as surety upon
the note.[6]   This is an application of the familiar rule that
the beneficiary of property which has been impressed with a
trust character may follow the proceeds of such property into
the hands of any one but a *bona fide* holder for value without
notice.[7]

[1] Austen v. Halsey, 6 Vesey, 475.
[2] Selby v. Selby, 4 Russ. 336.
[3] Turner v. Faucett, 6 Ired. Eq.
(Nor. Car.) 549.
[4] Clifford v. Campbell, 65 Tex.
243.
[5] Mason v. Pomeroy, 151 Mass.
164; Evertson v. Tappen, 5 John. Ch.
(N. Y.) 497; Van Horn v. Fonda, Id.

388; Breit v. Yeaton, 101 Ills. 242;
Shaw v. Thompson, 1 Sm. & M. Ch.
(Miss.) 628; Blake v. Chambers, 4
Neb. 90.
[6] Miller v. Birdsong, 7 Baxter
(Tenn.), 531.
[7] Hopper v. Conyers, L. R. 2 Eq.
549; Mount v. Suydam, 4 Sandf. Ch.
(N. Y.) 399; Green v. Givan, 33 N. Y.

§ 206. **Creditors subrogated to Rights of Executors to Reimbursement.** — Though creditors who have made advances or rendered services to a trust estate must ordinarily look to the trustee personally for their payment, yet if the trustee would be entitled to reimbursement from the estate for his payment, and is insolvent or a non-resident, equity will substitute the creditors to the rights of the trustee, and allow them to be paid directly out of the estate.[1]  On the same principle, since executors who are empowered by the will to carry on the testator's business after his decease, though personally liable for the trade-debts thereby contracted, may in equity reimburse themselves for their payment of such debts out of the property which has been lawfully embarked in the trade, the trade-creditors may themselves in equity resort to this fund if their remedy against the executors is unavailing,[2] and may even hold the fee-simple of land used for the purposes of the business;[3] but such creditors must look primarily to the property used in the business,[4] and cannot hold for the payment of their claims lands of the testator which he has not by his will subjected to the risks of trade,[5] merely because the executors have without authority used the proceeds of the business for the improvement of such land.  The rights of the creditors, being against the executors personally and only derivatively against the estate,[6]

343; Allen v. Russell, 78 Ky. 105; Gannaway v. Tarpley, 1 Coldw. (Tenn.) 572; Dodge v. Cole, 97 Ills. 338; Rose v. Schaffner, 50 Iowa, 483; Robinson v. Robinson, 22 Iowa, 427; Hunter v. Bosworth, 43 Wisc. 583; Whelan v. McCreary, 64 Ala. 319.

[1] Thomson v. Smith, 64 N. H. 412; Williamson's Appeal, 94 Penn. St. 231; Norton v. Phelps, 54 Miss. 467; Dickinson v. Conniff, 65 Ala. 581; Cannon v. Copeland, 43 Ala. 259; Reinstein v. Smith, 65 Tex. 247.

[2] Willis v. Sharp, 113 N. Y. 586, and 115 N. Y. 396, reversing s. c.,

46 Hun, 540; 43 Hun, 434; Clapp v. Clapp, 45 Hun, 451; Stewart v. Robinson, 21 Abbott, New Cas.(N.Y.), 63; Moseley v. Norman, 74 Ala. 422.

[3] Laible v. Ferry, 32 N. J. Eq. 791, reversing Ferry v. Laible, 31 N. J. Eq. 566.

[4] Wilson v. Fridenberg, 21 Fla.386.

[5] See Lucht v. Behrens, 28 Ohio St. 231.

[6] Lynch v. Kirby, 65 Ga. 279; Johnson v. Clarke, 15 So. Car. 72. So in Maybury v. Grady, 67 Ala. 147; Delaware, Lack. & W. R. Co. v. Gilbert, 44 Hun (N. Y.), 201.

cannot be greater than those of the executors for whom they
are substituted;[1] and accordingly if the executors, being
themselves in default - to the trust estate, would not be entitled to indemnity except upon condition of making good
their default, the creditors are in no better condition, and
cannot have their debts paid out of the fund unless the default is first made good.[2] Debts thus incurred by the executors, though having equal standing as among themselves,[3]
must be postponed to the proper debts of the deceased.[4] But
in the absence of such considerations, where trustees who are
authorized to carry on a business contract properly debts,
the creditors may not only hold the trustees personally, but
may also resort to the trust fund for their payment.[5]

§ 207. **Where the Creditor entitled to hold Two Funds.** — The
common-law rule that the personal estate of a deceased person will be applied to the payment of his debts to the relief
of his real estate[6] will not be enforced when it is in apparent
hostility to the intent of the deceased as expressed in his
will, and would defeat bequests made therein.[7] In a case
in New York, it appeared that a deceased citizen of that
State had by his will authorized his executors to reduce all
the property real and personal of which he should die pos-

[1] Evans v. Evans, 34 Ch. D. 597;
Strickland v. Symons, 22 Ch. D. 666;
Laible v. Ferry, *supra.*

[2] Dowse v. Gorton, 40 Ch. D. 536;
*in re* Johnson, 15 Ch. Div. 548.

[3] Mason v. Pomeroy, 151 Mass.
164.

[4] Jones v. Walker, 103 U. S. 444;
Morrow v. Morrow, 2 Tenn. Ch. 549.

[5] Owen v. Delamere, L. R. 15 Eq.
134; Thompson v. Andrews, 1 Myl.
& K. 116; Cutbush v. Cutbush, 1
Beav. 184; Richardson, *ex parte,* 3
Madd. 138; Garland, *ex parte,* 10
Ves. 110; Jones v. Walker, 103 U. S.
444; Smith v. Ayer, 101 U. S. 320,
330; Burwell v. Mandeville, 2 Howard, 560; Pitkin v. Pitkin, 7 Conn.
307.

[6] Hanson v. Hanson, 70 Maine,
508; Livingston v. Newkirk, 3 Johns.
Ch. (N. Y.) 312; Scott v. Morrison,
5 Ind. 551; Whitehead v. Gibbons,
10 N. J. Eq. (2 Stockt.) 230; McKay,
v. Green, 3 Johns. Ch. (N. Y.) 56.

[7] Graves v. Hicks, 6 Sim. 391;
Rogers v. Rogers, 1 Paige (N. Y.),
188; Manning v. Spooner, 3 Vesey, Jr.,
114; Harvey v. Steptoe, 17 Gratt.
(Va.) 289; Clinefelter v. Ayres, 16
Ills. 329; Marsh v. Marsh, 10 B.
Mon. (Ky.) 360; Iowa Loan Co. v.
Holderbaum, 52 N. W. Rep. 550;
Lightfoot v. Lightfoot, 27 Ala. 351.

sessed in America into divisible shape, and after the payment of debts and testamentary expenses to divide it into
seven shares, and distribute these in a specified manner.
When he executed his will his property was mostly personal;
but he afterwards purchased real estate in South Carolina,
paying part of the purchase-money in cash, and giving his
bond secured by a mortgage on the land for the remainder.
The will was admitted to probate in New York as a will of
both real and personal property, but in South Carolina only
as a will of personal property, not having the number of
witnesses required by the laws of that State for a will of real
estate.     All the legatees under the will were aliens, except
the beneficiaries of one of the shares, to whom as heirs-at-
law the real estate descended.     The holder of the mortgage-
bond presented it as a claim against the estate; and the
Court of Appeals held that to pay this bond out of the personal estate would defeat the obvious intent of the testator
to have all his real and personal estate in this country
divided equally among the beneficiaries under his will; and
that the doctrine of two funds would be applied by requiring
the bond-creditor to exhaust his remedy under his mortgage
against the real estate before resorting to the personal property, which alone was available to the claimants under the
will.[1]  When a court of equity has control of both the real
and the personal estate, it will, in order to save expense and
delay, apply them in the order in which, as between the heir
and the executor they are liable.[2]

§ 207 a.  **Subrogation between Tenant for Life and Remainder-
man.** — Where a testator devised all his estate both real and
personal to his wife for her life, with remainder over, and
directed his executrix to pay his debts as soon as possible
out of any funds which she might obtain for that purpose, it
was held that the tenant for life and the remainder-man

---

[1] Rice v. Harbeson, 63 N. Y. 493.     [2] Goodburn v. Stevens, 1 Md. Ch.
Dec. 420.

must contribute for the payment of debts according to their respective interests, and that advances made by the tenant for life for that purpose constituted a lien upon the estate as against the remainder-man.[1] The same rule has been applied in other courts.[2] Where a husband conveyed land which was subject to a mortgage for his own debt, to be held in trust for his wife for her life, with remainder in one half to her heirs or devisees and in the other half to his heirs or devisees, it was held that she might for the protection of her estate pay off this mortgage, and that she having done so, her devisees were entitled after her death to hold the mortgage lien upon the whole tract against her husband's heirs, until the latter should contribute their equitable proportions of the principal sum due on the mortgage-debt and of the interest accruing after her death, as it was her duty to keep down this interest during her life.[3] The redemption of the tenant for life is for the benefit of the remainder-man as well as of himself, upon the remainder-man's contributing his proportion of the expense; until this is done, the tenant for life can insist upon being subrogated to the original lien.[4]

§ 208. **Subrogation in Favor of Legatees.** — A legatee will be allowed the same right of subrogation as would be enjoyed by a creditor.[5] If the personal estate of a testator, not being sufficient to pay debts and legacies, has been exhausted by the executor in the payment of creditors whose debts are chargeable on both the real and the personal estate, a legatee, as between himself and the heirs, is entitled to stand in the place of the creditors *pro tanto*, and to receive

---

[1] Peck v. Glass, 6 How. (Miss.) 195; Watts v. Watts, 2 McCord Ch. (So. Car.) 77; Whitney v. Salter, 36 Minn. 103.

[2] Amory v. Lowell, 1 Allen (Mass.), 504; Durham v. Rhodes, 23 Md. 233, Hawkins v. Skeggs, 10 Humph. (Tenn.)

31; Jacocks v. Bosman, 1 Dev. & Bat. Eq. (Nor. Car.) 192.

[3] Ohmer v. Boyer, 89 Ala. 273.

[4] Allen v. De Groodt, 105 Mo. 442.

[5] Alexander v. Miller, 7 Heisk. (Tenn.) 65.

the amount of his legacy, or so much thereof as the personal estate but for such creditors would have paid, out of the real estate descended to the heir, unless it appears by the will that the testator intended the legacy to abate in the case of a deficiency in the personal property.[1]  Where a testator, having agreed to purchase an estate, died, leaving the greater part of the purchase-money unpaid, a legatee was allowed to have the assests marshalled in respect of the vendor's lien for the unpaid purchase-money, so that his legacy might be paid.[2]  And if such purchase-money has been paid by the executor, and the personal assets of the estate have thereby been exhausted, a pecuniary legatee will be subrogated to the vendor's lien upon the purchased estate against the devisees thereof.[3]  Where a debt of the testator is primarily chargeable upon lands which he has specifically devised, and the creditor obtains his payment out of the personal estate, or from other property which is only secondarily liable for the debt, the owners of such personal estate or other property are entitled to be subrogated to the rights of the creditor against the estate specifically devised.   And to prevent circuity of action, the court in such a case will permit and sometimes require the creditor who can hold two funds for the satisfaction of his demand to proceed at once against that fund which is primarily liable, without subjecting the owners of the secondary fund to useless litigation.[4]  If an annuity which was charged by the will upon both real and personal estate has been satisfied from the personalty, leaving that insufficient for the payment of the general legatees, the latter will, as against the heirs, but not against devisees, be subrogated to the lien of the annuitant upon the real estate.[5]

[1] Mollan v. Griffith, 3 Paige (N. Y.), 402.

[2] Sproul v. Prior, 8 Sim. 189.

[3] Lilford v. Keck, L. R. 1 Eq. 347.

[4] Smith v. Wyckoff, 11 Paige (N. Y.), 49; antea, § 61.

[5] Allen v. Allen, 3 Wallace, Jr. 289.

§ 209. **In Favor of a Purchaser from the Personal Representative.** — The purchaser of a deceased person's real estate at an invalid sale made thereof by the personal representative for the payment of debts, having paid his purchase-money and this having been applied to the payment of debts and charges of administration, is entitled, upon an avoidance of the sale, to be subrogated to the rights of the creditors and of the personal representative whom he has satisfied, and to charge the land with the debts and expenses so paid by him,[1] to the extent to which the land was liable for such debts and expenses.[2] The land will for the protection of a purchaser be charged with the debts which have thus been paid out of his purchase money.[3] A purchaser of personal property from a guardian will be protected in the same way.[4] This right of a purchaser has already been considered.[5] But it has been said that if the title of the purchaser fails by reason of a want of jurisdiction of the court ordering the sale over the heirs, the purchaser will not be so subrogated against them,[6] the debts paid not having been liens upon the land. Though a purchaser of land of a testator at a sale thereof made under a judgment against the executor acquires no title by his purchase, yet, if he pays his purchase-money in good faith under the belief that he is acquiring a good title, and this is applied

[1] Cathcart v. Sugenheimer, 18 So. Car. 123; Kinney v. Knoebel, 51 Ills. 112; Short v. Porter, 44 Miss. 533; Bland v. Bowie, 53 Ala. 152; Folts v. Ferguson, 77 Tex. 301; Wheeler v. Wheeler, 1 Conn. 51; Hudgins v. Hudgins, 6 Gratt. (Va.) 320.

[2] Springs v. Harven, 3 Jones Eq. (Nor. Car.) 96; Young v. Twigg, 27 Md. 621; Duncan v. Gainey, 108 Ind. 579; Jones v. French, 92 Ind. 138; Neel v. Carson, 47 Ark. 421; Waggener v. Lyles, 29 Ark. 47; Pool v. Ellis, 64 Miss. 555.

[3] Caldwell v. Palmer, 6 Lea (Tenn.), 652; Stults v. Brown, 112 Ind. 370; Gaines v. Kennedy, 53 Miss. 103; Hill v. Billingsley, Id. 111; Cunningham v. Anderson, 107 Mo. 371; Long v. Joplin Mining Co., 68 Mo. 422; Schaefer v. Causey, 8 Mo. Ap. 142; Brown v. Bouney, 30 La. Ann. pt. I. 174; Sharkey v. Bankston, Id. pt. II. 891.

[4] Harrison v. Ilgner, 74 Tex. 86.

[5] Antea, § 30 et seq.

[6] Bishop v. O'Conner, 69 Ills. 431; Jones v. Woodstock Iron Co., 10 So. Rep. 635.

to the payment of the judgment-debt, which was charged upon the land by the will, he will be subrogated to the benefit of this charge, and will be allowed to hold the land until he has been reimbursed to this extent.[1]  But the mere fact that the purchase-money has been applied to the payment of the debts of the deceased will not entitle the purchaser of his real estate from the administrator to a lien upon the land for his reimbursement upon the sale being set aside, if such debts do not appear to have been a charge upon the land.[2] Nor, if the administrator puts himself in the place of the purchaser, can he, as a relief against his own wrong in making the sale, claim the subrogation which might have been allowed to the innocent purchaser.[3]

§ 210.  **Where Legatees have paid Judgments against the Estate.** — Legatees who have paid a judgment rendered in favor of a creditor of the estate against the executor have for their reimbursement the right to be subrogated to the remedies of the judgment-creditor, if the claim of the creditor was reduced to a judgment, or otherwise made a lien upon the assets to which the legatees are entitled to look,[4] but not otherwise;[5] for one who pays a debt for which he was not personally liable, and which was not a charge upon his property will not be substituted to the benefit of a lien which the creditor had upon the estate of his debtor.[6]  So where an executor, who was also a devisee and legatee, died insolvent, having wasted a large portion of the estate, and leaving unpaid a debt of the testator and also a judgment against himself for his own debt, which judgment was a lien upon his

---

[1] McGee v. Wallis, 57 Miss. 638.

[2] Bennett v. Coldwell, 8 Baxter (Tenn.), 483; Hampton v. Nicholson, 23 N. J. Eq. 423; Neal v. Patten, 47 Ga. 73.

[3] Williams v. Stratton, 10 Sm. & M. (Miss.) 418. But see Weaver v. Norwood, 59 Miss. 665; Ebelmesser v. Ebelmesser, 99 Ills. 541.

[4] Place v. Oldham, 10 B. Mon. (Ky.) 400.

[5] Mitchell v. Mitchell, 8 Humph. (Tenn.) 359; Belcher v. Wickersham, 9 Baxter (Tenn.), 111; Alston v. Batchelor, 6 Ired. Eq. (Nor. Car.) 368.

[6] *Postea* § 240 *et seq.*

interest as devisee in certain real estate of the testator, it
was held that his co-devisees and legatees did not, by paying
the debt of the testator, acquire a right over his interest in
the real estate prior to the lien of his judgment-creditor,
either by substitution to the claim of the creditor whom they
had paid or by reason of the executor's waste.[1]  But if a
testator has bequeathed all his property to his widow in lieu
of her dower, and she has as his executrix paid from the
general assets notes given by him in payment for an estate
which he had bought subsequently to the execution of his
will, and which did not pass thereby, she will be subrogated
for her reimbursement to a lien retained by the vendor upon
the estate to secure to him the payment of these notes; and
this right will pass to her devisee.[2]  So if money of her
husband's estate that should have been paid to her for her
dower interest has been exhausted by the administrator in
the payment of debts, she may be subrogated to the rights of
the creditors who have thus been paid at her expense to hold
the real estate for her reimbursement.[3]

§ 211. Subrogation in Favor of Specific Devisees and Legatees.
— The devisee of a tract of land which by direction of the
testator had been levied upon in his lifetime to satisfy a debt
of his own, and was still bound by the levy at the time of
his death, is entitled after paying the debt, to be subrogated
to the claim of the creditor against the personal assets of
the estate;[4] and the lien-creditor of the devisee will have
the same right of subrogation;[5] for, unless the will mani-
fests a clear intention to the contrary,[6] it is the right of such
devisee to have the testator's indebtedness paid out of the
personal and undisposed-of assets of the estate,[7] though this

[1] Wilkes v. Harper, 1 N. Y. 586.

[2] Durham v. Rhodes, 23 Md.
233.

[3] Cronch v. Edwards, 52 Ark.
499.

[4] Redmond v. Burroughs, 63 Nor.
Car. 242.

[5] Morris v. Mowatt, 2 Paige (N.Y.),
586.

[6] Rogers v. Rogers, 1 Paige (N. Y.),
188 ; Brant's Will, 40 Mo. 266 ; Mire-
house v. Scaife, 2 Myl. & Cr. 695.

[7] Gould v. Winthrop, 5 R. I. 319 ;
Plimpton v. Fuller, 11 Allen (Mass.),

rule is reversed when devised property is subject to a charge which is not the proper debt of the testator.[1]  But this right will not extend to a grantee of the devisee whose grant is expressly made subject to the incumbrance upon the land.[2] And in England and New York real estate which is subject to a specific lien for the payment of a debt, as in the case of a mortgage, is *prima facie* the primary fund for the payment of such debt, to the exoneration of the personal property.[3] Since specific legatees are entitled to receive their bequests exonerated from incumbrances created by the testator,[4] they have likewise, if their legacies have been sold for the payment of the testator's debts, the right to resort to the general fund for their remuneration, upon the principles adopted in the marshalling of assets.[5]  If this general fund is made up partly of personal estate and partly of the proceeds of real estate not chargeable with the payment of simple-contract debts, that portion of it which comes from the personalty is liable in the first instance to make up for the loss of the specific legacies; and if that be insufficient, then the proceeds of the real estate are to be applied for the same purpose, so far, and so far only, as the specific legacies have been appropriated for the payment of specialty-debts which bound the real estate.[6]

139 ; Hewes v. Dehon, 3 Gray (Mass.), 205 ; Adams v. Brackett, 5 Met. (Mass.) 280 ; Hays v. Jackson, 6 Mass. 149 ; Lamport v. Beeman, 34 Barb. (N. Y.) 239 ; Keene v. Munn, 16 N. J. Eq. 398 ; Lennig's Estate, 52 Penn. St. 135 ; Phinney's Estate, Myrick's Prob. (Calif.) 239.

[1] Gould v. Winthrop, 5 R. I. 319 ; Andrews v. Bishop, 5 Allen (Mass.), 490.

[2] Keene v. Munn, 16 N. J. Eq. 398.

[3] Anthony, *in re*, 1 Ch. D. (1892) 450 ; Woolstencroft v. Woolstencroft,

2 De G., F. & J. 347 ; Brownson v. Lawrence, L. R. 6 Eq. 1 ; St. 17 & 18 Vic., ch. 113 ; 1 N. Y. Rev. Stats. 749 ; Mosely v. Marshall, 27 Barb. (N. Y.) 42 ; Jumel v. Jumel, 7 Paige (N. Y.), 591 ; Rogers v. Rogers, 1 Paige (N. Y.), 188 ; Cumberland v. Coddrington, 3 Johns. Ch.(N. Y.) 229.

[4] Johnson v. Goss, 128 Mass. 433 ; Richardson v. Hall, 124 Mass. 228.

[5] Cranmer v. McSwords, 24 W. Va. 594 ; Hope v. Wilkinson, 14 Lea (Tenn.), 21.

[6] Byrd v. Byrd, 2 Brock. C. C. 169.

§ 212. **Subrogation of Devisees to subsequently acquired Assets.** — Devisees who have lost the whole or part of the property devised to them by its being sold to pay the debts of the testator, in consequence of the insufficiency of the personal assets, will be subrogated to the rights of the creditors whom their property has thus satisfied, and entitled to reimbursement out of personal property subsequently discovered and received by the executors;[1] and such a devisee's right of subrogation will pass by an assignment of all his share and claim in and to the personal estate of the testator which then was in or might thereafter come into the hands of the executors, although not mentioned in the assignment, and not appearing to be then known to the assignor.[2] Accordingly, where a testator charged his personal estate with the payment of his debts, but, this being insufficient for that purpose, the testator's real estate, which had been devised, was sold to pay his debts, and afterwards the executors obtained a sum of money upon a claim which the testator had against the French government, it was held that this money was in equity to be considered a substitute for the real estate which had been sold for the payment of debts that were primarily chargeable upon the personal estate, and that in equity it must go exclusively to the devisees or their grantees, who were at the time of the sale the owners of the real estate that had been so sold, this money being regarded not as real estate, but as a fund to which they had an equitable right to compensate them for the loss of their land.[3] But creditors of such devisees, though having acquired a judgment-lien, can be subrogated to this right of the devisees only by bringing all parties before the court so that the rights of all may be properly protected.[4]

---

[1] Couch v. Delaplaine, 2 N. Y. 397; Graham v. Dickinson, 3 Barb. Ch. (N. Y.) 169.

[2] Couch v. Delaplaine, *supra.*

[3] Graham v. Dickinson, *supra.*

[4] Evans v. Duncan, 4 Watts (Penn.), 24.

§ 213. **Rights of Heirs, Devisees, or Legatees against each other.**
— If one of several devisees has lost the property devised to
him by its being taken to pay a debt of the testator, he will
be so far subrogated to the rights of the creditors whom he
has thus been forced to satisfy, as to be entitled to a contribution to his loss from the other devisees;[1] and an heir will
have the same right against the other heirs.[2] He will also
be subrogated to the rights of the creditor against another
debtor who was under a primary liability for the payment of
the debt.[3] The different devisees, if there be a deficiency of
assets, must contribute, to meet a charge upon all the estate
devised, in proportion to the value of their respective interests,[4] as to make up an annuity to the testator's widow, or to
pay debts of the testator which remain unsatisfied after the
personal property and the undevised real estate have been
exhausted.[5] A devisee whose estate has been taken for the
dower of the testator's widow has the same right to contribution as if it had been taken for a debt of the testator.[6] A
legatee who has advanced money to pay the testator's debts
under the mistaken supposition that they were charged upon
his property has been allowed to compel contribution from
his co-legatees.[7] Where legacies and devises are put upon

---

[1] Rhoads's Estate, 3 Rawle (Penn.),
420; Brigden v. Cheever, 10 Mass.
450; Armistead v. Dangerfield, 3
Munf. (Va.) 20; Foster v. Crenshaw,
3 Munf. (Va.) 514; Humphries v.
Shaw, 63 Nor. Car. 341; Gallagher v.
Redmond, 64 Tex. 622; Lancefield
v. Iggulden, L. R. 10 Ch. 136.

[2] Winston v. McAlpine, 65 Ala.
377; Chaplin v. Sullivan, 128 Ind. 50;
Falley v. Gribling, 128 Ind. 110; Mc-
Pike v. Wells, 54 Miss. 136; Taylor v.
Taylor, 8 B. Mon. (Ky.) 419; *Tilghman, C. J.*, in Guier v. Kelly, 2 Binney (Penn.), 294, 299; Lyles v. Lyles,
1 Hill Eq (So. Car.) 77; Brinson v.
Cunliff, 25 Tex. 760.

[3] Hancock v. Minot, 8 Pick.
(Mass.) 29, 38.

[4] Harris v. White, 5 N. J. Law,
422; Mitchell v. Blain, 5 Paige (N.
Y.), 588; Young v. Weldon, 1 Murph.
(Nor. Car.) 176; Snow v. Callum, 1
Desaus. (So. Car.) 542.

[5] Tomlinson v. Bury, 145 Mass.
346; Harland v. Person, 93 Ala. 274;
Livingston v. Livingston, 3 Johns.
Ch. (N. Y.) 148.

[6] Gallagher's Appeal, 87 Penn. St.
200; Eliason v. Eliason, 3 Del. Ch.
260; Blaney v. Blaney, 1 Cush. (Mass.)
107.

[7] McCampbell v. McCampbell, 5
Litt. (Ky.) 92.

an equality, they are equally liable to contribution among
themselves.[1]   But a residuary devisee is not entitled to contribution from the other devisees,[2] though a somewhat modified rule has been laid down in England.[3]   A devisee of land
who has been obliged to pay a debt of the testator which was
primarily charged upon the land devised to him cannot claim
contribution therefor from other specific devisees or legatees.[4]
In Mississippi it is said that the doctrine of the marshalling
of assets does not apply to the case of specific legatees under
a will when all the property bequeathed to them is subject to
an incumbrance paramount to the will of the testator, and
the property bequeathed to one of them has alone been seized
to satisfy this incumbrance; and accordingly such a specific
legatee will have no right to enforce contribution from his
co-legatees, though their property was equally liable with his
to the burden of the incumbrance,[5] thus leaving it to the
caprice of the creditor to determine at whose expense he
shall get his payment.[6]   And, on the principle that no one
can enjoy, by way of subrogation to a creditor, any greater
rights than the creditor himself possessed,[7] it was held that
where one died, leaving unincumbered real estate and also
real estate subject to a mortgage by the terms of which the
mortgagee could hold only the land for the satisfaction of
his demand, and the mortgagor's heirs made partition among
themselves of all his land in ignorance of the mortgage, the

[1] Powell v. Riley, L. R. 12 Eq.
175; Grim's Appeal, 89 Penn. St.
333; Dugan v. Hollins, 11 Md. 41;
Hammond v. Hammond, 2 Bland, Ch.
(Md.) 306; Brant's Will, 40 Mo.
266.

[2] Richardson v. Hall, 124 Mass.
228, 233; Blaney v. Blaney, 1 Cush.
(Mass.) 107; McMullin v. Brown, 2
Hill Eq. (So. Car.) 457.

[3] Lancefield v. Iggulden, L. R. 10
Ch. 136.  See Spong v. Spong, 3

Bligh, N. s. 84; Hensman v. Fryer,
L. R. 3 Ch. 420; s. c., L. R. 2 Eq.
627.

[4] Hocker's Appeal, 4 Penn. St.
497; Graves v. Graves, 106 Ind.
118.

[5] Peeples v. Horton, 39 Miss.
406.

[6] Antea, § 172 et seq.; Wright, is re,
16 Fed. Rep. 482.  And see 1 Story
Eq., § 493.

[7] Antea, § 6.

heir who afterwards lost his land by the mortgagee's taking it could not be indemnified for his loss from the personal estate of the deceased.[1]  Nor can a devisee who has lost his estate for lack of title in the testator be relieved out of other portions of the testator's property.[2]

§ 214. **Specific Devise or Legacy chargeable with Expense incurred for its Protection.** — If an executor has at the request of devisees relieved the devised property from an incumbrance resting upon it, he may for his reimbursement, as against the devisees, be subrogated to the original charge upon the property,[3] the general doctrine being that a trustee who removes a prior incumbrance upon the trust estate will be subrogated to the lien of that incumbrance for his protection.[4]  An executor who has properly paid out of the general estate taxes and liens primarily chargeable upon land specifically devised by the testator, and which should have been paid by the devisees thereof, may, in case of their failure to reimburse him, be subrogated to the liens upon the land, and may have these liens enforced for his protection.[5] Though co-legatees do not sustain to each other the relation of co-sureties for the testator's debts, each being responsible in any event only in proportion to the amount of his own legacy,[6] yet, if one of two residuary legatees has incurred in protecting their joint interest an expense which has proved to be beneficial to both of them, he will be entitled to recover from his co-legatee reimbursement to the amount of the expense incurred upon the latter's account,[7] at any rate if the latter neither objected to the incurring of the expense nor

---

[1] Fairman v. Heath, 19 Ind. 63.

[2] McKinnon v. Thompson, 3 Johns. Ch. (N. Y.) 307.

[3] Franklin v. Armfield, 2 Sneed (Tenn.), 305.

[4] Glide v. Dwyer, 83 Calif. 478; King v. Cushman, 41 Ills. 31; Freeman v. Tompkins, 1 Strobh. Eq. (So. Car.) 53.

[5] Hudson v. Gray, 58 Miss. 882; Mogan's Estate, Myrick's Prob. (Calif.) 80.

[6] Wilkes v. Harper, 1 N. Y. 586; De Ende v. Wilkinson, 2 Patt. & H. (Va.) 663.

[7] Miller's Appeal, 119 Penn. St. 620; New Orleans v. Baltimore, 15 La. Ann. 625.

himself provided for the protection of his interest.[1] The expenses of a necessary litigation will be thrown upon the whole fund which reaps the benefit thereof.[2]

§ 215. **Rights of Heirs among Themselves.** — If some of the heirs of an intestate held a mortgage upon his real estate to secure the payment of a debt due to them from him, and in order to prevent a sale of his real estate by his administratrix give bond for the payment of his debts, though they will thereby discharge the lien of their mortgage as a security for the debt due to themselves,[3] they may nevertheless hold the mortgaged premises against the other heirs as if the mortgage still subsisted, until these other heirs shall contribute their respective shares of the mortgage-debt.[4] If exempt property is sold by the administrator to pay debts, the heir is entitled to be reimbursed from such other property as is not subject to prior liens;[5] and if debts which were chargeable upon the personal property have been paid out of the real estate, the heir may, as against the distributees, be subrogated to the rights of the creditors upon the personal estate;[6] but he will not be so subrogated against the devisees to reimburse him for debts which he has paid out of his own pocket as a mere bounty.[7]

§ 216. **Rights of Purchaser from Heir or Devisee.** — If the purchaser from an heir-at-law of a portion of the real estate descended to the latter subsequently loses the land which he has purchased, by its being sold to pay the debts of the ancestor, such purchaser will have an equitable lien upon the residue of the property remaining in the hands of the heir for

[1] Thirlwell v. Campbell, 11 Bush (Ky.), 163.

[2] Florida Internal Improvement Co. v. Greenough, 12 Amer. & English R. R. Cas. 345.

[3] Robinson v. Leavitt, 7 N. H. 73.

[4] Jenness v. Robinson, 10 N. H. 215.

[5] McDougall v. Brokaw, 22 Fla. 98.

[6] Phipps v. Phipps, 3 Pa. Law Journal Rep. 275. So if the payment was made by the widow from her own means : McNally v. Weld, 30 Minn. 209. See also Deichman v. Arndt, 22 Atl. Rep. 799; Adams v. Smith, 20 Abbott, New Cas. (N. Y.) 60.

[7] Coleby v. Coleby, L. R. 2 Eq. 803.

his reimbursement: such a purchaser, as to the land remaining in the possession of the heir, stands in the position of a surety, and will be subrogated to the rights of the creditor whom his property has satisfied, as if he were a surety.[1] And if successive conveyances of lands have been made by an heir, or by a devisee thereof charged with the payment of debts or legacies; the lands thus conveyed are, in the hands of the purchasers thereof, liable among themselves to be resorted to for the payment of such debts or legacies in the inverse order of their alienation, the portion, if any, remaining in the hands of such heir or devisee being first taken, then the portion last conveyed by him, and so on.[2] In the same way *bona fide* purchasers of the property of the testator from executors who have power to sell the same will be protected from debts of the testator which are liens upon the purchased property, by compelling the executors, if they have assets, to pay such debts.[3]

§ 217. **Creditors subrogated to the Rights of Legatees.** — If a testator charges one estate with the payment of his debts, and another with the payment of legacies, and the legacies are paid out of the proceeds of the former estate, the creditors will be subrogated to the rights of the legatees against the latter estate, in the hands of a purchaser thereof who had constructive notice of the terms of the will; and sureties who have satisfied the creditors will have the same right which the creditors might have exercised.[4]   "The legatees," said Moncure, P.,[5] "having received payment out of the fund which belonged to the creditors, the latter had a clear and

---

[1] Eddy *v.* Traver, 6 Paige (N. Y.), 521.

[2] Jenkins *v.* Freyer, 4 Paige (N. Y.), 47; Livingston *v.* Freeland, 3 Barb. Ch. (N. Y.) 510; Conover *v.* Conover, 1 N. J. Eq. (Saxton) 403; Lewis *v.* Overby, 31 Gratt. (Va.) 601; Nellons *v.* Truax, 6 Ohio St. 97;

Ireland *v.* Miller, 71 Mich. 119; Finch *v.* Shaw, 19 Beav. 500; *antea*, § 75 *et seq.*

[3] Latrobe *v.* Tierman, 2 Md. Ch. Dec. 474.

[4] Burwell *v.* Fauber, 21 Gratt. (Va.) 446.

[5] In Burwell *v.* Fauber, *supra.*

plain right to compel the former to refund the money, so far
as it was necessary for the payment of debts. And the legatees, being thus disappointed in obtaining satisfaction out of
the fund which belonged to the creditors, would have as clear
and plain a right to be reinstated in their charge upon the
home place, and to be satisfied out of the same. But to
avoid circuity, a court of equity will subrogate the creditors
to the place of the legatees, and give the former a direct
decree against the home place." So, where an executor who
was also a trustee under the will applied the funds of the
estate which should have been used to meet the testator's
debts to pay charges which constituted a superior lien upon
the trust property, it was held that equity would give the
general creditors a charge upon the trust property to the
extent of such payments.[1]

§ 218. **Subrogation of Devisee or Legatee who is disappointed
by the Election of another.** — Beneficiaries under a will who
have, by the election of another legatee, been disappointed of
what they would otherwise have received, will be allowed
compensation for their loss out of what the latter would by
a different election have taken under the will.[2] If a legatee
under a will which devises away property belonging to himself elects to retain his own property and to waive the legacy,
the testator will not be thereby rendered intestate, or the
share of the residuary legatees, not being the parties disappointed in consequence of the election, increased, as to the
subject-matter of such legacy, but it will go to the disappointed devisee, so far as is necessary to the satisfaction of
his loss.[3] So, if a testator bequeaths the income of certain

---

[1] Ferris v. Van Vechten, 9 Hun
(N. Y.), 12.

[2] Pickersgill v. Rodger, 5 Ch. Div.
163; Wilkinson v. Dent, L. R. 6 Ch.
339, 341; Reeve v. Reeve, 1 Vern.
219; Welby v. Welby, 2 Ves. & B.
187, 190; Bor v. Bor, 3 Bro. P. C.

167; Dean v. Hart, 62 Ala. 308; Key
v. Griffin, 1 Rich. Eq. (So. Car.) 67;
Timberlake v. Parish, 5 Dana (Ky.),
345.

[3] Hamilton v. Hamilton, 1 Ch. D.
(1892) 396; Ker v. Wauchope, 1
Bligh, 1; Gilman v. Gilman, 111 N.

property to his wife for the support of herself and her children, and she waives the provisions of the will in her behalf and elects to take her dower-rights instead thereof, the children will be entitled to the whole of the income of that property for the time that she would otherwise have taken it.[1] Devisees whose interests are prejudiced by the widow's election to take her dower in preference to the provision made for her by her husband's will are equitably entitled to compensation for their loss out of the provision which she has thus rejected.[2] The ground of this doctrine was stated in an early case to be that where a testator in making provision for the different branches of his family, gives a fee-simple estate to one, and a settled estate to another, imagining that he had power to do so, a tacit condition is annexed to the devise of the fee-simple estate that the devisee thereof shall permit the settled estate to go according to the terms of the will; and if in that respect he should disappoint the will, what is devised to him will go to the person who is thereby disappointed, it being presumed that, if the testator had known of his lack of power to devise the settled estate, he would out of the estate in his power have provided for that branch of his family which had no interest in the settled estate, and have directed that no person should enjoy a devise or legacy who controverted his power as to a bequest given to another.[3] The will will thus be upheld, and the intent of the testator carried out, as far as this may be done.[4] Accordingly, this doctrine will not be applied to the case of

Y. 265; Batione's Estate, 136 Penn. St. 307; Lewis v. Lewis, 13 Penn. St. 79; Kinnaird v. Williams, 8 Leigh (Va.), 400; Macknett v. Macknett, 24 N. J. Eq. 277; Wilbanks v. Wilbanks, 18 Ills. 17. *Contra*, Hawley v. James, 5 Paige (N. Y.), 318.

[1] Plympton v. Plympton, 6 Allen (Mass.), 178; Adams v. Gillespie, 2 Jones Eq. (Nor. Car). 244; Roe v.

Roe, 21 N. J. Eq. 253. *Contra*, Hawley v. James, 5 Paige (N. Y.), 318.

[2] Sarles v. Sarles, 19 Abbott, New Cas. (N. Y.) 322; Jennings v. Jennings, 21 Ohio St. 56.

[3] Bor v. Bor, 3 Bro. P. C. 167.

[4] Sturtevant v. Bowker, 11 Met. (Mass.) 291; Allen v. Hannum, 15 Kans. 625.

a person who disappoints another by electing to take under
the instrument which gives rise to the election.[1]

§ 219. **Extent of this Right of Substitution.** — The substitution of the disappointed beneficiaries to the rights of the
legatee or devisee whose election has caused the disappoint-
ment will, if necessary, be to the extent of the rights which
were given by the will to the party making the election,[2] but
it can be carried no further.[3] If the widow of a testator who
has by his will, after various absolute devises and bequests,
bequeathed the income of a certain fund to his wife for her
life, with remainder to be distributed among various legatees,
and given the residue of his estate to his residuary devisees,
elects to take her statutory rights as widow in his estate instead of the provision made for her in his will, and thus
diminishes the share of the residuary legatees, these legatees
will, during the lifetime of the widow, by substitution to her
rights, be entitled to receive the income of the fund provided
for her, and after her death the fund will go to the legatees
named in the will, as if her election had operated no change
in carrying out the intentions of the testator.[4] The purchaser from a devisee of certain cottages in which the testator had only a life-estate, the remainder being in his wife,
will be entitled to compensation from the estate of the testator's wife, for her selling the cottages, to the extent of the
benefit taken by the wife under the will, the testator having
given all his estate to his wife for her life, and these cottages after her death to such purchaser's grantor.[5] A testator, having charged certain lands with a portion for his
daughter by his first wife, afterwards settled a portion of the

---

[1] Chesham, *in re*, 31 Ch. D. 466.
[2] Rogers *v.* Jones, 3 Ch. Div. 688;
Maskell *v.* Goodall, 2 Disney (Ohio),
282; Tiernan *v.* Roland, 15 Penn. St.
430, 451.
[3] Gretton *v.* Haward, 1 Swanst.
409; Upham *v.* Emerson, 119 Mass.
509; Sandoe's Appeal, 65 Penn. St.
314; Stump *v.* Findlay, 2 Rawle
(Penn.), 168.
[4] Firth *v.* Denny, 2 Allen (Mass.),
468; Brandenburg *v.* Thorndike, 139
Mass. 102.
[5] Rogers *v.* Jones, 3 Ch. Div. 688.

same lands as a jointure upon his second wife, who had no
notice of the prior charge. Believing that the charge would
have preference over the jointure, he then devised other
lands to his wife, in lieu of the jointure. After his death,
the wife, finding that her jointure was good against the
charge for the daughter's portion, because the latter was
merely voluntary, agreed with the heir to waive her devise,
and claim the jointure, for the purpose of depriving the
daughter of her portion. But the court decreed that the
daughter should have the lands devised to the wife, until her
portion was made up.[1]

§ 220. **This does not extend to a Devise merely upon Condition.** — If property is devised to one upon a condition with
which he fails to comply, and thus waives his right to the
devise, the performance of this condition by a stranger will
not substitute the stranger to the rights of the devisee.[2]
Thus, where a testator devised land to one of his sons on
condition that the devisee should support a second son during his life, but the devisee refused to accept the devise and
did not support the second son, and a stranger, having been
appointed guardian of the latter, advanced out of his own
means money for his support, to an amount equal to the
value of the estate so devised, it was held that these advances
could not rightfully be reimbursed out of the devised estate,
but that, on the refusal of the original devisee to accept the
same, it descended to the testator's heirs-at-law, free of any
charge thereon;[3] but elsewhere the right of a party furnishing support to the beneficiary of such a conditional devise or
conveyance to be subrogated to the title of the devisee has

---

[1] Reeve v. Reeve, 1 Vern. 219,
recognized by *Lord Hardwicke*, in Lanoy v. Athol, 2 Atk. 447.

[2] Temple v. Nelson, 4 Met. (Mass.)
584; Frederick v. Gray, 10 Serg. &
R. (Penn.) 182; Bugbee v. Sargent,
23 Maine, 269; Box v. Barrett, L. R.
3 Eq. 244.

[3] Temple v. Nelson, *supra;* Halstead v. Westervelt, 41 N. J. Eq. 100;
Savage v. McCorkle, 17 Oreg. 42.

been affirmed.[1] If a person to whom land is devised, on condition of his releasing a debt due to him from the testator, receives payment of the debt, he relinquishes the land; and the fact that he receives such payment from a stranger gives the latter no title to the land.[2] But if the money so paid by such stranger was the full value of the property, and immediately upon its payment he took possession of the land, and was suffered by all the heirs to hold possession, they knowing and acquiescing in his payment, and he incurred expense to make improvements, it has been intimated that eq ity would order the land to be conveyed to him, especially if the title was one which was then governed as to its transmission by the same rules as personal property.[3] And a devise of land on condition that the devisee shall pay certain specified debts and legacies creates a charge upon the land, to the exoneration of the personal property bequeathed by the will, although the devise be not accepted.[4]

[1] Ferre v. American Board, 53 Vt. 162; McArthur v. Gordon, 126 N. Y. 597; Huffmond v. Bence, 128 Ind. 131; Scott v. Hillenburg, 85 Va. 245. Some of these were cases of conveyances in which the consideration was a promise to give such support, or in which a lien was reserved or created therefor, to which subrogation might well be made; they were not upon a bare condition.

[2] Frederick v. Gray, 10 Serg. & R. (Penn.) 182. See also King v. Morris, 2 B. Mon. (Ky.) 99.

[3] Frederick v. Gray, supra.

[4] McFait's Appeal, 8 Penn. St. 290; Birdsall v. Hewlett, 1 Paige (N. Y.), 32; Bugbee v. Sargent, 27 Maine, 338; s. c., 23 Maine, 269.

# CHAPTER VII.

### SUBROGATION UNDER CONTRACTS OF INSURANCE.

§ 221. **Subrogation of Marine Insurers.** — Marine insurers acquire by the abandonment to them of the property insured and by the satisfaction of their policies all the ownership of the insured in the property abandoned,[1] with the *spes recuperandi*, and all the rights and remedies of the insured with respect thereto, and may prosecute all subsequent rights and remedies in their own names.[2] And the insurers may bring a libel to enforce this right even before their actual payment.[3] And their payment of a total loss without the

---

[1] The Mary E. Perew, 15 Blatchf. C. C. 58; Traders' Ins. Co. v. Propeller Manistee, 5 Biss. C. C. 381.

[2] Mutual Ins. Co. v. Brig George, Olcott (Adm.), 89; Sun Ins. Co. v. Hall, 104 Mass. 507; Union Ins. Co. v. Burrell, Anth. Cas. (N. Y.) 176; United Ins. Co. v. Scott, 1 Johns. (N. Y.) 106.

[3] The Manistee, 7 Biss. C. C. 35.

form of an abandonment will have the same effect.[1] "The law gives to the act of abandonment, when accepted, all the effects which the most carefully drawn assignment would accomplish. By the act of abandonment the insured renounces and yields up to the underwriter all his right, title, and claims to what may be saved, and leaves it to him to make the most of it for his own benefit. The underwriter then stands in the place of the insured, and becomes legally entitled to all that can be saved from destruction."[2] The insurers are entitled, upon settlement as for a total loss, to be subrogated for their own benefit to any rights of action of the insured against a third party for his negligence or wrong-doing causing the loss.[3] Nor can such third party in an action brought against him in the name of the insured set up the insurers' payment to the plaintiff as a defence, either wholly or *pro tanto*.[4] The abandonment has a retroactive effect, and vests in the insurers the title to the property or its proceeds from the time of the injury or loss as fully as if it had been the subject of a bill of sale.[5] The property vests in the insurers, with its benefits as well as its burdens,[6] if the abandonment has been rightfully made, though the loss has not been actually paid.[7]

[1] Dufourcet v. Bishop, 18 Q. B. D. 373; Holbrook v. United States, 21 Ct. of Claims, 434.

[2] *Story, J.*, in Comegys v. Vasse, 1 Peters, 193; Simonds v. Union Ins. Co., 1 Wash. C. C. 443.

[3] The City of Paris, 1 Benedicts, 529; Home Ins. Co. v. Western Transportation Co., 4 Robt. (N. Y.) 257; Mercantile Ins. Co. v. Clark, 118 Mass. 288; Georgia Ins. Co. v. Dawson, 2 Gill (Md.), 365; The Thyatira, 8 Prob. D. 155; Dickenson v. Jardine, L R 3 C. P. 639; Randal v. Cockran, 1 Ves. Sen. 98; North of England Ins. Association v. Armstrong, L. R. 5 Q. B. 244.

[4] Clark v. Wilson, 103 Mass. 219. The opinion of the court in this case, by Mr. Justice Gray, contains an exhaustive discussion of the question involved, both upon principle and upon authority.

[5] Sun Ins. Co. v. Hall, 104 Mass. 507; Union Ins. Co. v. Burrell, Anth. Cas. (N. Y.) 176; United Ins. Co. v. Scott, 1 Johns. (N. Y.) 106.

[6] Frothingham v. Prince, 3 Mass. 563; Sun Ins. Co. v. Hall, 104 Mass. 507; Heilner r. China Ins. Co., 13 N. Y. Supt. 177.

[7] Rogers v. Hosack, 18 Wend. (N. Y.) 319.

§ 222. **Subrogation to the Remedy for a Tort causing the Loss.**
— Accordingly the right of a ship-owner to indemnity for an
unjust capture will pass by his abandonment to the insurers
of the ship,[1] and on the latter's bankruptcy will vest in their
assignees.[2] The insurers of a ship which has been run down
and sunk by the fault of another ship are, upon their payment
of a total loss, subrogated to the right of the insured to recover therefor against the owners of the latter vessel,[3] and
will be entitled to any damages which the insured may have
recovered from such owners; and if their policy was a valued
one, their payment of this value will give to them the whole
*spes recuperandi* and the right to the whole damages, though
the insured vessel was in fact worth a larger sum than the
valuation named in the policy, this valuation being conclusive between the insurers and the insured.[4] Accordingly,
the defendants in an action to recover for the damage done
to the plaintiff's ship by a collision cannot deduct from the
damages to be paid by them the amount that has been paid to
the plaintiff for the same injury by insurers of the ship; the
plaintiff is entitled to recover as to this amount as a trustee
for the insurers.[5] So, too, if the insurers of goods have
stipulated to answer for a loss by theft, and the master and
ship-owners are also liable for this loss, the insurers, upon
a loss by theft and an abandonment to them or their payment
of a total loss, will be entitled to be subrogated to the remedy
of the insured therefor against the master and ship-owners;
and if the insured destroys this remedy after his recovery of
judgment against the insurers, equity will relieve the latter
*pro tanto* from this judgment.[6] And as the master or ship-

---

[1] Monticello v. Mollison, 17 Howard, 152.

[2] Comegys v. Vasse, 1 Peters, 193.

[3] The Potomac, 105 U. S. 630;
The Planter, 2 Woods, C. C. 490.

[4] North of England Ins. Association v. Armstrong, L. R. 5 Q. B. 244.

[5] Yates v. Whyte, 4 Bing. New
Cas. 272, following Mason v. Sainsbury, 3 Doug. 61.

[6] Atlantic Ins. Co. v. Storrow, 5
Paige (N. Y.), 285. See Phœnix Ins.
Co. v. Parsons, 129 N. Y. 86.

owners would have no right to claim from the owners of the
goods contribution for such a loss, the policy cannot, upon
their satisfying the insured, be legally assigned for their
benefit so as to enable them to recover from the insurers.[1]
Insurers will, upon satisfying a judgment recovered against
them for the total loss of a vessel occasioned by the barratry
of its master, be subrogated to the benefit of a judgment
obtained by the insured against the master for the same loss,
although they have, while the action against the master was
pending, refused an offer of the insured to transfer the control of that action to them, upon condition that they should
pay the expenses already incurred therein, and that the
transfer should not prejudice any rights of the insured.[2]

§ 228. **Limitations of this Subrogation.** — This subrogation
of the insurers to the remedy against a wrong-doer who has
caused the loss which the insurers have satisfied is only to
the remedies and rights of action which were vested in the
insured, or which the insured have succeeded in obtaining
from the party at fault,[3] subject to all the liabilities and
duties which rested on the insured,[4] even in favor of third
parties;[5] it is not an independent right of action in the insurers themselves,[6] and will not be subject to any personal
estoppel existing against the insurers in their own right.[7]
The insurers succeed merely to the means of redress which
were possessed by the party whom they have indemnified
against the party whose wrongful act caused the loss.[8]  Accordingly, where two ships belonging to the same owner came

[1] Atlantic Ins. Co. v. Storrow,
5 Paige (N. Y.), 285.

[2] Mercantile Ins. Co. v. Clark, 118
Mass. 288.

[3] New England Ins. Co. v. Dun-
ham, 3 Clifford, C. C. 332; Alliance
Ins. Co. v. Louisiana Ins. Co., 8
La. 1.

[4] Wilson v. Raffalovich, 7 Q. B. D.
553; The Bristol, 29 Fed. Rep. 867.

[5] Rice v. Cobb, 9 Cush. (Mass.)
302.

[6] Alliance Ins. Co. v. Louisiana Ins.
Co., 8 La. 1.

[7] Williams v. Hays, 64 Hun (N. Y.),
202.

[8] Magdeburg Ins. Co. v. Paulson,
29 Fed. Rep. 530; The Sam Brown,
Id. 650, which was a case of collision.

into collision, and one of them sank and became a total loss, the insurers of the latter ship did not, upon their payment of a total loss, become entitled to make any claim for the loss against the insured as the owner of the ship at fault in the collision; for their right existed only through the owner of the ship insured, and not independently of him; and as he could not have sued himself, they would have no remedy against him.[1] And the insurers' right of subrogation may be lost by their laches in failing seasonably to enforce it before the rights of others have accrued.[2] Nor will it be extended to cover a mere gift or gratuity subsequently received by the insured of what could not have been demanded as a right.[3]

§ 224. **Does not arise upon a Compromise of the Insurer's Liability.** — If the insurers do not accept an abandonment of the insured property, or pay a total loss, but make a compromise of the claim upon them, they will not be subrogated to the rights of action of the insured for the wrongful act which caused the loss, or entitled to the compensation that may afterwards be realized therefor.[4] Thus, where a cargo of merchandise which was insured was seized and condemned by the French government under the Berlin and Milan decrees, and a compromise was afterwards made between the underwriters and the insured, whereby the latter accepted from the former one-third of their claim under the policy, and surrendered the policy, but did not cede or assign to the underwriters their claim to indemnity from the French government, it was held, on the underwriters subsequently receiving the amount of their payment as an indemnity from the French government, that they received this money in trust for the insured, could not hold it by subrogation, and

---

[1] Simpson v. Thomson, 3 App. Cas. 279; Globe Ins. Co. v. Sherlock, 25 Ohio St. 50. .

[2] Mercantile Ins. Co. v. Corcoran, 1 Gray (Mass.), 76.

[3] Burnand v. Rodocanachi, 7 App. Cas. 333.

[4] Brooks v. McDonnell, 1 Yo. & Co. Ex. 500; New York Ins. Co. v. Roulet, 24 Wend. (N. Y.) 505.

must pay it over to them.[1] And if, under such circumstances, the insured should, after their compromise with the underwriters, receive full compensation for their loss from the parties at fault therefor, the underwriters would not be entitled to any part of this compensation.[2]

§ 225. **Effect of an Abandonment.** — After an abandonment, if it is a legal one, or if it is accepted, the insurers stand in the place of the insured, and the former agents of the insured become the agents of the insurers.[3] The master of the ship becomes the agent or servant of the insurers, and is answerable to them for his neglect or misconduct.[4] The consignee of goods insured becomes by the abandonment the agent of the insurers; and his acts done in good faith are at their risk and for their benefit.[5] An agent appointed by the insured after a capture to prosecute his claim becomes, after an abandonment, the agent of the insurers; and such agent's receipts of the proceeds of a sale of the captured property will be deemed to be a receipt thereof by the insurers, who must look to the agent for the amount, and pay to the insured the full amount of the loss, without any deduction therefor.[6] The wages of the crew, after an abandonment, will be chargeable to the insurers, not as insurers, but as owners of the

[1] New York Ins. Co. v. Roulet, 24 Wend. (N. Y.) 505.

[2] Brooks v. McDonnell, 1 Yo. & Co. Ex. 500.

[3] Chesapeake Ins. Co. v. Stark, 6 Cranch, 268; Hurtin v. Phœnix Ins. Co., 1 Wash. C. C. 400; Mutual Ins. Co. v. Cargo, Olcott, Adm. 89; Peirce v. Ocean Ins. Co., 18 Pick. (Mass.) 83; Badger v. Ocean Ins. Co., 23 Pick. (Mass.) 347; Gardiner v. Smith, 1 Johns. Cas. (N. Y.) 141; Curcier v. Phila. Ins. Co., 5 Serg. & R. (Penn.) 113; Cincinnati Ins. Co. v. Duffield, 6 Ohio St. 200; Norton v. Lexington Ins. Co., 16 Ills. 235; Gould v. Citizens' Ins. Co., 13 Mo. 534; Phillips v. St. Louis Ins. Co., 11 La. Ann. 459; Graham v. Ledda, 17 La. Ann. 45; Heilner v. China Ins. Co., 18 N.Y. Supt. 177.

[4] The Sarah Ann, 2 Sumner, 206; Mowry v. Charleston Ins. Co., 6 Rich. Law (So. Car.), 146; Jumel v. Marine Ins. Co., 7 Johns. (N. Y.) 412; Gardere v. Columbian Ins. Co., 7 Johns. (N. Y.) 514.

[5] Gardiner v. Smith, 1 Johns. Cas. (N. Y.) 141; Schmidt v. United Ins. Co., 1 Johns. (N. Y.) 249.

[6] Miller v. De Peyster, 2 Caines (N. Y.), 301.

ship.[1] Any purchase made by the insured or his agents of
the abandoned property which has been paid for by the insurers will be taken to have been made for the benefit of the
insurers.[2] And the insurers, as owners of the ship, will be
entitled to its earnings, if any are made after the abandonment.[3] But since the earnings of the ship up to the time of
the abandonment belong to the insured as its owner,[4] if the
owner of ship and goods rightfully abandons both to the
underwriters as for a total loss by perils insured against,
and part of the goods are saved, the insurers as owners of the
goods will be liable to the insured as owners of the ship for
freight *pro rata itineris* until the abandonment.[5] The freight
earned before and after the abandonment will be apportioned, so as to give to each party, the insured and the insurers, the earnings of the ship during the respective periods
of their ownership thereof.[6]

§ 226. **Abandonment of Ship and Freight separately insured.**
— If the owner of a ship has effected separate insurances
upon ship and freight, and afterwards rightfully abandons
both to the underwriters upon them respectively, the doctrine
generally adopted in this country is that he is entitled to
recover for a total loss of both,[7] and that the freight earned
prior to the loss goes to the ship-owner, or to his representatives, the insurers of the freight, to whom it has been
abandoned, while the freight, if any, earned subsequently to
the loss which has caused the abandonment goes to the insurers of the ship, who have by the abandonment become its

---

[1] McBride v. Marine Ins. Co., 7
Johns. (N. Y.) 431; Frothingham v.
Prince, 3 Mass. 563.

[2] United Ins. Co. v. Robinson,
2 Caines (N. Y.), 280.

[3] McBride v. Marine Ins. Co., 7
Johns. (N. Y.) 431; Stewart v. Greenock Ins. Co., 2 Ho. Lds. 159; Miller
v. Woodfall, 8 El. & Bl. 493.

[4] Miller v. Woodfall, 8 El. & Bl.
493.

[5] Teasdale v. Charleston Ins. Co.,
2 Brev. (So. Car.) 190.

[6] Kennedy v. Baltimore Ins. Co., 3
Harris & J. (Md.) 367.

[7] Coolidge v. Gloucester Ins. Co.,
15 Mass. 341.

owners.[1] The abandonment of the vessel to the insurers thereof will not preclude the insured from recovering upon the policy on the freight.[2] Accordingly, if a ship-owner, having insured the ship and the freight separately with two sets of insurers, upon a capture of the ship abandons the ship to the insurers of the ship, and the freight to the insurers of the freight, and then takes from the insurers of the ship half of his claim in cash, and for the other half an assignment of their interest in the ship, he will be entitled to the freight which would otherwise have been theirs, and may recover from the insurers of the freight to the full amount of their policy, deducting only the *pro rata* freight which had been earned before the abandonment.[3]

§ 227. **English Doctrine.** — In England, as in the United States, freight earned subsequently to the loss by reason of which the abandonment is made goes to the insurers as owners of the ship.[4] If, after the disaster and abandonment, the cargo is transshipped and carried by another vessel to the port of destination, and the freight is thus earned, this will not be for the benefit of the insurers of the ship,[5] nor will they be entitled to damages for the loss of this freight from a wrong-doer who has caused such loss.[6] But if, after the loss which is the cause of the abandonment, the original ship proceeds on her voyage, and earns the pending freight, both the vessel and the freight being separately insured, the title to the whole freight is vested by the abandonment in the insurers of the ship;[7] and, the freight having been earned in accordance with the true interpretation of the

[1] Marine Ins. Co. v. United Ins. Co., 9 Johns. (N. Y.) 186; Davy v. Hallett, 3 Caines (N. Y.), 16; Hammond v. Essex Ins. Co., 4 Mason, C. C. 196.

[2] Livingston v. Columbian Ins. Co., 3 Johns. (N. Y.) 49.

[3] Davy v. Hallett, 3 Caines (N. Y.), 16.

[4] Luke v. Lyde, 2 Burr. 882.

[5] Hickie v. Rodocanachi, 4 Hurlst. & Nor. 455.

[6] Sea Ins. Co. v. Hadden, 13 Q. B. D. 706.

[7] Stewart v. Greenock Ins. Co., 2 Ho. Lds. 159; Davidson v. Case, 8 Price, Exch. 542; s. c., 5 J. B. Moore, 116; s. c., in Exch. Chamber, 2 Brod. & B. 379.

policy upon the freight, and having been prevented from coming to the insured only by reason of his voluntary abandonment of the ship, the insured cannot recover anything in an action upon the latter policy.[1] The abandonment produces the same results upon the title to the freight as would follow from any other transfer of the ship.[2]

§ 228. **Subrogation of Insurers on Freight against the Insured.** — If, however, the rights of the insurers of the freight are not complicated by the effect of an abandonment of the ship to the insurers thereof, their right of subrogation, upon the abandonment to them of the insured subject, will, as against the insured, be the same as that of other marine insurers.[3] And however the question of priority of title as to the freight-money might be held as between the two sets of insurers, and however the weight of argument might be taken to preponderate in favor of the underwriters upon the ship over those upon the freight, yet the title of the latter is superior to that of the insured claiming in his own right.[4]

§ 229. **Subrogation against a Carrier of Insured Goods.** — As between a carrier and an insurer of the same goods, the primary responsibility for their loss or destruction is upon the carrier, and the liability of the insurer is merely secondary,[5] the owner and the insurer being considered as but one person, and having together the beneficial right to the indemnity due from the carrier for his breach of contract or non-per-

---

[1] Scottish Ins. Co. v. Turner, 4 Ho. Lds. 312; Benson v. Chapman, 8 C. B. 950; McCarthy v. Abel, 5 East, 388.

[2] Sea Ins. Co. v. Hadden, 13 Q. B. D. 706; Morrison v. Parsons, 2 Taunt. 407; Splidt v. Bowles, 10 East, 279; Chinnery v. Blackburne, 1 H. Blackst. 117, *note*.

[3] Dufourcet v. Bishop, 18 Q. B. D. 373; The Thyatira, 8 Prob. D. 155; Barclay v. Stirling, 5 Mau. & S. 6.

[4] Thompson v. Rowcroft, 4 East, 34; Puller v. Staniforth, 11 East, 232; Leatham v. Terry, 3 Bos. & P. 479.

[5] Bradburn v. Great Western Ry. Co., L. R. 10 Exch. 1; Liverpool and Great Western Steam Co. v. Phœnix Ins. Co., 129 U. S. 397; Garrison v. Memphis Ins. Co., 19 Howard, 312; North American Ins. Co., v. St. Louis Ry. Co., 9 Fed. Rep. 811; Mead v. Mercantile Ins. Co., 67 Barb. (N. Y.) 519; Kentucky Ins. Co. v. Western R. R. Co., 8 Baxter (Tenn.), 268.

formance of duty.[1]  Nor can the carrier raise the question
whether the insurers were bound under the policy to indemnify the insured for the loss sustained.[2]  If the insured, by
his act and contrary to the terms of the policy, defeats this
right of the insurers to be subrogated, the insurers' liability
will be terminated.[3]  "Standing, as the insurer does, practically in the position of a surety, stipulating that the goods
shall not be destroyed or injured in consequence of the perils
insured against, whenever he has indemnified the owner for
the loss he is entitled to all the means of indemnity which
the satisfied owner held against the party primarily liable.[4]
It is the doctrine of subrogation, dependent not at all upon
privity of contract, but worked out through the right of the
creditor or owner.    Hence it has been often ruled that an
insurer who has paid a loss may use the name of the insured
in an action to obtain redress from the carrier whose failure
of duty caused the loss.[5]  It is conceded that this doctrine
prevails in cases of marine insurance; but it is denied that
it is applicable to cases of fire insurance upon land; and the
reason for the supposed difference is said to be that the insurer in a marine policy becomes the owner of the lost or
injured property by the abandonment of the insured, while
in land policies there can be no abandonment.    But it is a
mistake to suppose that the right of insurers in marine

[1] Mobile R. R. Co. v. Jurey, 111
U. S. 584; Hall v. Nashville & Chatt.
R. R. Co., 13 Wallace, 367; Gales v.
Hailman, 11 Penn. St. 515.

[2] The Amazon Ins. Co. v. The Iron
Mountain, 1 Flippin, C. C. 616; Sun
Ins. Co. v. Mississippi Valley Co.,
17 Fed. Rep. 919; Pearse v. Quebec
Steamship Co., 24 Fed. Rep. 285.

[3] Carstairs v. Mechanics Ins. Co.,
18 Fed. Rep. 473; Fayerweather v.
Phœnix Ins. Co., 118 N. Y. 324; Ins.
Co. of North America v. Easton, 73
Tex. 167.

[4] Sun Ins. Co. v. Kountz Line,
122 U. S. 583; Hibernia Ins. Co. v.
St. Louis Transportation Co., 10 Fed.
Rep. 596; Lancaster Mills v. Merchants' Cotton-Press Co., 89 Tenn.
6; Railway Co. v. Manchester Mills,
88 Tenn. 653.

[5] This has been denied in one case,
and it is believed in only one; and in
that case no authority was cited for the
conclusion adopted, and two judges
dissented: Carroll v. New Orleans
R. R. Co., 26 La. Ann. 447.

policies to proceed against a carrier of goods after they have paid a total loss grows wholly or even principally out of any abandonment. There can be no abandonment where there has been total destruction; there is nothing upon which it can operate; and an insured party may recover for a total loss without it. It is laid down in Phillips on Insurance [1] that the payment of a loss, whether partial or total, gives the insurers an equitable title to what may afterwards be recovered from other parties on account of the loss, and that the effect of a payment of a loss is equivalent in this respect to that of an abandonment.[2] There is then no reason for the subrogation of insurers by marine policies to the rights of action of the insured against a carrier by sea which does not exist in support of a like subrogation in cases of insurance against fire upon land. Nor do the authorities make any distinction between the cases."[3] A marine insurer in such a case may in admiralty bring a libel against the carrier in his own name,[4] but at law the remedy of fire insurers against the carrier must be pursued in the name of the insured,[5] and is subject to all defences which might be made against the insured;[6] and the carrier may destroy the insurer's right by stipulating with the owner of the goods for the benefit of any insurance to be obtained by the owner against loss or damage to the goods for which the carrier would be liable.[7]

[1] Section 1723.

[2] Mobile R. R. Co. v. Jurey, 111 U. S. 584; The Sydney, 27 Fed. Rep. 119; Pearse v. Quebec Steamship Co., 24 Fed. Rep. 285; The Frank G. Fowler, 8 Id. 360.

[3] Strong, J., in Hall v. Nashville, & Chatt. R. R. Co., 13 Wallace, 367.

[4] Amazon Ins. Co. v. The Iron Mountain, 1 Flippin, C. C. 616; The Liberty, 7 Fed. Rep. 226.

[5] Hall v. Nashville & Chatt. R. R. Co., supra; Brighthope Railw. Co. v. Rogers, 76 Va. 443; Mercantile Ins.

Co. v. Calebs, 20 N. Y. 173; Gales v. Hailman, 11 Penn. St. 515; Georgia Ins. Co. v. Dawson, 2 Gill (Md.), 365.

[6] Hibernia Ins. Co. v. St. Louis Transportation Co., 120 U. S. 166, and 17 Fed. Rep. 478; The Frederick E. Ives, 25 Fed. Rep. 447; The B. B. Saunders, Id. 727; Germania Ins. Co. v. Memphis R. R. Co., 72 N. Y. 90.

[7] Inman v. So. Car. Ry. Co., 129 U. S. 128; Phœnix Ins. Co. v. Erie Transportation Co., 117 U. S. 312, affirming s. c., 10 Biss. 18; The Sydney, 27 Fed. Rep. 119; Rintoul v.

But the provision in a bill of lading that no damage that can be insured against will be paid for is not such a stipulation, and will not affect the rights of the insurer,[1] which are not to be taken away by implication.[2] Nor will the insurers be subrogated to any right of action which the insured may have against a third party for a breach of the latter's agreement to carry insurance on the property.[3]

§ 230. **Insurer against Fire subrogated to Remedy against Railroad.** — The insurers against fire of property which has been destroyed by fire communicated from a locomotive engine will, upon payment for the loss, be subrogated, to the extent of their payment, to the remedies of the insured, as the owners of the property insured and destroyed, against the railroad company for the loss.[4] But this remedy must also, like that against a carrier, be prosecuted at law in the name of the insured, since the right of action was already vested in the latter before the payment by the insurers,[5] except under those reformed codes of procedure which permit any action to be brought in the name of the real party in interest.[6] But since the insurers take by subrogation only the rights of the insured, and the action for a single tort is

N. Y. Central R. R. Co., 20 *Id.* 313 and 17 *Id.* 905; Jackson Co. *v.* Boylston Ins. Co., 139 Mass. 508; Platt *v.* Richmond R. Co., 108 N. Y. 358; Mercantile Ins. Co. *v.* Calebs, 20 N. Y. 173; Gulf, Colorado, & Santa Fe Ry. Co. *v.* Zimmerman, 81 Tex. 605; British Ins. Co. *v.* Gulf, &c. Co., 63 Tex. 475.

[1] The Hadji, 22 Blatchf. C. C. 235; s. c., 20 Fed. Rep. 875; 16 *Id.* 861.

[2] Phœnix Ins. Co. *v.* Liverpool Steamship Co., 22 Blatchf. C. C. 372; The Montana, 22 Fed. Rep. 715, and 17 *Id.* 377.

[3] Deming *v.* Merchants' Cotton-Press Co., 90 Tenn. 309.

[4] Hart *v.* Western R. R. Co., 13 Met. (Mass.) 99; Conn. Ins. Co. *v.* Erie Railw. Co., 73 N. Y. 399; Monmouth Ins. Co. *v.* Hutchinson, 21 N. J. Eq. 107.

[5] Swarthout *v.* Chicago R. R. Co., 49 Wisc. 625; Holcombe *v.* Richmond & Danville R. R. Co., 78 Ga. 776; Peoria Ins. Co. *v.* Frost, 37 Ills. 333; Hart *v.* Western R. R. Co., 13 Met. (Mass.) 99; Ætna Ins. Co. *v.* Hannibal & St. Joseph R. R. Co., 3 Dillon, C. C. 1.

[6] Conn. Ins. Co. *v.* Erie Railw. Co., 73 N. Y. 399; Hustisford Ins. Co. *v.* Chicago Railw. Co., 66 Wisc. 58; Swarthout *v.* Chicago & N. W. R. R. Co., 49 Wisc. 625; Railw. Co. *v.* Fire Association, 55 Ark. 164.

indivisible, a judgment against a railroad company for the destruction of one building by fire communicated from its locomotive engine will bar another action in the name of the same plaintiff against the same defendant for the destruction of another building by fire communicated from the first building, although the second action is really brought and prosecuted for the benefit of an insurance company which has, upon one of its policies, paid the plaintiff for the loss of the second building.[1] A release given by the nominal plaintiff pending the action will not be a bar to its further prosecution against the railroad company for the benefit of the insurance company.[2] Insurers of a building which has been destroyed by fire through the fault of a railroad company may restrain the insured from collecting or settling their claim against the railroad company without subrogation of the insurers.[3] If, before the payment by the insurance company of the amount due upon its policy, the owner of the property has received from the railroad company the amount of the loss above the insurance, and has given to the railroad company a discharge of its liability containing the statement that it was not intended thereby to release the insurance company from its liability to him, this will be treated as a limitation of the discharge to the amount of the loss over the insurance, retaining the claim upon the insurance company, and reserving its remedy over, and so not barring the insurance company's right of subrogation against the railroad company.[4]

§ 231. **Mode of enforcing this Right.** — This subject was fully discussed in New Jersey; and it was determined that where an insurance company pays the insured for a loss by fire occasioned by the fault of a railroad company, and the insured afterwards receives from the railroad company the

[1] Trask v. Hartford & N. H. R. R. Co., 2 Allen (Mass.), 331.

[2] Hart v. Western R. R. Co., 13 Met. (Mass.) 99; Monmouth Ins. Co. v. Hutchinson, 21 N. J. Eq. 107.

[3] Hartford Ins. Co. v. Pennell, 2 Ills. App. 609.

[4] Conn. Ins. Co. v. Erie Railw. Co., 73 N. Y. 399; reversing s. c., 10 Hun (N. Y.), 59.

amount in satisfaction of his damages, he holds this in trust
for the insurers, and they may recover it from him by a suit
in equity; and if the railroad company has not paid the insured his damages, or has paid them knowing that the insured
has already received his payment from the insurance company,
the latter may maintain a suit at law against the railroad
company in the name of the insured, even against his consent, to compel repayment of the damages to the amount of
their payment; and a release given by the insured to the
railroad company would be no defence to this suit. But
these two remedies cannot be pursued on a single bill in
equity; neither the insured nor the railroad company is a
necessary party to the suit against the other; they are not
jointly liable, and no judgment could be rendered or decree
made against both. The insurers may, however, before be-
ginning their suit against the railroad company, bring a bill
in equity to have a release given by the insured to the railroad company, when the latter knew of the payment by the
insurers, declared void as a fraud upon their rights; and to
this bill both the insured and the railroad company would be
proper parties.[1]

§ 232. **Subrogation against other Parties liable for a Loss by
Fire.** — In like manner the insurers of a building, which has
been burned in such a manner as to create a liability therefor
in a muncipality or in other parties at fault, cannot, upon
their payment of a loss, maintain in their own names an action therefor against the parties ultimately responsible for
the loss,[2] but may do so in the names of the insured owners
of the property, whom they have indemnified.[3] The insurer
takes by substitution all the rights and remedies of the insured;[4] and under some of the reformed codes of procedure,

[1] Monmouth Ins. Co. v. Hutchinson, 21 N. J. Eq. 107.
[2] London Ass. Co. v. Sainbury, 3
Doug. 245; Rockingham Ins. Co. v.
Bosher, 39 Maine, 253.

[3] Mason v. Sainsbury, 3 Doug. 61.
[4] Burnand v. Rodocanachi, 7 App.
Cas. 333, 339; Castellain v. Preston,
11 Q. B. D. 380, reversing s. c., 8 Id.
613; Niagara Ins. Co. v. Fidelity Ins.

though not at common law, may after full payment maintain
action thereon in their own names.[1]  The payment by the
insurers will be no defence in an action brought by the owner
of the property against the party who is answerable for the
loss, either in bar of the action or in mitigation of damages.[2]
The insurers' payment gives them by subrogation an equitable interest in the claim against the wrong-doer.[3]  But this
subrogation of the insurers is strictly limited to the existing
rights of the insured,[4] and is subject to the right of the owner
to be fully compensated for the loss of his property;[5] if he
has obtained a partial indemnity from a municipality whose
liability is less extensive than that of the insurers, this will
be a defence only *pro tanto* to the insurers; they will still be
liable to him within the limits of their policy for the amount
of his loss, deducting therefrom the net proceeds of his recovery against the municipality.[6]  And if the insured owner of
the property, after receiving payment of the insurance, is fully
indemnified for his loss by the wrong-doer or from the latter's
means, he must then account to the insurers for what they
had previously paid him;[7] the insurers' liability is merely
a secondary one.[8]  On the same principle, where a building which was insured against fire, but not to its full value,

Co., 123 Penn. St. 516; Home Ins.
Co. *v.* Oregon Ry. & Nav. Co., 20
Oreg. 569.

[1] Marine Ins. Co. *v.* St. Louis Ry.
Co., 41 Fed. Rep. 643.

[2] Clark *v.* Blything, 2 Barn. &
Cress. 254; Perrott *v.* Shearer, 17
Mich. 48; Cunningham *v.* Evansville
R. R. Co., 102 Ind. 478; Weber *v.*
Morris & Essex R. R. Co., 35 N. J.
Law, 409; Hayward *v.* Cain, 105
Mass. 213; Harding *v.* Townshend, 43
Vt. 536.

[3] Castellain *v.* Preston, 11 Q. B. D.
380; Chicago, St. Louis & N. O. R.
Co. *v.* Pullman Car Co., 139 U. S.
79; Pratt *v.* Radford, 52 Wisc. 114.

[4] St. Louis & Iron Mountain R.
Co. *v.* Commercial Union Ins. Co.,
139 U. S. 223.

[5] Home Ins. Co. *v.* Oregon Ry. &
Nav. Co., 20 Oreg. 569; People's
Ins. Co. *v.* Straehle, 2 Cincinnati Sup.
Ct. 186; Newcomb *v.* Cincinnati Ins.
Co., 22 Ohio St. 382.

[6] Pentz *v.* Ætna Ins. Co., 9 Paige
(N. Y.), 568.

[7] Darrell *v.* Tibbetts, 5 Q. B. Div.
560.

[8] Friemandorf *v.* Watertown Ins.
Co., 9 Biss. C. C. 167; Hardman *v.*
Brett, 37 Fed. Rep. 803; Fidelity Ti-
tle Co. *v.* People's Gas Co., 150 Penn.
St. 8.

had been burned through the fault of a municipality, and the
owner had brought an action therefor against the municipality, and undertook to sue for the whole damage, as he may
do,[1] he was allowed to conduct the action without the interference of the insurers, though he would be liable to the insurers for anything that he might do in violation of his
equitable duty towards them.[2] So he could release the wrong-
doer from liability for any injuries not covered by the insurance.[3] By the civil law, as adopted in Canada, the subrogation of the insurers is more extensive than has been
already stated; and, though liable for and paying only a
part of the damage done, they may be subrogated *pro tanto*
to the remedy of the insured against the wrong-doer who has
caused the loss, and may thereupon maintain a suit in their
own names for the recovery of their payment from such
wrong-doer.[4]

§ 233. Subrogation of Mortgagee to Insurance procured by
Mortgagor. — A mortgagee as such has no claim to the benefit
of a policy of insurance procured upon the mortgaged property by and for the mortgagor;[5] and the same is the case
with the holder of a mechanic's lien.[6] But an agreement,
express or implied, on the part of the mortgagor, that he will
keep the mortgaged premises insured for the protection of the
mortgagee, will create an equitable lien upon the money due
for a loss,[7] though the policy was procured by the mortgagor

---

[1] Dillon v. Hunt, 105 Mo. 154.

[2] Commercial Ass. Co. v. Lister,
L. R. 9 Ch. 483.

[3] Insurance Co. of North America v.
Fidelity Title Co., 123 Penn. St. 523.

[4] Quebec Ass. Co. v. St. Louis, 7
Moore, P. C. 286, *Parke, B.*, citing
Alauzel on Assurance, p. 384, § 477;
Pardessus, *Cours de Droit Commerciel*,
595; Quinault, p. 248; Toullier, tit.
IV. § 175; Emerigon (English trans.,
1850), Ch. XII. § 14, pp. 329–336;
Pothier on Assurance, p. 248.

[5] Columbia Ins. Co. v. Lawrence,
10 Peters, 507; Nichols v. Baxter, 5
R. I. 491; Franklin Savings Institution v. Central Ins. Co., 119 Mass.
240; Wilson v. Hill, 3 Met. (Mass.)
66; McDonald v. Black, 20 Ohio, 185;
Nordyke & Marmon Co. v. Gery, 112
Ind. 535; Ryan v. Adamson, 57 Iowa,
30; Carter v. Rockett, 8 Paige (N.
Y.), 437.

[6] Rackley v. Scott, 61 N. H. 140.

[7] Reid v. McCrum, 91 N. Y. 412.

in his own name upon the mortgaged property,[1] and whether
the policy existed at the time of the mortgage or was afterwards taken out by the mortgagor,[2] although, by a clause in
the condition of the mortgage, the mortgagee was permitted,
upon the mortgagor's default, himself to take out a policy
for his protection at the expense of the mortgagor, adding
any premiums that he might pay to the mortgage-debt;[3] and
this equitable lien of the mortgagee will avail against both
the insurance company and an assignee of the policy, if they
were prior to the assignment notified of the rights of the
mortgagee.[4] And this lien in favor of the mortgagee upon
insurance procured by the mortgagor will be valid against
the latter's assignee in bankruptcy.[5] If in such a case a suit
at law to recover the loss under the policy is pending between
the legal owner of the policy and the insurance company,
equity will not enjoin the further prosecution of this suit,
but will, to avoid delay and expense and ascertain the rights
of the parties, allow the suit to proceed to judgment, enjoin-
ing, however, the company from making payment to the
plaintiff in that suit, and the plaintiff from receiving such
payment, and allowing the mortgagee to appear and prosecute
the suit, for the protection of his equitable lien upon the loss
contested in it.[6] If the mortgagor's covenant was to keep
the buildings insured, and in case of loss to apply the insurance-money to rebuilding, and after a loss the mortgagee has
sold the land under his mortgage for less than is due upon
the mortgage-debt, he will still be entitled to his equitable
lien upon the insurance-money for the balance due to him,

[1] Hazard v. Draper, 7 Allen (Mass.),
267 ; Doughter v. Van Horn, 29 N. J.
Eq. 90.

[2] Dunlop v. Avery, 89 N. Y. 592,
and 23 Hun (N. Y.), 509 ; Ames v.
Richardson, 29 Minn. 330.

[3] Wheeler v. Factors' Ins. Co., 101
U. S. 439.

[4] Nichols v. Baxter, 5 R. I. 491 ;
Thomas v. Vonkapff, 6 Gill & J. (Md.)
372 ; Vandegraaff v. Medlock, 3 Porter (Ala.), 389.

[5] Sands Ale Brewing Co. in re, 3
Biss. C. C. 175.

[6] Nichols v. Baxter, supra.

although he has, by his sale, made rebuilding by the mortgagor or his representatives impossible.[1]  But the mortgagee
cannot hold the insurers liable for the amount of a loss under
such a policy which they have paid to the mortgagor before
they had notice of the terms of the mortgage.[2]

§ 234. **Where a Creditor obtains Insurance upon Property
on which he has a Lien.** — Where a creditor effects insurance
upon property mortgaged or pledged to him to secure the
payment of his demand, the insurers do not become sureties
for the debt, nor do they acquire all the rights of such sureties.[3]  They are insurers of the particular property only; and
so long as the property remains liable for the debt, so long
its destruction by fire will be a loss to the creditor within the
terms of the policy.[4]  Accordingly, it has been held in Massachusetts that a mortgagee who has, at his own expense,
insured his interest in the mortgaged property against loss
by fire may, in case of such a loss before he has received payment of his demand, collect the amount of the loss from the
insurers for his own use, without first assigning the mortgage
or any interest therein to the insurers;[5] nor can the insurers,
upon offering to pay the loss and the additional amount due
upon the mortgage above the loss, require the mortgage to be
assigned to them, and thus be subrogated to the rights and
remedies of the insured under his mortgage.[6]  But this Mas-

[1] Thomas *v.* Vonkapff, 6 Gill & J.
(Md.) 372.

[2] Stearns *v.* Quincy Ins. Co., 124
Mass. 61.

[3] Cone *v.* Niagara Ins. Co., 60
N. Y. 619; Excelsior Ins. Co. *v.* Royal
Ins. Co., 55 N. Y. 343, 359; Hadley
*v.* N. H. Ins. Co., 55 N. H. 110. But
see Kip *v.* Mutual Ins. Co., 4 Edw.
Ch. (N. Y.) 86.

[4] *Bradley, J.*, in Insurance Co. *v.*
Stinson, 103 U. S. 25; International
Trust Co. *v.* Boardman, 149 Mass.

158; Cassa Marittima *v.* Phœnix Ins.
Co., 129 N. Y. 490.

[5] King *v.* State Ins. Co., 7 Cush.
(Mass.) 1, citing and considering
Columbia Ins. Co. *v.* Lawrence, 10
Peters, 507; Roberts *v.* Traders' Ins.
Co., 17 Wend. (N. Y.) 631; Ætna
Ins. Co. *v.* Tyler, 16 Wend. (N. Y.)
385; Carpenter *v.* Providence Ins.
Co., 16 Peters, 495.

[6] Suffolk Ins. Co. *v.* Boyden, 9
Allen (Mass.), 123; Provincial Ins.
Co. *v.* Reesor, 21 Grant Ch. (Up. Can.)
296; 33 Up. Can. Q. B. 357.

sachusetts rule has not been generally followed elsewhere.[1]
And in New Jersey the insurers will, in such a case, upon
their payment of the loss, be subrogated *pro tanto* to the
benefit of the mortgage or other security held by the insured,
and by paying to the insured the whole amount of the claim
for which the latter holds his securities, they will become
entitled to all such securities;[2] and if after effecting the insurance the insured has parted with any of his securities or
received partial payment of the debt for which they are held,
and which gives him his insurable interest, the liability of
the insurers will be proportionally diminished,[3] unless the
insurance was really intended for the benefit of the debtor.[4]

§ 235. **Rights of Mortgagor in Insurance obtained by Mortgagee.** — A mortgagor is not entitled to the benefit of insurance in the mortgaged property obtained by the mortgagee
in his own name, at his own expense, and without the privity
of the mortgagor, and in the event of a loss cannot require
the amount received by the mortgagee upon such insurance
to be applied in reduction of the mortgage-debt.[5] The interests of the mortgagee and of the mortgagor, though both
insurable, are separate and distinct from each other.[6] But
if the mortgagee has procured the insurance, though in his
own name, at the request and expense and for the benefit of

[1] Castellain v. Preston, 11 Q. B. D. 380, reversing s. c., 8 Q. B. D. 613, which followed the Massachusetts cases cited *supra*; Thomas v. Montauk Ins. Co., 43 Hun (N. Y.), 218; Pendleton v. Elliott, 67 Mich. 496; Baker v. Fireman's Ins. Co., 79 Calif. 34.

[2] Boundbrook Ins. Co. v. Nelson, 41 N. J. Eq. 485.

[3] Sussex Ins. Co. v. Woodruff, 26 N. J. Law (2 Dutch.), 541, criticised in Ins. Co. v. Stinson, 103 U. S. 25.

[4] Nelson v. Boundbrook Ins. Co., 43 N. J. Eq. 256, reversing for that reason s. c., 41 N. J. Eq. 485.

[5] Russell v. Southard, 12 Howard, 139; Honore v. Lamar Ins. Co., 51 Ills. 409; Stinchfield v. Milliken, 71 Maine, 567; Concord Ins. Co. v. Woodbury, 45 Maine, 447; Burlingame v. Goodspeed, 153 Mass. 24; White v. Brown, 2 Cush. (Mass.) 412; Cushing v. Thompson, 34 Maine, 496.

[6] Johnson v. North British Ins. Co., 1 Holmes, C. C. 117; Tuck v. Hartford Ins. Co., 56 N. H. 326; Wheeler v. Watertown Ins. Co., 131 Mass. 1; Carpenter v. Continental Ins. Co., 61 Mich. 635; Westchester Ins. Co. v. Foster, 90 Ills. 121; Niagara Ins. Co. v. Scammon, 28 No. E. Rep. 919.

the mortgagor, as well as for his own protection,[1] though this is by a parol agreement unknown to the insurers, the mortgagor will have the right, in case of a loss, to have the avails of the policy applied for his relief towards the discharge of his indebtedness.[2] So, if the owner of land, after executing an agreement for its sale, but before making a conveyance, insures the buildings standing upon the land, and not merely the purchase-money agreed to be paid to him, he may upon a loss recover the whole amount of the insurance, and will hold any surplus over the balance of the purchase-money due to him in trust for the vendee of the premises;[3] and the insurance company will have no right of subrogation to his claim upon the vendee for such purchase-money.[4] Where the owners of real estate holding insurance against the loss of the buildings by fire, assigned the policy to a mortgagee of the estate, and a loss having occurred, the assignee brought suit upon the policy in the name of the insured, and obtained judgment thereon, and then, instead of collecting this judgment, coerced the payment from the insured by a foreclosure of his mortgage, the insured was held to be entitled to the benefit of this judgment although, while the assignee held the policy, he had effected other insurance upon the property, without notice to the insurers.[5]

[1] Waring v. Loder, 53 N. Y. 581; Clinton v. Hope Ins. Co., 45 N. Y. 454, 467; De Wolf v. Capital City Ins. Co., 16 Hun (N. Y.), 116.

[2] Holbrook v. Am. Ins. Co., 1 Curtis, C. C. 193; Phœnix Ins. Co. v. Chadbourne, 31 Fed. Rep. 300; Hay v. Star Ins. Co., 77 N. Y. 235; Kernochan v. N. Y. Ins. Co., 17 N.Y. 428 (affirming s. c. 5 Duer (N. Y.), 1); Phœnix Ins. Co. v. Parsons, 56 N. Y. Super. Ct. 423; Grosvenor v. Atlantic Ins. Co., 17 N. Y. 391; Norwich Ins. Co. v. Boomer, 52 Ills. 442; Concord Ins. Co. v. Woodbury, 45 Maine, 447; Honore v. Lamar Ins. Co., 51 Ills. 409; Ætna Ins. Co. v. Baker, 71 Ind. 102; Klein v. Union Ins. Co., 3 Ontario, 234; Richardson v. Home Ins. Co., 21 Upper Canada (C. P.), 291; Hazard v. Canada Ins. Co., 39 Upper Canada (Q. B.), 419. See Morrison v. Tenn. Ins. Co., 18 Mo. 262.

[3] Reed v. Lukens, 44 Penn. St. 200.

[4] Ins. Co. v. Updegraff, 21 Penn. St. 513.

[5] Roberts v. Traders' Ins. Co., 17 Wend. (N. Y.) 631.

§ 286. **Insurance obtained by Mortgagor for Benefit of the Mortgagee.** — If the owner of an equity of redemption has procured insurance upon the buildings standing on the mortgaged premises, payable in case of loss to the mortgagee, as additional security to the latter, it is the right of the former to have the proceeds of the policy, in case of a loss, applied to the payment of the mortgage-debt;[1] nor will this right be affected by the fact that the policy contains a stipulation that no conveyance of the property shall affect the right of the mortgagee to recover for a loss; but if, after the issuing of such a policy, the equity of redemption is sold and conveyed, and a loss then occurs, and the insurance company, upon paying the amount of this loss to the mortgagee, takes from him an assignment of the mortgage and of the policy, the purchaser of the equity of redemption may redeem from the mortgage by paying to the insurance company as assignee of the mortgage the amount remaining due upon the mortgage-debt after deducting therefrom the payment received by the mortgagee from the company.[2] An action at law upon a policy insuring the mortgagor, but made payable in case of loss to the mortgagee, and remaining in force for the protection of both, may be maintained in the name of either of them,[3] though it has been intimated that the consent of the mortgagee is necessary to the maintenance of an action upon such a policy by the mortgagor in his own name.[4] So long

[1] Conn. Ins. Co. v. Scammon, 117 U. S. 634; Pearman v. Gould, 42 N. J. Eq. 4.

[2] Graves v. Hampden Ins. Co., 10 Allen (Mass.), 281.

[3] Marten v. Franklin Ins. Co., 38 N. J. Law (9 Vroom), 140; State Ins. Co. v. Maackens, 38 N. J. Law, 564. See Meriden Bank v. Stone Ins. Co., 50 Conn. 396; Kane v. Hibernia Ins. Co., 38 N. J. Law, 441; Hopkins Mfg. Co. v. Aurora Ins. Co., 48 Mich. 148; St. Paul Ins. Co. v.

Johnson, 77 Ills. 598; Travellers' Ins. Co. v. California Ins. Co., 1 Nor. Dak. 151; North British Ins. Co. v. Felrath, 77 Ala. 194; Winne v. Niagara Ins. Co., 91 N. Y. 185; Ennis v. Harmony Ins. Co., 3 Bosw. (N. Y.) 516; Flynn v. North Amer. Ins. Co., 115 Mass. 449.

[4] Patterson v. Triumph Ins. Co., 64 Maine, 500; Coates v. Pennsylvania Ins. Co., 58 Md. 172; Graves v. American Live Stock Ins. Co., 46 Minn. 130; Jackson v. Farmers' Ins.

23

as the mortgagee is unsatisfied, he has the right to keep the
control of such an action, and to receive the avails thereof.[1]

§ 237. **Where the Policy stipulates for the Subrogation of the
Insurers.** — A policy of insurance taken out by the mortgagor
or the owner of the equity of redemption, and made payable
in case of loss to the mortgagee, which, besides a stipulation
that a forfeiture as to the mortgagor shall not affect the right
of the mortgagee to recover for a loss, contains also the provision that, in case of the payment to the mortgagee of a loss
for which the insurers would not be liable to the mortgagor,
the insurers shall be subrogated to the rights of the mortgagee and entitled to an assignment of the mortgage, is not
available to the mortgagor, after a forfeiture of his right
under the policy;[2] and, upon the payment of such a loss by
the insurers to the mortgagee, they may take an assignment
of the mortgage, and collect from the mortgagor the whole
amount of the debt secured thereby.[3] If the mortgagee has
destroyed the insurers' right of subrogation to the mortgage,
he can no longer hold the insurers liable upon the policy.[4]
The same rule will be applied to a policy of insurance procured by a mortgagor and made payable in case of loss to a
mortgagee, which has become forfeited by its terms, but
which has been kept alive as to the mortgagee by an agree-

Co., 5 Gray (Mass.), 52; Turner v.
Quincy Ins. Co., 109 Mass. 568. But
see Friemansdorf v. Watertown Ins.
Co., 9 Biss. C. C. 167; Chrisman v.
State Ins. Co., 16 Oreg. 283.

[1] Ripley v. Astor Ins. Co., 17 How.
Pr. (N. Y.) 444; Cone v. Niagara Ins.
Co. 60 N. Y. 619; Frink v. Hamp-
den Ins. Co., 45 Barb. N. Y. 384;
Hammel v. Queen Ins. Co., 50 Wisc.
240; Hartford Ins. Co. v. Olcott, 97
Ills. 439; Hadley v. N. H. Ins. Co.,
55 N. H. 110; Chamberlain v. N. H.
Ins. Co., 55 N. H. 249; Motley v.
Manufacturers' Ins. Co, 29 Maine,
337; Brown v. Roger Williams Ins.

Co., 5 R. I. 394; National Ins. Co. v.
Crane, 16 Md. 260; Richelieu Nav.
Co. v. Thames Ins. Co., 58 Mich. 132;
Price v. Phœnix Ins. Co., 17 Minn.
497; *Fletcher, J.*, in Barrett v. Union
Ins. Co., 7 Cush. (Mass.) 175, 181;
cited approvingly in Phillips v. Mer-
rimack Ins. Co., 10 Cush. (Mass.) 353.

[2] Phœnix Ins. Co. v. Floyd, 19 Hun
(N. Y.), 287.

[3] Allen v. Watertown Ins. Co., 132
Mass. 480; Ulster Ins. Co. v. Leake,
73 N. Y. 161; Springfield Ins. Co. v.
Allen, 43 N. Y. 389.

[4] Lett v. Guardian Ins. Co., 52
Hun, 570.

ment between him and the insurers that his interest shall be
absolutely insured, and that the insurers may be subrogated
to his rights upon their payment to him of a loss, if the
policy become avoided as to the mortgagor.[1] This stipulation for the benefit of the mortgagee, though contained in a
policy issued to the mortgagor, is an independent agreement
between the insurers and the mortgagee, which is binding
upon them,[2] but with which the mortgagor has no concern.[3]
And if the mortgagee has himself insured his interest as such
by a policy providing that upon the payment to him of a loss
he shall assign his mortgage to the insurers, they will, upon
paying to him the amount of a loss and taking an assignment
of his mortgage, be entitled to all his original rights under
the mortgage for the whole of the debt secured thereby.[4] But
the mortgagee's debt must be paid in full before the insurers
can compel him to make over to them any share or proportion in the mortgage or the mortgage-debt.[5]

§ 238. **Between Lessor and Lessee or Vendor and Purchaser.**
— If the lessee of buildings has by the terms of his lease the
option to purchase them, and they are insured for the benefit
of the lessor, the lessee cannot, after the buildings have been
burned, and the lessor has received the amount of his insurance, require, by then exercising his option to purchase, the
insurance-money to be applied towards the satisfaction of his
purchase-money and the arrears of his rent.[6] But if the insurance was procured by the lessee in accordance with his
agreement, and for his benefit after exercising his option to

[1] Ulster Savings Institution v.
Leake, 73 N. Y. 161. See Foster v.
Equitable Ins. Co., 2 Gray (Mass.),
216.

[2] Dick v. Franklin Ins. Co., 81 Mo.
103, affirming s. c., 10 Mo. Ap. 376.

[3] Phœnix Ins. Co. v. Floyd, 83 N.Y.
613, affirming s. c., 19 Hun (N. Y.),
237. See Graham v. Firemen's Ins.
Co., 8 Daly (N. Y.), 421.

[4] Foster v. Van Reed, 70 N. Y. 19;
Thornton v. Enterprise Ins. Co., 71
Penn. St. 234; Dick v. Franklin Ins.
Co., 10 Mo. Ap. 376; affirmed in 81
Mo.103. See Traders Ins. Co. v. Race,
31 No. E. Rep. 392.

[5] Phœnix Ins. Co. v. First National Bank, 85 Va. 765.

[6] Gilbert v. Port, 28 Ohio St. 276.
See Poole v. Adams, 12 W. R. 683.

purchase, he will, upon the exercise of this option after the occurrence of a loss, be entitled to the benefit of such insurance.[1] In one case, it appeared that a lessee had by the terms of his lease the option of purchasing the leased premises for a stipulated price by giving certain notice of his intention to do so. The lessor covenanted to insure, and did insure. The buildings were burned down; and the lessor received the insurance-money. The lessee then gave seasonable notice of his intention to purchase, and claimed the benefit of the insurance-money as part payment of the stipulated price; but, the lease containing no provision as to the disposition of the insurance-money, it was held that the lessee was not entitled to it.[2] If in such a case the purchase is completed after the insurers have paid to the vendor the amount of the loss, and the vendor receives from the purchaser the full amount of the agreed price without any abatement for the loss of the buildings destroyed, the insurers may by subrogation claim from the insured vendor the full benefit of the salvage that he has thus received from the purchaser, and so recover back from him the amount of the loss which they have previously paid him.[3] The tenant has no interest in insurance procured for the benefit of the landlord,[4] just as the landlord has no equitable claim upon the tenant's insurance of his own interest,[5] and just as vendor and vendee have respectively no equitable claim upon insurance procured by either upon his own interest,[6] unless by agreement be-

---

[1] Reynard v. Arnold, L. R. 10 Ch. 386.

[2] Edwards v. West, 7 Ch. Div. 858, criticising Lawes v. Bennett, 1 Cox, 167, and explaining Reynard v. Arnold, supra.

[3] Castellain v. Preston, 11 Q. B. D. 380, reversing s. c., 8 Q. B. D. 613, and distinguishing Burnand v. Rodocanachi, 7 App. Cas. 333, on the ground that the payment there made by the U. S. Government was not salvage, not demandable of right, but a mere gift, and so not the subject of subrogation.

[4] Darrell v. Tibbetts, 5 Q. B. Div. 560; Leeds v. Cheetham, 1 Sim. 146; Miltenberger v. Beacom, 9 Penn. St. 198; Tongue v. Nutwell, 31 Md. 302; Ely v. Ely, 80 Ills. 532.

[5] Merchants' Ins. Co. v. Mazange, 22 Ala. 168; Ely v. Ely, 80 Ills. 532.

[6] King v. Preston, 11 La. Ann. 95; Hammer v. Johnson, 44 Ills. 192; Wood v. Northwestern Ins. Co., 46

tween them;[1] such as a provision that any money received upon the policy shall be applied to repair the injury.[2]

§ 239. **Subrogation of Life Insurers.** — The doctrine of subrogation of the insurer has no application to an ordinary contract of life insurance;[3] though this is probably because a contract of life insurance is not, like other insurance, a contract of indemnity merely, and it cannot be supposed to have been contemplated by the contracting parties that the insurer should be subrogated to the remedy of the insured for any wrong or injury which might cause a loss.[4] Accordingly, where a railroad company has by its negligence caused the death of a passenger upon its road, insurers who have thereby been compelled to pay a policy of insurance issued by them upon his life cannot maintain an action against the railroad company for the reimbursement of such payment;[5] for though the loss of the insurers was caused by the railroad company's wrongful acts, yet, as these wrongful acts affected the insurers only by reason of their artificial contractual relation with the insured, to whom the wrong was done, their loss is too remote and indirect a consequence of the wrong to be the foundation of an action.[6] Nor can the railroad company set up the insurance in diminution of the damages for which it is liable, unless so provided by the statute creating the liability.[7] But, as has been already intimated, these

N. Y. 421; Rayner v. Preston, 18 Ch. D. 1, affirming s. c., 14 Ch. D. 297.

[1] Benjamin v. Saratoga Ins. Co., 17 N. Y. 415; Washington Ins. Co. v. Kelley, 32 Md. 421.

[2] Garden v. Ingram, 23 L. J. N. s. Ch. 478.

[3] See the general language in Ætna Ins. Co. v. Hannibal & St. Joseph R. R. Co., 3 Dillon, C. C. 1; Harding v. Townshend, 43 Vt. 536; Pittsburg R. R. Co. v. Thompson, 56 Ills. 138.

[4] See per Lord Blackburn, in Bur-

nand v Rodocanachi, 7 App. Cas. 333, 340, 341, citing Godsall v. Boldero, 9 East, 72; and Dalby v. India Life Ins. Co., 15 C. B. 365.

[5] Conn. Ins. Co. v. N. Y. & N. H. R. R. Co., 25 Conn. 265; postea, § 244. And see Mobile Ins. Co. v. Brame, 95 U. S. 754.

[6] Conn. Ins. Co. v. N. Y. & N. H. R. R. Co., supra; postea, § 244.

[7] Grand Trunk Railw. Co. v. Jennings, 13 Ap. Cas. 800; Hicks v. Newport Railw. Co., 4 B. & S. 403, note; Kellogg v. N. Y. Central R. R.

decisions might perhaps better be sustained by the apparent fact that no subrogation of the insurers could have been intended by the parties to this insurance than upon the reasons assigned by the court; for it has already been shown that the doctrine of subrogation is wholly independent of any privity or contractual relations between the parties to be affected by it.[1] And in almost all cases of the subrogation of marine or fire insurers .to the remedies of the insured against a wrong-doer whose tort has caused the loss, this tort has affected the insurers "only by reason of their artificial contractual relations with the insured, to whom the wrong was done." But in these cases the subrogation of the insurers is contemplated, or must be presumed to have been contemplated, by the parties to the contract of insurance, since otherwise the insured would, contrary to the intent of the parties, receive more than an indemnity for the loss, or else the mere wrong-doer, the party primarily liable for the injury, would obtain the benefit of the insurers' subsidiary liability; a result which would be at variance with the principles of manifest justice from which the equitable doctrine of subrogation has been evolved. The payment by a life insurance company to a creditor of the amount of an insurance policy issued by it to him upon the life of his debtor, is not *pro tanto* a satisfaction of the debt,[2] unless the premiums have been paid by or for the debtor.[3] If the debtor pays off the indebtedness in his lifetime, he cannot require from the creditor an assignment of such a policy,[4] unless it was really obtained for him or at his expense.[5] One who, not being the owner of a policy

---

Co., 79 N. Y. 72; Baltimore & Ohio R. R. Co. *v.* Wightman, 29 Gratt. (Va.) 431; Sherlock *v.* Alling, 44 Ind. 184.

[1] *Antea*, §§ 1, 11, 93.

[2] Humphrey *v.* Arabin, 2 Lloyd & Gould, Ir. Ch. Plunkett, 318.

[3] Bruce *v.* Garden, 22 L. T. (N. S.) 595, overruling s. c., 20 L. T. (N. S.)

1002; Morland *v.* Isaac, 20 Beav. 388; Coon *v.* Swan, 30 Vt. 6.

[4] Gotlieb *v.* Cranch, 4 De G., M. & G. 440; Knox *v.* Turner, L. R. 9 Eq 155.

[5] Courtenay *v.* Wright, 2 Giff. 337; Drysdale *v.* Piggott, 8 De G., M. & G. 546; Page *v.* Burnstine, 102 U. S. 664; Cammack *v.* Lewis, 15 Wallace,

of insurance, has paid the premiums thereon, will not by substitution to the rights of the owner be entitled to a lien thereon unless by reason of a contract with the owner, or by reason of the right of a trustee to indemnity out of the trust property for money expended by him in its preservation, or the right of a mortgagee to hold his lien for any money paid by him for the preservation of the property, or by the subrogation to the rights of such a mortgagee or trustee of one who has made such advances at their request and in their right.[1]

643.  See McKenty *v.* Universal Ins. Co., 3 Dillon, C. C. 448.

[1] Leslie *v.* French, 23 Ch. D. 552, commenting on Tharp, *in re,* 2 Sm. & Giff. 578, note ;  Swan *v.* Swan, 8 Price, 518 ; and Gill *v.* Downing, L. R. 17 Eq. 316.

# CHAPTER VIII.

### SUBROGATION OF STRANGERS.

§ 240. **Strangers or Volunteers not entitled to Subrogation.** — The doctrine of subrogation is not applied for the mere stranger or volunteer, who has paid the debt of another, without any assignment or agreement for subrogation, being under no legal obligation to make the payment, and not being compelled to do so for the preservation of any rights or property of his own.[1] One person cannot, by his unauthorized payment of the price of land which another has agreed to buy, substitute himself to the vendor's lien upon the land.[2] "The doctrine of subrogation," said Mr. Chancellor Johnson,[3] "is a pure unmixed equity, having its foundation in the princi-

[1] Webster's Appeal, 86 Penn. St. 409; Hoover v. Epler, 52 Penn. St. 522; Clark v. Moore, 76 Va. 262; St. Francis Mill Co. v. Sugg, 83 Mo. 476; Sanford v. McLean, 3 Paige (N. Y.), 117; Griffin v. Orman, 9 Fla. 22; Shinn v. Budd, 14 N. J. Eq. 234.

[2] Truesdell v. Callaway, 6 Mo. 605.

[3] Gadsden v. Brown, Speers Eq. (So. Car.) 37, 41.

ples of natural justice, and from its very nature could never have been intended for the relief of those who were in a condition in which they were at liberty to elect whether they would or would not be bound; and, so far as I have been able to learn its history, it has never been so applied. If one with a perfect knowledge of the facts will part with his money, or bind himself by his contract in a sufficient consideration, any rule of law which would restore him his money or absolve him from his contract would subvert the rules of social order. It has been directed in its application exclusively to the relief of those that were already bound, who could not but choose to abide the penalty. Sureties, for example, who have before become bound, are among the special subjects of its care.[1] .·. . Another example of the application of the same principle will be found in the case where two creditors have mortgages or other liens upon the same property of the same debtor. Thus, if the subsequent creditor pay the prior debt, he is entitled to be substituted to the rights of the prior creditor, as a means, without injury to the prior creditor, of enabling him to secure payment of his own debt.[2] But I have seen no case, and none has been referred to in the argument, in which a stranger, who was in a condition to make terms for himself, and demand any security he might require, has been protected by the principle."

§ 241. **The Voluntary Payment of a Debt by a Stranger extinguishes it.** — Subrogation by operation of law exists in favor, not of all who pay the debt of another, but only in favor of those who, being bound for it, have therefore discharged it.[3] The demand of a creditor which is paid with the money of a third person, and without any agreement that

---

[1] *Antea,* § 86 *et seq.*

[2] *Antea,* § 12 *et seq.*

[3] Nolte *v.* Creditors, 19 Mart. (7 Mart. N. s.), La. 602; Harrison *v.* Bisland, 5 Rob. (La.) 204; Hough *v.* Ætna Ins. Co., 57 Ills. 318; Boyd *v.* McDonough, 39 How. Pr. (N. Y.) 389; Kuhn *v.* North, 10 Serg. & R. (Penn.) 399; United States Bank *v.* Winston, 2 Brock. C. C. 252; Kleimann *v.* Geiselmann, 45 Mo. App. 497; Guy *v.* Du Uprey, 16 Calif. 195.

the security shall be assigned or kept on foot for the benefit
of such third person, is absolutely extinguished by the payment.[1] It is well settled that no one can be allowed to
obtrude himself upon another as his surety; and therefore
if a man voluntarily pays the debt of another, without any
agreement to that effect with the debtor, he cannot take the
place of the creditor or recover the money so paid of the
debtor, because the law does not permit one man thus officiously and without solicitation to intermeddle with the
affairs of another.[2]   One cannot, by voluntarily paying
money or rendering service for another, not having been requested so to do, make that other his debtor,[3] or subrogate
himself to the rights of the creditor.[4]   A drayman, having
contracted to haul and deliver to a·vessel certain cotton,
hauled it to the vessel and deposited it on the levee, at a
place pointed out to him by the officers of the vessel, and left
it there at their request, they declining to receipt for it on
the ground that it was too late in the day.   The cotton having been stolen in the night, the drayman paid its value to its
owners, and brought his action against the vessel, to recover
the amount of this payment.   But it was held that he could
not recover; for the cotton had been delivered to the vessel;
the vessel was liable to the owners of the cotton; and the
payment by the drayman, being one which he was not bound
to make, did not subrogate him to the right of those owners.[5]

---

[1] Shinn v. Budd, 14 N. J. Eq. 234;
Conrad v. Buck, 21 W. Va. 396;
Woods v. Gilson, 17 Ills. 218; Kitchell v. Mudgett, 37 Mich. 82; Simmons v. Walker, 18 Ala. 664; Morris
v. Lake, 9 Sm. & M. (Miss.) 521;
Moran v. Abbey, 63 Calif. 56; Terry
v. O'Neal, 71 Tex. 592.

[2] United States v. Keehler, 9 Wallace, 83; Bancroft v. Abbott, 3 Allen
(Mass.), 524; South Scituate v. Hanover, 9 Gray (Mass.), 420; Bland,
Ch., in Winder v. Diffenderffer, 2

Bland, Ch. (Md.) 199, citing Stokes
v. Lewis, 1 T. R. 20; Norton v. High-
leyman, 88 Mo. 621.

[3] Binford v. Adams, 104 Ind. 41;
Fay v. Fay, 43 N. J. Eq. 438 ; Webb
v. Cole, 20 N. H. 490.

[4] Homestead Co. v. Valley R. R.
Co., 17 Wallace, 153; Langley v.
Chapin, 134 Mass. 82; Hungerford
v. Scott, 37 Wisc. 341; Traders' Ins.
Co. v. Race, 31 No. E. Rep. 392.

[5] Roth v. Harkson, 18 La. Ann.
705.

§ 242. **Application of this Principle to the Case of one who binds himself for a Pre-existing Debt.** — The owner of an equity of redemption which was subject to several mortgages gave his notes with an indorser to the first mortgagee for the interest which was due on that debt. The indorser paid these notes at their maturity; but no assignment of the mortgage was made to him. On a subsequent sale of the property, he claimed to be subrogated to the rights of the first mortgagee to the amount which he had thus paid, and so to have a preference over the subsequent mortgagees in the surplus proceeds of the sale after the payment of the first mortgage. But it was held, that, as he was not a party to the original transaction, and there was nothing in the mortgage which provided for making him a surety, so as to subrogate him to the rights of the mortgagee, he was merely a volunteer, and accordingly was not entitled to the priority which he claimed. He could entitle himself to the benefit of the security held by the creditor only by an agreement to that effect, or by taking an assignment of a corresponding interest in the mortgage when he paid the note.[1] The same principle has been declared in South Carolina.[2]

§ 243. **Application of this Principle to the Case of one who loans Money to the Debtor for the Payment of his Debt.** — The mere loaning of money to a debtor to be applied by him in or towards payment of a debt which was a lien upon his estate does not of itself subrogate the lender in whole or in part to this lien,[3] even though it was understood between the parties to the transaction that it would have this effect,[4] unless there was such an agreement as to operate a conventional subrogation.[5] One who has advanced money to pay off liens upon a

---

[1] Swan v. Patterson, 7 Md. 164.
[2] Gadsden v. Brown, Speers Eq. 37.
[3] Nash v. Taylor, 83 Ind. 347; Price v. Courtney, 87 Mo. 387; Kline v. Ragland, 47 Ark. 111.

[4] Unger v. Leiter, 32 Ohio St. 210; Riffle's Appeal, 3 Brewst. (Penn.) 94; Bowen v. Barksdale, 33 So. Car. 142.
[5] Murphree v. Countiss, 58 Miss. 712; Baker v. Ward, 7 Bush (Ky.), 240.

ship will not by reason of this bare fact be subrogated to the
benefit of the liens,[1] unless at any rate it is clearly shown
both that the money was so used and that it was advanced
for that purpose on the credit of the vessel.[2] The lender of
money which is applied by the borrower in part payment of
the purchase-money of land is not thereby subrogated to the
vendor's lien upon the land,[3] especially if this would prejudice the vendor's security for the amount unpaid,[4] unless the
parties appear to have so intended,[5] or unless a fraud would
otherwise be operated.[6] One who pays off a prior incumbrance upon property in which he has himself no interest to
be protected will not by his payment be subrogated to the
lien which he has discharged, as against those having intervening interests in the property,[7] even though, after the incumbrance had been really discharged by his payment of the
debt, but not formally released, he took an assignment
thereof, without the consent of the owner of the property.[8]
Nor is the rule changed by the fact of his acquiring an interest immediately upon his payment.[9] If a guardian pays off
an incumbrance upon his own land with his ward's money, it
has been held that the ward is not thereby subrogated to the
lien thus discharged.[10] But if, when he made his payment,

[1] The William A. Harris, 8 Bene-
dicts, 210; The City of Salem, 31
Fed. Rep. 616.
[2] The Heinrich Bjorn, 8 Prob. D.
151; The St. Lawrence, 5 Prob. D.
250; The Anna, 1 Prob. D. 253;
The Lime Rock, 49 Fed. Rep. 383;
Nippert v. The J. B. Williams, 42
Id. 533, reversing s. c., 39 Id. 823;
The Augustine Kobbe, 39 Id. 559,
and 37 Id. 702; The Menominie, 36
Id. 197; The Wyoming, 36 Id. 493;
The Tangier, 2 Lowell, 7.
[3] Griffin v. Proctor, 14 Bush (Ky.),
571; Durant v. Davis, 10 Heisk.
(Tenn.) 522; Jones v. Lockard, 89
Ala. 575; Pettus v. McKinney, 74

Ala. 108; Nichols v. Dunn, 25 Ark.
129.
[4] Brower v. Witmeyer, 121 Ind. 83.
[5] See Carey v. Boyle, 53 Wisc. 574.
[6] Otis v. Gregory, 111 Ind. 505;
Netterville v. Barber, 52 Miss. 168;
antea, § 8.
[7] Downer v. Wilson, 33 Vt. 1;
Wilson v. Soper, 44 Maine, 118;
North River Construction Co., in re,
38 N. J. Eq. 433; Woods v. Gilson,
17 Ills. 218; Wolff v. Walter, 56 Mo.
292.
[8] Moody v. Moody, 68 Maine, 155.
[9] Gardenville Association v. Walker, 52 Md. 452.
[10] French v. Sheplor, 83 Ind. 266.

he manifested an intention to keep the prior lien alive for
his protection, as by taking a quitclaim deed or an assignment from the prior incumbrancer, his payment will be
deemed to have been made, not in extinguishment, but as a
purchase, of the charge, and he may hold under it.[1] And
one who has lent money to an infant to be used in purchasing necessaries or in paying debts incurred for necessaries,
the money having been actually used for that purpose, has
been allowed to hold the infant liable therefor by subrogation to the rights of the person furnishing the necessaries,[2]
though it may be doubted whether this was necessary for his
protection.[3]

§ 243 a.  **Application of this Principle to the Purchase of
Coupons on Secured Bonds.** — Where matured coupons on
secured bonds of a railroad or other corporation are taken up
with money furnished without the knowledge of the bondholders by a third party, without any assent on the part of
the bondholders that this transaction should be regarded as
a purchase of the coupons, they will not afterwards in the
hands of such third party be allowed to share in the security
to the prejudice of the bondholders.[4]  If the coupons have
been paid on presentation at the place of payment with the
money of a third party, a private arrangement between him
and the debtors that he should be regarded as the purchaser
of the coupons will not be enforced against the bondholders.[5]
Such a voluntary act will be regarded as a payment, not as a
purchase, unless so intended by all parties.[6]  So the mere
fact that money loaned to a railroad company was actually

[1] Cole v. Edgerly, 48 Maine, 108;
Capen v. Richardson, 7 Gray (Mass.),
364; Freeman v. McGaw, 15 Pick.
(Mass.) 82; Borland v. Meurer, 139
Penn. St. 513; Loewenthal v. Mc-
Cormick, 101 Ills. 143.

[2] Price v. Sanders, 60 Ind. 310;
Martin v. Gale, 4 Ch. D. 428.

[3] Randall v. Sweet, 1 Denio (N.
Y.), 460; Conn v. Coburn, 7 N. H.
368; Haine v. Tarrant, 2 Hill Law
(So. Car.), 400.

[4] Wood v. Guarantee Trust Co.,
128 U. S. 416.

[5] Fidelity Co. v. West Penn. Railw.
Co., 138 Penn. St. 494.

[6] Cason v. Heath, 86 Ga. 438.

applied towards the payment of interest upon its first mortgage bonds or of operating expenses will not entitle the
lender to any preference over the first mortgage bonds by
way of subrogation.[1]

§ 244. **Creditor not substituted to Remedy of his Debtor
against a Wrong-doer.** — One who has been injured by the act
of a wrong-doer has no right, in consequence thereof, to be
subrogated to the benefit of an indemnity which the wrong-
doer may have taken against the consequences of his wrongful act;[2] nor, though his debtor may by reason of the wrong
have become unable to pay him,[3] or he may have been put to
expense about the person to whom the wrong has been done,[4]
will he therefor be substituted to the remedy of such person
against the wrong-doer.[5] A plaintiff cannot recover against
a defendant for injury done by the latter to a third person,
though this injury causes also a loss to the plaintiff, by reason of his contract relations with or for such third person.[6]
A judgment-creditor can maintain no action against one who
has converted to his own use the goods of the debtor, though
the latter had no other property, and the creditor is thus
prevented from obtaining the satisfaction of his demand,[7]
unless this was done by fraudulent arrangement between the
debtor and the wrong-doer,[8] or unless the creditor has before
the conversion acquired a legal interest in the property by

[1] Morgan's Company v. Texas Central R. R. Co., 137 U. S. 172.

[2] McGay v. Keilback, 14 Abbott
Pr. (N. Y.) 142.

[3] Green v. Kimble, 6 Blackf. (Ind.)
552.

[4] Anthony v. Slaid, 11 Metc.
(Mass.) 290; Butler County v. Mc-
Cann, 23 Ala. 599.

[5] Barker v. Mathews, 1 Denio
(N. Y.), 335.

[6] Lumley v. Gye, 2 El. & Bl. 216;
Smith v. Hurd, 12 Met. (Mass.) 371;
Cunningham v. Brown, 18 Vt. 123;

Conn. Ins. Co. v. N. Y. & N. H. R. R.
Co., 25 Conn. 265; Braem v. Merchants Bank, 127 N. Y. 508; Ashley
v. Dixon, 48 N.Y. 430; Dale v. Grant,
34 N. J. Law, 42; Jemmison v. Gray,
29 Iowa, 537.

[7] Green v. Kimble, 6 Blackf. (Ind.)
552; Wellington v. Small, 3 Cush.
(Mass.) 145; Lamb v. Stone, 11 Pick.
(Mass.) 527; Murtha v. Curley, 47
N. Y. Super. Ct. 393.

[8] Adams v. Paige, 7 Pick. (Mass.)
542. But see Klous v. Hennessy, 13
R. I. 332.

means of an attachment or levy thereon;[1] and then he sues in his own right, and not by substitution to the remedy of his debtor.[2] The same principle applies to an action by a carrier against his servant for damages done by the latter to goods in his possession, for which the carrier has satisfied the owner of the goods;[3] the action is maintained in the carrier's own right.

§ 245. **When the Person making Payment of the Debt of another regarded as a Stranger or Volunteer.** — It is sometimes difficult to ascertain when one who has paid a debt will be considered to have been a mere stranger or volunteer. A payment made in pursuance of a moral obligation,[4] or by one who was liable to be compelled to make it, will not be regarded as made by a stranger, and will not extinguish the indebtedness of the party on whom rests the ultimate liability.[5] So, where a guardian has been compelled to pay to his ward a sum of money due from a former guardian, on account of his having neglected to compel the payment thereof by the former guardian, he is by his payment subrogated to the right of the ward, and may recover the amount from the former guardian or the sureties upon the latter's bond.[6] Neither directors[7] nor stockholders are strangers to the corporation; they may be subrogated against both the corporation and other stockholders for payments of its debts made by them in a fair effort to protect their own interests in the corporate property.[8] If the corporate officers take no steps to

[1] Brown v. Casetes, 11 Cush. (Mass.) 348; Bates v. Blonsky, 62 How. Pr. (N. Y.) 429; Yates v. Joyce, 11 Johns. (N. Y.) 136.

[2] See Smith v. Blake, 1 Day (Conn.), 258; Platt v. Potts, 13 Ired. Law (Nor. Car.) 455; Matthews v. Pass, 19 Ga. 141.

[3] See Gray v. Boston Gas Co., 114 Mass. 149; Smith v. Foran, 43 Conn. 244.

[4] Slack v. Kirk, 67 Penn. St. 380.

[5] Heritage v. Paine, 2 Ch. Div. 594; The Jersey City, 43 Fed. Rep. 166; Rindge v. Coleraine, 11 Gray (Mass.), 158; Farmers' Bank v. Erie R. R. Co., 72 N. Y. 188; Gillett v. No. Am. Ins. Co., 39 Ills. App. 284; Jacques v. Fackney, 64 Ills. 87.

[6] Smith v. Alexander, 4 Sneed (Tenn.), 482.

[7] Harts v. Brown, 77 Ills. 226.

[8] Redington v. Cornwell, 90 Calif. 49.

redeem within the time allowed by law corporate property
which has been sold on execution, a stockholder will, upon
paying the judgment and redeeming the property, be subrogated to all the rights of the original purchaser at the
sheriff's sale.[1] If trust-money is used by a trustee to pay
off liens upon his own property, the *cestuis que trustent* cannot be called volunteers, and may be subrogated to the liens
thus discharged.[2] An agent who pays money out of his own
pocket to protect the estate of his principal that is in his
charge is not a mere volunteer, and is entitled to all the
equities that the same payment would have given to his
principal.[3] The wife and children of one deceased who pay
valid demands against his estate out of their individual
means have been held not to be mere volunteers, and may be
subrogated.[4] Said Thompson, C. J.,[5] "The principles of subrogation do not apply in favor of volunteers. They can obtain the right of substitution only by contract. The cases
which I have referred to[6] illustrate who are not to be regarded
as volunteers and strangers. One was the case of an indorser, who was substituted to the judgment-creditor whose
judgment the proceeds of his note had paid. His indorsement
was voluntary. Another paid for his own protection an execution on a prior judgment. He was not legally compelled
to pay. A third and fourth advanced money, one in favor of
an estate, and one to his ward. They were all subrogated,
and not regarded as strangers. I regard the doctrine as ap-

---

[1] Wright *v.* Oroville Mining Co.,
40 Calif. 20; Bush *v.* Wadsworth, 60
Mich. 255. But see Eastman *v.*
Crosby, 8 Allen, 206.

[2] Oury *v.* Sanders, 77 Tex. 278.

[3] Curry *v.* Curry, 87 Ky. 667.

[4] Burwell *v.* Snow, 107 Nor. Car.
82; Brown *v.* Frost, 95 Ind. 248;
Carithers *v.* Stuart, 87 Ind. 424;
Bayles *v.* Husted, 40 Hun (N. Y.),
376.

[5] Mosier's Appeal, 56 Penn. St.
76.

[6] Cheeseborough *v.* Millard, 1
Johns. Ch. (N. Y.) 409; Cottrell's
Appeal, 23 Penn. St. 294; Silver
Lake Bank *v.* North, 4 Johns. Ch.
(N. Y.) 370; Payne *v.* Hathaway, 3
Vt. 212; Wallace's Appeal, 5 Penn. St.
103; Kelchner *v.* Forney, 29 Penn.
St. 47; Greiner's Estate, 2 Watts
(Penn.), 414.

plicable in all cases where a payment has been made under a legitimate and fair effort to protect the ascertained interests of the party paying,[1] and where intervening rights are not thereby jeopardized or defeated. Such payments, whatever their effect might be at law in extinguishing the indebtedness to which they apply, will not be so regarded in equity, if contrary to equity to regard them so." But the payment must be made by one who really has an interest in discharging the demand which he pays;[2] otherwise there will be no subrogation,[3] as if he makes his payment under the mistaken belief that he is bound as surety.[4]

§ 246. Instances of the Subrogation of a Person on his Paying the Debt of another. — A groom who has paid a farrier's bill for shoeing a horse under his charge will not be regarded as a volunteer, but will, after he has fully satisfied the farrier, be subrogated for his reimbursement to the farrier's lien upon the horse.[5] The clerk of a steamboat who has advanced the money for the payment of the wages of the crew on an order drawn by the captain upon the owners of the boat, will be substituted to the rights of the crew as their equitable assignee;[6] but not so if the money had been advanced by one not connected in any manner with the boat,[7] or under circumstances showing that no such subrogation was contemplated.[8] The payment of a planter's drafts in favor of his laborers will not subrogate the party paying the drafts to the privilege of the workmen.[9] A county, having paid to the State the

---

[1] Pease v. Egan, 131 N. Y. 262; Dodge v. Zimmer, 110 N.Y. 43; Drake v. Paige, 52 Hun (N. Y.), 292.

[2] Clingman v. Hopkie, 78 Ills. 152.

[3] Bayard v. McGraw, 1 Ills. Ap. 134.

[4] Dawson v. Lee, 83 Ky. 49. Contra, Capehart v. Mhoon, 5 Jones Eq. (Nor. Car.) 178.

[5] Hoover v. Epler, 52 Penn. St. 522.

[6] Abbott v. Baltimore Steam Packet Co., 4 Md. Ch. Dec. 310. See The Woodland, 104 U. S. 180; The J. A. Brown, 2 Lowell, 464.

[7] Steamboat White v. Levy, 10 Ark. (5 English) 411.

[8] The Sarah J. Weed, 2 Lowell, 555.

[9] Shaw v. Grant, 13 La. Ann. 52; Rheeling's Appeal, 107 Penn. St. 161.

amount of a State tax for which its treasurer was in default,
may be subrogated to the remedy of the State against the
sureties upon the treasurer's official bond; for, while the
ultimate liability was upon the treasurer, the payment was
for the relief of the county, and so could not be deemed to
have been voluntarily made.[1] So, where the general agent
of an insurance company had appointed a local agent and
taken from him a bond running to the company, conditioned
that the local agent should pay over to the company all
moneys received by him, and the general agent had paid to
the company certain premiums received by the local agent
but not accounted for by him, it was held, in a suit upon this
bond brought in the name of the company for the benefit of
the general agent, that since the latter had the appointment
of the local agents, and was bound, not only by contract with
the company, but in order to keep his own position, to pay
over all moneys received by his subordinates, his settlement
with the company for the local agent's defalcation did not
discharge the bond, but he should be subrogated to the rights
of the company against the sureties upon the bond.[2] A new
corporation, having paid the debts of an old corporation
whose place it was organized to take, may be subrogated to
the rights of the old corporation, though its only title was
under an invalid receiver's deed.[3] Where one, believing
that he was a surety upon an administrator's bond, settled
with the next of kin, who entertained the same belief, it was
held, the discovery having been made that he was not such
surety, and the administrator having become insolvent, that,
having made the settlement and paid his money under a mistake of fact, he was not to be deemed an intermeddler, but
must be regarded in equity as a purchaser for value of the

[1] Elder v. Commonwealth, 55 Penn.
St. 485; Hughes v. Commonwealth,
48 Penn. St. 66.

[2] Hough v. Ætna Ins. Co., 57 Ills.
318.

[3] St. Louis Coal Co. v. Sandoval
Coal Co., 116 Ills. 170.

claims of the next of kin against the administrator and the real sureties, and that he had an equity to be subrogated to the rights of the next of kin under the administration-bond.[1] And the general proposition has been laid down that one whose money has discharged claims against a trust estate, which it was bound to pay, though he cannot maintain an action at law against the trust estate or the *cestui que trust*, will be subrogated in equity to the rights of the holders of such claims;[2] but this must be limited to the case of one who has an interest in making the payment on which he rests his claim.[3]

§ 247. **Subrogation of one paying a Debt at the Instance of the Debtor.** — One who pays a debt at the instance of the debtor, under such circumstances that it appears to have been contemplated by the parties that he should become entitled to the benefit of the security for the debt held by the creditor from the debtor, may, as against the debtor and the debtor's estate,[4] be subrogated to the benefit of such security and of the debt which he has discharged.[5] And a party who has paid a debt at the request of the debtor, under circumstances which would operate a fraud upon him if the debtor were afterwards allowed to insist that the security for the debt was discharged by his payment, may also be subrogated to the security, as against that debtor.[6] But this subrogation will not be allowed against one interested in the property held as security, who was a stranger to the transaction by which the payment was made, and who was under no obliga-

[1] Capehart *v.* Mhoon, 5 Jones, Eq. (Nor. Car.) 178. *Contra*, Dawson *v.* Lee, 83 Ky. 49.

[2] Hines *v.* Potts, 56 Miss. 346.

[3] *Antea*, §§ 12, 245. See Parks *v.* Watson, 20 Fed. Rep. 764.

[4] Pearl *v.* Hervey, 70 Mo. 160.

[5] Stebbins *v.* Willard, 53 Vt. 665; Zell's Appeal, 111 Penn. St. 532; Denton *v.* Cole, 30 N. J. Eq. 244;

Wilson *v.* Brown, 13 N. J. Eq. 277; Caudle *v.* Murphy, 89 Ills. 352; Lily *v.* Dunn, 96 Ind. 220; Rodman *v.* Sanders, 44 Ark. 504; Roy *v.* Clarke, 75 Tex. 28; Wahrmund *v.* Merritt, 60 Tex. 24, 27; Dillon *v.* Kauffman, 58 Tex. 696.

[6] Stevens *v.* King, 84 Maine, 291; Lockwood *v.* Marsh, 3 Nevada, 138; Oury *v.* Sanders, 77 Tex. 278.

tion for the payment of the debt,[1] unless it appears that the
payment was made, not as an extinguishment of the debt,
but in reliance upon, and as a purchase of, the security.[2]
This is a species of conventional subrogation, being a subrogation by an implied convention or agreement.[3] Accordingly, it will not be allowed if it appears not to have been
intended by the parties,[4] though this intention, if not expressed, may ordinarily be determined from the circumstances
attending the transaction.[5] Nor can one be subrogated to an
equitable lien merely because he has advanced to the real
creditor the money with which the loan was made.[6]

§ 248. Conventional Subrogation. — It has been said that
whenever a payment is made by a stranger to a creditor in
the expectation of being substituted to the place of the creditor, he is entitled to such substitution.[7] But the doctrine
generally adopted, and that of these very cases when limited
to the point actually decided, is that a conventional subrogation can result only from a direct agreement, express or
implied, made with either the creditor or the debtor,[8] and
that it is not sufficient that a person paying the debt of another should have merely the understanding on his part that
he is to be subrogated to the rights of the creditor,[9] though,
if the agreement has been made, a formal assignment will
not be necessary.[10] And the agreement may be shown by
subsequent acts which indicate a prior agreement. Thus,

[1] Wolff v. Walter, 56 Mo. 292.
[2] Caudle v. Murphy, 89 Ills. 352.
[3] Brice's Appeal, 95 Penn. St. 145.
[4] White v. Cannon, 125 Ills. 412;
White v. Curd, 86 Ky. 191; Bunn v.
Lindsay, 95 Mo. 250; Ashton v. Clayton, 27 Kans. 626.
[5] Wilcox v. Logan, 91 Nor. Car.
449.
[6] Van Winkle v. Williams, 38 N.
J. Eq. 105.
[7] Tradesmen's Building Association v. Thompson, 32 N. J. Eq. 133;

Coe v. New Jersey Midland R. R. Co.,
27 N. J. Eq. 110; Owens v. Bedell, 19
Can. S. C. 137.
[8] Texas & St. Louis R. R. Co. v.
McCaughey, 62 Tex. 621.
[9] New Jersey Midland R. R. Co. v.
Wortendyke, 27 N. J. Eq. 658, reversing in part Coe v. New Jersey Midland R. R. Co., supra.
[10] Neely v. Jones, 16 W. Va. 625;
Woods v. Ridley, 27 Miss. 120; Morrow v. U. S. Mortgage Co., 96 Ind.
21.

where a stranger pays the amount of an execution which has been put into the hands of a sheriff, a subsequent assignment of the judgment by the plaintiff therein to the person making the payment will be regarded as showing that the payment was made in purchase, and not in discharge of the judgment.[1] And no claim by subrogation, whether conventional or by operation of law, to the securities held or the remedies enjoyed by a creditor for the collection of his demand, can be enforced, until the whole demand of the creditor has been satisfied.[2] Until then there can be no interference with the creditor's rights or securities which might, even by possibility, prejudice or in any way embarrass him in the collection of the residue of his demand.[3] Subject to these limitations, any agreement, whether made by the debtor or the creditor, for the substitution of the person advancing money for the payment of a debt to the securities, remedies, or priorities of the creditor, will, to the extent of the agreement, be enforced in equity,[4] even against parties having intervening interests in the property held as security.[5]

§ 249. **Conventional Subrogation upon Payment of a Debt, and a Remedy for the Payment itself, cannot co-exist.** — One who claims under an assignment of a debt and of the securities which were held for its payment, or under a conventional subrogation to the rights of the creditor, which is equivalent to such an assignment,[6] cannot also claim the benefit of the payment which he has made for such assignment or conventional subrogation as a distinct ground of relief against the debtor. If he elects one remedy, he cannot also enjoy the

[1] Carter v. Halifax, 1 Hawks (Nor. Car.), 483.

[2] Antea, §§ 70, 118, 127.

[3] New Jersey Midland R. R. Co. v. Wortendyke, 27 N. J. Eq. 658; Peters v. Bourne, 11 Bush (Ky.), 55.

[4] Grant, in re, U. S. Dist. Court, Mass., 14 Am. Law Rev. 801; Mitchell v. Butt, 45 Ga. 162; Worner v.

Waterloo Society, 50 Iowa, 262, and 62 Iowa, 700; Bruce v. Bonney, 12 Gray (Mass.), 107; Fuller v. Hollis, 57 Ala. 435; McMillan v. Gordon, 4 Ala. 716; Owen v. Cook, 3 Tenn. Ch. 78; Wahrmund v. Merritt, 60 Tex. 24.

[5] Shreve v. Hankinson, 34 N. J. Eq. 76.

[6] Antea, § 5.

other.[1] He cannot, at the same time that he takes the benefit of the securities, claim also the advantages of having extinguished them by his payment. This principle was confirmed in a case in which it appeared that property was conveyed to trustees, to raise £75,000, with which to pay off prior mortgages, which, with arrears of interest, amounted to that sum. The trustees did not raise the money, but allowed a third party to pay off the mortgages and to take transfers of them, and then made a deed, purporting to assign to him the charge of £75,000, and to mortgage the property to him for that sum. But it was held that he could not charge interest on that sum, but that his right to stand as mortgagee was limited to the principal and interest due upon the mortgages that had been thus transferred to him.[2] On the same principle, it has been held that a creditor who has obtained possession of property of an insolvent debtor held in pledge by another creditor, by paying off the debt due to the latter, cannot afterwards maintain an action to recover the amount thus paid by him without offering to give up the pledged property.[3]

§ 250. Conventional Subrogation in Louisiana.— In Louisiana conventional subrogation to the rights and securities of a creditor in favor of a third person paying the debt can take place only by an express and formal agreement to that effect entered into by the creditor[4] at the time of the payment.[5] Accordingly, in that State, one who advances money to a debtor for the purpose of paying an indebtedness secured by a mortgage, under an agreement with the debtor that he shall, for his security, be subrogated to the benefit of the

---

[1] *Antea*, §§ 41, 110.

[2] Thompson *v.* Hudson, L. R. 2 Ch. 255, affirming s. c., L. R. 2 Eq. 612.

[3] Byrne *v.* Hibernia Bank, 31 La. Ann. 81.

[4] Hoyle *v.* Cazabat, 25 La. Ann.

438; Sewell *v.* Howard, 15 La. Ann. 400.

[5] Brice *v.* Watkins, 30 La. Ann., Pt. I., 21; Levy *v.* Baer, 19 La. Ann. 468; Durac *v.* Ferrari, 26 La. Ann. 114; Surghnor *v.* Beauchamp, 24 La. Ann. 471.

mortgage, will nevertheless have no such right of subrogation, unless the creditor was also a party to the agreement in
the prescribed form.[1] Nor will facts showing the intention
of the parties that the person making the payment should be
subrogated to the benefit of the securities held by the creditor
be sufficient to effect this substitution, unless this intention
appears to have been actually executed by a conventional subrogation.[2] But since a conventional subrogation invests the
person in whose favor it is made with all the rights and
privileges of the creditor as fully as an assignment would
do,[3] one who has paid a judgment to the plaintiff therein,
and has been expressly subrogated to his rights, may take
out an execution thereon to his own use; for such an express
subrogation is a sufficient authority to use the creditor's
name for the recovery of the debt from the judgment-debtor.[4]

[1] Hoyle v. Cazabat, 25 La. Ann.
488; Virgin's Succession, 18 La.
Ann. 42.

[2] Harrison v. Bislands, 5 Rob. (La.)
204; Chambliss v. Miller, 15 La. Ann.
718; Shaw v. Grant, 13 La. Ann. 52.

[3] Antea, § 5. Smith v. Wilson,
11 Rob. (La.) 522; Oakey v. Sheriff,
13 La. Ann. 273.

[4] King v. Dwight, 3 Rob. (La.)
2; Nugent v. Potter, 21 La. Ann.
746.

# INDEX.

[THE REFERENCES ARE TO THE SECTIONS.]

## A.

ACTION — *continued.*

**APPROPRIATION,**
>of deposits to payment of debt to bank, 123, 124.
>of security by one co-surety, 140 *et seq.*
>of surety's security to payment of debt, 154 *et seq.*
>of security to payment of note, 187.
>of merchandise to payment of bill drawn against it, 189.
>>what is sufficient, 193 *et seq.*
>>direction to charge bill to consignment not enough, 195.
>>or that bill was given in partial payment for property, 195.
>>or that bill was taken on credit of the fund, 197.
>to railroad, bondholders not subrogated to, 167 *a.*

**ARKANSAS,**
>original obligation destroyed at law by surety's payment, 137.
>>preserved in equity, 137.
>>but not against co-sureties, 137.

**ASSESSMENTS.** *See* TAXES.

**ASSETS.** *See* MARSHALLING OF ASSETS.

**ASSIGNEE IN BANKRUPTCY.** *See* BANKRUPTCY AND INSOLVENCY.

**ASSIGNMENT,**
>conventional subrogation equivalent to, 5.
>to be distinguished from subrogation, 6, 45.
>subrogation of insurer equivalent to, 6.
>of judgment paid by a sheriff, 7.
>release to one entitled to subrogation equivalent to, 13, 14, 20, 24.
>discharge fraudulently made equivalent to, 19.
>of mortgage to mortgagor, when no extinguishment, 22.
>not needed where one entitled to subrogation, 28.
>when necessary for preservation of incumbrance, 29.
>of mortgage, by foreclosure sale, 31.
>of debt, carries collateral security, 34.
>right of one entitled to subrogation to demand, 45.
>to one bound to pay debt, tantamount to discharge, 47, 50, 74.
>of mortgage to purchaser, effect upon dower, 49 *et seq.*
>>to widow, effect of, 51.
>>>*See* DOWER.
>of mortgage to owner of equity, how far an extinguishment, 53.
>>>*See* MERGER.
>surety's subrogation equivalent to, 87.
>no subrogation to unassignable lien, 97.
>by principal of debt due to him from surety, 102.
>of surety's right of subrogation, 107.
>of original obligation, right of surety to require, 137.
>of surety's indemnity, when an extinguishment, 139, 158, 159.
>of joint debt, after payment by one debtor, 180.
>of fund, by bill drawn against it, 193, 197.
>>by check drawn for it, 200 *a.*
>to indorser, of judgment against maker of note, 201.

**ASSIGNMENT** — *continued.*
>abandonment to insurers equivalent to, 221 *et seq.*
>may be evidence of conventional subrogation, 248.

**ASSUMPTION,**
>of mortgage by purchaser of premises, 22 *et seq.*
>>*See* PURCHASER.
>of mortgage prevents subrogation against it, 46.
>>exception in Pennsylvania, 35.
>>by purchaser of part of premises, 82.
>remedy of mortgagee against one assuming mortgage, 85.
>of debt by a surety, effect of, 112.

**ATTACHMENT,**
>rights of successive attaching creditors in mortgaged premises, 22.
>dissolved by bankruptcy, subrogation to, 23.
>subrogation of one purchasing property under, 38.
>upon property conveyed in fraud of creditors, rights of grantee, 40.
>subrogation of first purchaser subject to, 84.
>how far surety discharged by creditor's release of, 122.
>against principal, preserved after surety's payment, 137.

**ATTORNEY,**
>subrogated to rights of client, 10 *a.*
>subrogation upon payment to attorney, 15.
>creditor bound by notice to his, 81.

**AVOIDANCE OF SALE.** *See* PURCHASER.

### B.

**BAIL,**
>sheriff's neglect to assign bond of, ground of subrogation, 7.
>of one defendant has no right against another, 113.
>of shipmaster not subrogated against owners, 113.
>subrogation of, against prior sureties, 131 *et seq.*
>>*See* SUCCESSIVE SURETIES.
>can recover contribution only for actual payment, 151.
>of one partner not subrogated against the firm, 171.
>in criminal cases, not subrogated, 168.

**BANK,**
>carrier subrogated against, upon paying for destroyed bills, 10.
>subrogation of depositor against, 10 *a.*
>right to apply deposits of its debtor against surety, 123.
>how far surety discharged by neglect of, to apply deposits, 124.
>not compelled to apply surety's deposits, 124.
>securities held by, against acceptances, available to holders of bills, 190.
>rights of, to deposits, against equities of third parties, 192, 197.
>subrogation upon payment of check, 4.
>subrogation of holder of check, 200 *a.*
>indorser subrogated against, for its negligence, 181.

## BANKRUPTCY AND INSOLVENCY,

assignee redeeming pledges subrogated to rights of pledgee, 23.
    subrogated to security waived by proof of claim, 23.
    to lien of dissolved attachments, 23.
    and to action against primary debtor, 23.
assignee's avoidance of prior lien will not advance junior, 23.
purchasers subrogated to lien of taxes in, 35.
assignment of incumbrance to debtor's assignee in, not a merger, 49.
subrogation of surety before payment, in case of, 97.
entitles surety to benefit of principal's set-off, 101.
of principal, rights of surety upon, 102.
rights of wife as surety against husband's estate in, 104.
creditor's waiver of security by proof in, how far discharges surety, 120, 122.
effect of surrender of lease in, 126.
surety may have debt proved against estate of principal in, 130.
surety's indemnity available to creditor upon, 160–162.
proof in, against maker of note after payment by indorser, 182.
indorser subrogated to proof by maker, 182.
security of indorser available to holder on, 187.
securities held by acceptor in, available to holders of bills, 190.
    *See* NOTES AND BILLS.
acceptor's indemnity available to holder of bill only upon, 198.
acceptor subrogated to securities of holder upon, 198.
rights of mortgagee to mortgagor's insurance in, 233.

## BILL OF LADING,

rights of holder of bill drawn against, 189 *et seq.*

## BILL IN EQUITY. *See* EQUITY.

## BILLS. *See* BANK.

## BILLS AND NOTES. *See* NOTES AND BILLS.

## BONA FIDE HOLDER,

of note, transferee of, substituted to rights of, 183.
of securities for payment of note, 192.

## BOND. *See* INCUMBRANCE; RAILWAY SECURITIES; SUCCESSIVE CLAIMS.

issued *ultra vires*, subrogation for, 19.
for title, rights of grantee of one who holds, 34.
subrogation of surety on, 86 *et seq.*
on appeal, rights of sureties against creditor, 117.
    against each other, 131 *et seq.*
secured by mortgage to government, subrogation of holders of, 167 *a.*
surety on, how discharged by act of creditor, 119 *et seq.*, 126 *a.*
bondholders not subrogated to appropriation to railroad, 167 *a.*
purchase of coupons, 243 *a.*
loan of money to pay coupons, 243 *a.*

# C.

**CALIFORNIA,**
surety subrogated to original obligation in, 137.
but not mere joint debtor, 137.
rights of purchaser at foreclosure in, 32.

**CANADA,**
subrogation of insurers in, *pro tanto*, 232.

**CAPTURE,**
insurers subrogated to remedy of insured for, 222 *et seq.*

**CARRIER,**
subrogated to rights of owners of goods whom he has satisfied, 10.
and to lien of antecedent carrier, 10.
agent of, subrogated like, 10.
charges of, pledgee subrogated to, 12.
sheriff subrogated to charges of, which he has paid, 12.
how far bound by fraudulent bill of lading, 189 a.
of insured goods, insurers subrogated against, 229.
not subrogated upon payment for which he was not liable, 241.
action against servant for injury to goods, 244.

**CESSION.** *See* Assignment.
of creditor's remedies by subrogation, 11.

**CHECK,**
subrogation upon payment of, 4.
application of deposits to pay checks, when release of surety, 128.
subrogation of holder of, to rights of drawer, 200a.

**CHILD.** *See* Parent.
subrogation against, for necessaries, 243.

**CIRCUITY OF ACTION,**
creditor thrown upon primary fund to avoid, 208.

**CITY.** *See* Government.

**CIVIL LAW,**
definition of subrogation in the, 2.
allows subrogation for whose benefit, 2.
subrogation of insurers by, 232.

**CLERK OF COURT,**
subrogation of sureties of, 89.
laches of, in official act, no defence to surety, 121.

**COLLATERAL SECURITY.** *See* Securities.

**COLLECTOR,**
not subrogated to claim of government, growing out of his own wrong, 4.
may be subrogated to lien of taxes after payment, 7.

**COLLISION,**
insurers subrogated to remedy of insured for, 222, 223.

COMPROMISE,
of insurers' liability no ground of subrogation, 224.

CONDITION,
waiver of devise upon, 220.
performance of, by stranger, gives him no right to devise, 220.
unless accompanied by claim and recognition, 220.

CONNECTICUT,
right of solvent surety to surrender indemnity, 161.

CONSIDERATION. *See* CONTRACT.

CONSIGNMENT,
subrogation of consignee, 10 *a*.
against which bill drawn, lien of holder upon, 189.

CONSTABLE. *See* SHERIFF.

CONTRACT. *See* CONVENTIONAL SUBROGATION.
subrogation does not depend on, 1, 11, 93.
to assume mortgage, rights of parties to, 24 *et seq.*, 46.
for conveyance, not to be rescinded after accruing of others' interests, 34.
invalid, holder of, subrogated, 36 *a*.
waiver of right of subrogation by, 41, 42.
for benefit of another, remedy upon, 85, 171 *a*.
surety subrogated independently of privity, 93.
made by creditor, surety subrogated to benefit of, 95.

CONTRIBUTION,
subrogation for the purpose of obtaining, 45.
by and to dowress, upon redemption of incumbrance, 49 *et seq.*
purchaser of part of incumbered estate, when entitled to, 74.
*See* PURCHASER.
between successive purchasers in Iowa and Kentucky, 76.
from prior to subsequent purchaser of parts of incumbered estate, 79–82.
among purchasers and devisees, 84.
to and against subsequent and judicial sureties, 131 *et seq.*
*See* SUCCESSIVE SURETIES.
obtained by subrogation among co-sureties, 140 *et seq.*
not enforced between guarantor and surety, 150.
*See* CO-SURETIES.
among joint debtors, 169 *et seq.*
*See* JOINT DEBTORS.
among heirs, devisees, or legatees, 213.

CONVENTIONAL SUBROGATION,
what it is, 5.
equivalent to absolute assignment, 5.
must be made at same time as payment, 5.
necessary to pass claim for damages, 87.
of acceptor of bill to security of prior parties, 199.

25

CREDITOR — *continued*.
 substituted to security held by a surety, 154 *et seq.*
    *See* SUBSTITUTION.
 subrogation of joint debtors, 169 *et seq.*
 creditor may hold all until fully paid, 169.
 of deceased person, marshalling of assets for, 204.
 may follow property purchased with funds of estate, 205.
 substituted to rights of executors, 206.
    *See* ADMINISTRATION OF ESTATES.
 devisees subrogated to rights of, 212.
 right to insurance between debtor and, 233 *et seq*
 holding insurance on his debtor's life, 239.
 not substituted to debtor's remedy against wrong-doer, 244.

CRIMINAL PROCEEDINGS,
 subrogation not applied to bonds in, 168.

CUSTOMS. *See* TAXES.

## D.

DEBT. *See* CREDITOR; PRINCIPAL AND SURETY; SUCCESSIVE CLAIMS.
 held to subsist for one entitled to subrogation who has paid it, 13.
 when, must be due and payable, to give ground for subrogation, 18.
 how far extinguished by surety's payment, 185 *et seq.*
  by joint debtor's payment, 180.

DEBTOR. *See* CREDITOR.

DECEASED PERSONS. *See* ADMINISTRATION OF ESTATES.

DECREE. *See* PRACTICE.

DEED. *See* RECORDS.
 neglect to record, no bar to subrogation, 9, 30.
 holder under invalid, subrogated, 36 *a.*
 subrogation of a purchaser limited by terms of, 37.
 given in fraud of creditors, subrogation under, 40.
 quitclaim, of mortgage, operating as assignment, 40.
 estoppel by, not enforced for one claiming against, 58.

DEFINITION,
 of subrogation, 1.
 in civil law, 2.

DELAWARE,
 surety on bond entitled to assignment on payment, 137.
  and to original judgment against principal, 137.

DEPOSITS. *See* BANK.

DEPUTY SHERIFF. *See* SHERIFF.

DEVISE,
 subrogation of purchaser from devisee, 35.
 devisee of contingent remainder subrogated, 36 *a.*

### E.

ELECTION,
  mortgagee, when not compelled to make, 25.
  of one entitled to subrogation, 41.
  of creditor between different remedies, 41.
  of surety to take subrogation, 110.
        *See* MARSHALLING OF ASSETS, WAIVER.
  of surety between subrogation and indemnity, 110.
  subrogation of devisee or legatee disappointed by, 218.
    for compensation out of right waived by, 218.
    where widow waives provisions of will, 218.
  extent of this subrogation, 219.
    to the rights of party making the, 219.
  does not include bequest merely upon condition, 220.
  between subrogation and indemnity, 249.

ENDORSER. *See* NOTES AND BILLS.

ENGLAND,
  rights of junior incumbrancer in, 16.
  restriction of surety's subrogation in, 119.
  original obligation not extinguished by surety's payment, 185.
  mortgaged real estate of deceased first applied on debt, 211.
  rights of separate insurers on ship and freight, 227.

EQUITY,
  subrogation is a doctrine of, 1.
    but extended to common law, 1.
    to be carried out with equitable discretion, 4.
  will subrogate sheriff to judgment which he has been compelled to
    pay, 7.
  throws by subrogation debt upon party who ought to pay it, 11.
  treats purchaser who has assumed mortgage as principal debtor, 24, 25.
  reinstates incumbrance discharged in ignorance of intervening lien, 29.
  subrogates holder under invalid decree, 36 a.
  reinstating discharged mortgage, 20, 55.
  when, requires assignment to carry out subrogation, 45.
  rules of, as to merger, 53 *et seq.*
        *See* MERGER.
  marshalling of assets in, 61.
        *See* MARSHALLING OF ASSETS.
  rights in, of purchasers of parts of mortgaged estates, 74 *et seq.*
        *See* PURCHASERS.
  remedy of mortgagee in, against one assuming mortgage, 85.
  subrogation of sureties in, 86 *et seq.*
        *See* PRINCIPAL AND SURETY.
  lien of surety in, upon funds in hands of principal, 100.
  surety may come to, to compel principal to pay debt, 130.
  will give relief to surety, how, 130 a.

EQUITY — *continued.*
will enforce rights of co-sureties to securities of each other, 140.
enables creditor to reach security held by surety, 154 *et seq.*
   *See* SUBSTITUTION.
gives compensation to devisee disappointed by election of another, 218 *et seq.*
will enforce agreement for conventional subrogation, 248.

EQUITY OF REDEMPTION. *See* REDEMPTION.

ERROR. *See* WRIT OF ERROR.

ESTATES OF DECEASED PERSONS. *See* ADMINISTRATION OF ESTATES.

ESTOPPEL. *See* WAIVER.
no subrogation against interests taken on faith of record, 17, 20.
discharge of mortgage bars mortgagee, 20.
formal discharge may not be, if no other rights intervene, 20.
subrogation upon, of incumbrancer, 29.
usury in taking new security no bar to subrogation, 42.
   in original transaction would be a bar, 42.
how far negligence will be an, 43.
subrogation will not relieve one against his own wrong, 44.
one cannot be subrogated against his own warranty, 46.
by release of dower, 49.
of owner of equity to claim a merger, 56.
by deed, not enforced for one claiming against the deed, 58.
of mortgagee against purchaser of part of the estate, 78.
surety subrogated to principal's rights by, 101.
of surety, against a purchaser of security for the debt, 109.
of carrier by fraudulent bill of lading, 189 *a.*
of insurer no bar to subrogation, 223.

EVIDENCE,
right of subrogation must be shown by, 11.
parol, that conveyance subject to mortgage, 82.
of intent as to security held for debt by surety, 156.
right of joint debtor must be shown by, 179.
of relation to each other of parties to note, 181.

EXECUTION,
payment of, by officer, when a ground of subrogation, 7.
interest taken by purchaser at sale under, 17.
subrogation upon levy of, upon mortgaged lands, 21, 22.
levy of, upon parts of an equity of redemption, 22.
assignee in bankruptcy subrogated against levies under, 23.
subrogation of purchaser of property sold on, 38.
   allowed against the debtor's claims, 38.
   where the property recovered by third parties, 39.
release of debtor's land from levy, how far releases land of his grantee, 80.

**FRAUD,**
    fraudulent discharge of incumbrance will not bar subrogation, 8, 19.
    subrogation for prevention of, 19, 20, 58.
    of mortgagor obtaining note and mortgage, no bar to foreclosure, 20.
        except against innocent purchasers for value, 20.
    purchaser not subrogated to vendor's action for, 37.
    rights of purchaser in, of vendor's creditors, 40.
    when subrogated to charges which he has paid, 40.
    payment of debt by one guilty of, no ground of subrogation, 44.
    of husband, not imputed to wife, 49.
    prior incumbrance discharged by, may be reinstated, 58.
    where agreement to assume incumbrance obtained by, 79.
    where draft secured by fraudulent bill of lading, 189 a.

**FREIGHT,**
    subrogation to carrier's lien for, 10, 12.
    insurers of ship entitled to, after abandonment, 225 et seq.
    abandonment of ship will not release insurers of, 226.
    rights of insurers of, against insurers of ship, 226, 227.


## G.

**GEORGIA,**
    rights in, of purchasers of parts of incumbered estate, 76.
    original debt preserved in equity after surety's payment, 137.
        but extinguished at law, 137.
    surety's right does not extend to joint debtors, 137.
    subrogation refused against grantee of a co-purchaser, 174.

**GOVERNMENT,**
    officer not subrogated to claim of, growing out of his own wrong, 4.
    priority of, passes to purchasers of goods on paying duties, 35.
    surety to, subrogated to priority of, 88.
        but not in competition with, 88.
    laches not to be imputed to, 121.
    holders of bonds secured by mortgage to, subrogated, 167 a.
    certificates of indebtedness issued by, subrogation upon, 183.

**GRANTOR.** *See* PURCHASER.

**GUARANTY.** *See* PRINCIPAL AND SURETY.
    guarantor and surety need not contribute, 150.

**GUARDIAN,**
    surety of, subrogated to rights of ward, 89.
    not discharged by act against which bond taken, 126 a.
    ward substituted to mortgage given by, to his surety, 166.
    but not in New Jersey, 166.
    subrogated to liability of former, which he has paid, 245.

# H.

# I.

INCUMBRANCE — *continued*.
  effect of payment of, by one not the debtor, 13.
  may be treated as subsisting though formally discharged, 14.
  right of junior on payment of prior incumbrancer, 15, 16, 17.
  limitations of right of junior incumbrancer, 18.
  subrogation of one advancing money to pay, 19.
  where new, given for old, 20.
  rights and liabilities of purchaser of incumbered property, 22 *et seq.*,
    28 *et seq.*
          *See* PURCHASER.
  rights of co-mortgagees against each other, 27.
  need not be assigned to one entitled to subrogation, 28.
          *See* ASSIGNMENT.
  when extinguished by taking discharge, 29.
  subrogation of one purchasing under, 31, 32, 33.
  holder of invalid, subrogated, 36 *a*.
  no subrogation to, if excluded by terms of sale, 37.
  transfer of, to purchaser in fraud of creditors, 40.
  when subrogation to, gives right to assignment of, 45.
  real debtor cannot be subrogated to, 46.
  assignment to one bound to pay, tantamount to discharge, 47.
  payment of, by dowress, entitles her to subrogation, 48.
  effect of payment of, upon dower, 49 *et seq.*
          *See* DOWER.
  not merged by assignment to debtor's assignee in insolvency, 49.
  when extinguished by assignment to owner of equity, 53 *et seq.*
          *See* MERGER.
  when prior incumbrancer postponed by his purchase of equity,
    57 *et seq.*
  subrogation of junior incumbrancer whose security pays prior, 61.
        *See* MARSHALLING OF ASSETS.
  effect of release of, upon junior incumbrancer, 72 *et seq.*
  lien of judgment treated like other, 77.
  effect of partial release of, upon other part conveyed, 72 *et seq.*, 78.
    no effect, unless prior creditor had been notified, 81.
  surety upon payment subrogated to, 86 *et seq.*
  subrogation of co-purchasers of incumbered property, 172 *et seq.*
        *See* JOINT DEBTORS.
  no subrogation to, after extinguishment of, 176.
  upon estate of deceased, heirs or devisees subrogated to, 213.
  trustee subrogated to one, which he has paid, 214.

INDEMNITY. *See* CONTRIBUTION.
  obtained by subrogation, 11.
  of surety who is held to pay debt, 86 *et seq.*
  subrogation of surety's indemnifier, 106.
  of surety extinguished by his release from liability, 139.
    co-sureties entitled to share in, 141.
        *See* CO-SURETIES.

LEASE,
subrogation of lessee, on redeeming from prior mortgage, 14.
or of mortgagee of lessee, 14.
surety of lessee cannot compel distress by landlord, 115.
    whether subrogated to right of distress, 115.
    discharged by surrender of lease, 126.
    but not as to rent already due, 126.
    rule limited in bankruptcy, 126.
right of lessor and lessee to each other's insurance, 233.

LEGACY,
subrogation to lien of, upon purchased land, 21.
rights of purchaser of land charged with, 77.
surety paying, entitled to property held for, 100.
lien on, of surety's executors who have paid debt of legatee, 100.
legatee of partner subrogated like him, 171.
charged with debt of legatee paid by executor, 202.
subrogation in favor of legatees, 208.
legatees subrogated to liens which they have paid, 210.
    if they pay to preserve property to which they look, 210.
    where specific legacies sold for testator's debts, 211.
contribution among legatees, 213.
charged with expense incurred for its protection, 214.
creditors subrogated to rights of legatees, 217.
subrogation for, lost by election of another, 218.
    *See* ELECTION.

LEGAL PROCEEDINGS,
subrogation of sureties in, against prior sureties, 131 *et seq.*
    *See* SUCCESSIVE SURETIES.

LESSEE. *See* LEASE.

LETTER–CARRIER,
subrogation of, 10.

LEVY OF EXECUTION. *See* EXECUTION.

LIBEL,
insurers subrogated may bring, in own name, in admiralty, 221.

LIEN. *See* INCUMBRANCE; SUCCESSIVE CLAIMS.
subrogation of one discharging, 8, 9, 19.
of carrier, subsequent carrier subrogated to, 10.
pledgee subrogated to carrier's, 12.
creditor satisfying prior, subrogated to it, 3, 12.
sheriff subrogated to carrier's, 12.
of taxes, passing to one who has paid them, 14.
of dower, party redeeming from, subrogated to, 15.
subrogation of one who has discharged, 19, 20.
prior, avoided by bankruptcy ; junior, not advanced, 23.
discharge of, of record, when set aside, 20.
subrogation of one purchasing under, 31–33.
rights of assignee of, 34.

LIEN — *continued.*
    assignment of maritime, 34.
    holder of invalid, subrogated, 36 *a.*
    subrogation to, not allowed, if excluded by terms of sale, 37.
    of purchaser at execution sale, 38.
    when one subrogated to, may require assignment of, 45.
    one who has assumed, not subrogated, 46.
    destroyed by assignment to one bound to pay it, 47.
                *See* MERGER.
    rights of holder of single, against prior holder of two, 61 *et seq.*
    of corporation on its own stock, subrogation of creditor to, 61.
        subrogation of surety to, 92.
                *See* MARSHALLING OF ASSETS.
    effect of release of, upon holder of subsequent, 72.
    on property of purchaser, released by release to debtor, 78–80.
    surety subrogated to, of corporation upon its stock, 92.
    surety of purchaser subrogated to, of vendor, 96, 97, 109.
    no subrogation to, unassignable, 97.
    equitable, surety subrogated to, 98.
    vendor's surety subrogated to, of purchaser, 98.
    surety's right to, of corporation when not enforced upon stock, 123.
    of government, bondholders subrogated to, 167 *a.*
    of holder of bill upon property against which drawn, 189 *et seq.*
    of mortgagee upon mortgagor's insurance, 233.
    insurance by creditor upon property subject to, 234 *et seq.*

LIFE ESTATE. *See* TENANT FOR LIFE.

LIFE INSURANCE. *See* INSURANCE.

LIMITATIONS, STATUTE OF,
    a bar to surety's subrogation, 110.
    when statute begins to run, 110.
    no subrogation to lien barred by lapse of time, 176.

LOUISIANA,
    doctrine of subrogation, 5.
    subrogation in, of later against prior surety, 134.
    surety subrogated to original obligation on payment, 137.
    conventional subrogation in, 250.

### M.

MAINE,
    no remedy allowed in, between successive sureties, 134.
    subrogation in, of surety, to satisfied judgment, 138.

MARINE INSURANCE. *See* INSURANCE.

MARRIED WOMEN. *See* HUSBAND AND WIFE.

MARSHALLING OF ASSETS,
    not required in favor of debtor or his grantees, 25.
    where wife's property held for husband's debt, 51.

MARSHALLING OF ASSETS — *continued*.
>> waste or misapplication same as release, 72.
>> not if made in good faith and without notice, 73.
>> or if remaining fund sufficient for all demands, 73.
> purchaser's fund exonerated by release of primary fund, 78.
> rights of successive purchasers of parts of incumbered estate, 74 *et seq*.
>> *See* PURCHASERS.
> of different securities, in favor of surety against creditor, 114.
>> in favor of creditor against surety, 117, 129.
> among co-sureties, 141.
> among creditors of deceased persons, 204.
> in favor of legatees, 208.
> among heirs, devisees, or legatees, 213.

MARYLAND,
> no contribution in, between prior and later sureties, 134.
> surety on payment entitled to benefit of original obligation, 137.
> surety subrogated against co-sureties in, 137.

MASSACHUSETTS,
> rules as to widow's dower in incumbered estate, 52.
> no remedy allowed between prior and later sureties, 134.
> original obligation extinguished by surety's payment, 138.
> judgment not to be assigned to one debtor on his payment, 138.
> surety how far subrogated against his co-sureties, 140.
> right of creditor to security of surety who is also a creditor, 156.
> rule as to mortgagee's insurance in, 234.

MAXIM,
> *sic utere tuo ut alienum non lædas*, 4.

MECHANIC'S LIEN,
> marshalling of assets for protection of, 61.
> holder of, not subrogated to owner's insurance, 233.

MERGER,
> when caused by payment by one not the debtor, 18.
> when not caused by release of mortgage to mortgagor, 22.
> by assignment of mortgage to a purchaser of the premises, 26, 37.
> not caused by quitclaim of mortgage to purchaser in fraud of creditors, 40.
> created or not by assignment, as required by justice, 47, 49 *et seq*.
> when operated by sale of equity to mortgagee, 49.
>> by assignment of mortgage to owner of equity, 53 *et seq*.
>> according to justice and intent of parties, 53.
>> prevented by intervening incumbrance, 53, 57, 60.
> tests by which determined, 54.
> not presumed, if contrary to interest, 54.
> or where interest held in different rights, 54.
> prevented only for innocent purpose, 54, 55.
> not prevented to prejudice of *bona fide* purchaser, 55.
>> though discharge taken, 55.

## N.

NOTES AND BILLS — *continued*.

NOTICE — *continued.*
  to prior creditor, of rights of junior, 72.
  to agent of prior creditor, 72.
  of junior interest must be given to prior creditor, 78.
  of rights of prior purchaser of part of mortgaged estate, 75.
  to mortgagee, of subsequent conveyances of premises, 81.
  mere recording of subsequent conveyances not sufficient, 81.
  unless special duty to examine records, 81.
    but knowledge of attorney in that matter is, 81.
    possession of subsequent grantee is not, to prior incumbrancer, 81.
  of rights of creditor by record of mortgage to surety, 155.

## O.

OFFICER. *See* COLLECTOR; POST-OFFICE; SHERIFF.
OHIO,
  original obligation may be preserved after surety's payment, 137.
ORDERS,
  payment of, when subrogates to original rights, 246.

## ' P.

PARENT,
  not subrogated for expense of supporting child, 8.
  son subrogated upon paying debt of, in So. Car., 137.
PARTNERSHIP,
  marshalling of assets among creditors of, 66, 69.
  subrogation of one partner's creditors, 69.
  surety of one partner not subrogated against firm, 113.
  rights of surety both of one partner and of firm, 113.
  surety of, subrogated to bonds given by one partner to another, 163.
  subrogation among the partners, 171.
  right extends to their creditors and legatees, 171.
  creditors substituted to security of partners, 171 a.
  and to agreements of retiring partner, 171 a.
  action on promise to pay debts of old firm, 171 a.
PAYMENT,
  obligation extinguished by, kept alive by subrogation, 2, 28.
  when, operates extinguishment, 3.
  essential to subrogation, 3, 5, 6, 45, 89, 118, 127.
  must be compulsory, 3, 11.
  of dishonored check, subrogation upon, 4.
  by agent, of debt due to principal, extinguishes it, when, 5, 10 a.
  if not made under obligation, 5.
  by sheriff, of execution for which he has become liable, subrogates him, 7.

PAYMENT — *continued.*

PAYMENT — *continued.*
>    of indebtedness to principal necessary to surety's subrogation, 112.
>    of debt by principal extinguishes security, 116.
>    of independent claim to debtor will not discharge surety, 123.
>    by principal, when no discharge of surety, 123.
>    by principal, made after, by surety, 125.
>    need not come wholly from surety, 128.
>    by surety, how far extinguishes original obligation, 135–138.
>    by indorser of note, effect on suit pending against maker, 137, 182.
>    when, entitles third person to surety's indemnity, 139.
>    subrogation of surety against his co-sureties, upon, 140 *et seq.*
>    See CO-SURETIES.
>    by a co-surety, taken at money value, 151.
>    upon, subrogation of joint debtor against the others, 169 *et seq.*
>    See JOINT DEBTORS.
>    by one debtor, how far an extinguishment of debt, 180.
>    by indorser of note, subrogates him to rights of payee, 181.
>        maker not entitled to benefit of, 182.
>    by prior parties, subsequent parties have benefit of, 182.
>    of note by stranger, 186.
>    of bill, by property appropriated therefor, 189 *et seq.*
>    of debts of deceased, personal representative subrogated upon, 202.
>    by legatee, a ground of subrogation, 208, 210.
>    of loss by insurers entitles them to subrogation, 221 *et seq.*
>    of debt by a stranger extinguishes it, 1, 240.
>    in full, essential to conventional subrogation, 248.
>    action for, cannot coexist with subrogation, 249.

PENNSYLVANIA,
>    purchaser subrogated to debt assumed by him, 35.
>    judgment not extinguished by surety's payment, 137.

PLEDGE. *See* LIEN; SECURITY.

POLICY. *See* INSURANCE.

POSSESSION,
>    of subsequent purchaser, not notice to prior incumbrancer, 81.

POST-OFFICE,
>    subrogation of letter-carrier, 10.

PRACTICE,
>    subrogation to be carried out with equitable discretion, 4.
>        not to be enforced against legal right, 4.
>        of sheriff upon paying a judgment, 7.
>        of attorney to rights of client, 10 *a.*
>        burden of proof on one claiming subrogation, 11.
>        how far barred by decree of foreclosure, 18.
>    two co-mortgagees may redeem from third, who holds prior mortgage, 27.
>    remedies of purchaser under decree of foreclosure, 30, 31.

PRACTICE — *continued.*
  creditor's election of remedies, 25, 41.
                    •    *See* WAIVER.
  when right of subrogation gives right to assignment, 45.
  remedy of purchaser of part of land subject to lien, 83.
  surety subrogated before payment if debtor insolvent, 97.
      allowed benefit of principal's set-off or defence, 101.
      allowed writ of error on judgment against principal, 101.
      must elect between subrogation and remedy at law, 110.
      may in equity compel payment of debt by principal, 130.
      equitable rights of, 130 *a.*
  rights of sureties on successive appeals, 131.
                    *See* SUCCESSIVE SURETIES.
  whether original debt extinguished by surety's payment, 135–138.
  equity enforces rights to co-surety's security, 140 *et seq.*
      whether extinguished by one joint debtor's payment, 180.
  substitution of creditor to security held by surety, 154 *et seq.*
  subrogation of accommodation acceptor, 199.
  creditors of devisees, how subrogated, 212.
  insurers may bring libel in own names, 221.
  subrogation of insurers against fire in name of insured, 229, 230.
      mode of enforcing their remedy, 231, 232.
      action upon policy procured by mortgagor for mortgagee, 236.

PREFERENCE. *See* PRIORITY.

PRIMARY FUND. *See* MARSHALLING OF ASSETS.

PRINCIPAL AND AGENT. *See* AGENCY.

PRINCIPAL AND SURETY,
  subrogation of surety by civil law, 2, 3, 5.
  surety not subrogated if his claim barred at law, 4.
  surety of tax-collector subrogated, 7.
  subrogation of one who has lent his notes, 8.
      of agent bound as guarantor or surety, 10 *a.*
  subrogation not confined to cases of suretyship, 11.
  surety postponed to one whose money has paid prior lien, 19, 36.
  action against primary for benefit of subsidiary debtor, 23.
  mortgagor regarded as surety of one who has assumed mortgage,
      24, 25.
  principal becoming surety, 25.
  surety entitled to assignment, to carry out his subrogation, 45.
  security merged by assignment to principal or his agent, 56.
  apparent principal when really surety, 182 *a.*
  surety's right of subrogation against his principal, 86.
      will pass to his assignees or creditors, 86.
      and to his heirs and grantees, 86.
      not to be defeated by creditor, 86.
  surety discharged if creditor interferes with his subrogation, 86.
  takes no greater rights than creditor had, 86.

PROMISSORY NOTE. *See* Notes and Bills.
PUBLIC OFFICER. *See* Collector; Sheriff.
PURCHASER. *See* Successive Claims.
    paying incumbrance on purchased estate, subrogated, 3, 5, 9, 28.
    subrogation against, for price, 8.
    payment of mortgage by one who has bargained for premises, 16.
    subrogation not allowed against record, 17.
    latent equity not enforced against, 17.
    of mortgaged lands under junior lien, rights of, 21, 22.
    of land subject to a legacy, subrogated to that charge, 21.
    subrogation of original debtor against, 22.
    not personally liable for debt he has not assumed, 22.
    of part of an equity of redemption, rights of, 22.
    assuming mortgage, mortgagor subrogated against, 24.
    grantee of, with warranty, rights of, 24.
    rights of mortgagee against, assuming mortgage, 24, 85.
    rights of mortgagor against mortgagee and such purchaser, 25.
    how far rights of mortgagee affected, 25.
    subject to mortgage, mortgagor subrogated against, 26.
    but not against mortgagor's warranty, 26.
    subrogated upon paying incumbrance which he did not assume, 28.
    his right of subrogation will pass to his grantee, 28.
    rights of, upon discharge of incumbrance, 29.
    of bare equity, acquires no interest in other securities for debt, 29.
    subrogated upon avoidance of his purchase, 30.
    under decree in favor of creditors subrogated, 31.
    under a mortgage or lien subrogated to lien, 31, 33.
    but not if purchased under adverse title, 31.
    with notice, takes rights of creditor without notice, 31.
    under adverse title, when not subrogated, 31.
    how allowed such subrogation in California, 32.
    ordinarily subrogated to rights of vendor, 34.
    with notice, takes rights of vendor without, 34.
    subrogated upon paying debts with which property chargeable, 85.
    subrogated to rights of creditor against vendor, 36.
    right of set-off against notes given for price, 36.
    set-off must be *pro rata* against holders of notes, 36.
    subrogated, although title invalid, 36 *a*.
    limitations of his right of subrogation, 37.
    does not take vendor's remedy for mere tort, 37.
    not subrogated to title superior to what he bought, 37.
    by quitclaim, cannot defend against mortgage, 37.
    under execution-sale subrogated against debtor, 88.
    not if property recovered by third parties, 39.
    subrogated where purchase avoided by vendor's creditors, 40.
    not subrogated against his own wrong, 44.
        nor against mortgage which he has assumed, 46.
        or any charge which bound to pay, 46.

RECORD — *continued.*
  unless it would prejudice subsequent interests, 43.
  right of purchaser of part of incumbered estate shown by, 75.
  of subsequent deeds, mortgagee not affected by, 81.
  unless special duty to examine, 81.
  discharge of surety by creditor's failure to make, 121.
    not by failure of public officer to make, 121.
  of mortgage to surety, notice of creditor's rights, 155.
  no subrogation to lien lost for lack of, 176.

REDEMPTION.  *See* INCUMBRANCE ; MORTGAGE ; SUCCESSIVE CLAIMS.
  of incumbrance, subrogation upon, 13 *et seq.*
  limitations of right of junior creditor, 18.
  when incumbered lands sold under junior lien, 21, 22.
  of pledge by assignee in bankruptcy, 23.
  by co-mortgagees from each other, 27.
  from prior incumbrance, effect of, upon dower, 49 *et seq.*
  right of dowress to make, 49 *et seq.*
            *See* DOWER.
  by different owners of securities for same debt, 172 *et seq.*
  by co-tenant, rights upon, 172.
        •         *See* JOINT DEBTORS.

REIMBURSEMENT,
  of one who has paid off prior incumbrance, 12 *et seq.*
            *See* SUCCESSIVE CLAIMS.
  subrogation allowed only for purpose of obtaining, 21.
  of surety upon his payment of debt, 86 *et seq.*
            *See* PRINCIPAL AND SURETY.
  creditor substituted to his debtor's claim for, 167.
    but not to his debtor's remedy for a tort, 244.
    implied agreement for, avoided by subrogation, 249.

RELEASE,
  from prior to junior mortgagee extinguishes lien, 12.
  to one entitled to subrogation treated as assignment, 13, 14, 22, 24.
  of incumbrance fraudulently made treated as assignment, 19.
  of mortgage to purchaser in fraud of creditors, 40.
  of dower operating estoppel, 49.
  by prior creditor of fund primarily liable, 72.
  waste or misapplication regarded as, 72.
  will not prejudice creditor without notice of junior interest, 73.
  of primary fund discharges secondary fund *pro tanto,* 78.
    but not as between real debtor and creditor, 78.
    or unless it ought in justice to do so, 79.
  discharges purchaser entitled to subrogation, 80.
    if creditor has notice of purchaser's right, 81.
  of surety by interference with his subrogation, 119 *et seq.*
    by interference with co-sureties' subrogation, 151.
  given to surety for transfer of his indemnity, 158, 159.

SUBROGATION — *continued.*
 gives only rights already existing, 6.
 subrogation of sheriff compelled to pay a judgment, 7.
  of tax-collector, 7.
  of one who has advanced money to pay incumbrance, 8, 19.
  of one compelled to pay debt of another, 9.
  of a carrier, 10.
  of carrier's agent, 10.
  of letter-carrier, 10.
  of consignee or agent, 10 *a.*
 general doctrine of, 11.
 compels discharge of debt by party ultimately liable, 11.
 allowed only on sustaining burden of proof, 11.
 where there are successive claims on same property, 12 *et seq.*
    *See* SUCCESSIVE CLAIMS.
 of one who has paid off an incumbrance, 13 *et seq.*
 not allowed against interest taken on faith of record, 17.
 latent equity of, against purchaser, 17.
 allowed only for protection and reimbursement, 18, 21.
 of one advancing money to pay incumbrance, 19.
 of one taking new incumbrance for old, 20.
 allowed only if intended or necessary, 19.
 against corporation for money borrowed *ultra vires*, 19.
 against one at whose request money paid, 19, 20.
 of and against a purchaser under a junior lien, 21, 22.
 of an assignee in bankruptcy, 23.
 of mortgagor paying his own mortgage, 24, 25, 26.
 of and against purchaser of incumbered property, 24–28 *et seq.*
  upon estoppel of incumbrancer 29.
    *See* PURCHASER.
 of co-mortgagees against each other, 27.
 right of, will pass to grantee of one entitled to, 28.
 of purchaser under decree, 31.
 upon payment made to protect one's interest, 33.
 not allowed for claims which could not have been enforced, 35.
 of one whose title invalid, 36 *a.*
 of purchaser of property sold on execution, 38, 39.
 voluntary purchaser of debtor's interest not entitled to, 39.
 waiver of right of, 41, 42.
 right of, lost by negligence prejudicial to others, 43.
 party seeking, must not be in his own wrong, 44.
 when one entitled to, may require assignment, 45.
 the real debtor not entitled to, 46.
 dowress entitled to, on paying prior incumbrance, 48.
 of purchaser against widow's dower, 49 *et seq.*
    *See* DOWER.
 of purchaser, to mortgage assigned to him, 53 *et seq.*
    *See* MERGER.